A Comprehensive Guide
to Career Assessment

SEVENTH EDITION

Kevin B. Stoltz and Susan R. Barclay, Editors

NCDA | National Career Development Association

National Career Development Association

Library of Congress Cataloging-in-Publication Data

Names: Stoltz, Kevin B., editor. | Barclay, Susan R., editor. | National
   Career Development Association (U.S.), issuing body.
Title: A comprehensive guide to career assessment / Kevin B. Stoltz & Susan
   R. Barclay, editors.
Other titles: Counselor's guide to career assessment instruments.
Description: Seventh edition. | Broken Arrow, OK : National Career
   Development Association, [2019] | Includes bibliographical references.
Identifiers: LCCN 2019010652 | ISBN 9781885333605 (hardcover)
Subjects: LCSH: Occupational aptitude tests--Evaluation. | Vocational
   interests--Testing--Evaluation.
Classification: LCC HF5381.7 .C68 2019 | DDC 153.9/4--dc23
LC record available at https://lccn.loc.gov/2019010652

DEDICATION

We dedicate *A Comprehensive Guide to Career Assessment* to all the workers who situate themselves in workplaces across the world. Without you – the worker – the profession of providing career counseling and assessment would not exist. Our desire is that you grow in your work identity continually and that you find meaning in all you do as you contribute purposefully to the vocational world.

We want to thank and dedicate *A Comprehensive Guide to Career Assessment* to the spirit of human endeavor, for in the final analysis, humans cannot be still but must advance, and this advance is our work.

ACKNOWLEDGEMENTS

Both of us came to career development work by a long and circuitous trail and each having experience in corporate, practice, and academic positions. Through these experiences, we grew from observing the many people who touched our lives. We want to thank the teachers, professors, supervisors, managers, and mentors who helped shape our work and careers.

We could not imagine the amount of time and energy editing the 7th edition of *A Counselor's Guide to Career Assessment* would take when NCDA approached us with their request to serve as editors. As we contemplated our approach to the newest edition, we conceptualized many changes we wanted to make considering the protean and boundaryless times in which we all work and live. First, we wanted to update the name of the publication as a way of recognizing the diversity of career professionals who provide career assessment. Next, we wanted to extend the publication to recognize the global nature of work. We accomplished this by soliciting experts from across the world to contribute their writings concerning career assessment in their prospective nations. Finally, we knew we wanted to launch the 7th edition in electronic format to respect the technological context in which people work and live, and to create a "living" document that provides greater opportunity to update, as needed, and keep pace with the changing nature of career research and assessment instrument development.

A project of this magnitude requires the assistance and support of many individuals. Our first meeting with NCDA included Deneen Pennington, Melanie Reinersman, and Mary Ann Powell. We appreciate the brainstorming that took place that day and the many ideas we generated during that meeting. In addition, Melanie worked alongside us, throughout the editing process, as the three of us read, edited, re-read, and re-edited until we knew the documents were ready for publication. Melanie worked to secure publisher materials for the many assessments we wanted to include in the publication, and often, this was a challenging task. Thank you, Melanie, for your support and the many emails and conference calls as we hammered out details and forged the 7th edition. We thank Alicia Cheek for delivering the publisher materials we were able to secure to the many reviewers who agreed to contribute their time, energy, and writing talent to this project.

We appreciate the support the NCDA Board gave to this newest edition and the encouragement to our many ideas, even when we were still conceptualizing many of them. You did not waiver in your support of us, as editors, and perhaps more important, you did not waiver in your support of a completed project that would generate the e-version and its availability to researchers, educators, practitioners, and many others who engage in career assessment.

We were fortunate to have editorial assistance throughout much of this project. For that, we thank Baylee Shaw, Tanupreet Suri, and Samantha Sartain. You helped us with the fine details and the many moving pieces that, otherwise, we might have misplaced long ago.

Perhaps our greatest appreciation goes to the many individuals and teams of individuals who contributed to this project. The resounding positive responses, when asked to contribute, encouraged us and reaffirmed how important this project was. You spent time and energy you could have spent elsewhere, probably, and you endured the many rounds of editing and rewriting. "Thank you" seems insufficient for the amount of work each of you invested in helping us bring this project to fruition; yet, we thank you. Your contribution goes well beyond this project by enabling qualified career professionals, who access this publication, to collaborate effectively and intentionally with the diverse workers of the world.

Kevin B. Stoltz, Co-editor

Susan R. Barclay, Co-editor

FOREWORD

A Comprehensive Guide to Career Assessment (7th ed.) represents a major leap forward for a resource that already enjoys a stellar reputation as the leading career assessment book in the field. Aptly titled, the current edition stands as arguably the most thorough and, indeed, comprehensive book yet to address incorporating assessments into the career intervention process. I know of no other resource, for example, addressing topics ranging from the history of career assessment to the use of career assessments across global contexts, to how career assessments can be effectively integrated into various practice settings, to specific reviews of an impressive number and variety of career assessment instruments.

The editors, Drs. Stoltz and Barclay, use an innovative strategy to provide portions of the book on-line and/or in hard copy to accommodate the extensive coverage of assessment topics in a way that makes access to the entire book efficient and effective. Additionally, authors contributing to this edition are a veritable "who's who" of leading career development experts from around the globe. The collective result is a book that stands as the gold standard among books addressing career assessment.

As President of the National Career Development Association, I extend my heartfelt gratitude to the editors for their impressive accomplishment. Additionally, as President of NCDA, I encourage all career practitioners, theorists, educators and researchers to make this book a required resource within your professional toolkit. It is guaranteed to be a book that you return to multiple times as you construct career interventions, create career-related research studies, or simply desire to learn more about the broad topic of career assessment.

Spencer Niles
President, National Career Development Association, 2018-19
Dean and Professor
College of William and Mary

PREFACE

We believe work is a central life undertaking in human experience and that working behavior reflects the individual's personal contribution to this venture. Helping individuals identify and seek work that actualizes the person's ability to make significant contributions to human projects is the key goal in the career-focused helping endeavor. An integral part of this process is career assessment. In the career development professions, career assessment continues to evolve, and this new edition of the *Guide* offers many innovations that represent the positive developments in the science and practice of career development work.

Similar to the editors before us, we have assembled a collection of chapters and instrument reviews that represent much of the work of career assessment. We have broadened the scope of the work by including chapters and reviews from around the world. Additionally, in the 7th edition of the *Guide*, we have incorporated the use of technology and reconceptualized the book into an online reference tool designed to serve career practitioners, counselor educators, and researchers as they go about their work of assisting individuals in finding meaningful work.

The first six chapters represent foundational information about career assessment. Chapter 1 provides a broad and rich history of career assessment in the United States. Following this historical account of career assessment, Chapter 2 provides a glimpse of the future for career assessment by introducing trends and emerging concepts important to career work. Chapter 3 allows readers to view the important developments of integrating technology into the work of career counseling and career practitioner services. Recognizing that technology helps introduce the diverse peoples of the earth to each other, Chapter 4 presents the important content of diversity and cultural considerations to the work of career practitioners. With a focus on the complexity of creating and understanding career assessment construction, Chapter 5 provides a brief review of the steps and considerations when choosing career assessments for use in practice. Finally, Chapter 6 presents the steps and procedures of administering, scoring, and communicating results to clients with a focus on holistic career assessment.

To highlight the specializations in career development work, we included seven chapters on the companion website that present career assessment within specific professional foci. Chapter 7 provides the unique perspectives of career assessment with children in K-12 settings in the US. Following this developmental line, we present Chapter 8, which includes career assessment processes in higher education. Chapter 9 continues with a focus on career assessment in business, industry, and workforce development. Another unique addition to the *Guide* is Chapter 10, which includes perspectives from an individual who works in private practice as a career counselor and a consultant. Understanding the outcomes of career counseling and other helping systems is critical to the survival of the profession and, thus, we include Chapter 11, which provides information on career assessment in research and program evaluation. Knowing that advocacy and public policy is a central function of career practitioners, we include Chapter 12 that presents critical information concerning career assessment in public policy. Chapter 13 was included to highlight the integration of mental health and career counseling and to acknowledge the indivisible nature of human experiences. We believe that including these focused chapters on the specializations in the profession provides a detailed view of the practice of career assessment across work environments in the US.

To respect and represent the great diversity of career-focused work across the world, we have included contributions from seven key areas around the globe on the companion website. These chapters shed light on the various approaches to career assessment from unique and diverse viewpoints. Chapter 14 offers detailed perspectives of career assessment from Asia. From the land down under, Chapter 15 provides the practices of career assessment in Australia. Next, Chapter 16 introduces career assessment methods in Canada. Remaining in the northern hemisphere, Chapter 17 provides a rich history and practice of career assessment in Europe. Latin American comes next, with Chapter 18 outlining career assessment in these southern hemisphere nations. At the confluence of Asia and Europe, the Middle East is represented in Chapter 19 and details accounts of career assessment in the region. Finally, career assessment in South Africa, Chapter 20, provides an important conversation of post-colonial advocacy for career assessment. We believe these chapters are fundamental to understanding work in the diverse lives being served by the practitioners of career assessment across the globe.

Following the international focus of these chapters are the reviews of career assessments that represent another innovation to the 7th edition of the *Guide*. Earlier editions focused on the area of formal assessment. Career practice in the 21st century includes other forms of assessment. We have broadened the foci of the *Guide* to include traditional formal assessment, informal assessment, and emerging constructs that are important to understanding the career experience. The reviews of assessments included in this book and on the companion website are arranged into four general categories and include some overlap. The categories consist of quantitative assessments, qualitative assessments and processes, research assessments, and open source assessments. The reviews include assessments from around the world. The quantitative assessment category includes the most familiar career assessments offered commercially for use by career practitioners. The qualitative assessment section includes descriptions and research of counseling processes used for assessment in exploring career development. The research category provides insights into the continuing study and new developments in career assessments. Finally, the open source section introduces many assessment resources that are available at no cost to practitioners and our clients.

In closing, we are humbled by the broad array of career assessments available in our profession. The combined work and knowledge are formidable, and we have attempted to organize this work as a catalogue of helpful and useable information for the many career practitioner specialties in the profession. We offer the 7th edition as an updated professional tool that will serve the variety of professionals active in career assessment and practice worldwide.

Kevin B. Stoltz, Co-editor

Susan R. Barclay, Co-editor

STRUCTURE OF THE BOOK

The National Career Development Association (NCDA) is excited to release its newest publication regarding career assessment – the 7th edition of *A Counselors Guide to Career Assessment*. We, as editors, are excited about the changes to the well-known publication. First and foremost is the change in the name to *A Comprehensive Guide to Career Assessment*. Originally conceptualized in 1982 as a guide for counselors, we designed the 7th edition for use by a wide variety of career practitioners, including those in training. This change keeps pace with the continual evolution of the workplace in the 21st century. Second, we wanted to highlight the global focus of career development work and NCDA membership, and we did this by including chapters and instrument reviews from leading scholars and practitioners located around the world. This global perspective expanded the book significantly and led to a reconceptualization of how to deliver the new edition. Recognizing the full potential of the book when combined with technological advances, we developed an online format as a companion to the print book that we believe will serve practitioners, researchers, counselor educators, students, and NCDA members worldwide.

This advancement starts with a printed book that holds the first six chapters of the new edition and reviews of over two dozen career assessments. These first six chapters consist of foundational knowledge of career assessment that the authors have updated for current use in the profession. Along with those six chapters are reviews of career development assessments that include not only reviews of traditional instruments but offer expanded variety with new assessment categories (i.e., quantitative, qualitative, research, and open source). These reviews are representative of the variety that will be available on the book's new companion - an official website. To control cost, while offering valuable content, we offer this comprehensive resource in two formats. Individuals can purchase the print book as a stand-alone item; they can purchase website access as a stand-alone item; or, individuals can purchase both the print copy and website access for the greatest coverage of content. We believe the unique features of the combined option represent the most value to users of this *Guide*.

The website offers expanded content including career assessment in specific work environments, global perspectives on career development, and reviews of assessments used in diverse cultures. Of the 14 additional chapters, the first seven represent many professional environments in which career specialists work. These include K-12 schools; higher education; business and workforce development; private practice; research and evaluation; public policy; and mental health counseling. The remaining seven chapters, which were written by authors from around the world, present career assessment from their diverse cultures and settings. These include Asia, Australia, Canada, Europe, Latin America, the Middle East, and South Africa.

In addition to the new chapter content, the website houses more reviews in the same four categories as the print version. These categories are quantitative assessments offered commercially for use, qualitative assessments documented in the professional literature, research assessments that focus on continuing inquiry in the profession, and open source assessments available at no cost on the world-wide-web. In addition to the usual keyword searches, the online assessment reviews are searchable three ways: alphabetically, categorically, and via instrument type (search by key constructs, such as interests, adaptability, or meaning). We will add additional reviews to the website as they become available. Each review includes a relevant literature search, updated test descriptions and quality markers, and contact information to explore access and further information from the publisher of the assessment. Of course, the online technical features make for a user-friendly 21st century resource, yet the print book's foundational content is a valuable reserve for both students and experienced professionals.

We envision this book and the website as the go-to-source for career assessment now and in the future. With the incorporation of technology into this project, NCDA can offer ongoing reviews and updates that will build a current accounting and a historical record of career assessment worldwide. This is truly a comprehensive work that will live up to its name.

Kevin B. Stoltz, Co-editor

Susan R. Barclay, Co-editor

Expert contributors provided the chapter content and the instrument reviews in both the print and online companion. The instrument publisher provided the information about the assessment that appears in a box prior to select reviews. Using the Table of Contents and Index as a guide, readers can determine the most helpful parts and where to find them. The print and online companion can be purchased separately or together for the optimal resource.

TABLE OF CONTENTS

Part III – Global Perspectives on Career Assessment 107
ONLINE ONLY

Part IV – Career Assessment Instrument Reviews 109
PRINT ONLY (unless otherwise noted; see the online companion for
the reviews that appear online only)

Quantitative

PART I

FOUNDATIONS
IN
CAREER
ASSESSMENT

CHAPTER 1

HISTORY AND USES OF CAREER ASSESSMENT

Mark Pope

Yang Ai

Courtney R. Boddie

Carol A. Miller

University of Missouri – Saint Louis

History and Uses of Career Assessment

Pope (2015a) discussed the roots of career assessment as part of the array of career interventions that have arisen over the last 100 years in the emergence and development of the vocational guidance movement in the United States and around the planet. These developments followed the course of that movement through the social transformations of, and transitions between, the agrarian and industrial periods, as well as between the industrial and digital/global eras of US history (Pope, 2000, 2015a).

Historians identified three general career intervention periods of career counseling: *vocational guidance, career education*, and *life design* (Duarte, 2009; Pope, 2015a; Savickas, 2010, 2012). Savickas characterized the tasks of each period in this manner:

The vocational guidance model works to (a) enhance self-knowledge, (b) increase occupational information, and (c) match self to occupation....

Career education and counselling works to (a) assess development status, (b) orient the individual to imminent developmental tasks, and (c) develop the attitudes, beliefs, and competencies needed to master those tasks....

Life-design interventions (a) construct career through small stories, (b) reconstruct the small stories into a large story or identity narrative, and (c) co-construct the next scenario in that life portrait. (2010, p. xi)

Hartung (2010) described these periods, respectively, as individual differences, individual development, and individual design, or termed another way, that "these three perspectives include differential, developmental, and constructivist views" (p. 1). They also correspond to historical periods of modernity, high modernity, and post-modernity (Savickas, 2011) (See Table 1). More important, the interventions of these periods are additive, not mutually exclusive. Previous interventions that were appropriate for an earlier period are not lost in such a construction of this history. Each builds upon, and supplements, the work of the preceding period and might even be appropriate depending on the specific life/career issues of the client presenting for career counseling.

Table 1

A Comparison of Historic Eras in the Vocational Guidance Movement

Period	Theme	Types of Assessments	Historical Category
Vocational guidance	Individual differences	Differential	Modernity
Career education	Individual development	Developmental	High modernity
Life design	Individual design	Constructivist	Post-modernity

This chapter traces the evolution of career assessment from its roots in that early 20th-century vocational guidance movement to contemporary times. Also, the chapter includes a discussion of the historical and political context of the period.

The Vocational Guidance Period

The initial foray into helping others with problems in their careers was based on the ideas of Frank Parsons, the founder of the Breadwinner's Institute of the Vocation Bureau of the Boston Civic Service House (Aubrey, 1977; Brewer, 1919, 1942; Briddick, 2009a,b; Davis, 1969; Pope, 2000; Pope & Sveinsdottir, 2005; Whiteley, 1984). The Boston Civic Service House was a Jane Addams' styled settlement house that arose to help individuals and their families who were migrating from rural areas to resettle in urban centers, as well as immigrants coming to the US. Parsons and his small group of disaffected social workers realized that case management, the traditional focus of that field, was simply not enough (Pope, 2000). People also needed a place to gain knowledge about themselves to consider how to overcome the many barriers they faced and to gain knowledge of the current occupational structure of their society. In so doing, they could learn to apply their internal, personal resources to their vocational problems, especially choosing a vocation (Parsons, 1909). They termed this process "vocational guidance" (Bloomfield, 1915; Brewer, 1919, 1942).

Historical and Political Context

The Boston Civic Service House, like other urban settlement houses of that time, grew from great social upheaval and social inequality, when individuals were simply being ground down. It developed as a direct response to the deeply felt need to help people who were having difficult financial, employment, and personal problems as a result of the social transition from an agrarian society to an industrial one at the end of the 1800s and beginning of the 1900s (Pope, 2000; Pope, Briddick, & Wilson, 2013). Vocational guidance arose in response to, and as an immediate outcome, of this transition, a transition Pope (2000) characterized:

> The societal upheaval giving birth to (vocational guidance) was characterized by the loss of jobs in the agricultural sector, increasing demands for workers in heavy industry, the loss of permanent jobs on the family farm to new emerging technologies, such as tractors, the increasing urbanization of the USA, and the concomitant calls for services to meet this internal migration pattern, all in order to retool for the new industrial economy. (p. 195)

Parsons' (1909) model of vocational guidance was largely without theoretical or empirical foundations, and the interventions developed during this period were grounded in "simple logic and common sense and relied predominantly on observational and data-gathering skills" (Aubrey, 1977, p. 290). Parsons (1909) wrote that "in the choice of a vocation there are three broad factors: (1) a clear understanding of yourself; ... (2) a knowledge of the requirements and conditions for success ... in different lines of work; (3) true reasoning on the relation of these two groups of facts" (p. 5). This was the first institutionalization of career counseling in the US (Ginzburg, 1971) and this approach, as well as the interventions that arose during this period, have had a profound and enduring effect on the field to this day. Later historians and theorists would term this approach *trait-factor*, or simply *matching*, and even later, *person-environment fit*, but it was a critical component in the acceptance and institutionalization of this new field, because it gave a scent of scientific methods to the practice of vocational guidance.

The vocational guidance period began as a direct result of the social transformation from the agrarian to the industrial era. The transition to the new industrial organization was fraught with instability and insecurity on the part of the individual worker, as occurs with most transitions. The promise of this new industrial society was secure employment and stable organizations. No matter if this was an illusion developed and perpetuated by the owners of these new industries, it became part of the new American ethos.

The idea of a company that provides long-term economic security and lifetime employment became the social ideal. This ideal "offered a firm basis for building a life and envisioning a future" for these new industrial workers (Savickas, 2012, p. 14). But this required that their careers be "established within the social order, which permitted individual choices but fitting determined patterns. This was the notion of a career concomitant with social reality, such as Parsons had sought in order to respond to social necessities" (Duarte, 2009, p. 261).

Vocational Guidance Assessments

Parsons was the grandparent of the trait-factor or person-environment fit approach to career assessment. This approach was important to the success of the new vocational guidance movement. The trait-factor model is characterized by the extensive reliance of the career counselor on psychological tests as a method to get what is termed objective career assessment data on the individual. Psychological tests, therefore, became an important and necessary part of the first functional stage in vocational guidance, that is, self-assessment (Pope, 2000). Testing gave vocational guidance respectability in American society (Whiteley, 1984). Without a scientific procedure to justify the first step of the vocational guidance process (i.e., self assessment), it is unlikely that vocational guidance would have been so popularly accepted (Pope, 2000; Super, 1954). Francis Galton (1874), Wilhelm Wundt (1879), James McKean Cattell (1890), and Alfred Binet (1896) made important contributions to the newly emerging field of psychological testing and, through extension, to vocational guidance.

It is, however, important to note that many of the early founders of vocational guidance were hesitant to prescribe psychological tests because many popularly available tests of that time had not been studied and researched rigorously for specific application to vocations (Bloomfield, 1915; Brewer, 1919). They were not against testing *per se,* only testing done badly.

Intelligence testing. During this time, scholarly attention to the measurement of both intelligence and interests was emerging. Intelligence was important because results might predict, successfully, both those who were very gifted and those who needed additional help in their studies in order to become contributors to society. Alfred Binet and Theophile Simon published the first validated intelligence scale – the *Binet-Simon Scale* (1905). They defined intelligence much more specifically as how individuals deal with tasks that require reasoning, judgment, and problem-solving – all directly related to vocational guidance.

Lewis Terman and H. G. Childs (1912) of Stanford University published preliminary results on an American adaptation of the *Binet-Simon Scale*, called the *Stanford-Binet Intelligence Scale*. This scale was where the concept of intelligence quotient (I.Q.) was introduced (i.e., the ratio between a person's mental age and chronological age). The *Stanford-Binet* became the most viable of the American revisions to this instrument.

Prior to 1917, all intelligence tests were categorized as being *individually administered*, because they were designed to be administered to one person at a time, which was a very costly process in both time and resources. During World War I, *group administered intelligence tests* were produced under the direction of Robert M. Yerkes, who chaired the American Psychological Association committee established to help with the war effort by assisting with the needed rapid classification of the 1.5 million recruits with respect to general intellectual level. Tests developed by Army psychologists used Arthur S. Otis' work (now *Otis-Lennon Tests*). Otis had been a student of Lewis Terman at Stanford University. The outcome of this effort was the development of two multiple choice tests of cognitive ability -- *Army Alpha*, for general routine testing, and *Army Beta*, a non-language scale for both recruits who were functionally illiterate and for foreign-born recruits for whom English was not their first language.

Vocational interests and their assessment. In 1912, Edward Lee Thorndike published a study on the permanence of vocational interests and their relationship to abilities. This work marked the beginning of what would become a burgeoning field of study in vocational interest assessment. Edward Kellogg Strong, Jr., who would later go on to develop the *Strong Vocational Interest Blank* in the 1920s, was a doctoral student in psychology at Columbia University and studied with Thorndike during this time. From 1917 to 1919, Strong served with the Army Committee on Classification of Personnel. He then took an academic position at Carnegie Institute of Technology (Carnegie Tech) in Pittsburg. Walter Bingham, from Carnegie Tech, led a group of industrial psychologists, in 1919, who worked on many applied problems in psychology including the challenge of measuring vocational interests. C. S. Yoakum, at Carnegie Tech, led a graduate seminar that prepared an extensive pool of nearly 1,000 items for interest inventories that, in turn, provided the items and the impetus for several other inventories, including the *Carnegie Interest Inventory* and the *Carnegie Interest Analysis*.

Unfortunately, the Industrial Psychology program at Carnegie Tech was discontinued in 1923, and, at that time, Strong took a position as Professor of Psychology in the School of Business at Stanford University. In 1927, Strong published the 420-item *Strong Vocational Interest Blank* for men, which was the first of many such interest inventories that would follow during this period. Inventories included the *Purdue Interest Report Blank* (Remmers, 1929), the *Minnesota Vocational Interest Inventory* (Paterson, 1930), the *Interest Analysis Blank* (Hubbard, 1935), and the *Kuder Preference Record – Vocational* (Kuder, 1934). In 1933, Strong published the *Strong Vocational Interest Blank* for women that included 410 items, 262 of which were the same as the men's version.

Between the 1920s and 1950s, thousands of tests were in print to measure intelligence, personality, abilities, and vocational interests, including the *Minnesota Multiphasic Personality Inventory* (Hathaway & McKinley, 1943), the *Thematic Apperception Test* (Murray, 1955), and the *California Psychological Inventory* (Gough, 1956). The boom in development and publication for commercial purposes of all psychological tests led, in 1938, to the development and publication of the *Mental Measurements Yearbook* (MMY). Oscar Kriesen Buros published the first MMY to provide objective reviews of psychological tests in response to the extraordinary growth in the commercial publication of such tests as well as the lack of data on the efficacy of such instruments. The MMY continues today as the preeminent source for objective reviews of such instruments.

Role of occupational information in assessment. Accurate occupational information –the second of Parsons' three pillars was difficult to find in the early 1900s. Probably the first published work on guidance, *Choosing a Vocation* by Frank Parsons (1909), described a number of exercises intended to help clients prepare for vocational choices. Today, this is called *cognitive education activities* aimed at preparing people to make choices. For example, Parsons described (p. 10) an exercise for groups of young people, who were asked to read a good book and respond to twelve activities in writing, in one page or more. Here are three of those activities:

- Enumerate half a dozen facts that seem fundamental in the book.
- Describe its main characters and their most striking personal traits.
- Compare the book with others you have already read and classify it in relation to those other books.

The formulation of these activities highlights Parsons's educational approach of enabling clients to develop their analysis skills, selection of information, synthesis, and comparison. Parsons thought these skills would be transferable to self-analysis and occupational analysis.

In 1938 the U.S. Department of Labor, through its Bureau of Labor Statistics, published the first *Dictionary of Occupational Titles,* an objective classification system for occupations in the US. The DOT was an important staple of the vocational guidance period with its nine-digit numeric code used to describe each of the thousands of occupations in the US, as that code allowed for ease of job matching. The DOT had a distinctive industrial manufacturing focus, as would be expected for such a document from this period. The DOT "emerged in an industrial economy and emphasized blue-collar jobs. Updated periodically, the DOT provided useful occupational information for many years. But its usefulness waned as the economy shifted toward information and services and away from heavy industry" (Mariani, 1999, p. 2).

The DOT was followed in 1949 with the first edition of its sister publication, the *Occupational Outlook Handbook* (OOH) that provided occupational outlook information on single occupations. A major motivation for the development of the OOH was the need to help returning armed services members find work after World War II. Goldstein (1999) reported that the impetus came directly from the Veterans Administration (VA) that wanted to ensure that these veterans would have the kind of information that would lead to actual employment opportunities, not simply education that was mandated by the Serviceman's Readjustment Act of 1944 (the "G.I. Bill of Rights").

This predecessor to the OOH was provided to VA vocational counselors in educational program centers as *VA Manual M7-1: Occupational Outlook Information* and was three-hole punched and bound between a front and back cover by long black shoelaces (Goldstein, 1999). OOH's first print run was 40,000 copies, considered a best-seller for a government agency that usually only printed and sold 500 to a very few thousand of any one of its many publications.

Societal institutions, including schools, government, and community-based organizations, approached career assessment during this period as vocational guidance, helping match individuals to the best occupation (Pope, 2000). Government, in particular, focused on developing better occupational information so as to aid this process, including such projects as the 1938 publication of the *Dictionary of Occupational Titles* and it's nine-digit coding system used to categorize the characteristics of each occupation in the US. The matching paradigm that defined this period would achieve its zenith in the work of John Holland (1997). But even today, "in conducting actual career interventions, the profession of career counseling has relied on Parsons' (1909) matching model for vocational guidance as its core 'counseling' model" (Savickas, 2011, p. 5).

The Career Education Period

The second career intervention period – career education – flowed from the work of Donald Super (1957, 1975, 1990) and Kenneth Hoyt (1977, 2005; Hoyt, Evans, Mackin, & Magnum, 1972) and was characterized by a focus on the development of the individual (Hartung, 2010; Savickas 2010). Savickas (2011) characterized the primary interventions of this period in this manner:

Practitioners apply Super's (1957) model of vocational development when they perform career education to help clients (a) understand career stages; (b) learn about imminent developmental tasks; and (c) rehearse the attitudes, beliefs, and competencies needed to master those tasks. (p. 4)

The quite effective content approach of the vocational guidance period was supplemented with the more process-oriented approach of career education beginning in the late 1940s and early 1950s (Savickas, 2011). This approach focused on *how* to make career decisions rather than on *which* occupation an individual might choose. Career development practitioners during this period focused on the tasks that Savickas outlined above, including teaching those attitudes, beliefs, and competencies that practitioners believed would lead to more realistic career decisions.

Historical and Political Context

In the United States, this stage in the development of career counseling was characterized by the focus of societal resources on colleges and universities and the training of professional counselors as a direct result of, and response to, a new social transition engendered by two major events that set the tone for all subsequent world-wide actions: the end of World War II and the Union of Soviet Socialist Republics' (USSR, including Russia and other European communist nations) successful launching of satellites that orbited the Earth and even landed on the moon (Pope, 2000).

World War II focused the energy and attention of all nations of the world on this contest between nationalistic fascism (Germany, Japan, and Italy) and capitalism/communism (USA, Great Britain, France, USSR) that were politically allied at this time (Pope, 2000). President Truman's Fair Deal program was a response to the problems encountered by returning armed services veterans. The lack of jobs and the subsequent displacement of current workers by these returning veterans were important societal problems that the Truman program attempted to address.

Then, the USSR launched the first space probe, Sputnik I, successfully in 1957 and followed that by landing Lunik II on the moon in 1959 (Pope, 2000). These two events, more than any other, humbled American capitalism for a time. The United States had considered itself far superior technologically to any other country on Earth; however, when the USSR succeeded in its space program, this impelled the U.S. Congress to begin to address the deficits in science and math education across the nation. The passage of the National Defense Education Act (NDEA) in 1958 was a direct response to the successful launching of Sputnik and the desperation of American government officials at the loss of what was claimed to be U.S. superiority in technology to a relatively underdeveloped country – the USSR.

Under the NDEA, the Counseling and Guidance Training Institutes were established to provide improved training for counselors who were to identify and encourage science and math majors for college education. This was a boom period for the training of career counselors, and almost 14,000 counselors received training in these NDEA Institutes (Borow, 1964).

In 1944, in response to the unique vocational needs of the U.S. population during that time, the Veterans Administration established a network of vocational guidance services, including vocational rehabilitation, training, counseling, and advisement that spanned the entire nation. Also at that same time, the U.S. Employment Service was developed under the direct administration of the War Manpower Commission, which included 1,500 offices staffed by employment counselors.

Then, in the mid- to late-1950s, the Vocational Rehabilitation Act (VRA, 1954), and National Defense Education Act (NDEA, 1958) were enacted into law. Both of these laws had an important influence on the professional practice of career counseling. The VRA recognized the needs of people with disabilities, in particular the needs of World War II veterans. In addition, the VRA mandated the development of rehabilitation counselors and authorized funds for their training. NDEA was passed as a direct response to the USSR's successes in space technology, and focused on improving science and math performance by students in the public schools. Guidance counseling was seen as a critical component of such a program and would encourage students to explore their career interests, abilities, and opportunities. Grants were given to schools to provide guidance activities and to institutions of higher education to improve the training of guidance counselors.

Looking back at the career education period, Savickas (2011) characterized work and workers in this manner: "(f)ollowing World War II, the United States experienced the rise of suburban, middle-class individuals employed by hierarchical bureaucracies located in horizontal skyscrapers" (p. 4). The main question for workers during this period was "how to climb the career ladders in hierarchical professions and bureaucratic organizations" (p. 4).

This bureaucratic organizational framework was instrumental in the development of not only a new process for individuals to find a job that was consistent with their personal traits, but also the possibility of an occupational promotion up the career ladder if certain criteria were met. At this time, and for the first time historically, career development was defined as a succession of related jobs that, in a somewhat predictable sequence, offered the possibility of upward mobility, leading to the attainment of status and prestige in society (Duarte, 2009; Wilensky, 1961).

Career Education Assessments

Many career assessments were developed and rose to prominence with career practitioners during this period. With the focus of this period on the process of individual career development, many of the assessments of this period had a distinctive psychoeducational flavor focusing on the developmental aspects of the individual's career.

Career development. Donald Super's work on career development stages came out of the longitudinal Career Pattern Study that began in 1951 following a cohort of ninth grade males (Patton & Lokan, 2001). In the late 1960s and early 1970s, Super developed his *Career Development Inventory* (CDI), with three experimental versions leading to its first commercial publication in 1981. Following the publication of the CDI, the measurement of other Super constructs followed, including the *Adult Career Concerns Inventory* (Super, Thompson, & Lindeman, 1988), *Salience Inventory* (Nevill & Super, 1986), *Work Values Inventory* (now *Values Scale*), and *Career Maturity Inventory* (Crites, 1973; Crites & Savickas, 1996). Each of these instruments was designed to help career practitioners apply Super's career development theory to problems of practice.

Career interest patterns. Research on career interests blossomed during this period. In 1955, the University of Minnesota Press published a number of books on career interests, including Wilbur L. Layton's *The Strong Vocational Interest Blank: Research and Uses*, based on a University of Minnesota-sponsored symposium on the *Strong Vocational Interest Blank* (SVIB); John G. Darley and Theda Hagenah's *Vocational Interest Measurement*; and Edward K. Strong's classic longitudinal study, *Vocational Interests Eighteen Years after College*. Strong's study provided the research basis to justify the use of career interest measurement as a powerful intervention tool for career practitioners.

In 1963, the University of Minnesota established the Center for Interest Measurement Research to lead the development of major revisions of the SVIB Men's Form in 1966 and Women's Form in 1969. Then in 1974, David Campbell developed the merged form of the SVIB that combined the men's and women's forms into one inventory, called the *Strong-Campbell Interest Inventory*.

Later, one of the seminal contributions to the study of career interests emerged from the work of John Holland (1973, 1985, 1997). Holland found there were identifiable patterns of career interests and suggested a six-factor structure to house them – his RIASEC model. He wrote that work environments corresponded similarly to this model, further simplifying the matching career intervention. Holland developed the *Self-Directed Search, My Vocational Situation*, and *Vocational Preference Inventory* as instruments to help operationalize his new theory. As a complement to Holland's work, Gary Gottfredson developed the *Dictionary of Holland Occupational Codes* (1982, 1996), which cross-matched a three-letter career interest code, based on the RIASEC model, with over 14,000 occupations from the *Dictionary of Occupational Titles* to enable greater efficiency in occupational matching.

The Life Design Period

In the 21st century, at the end of the industrial era and with the rise of the digital/global era, a new period in the history of career assessment began, termed the Life Design period (Duarte, 2009; Hartung, 2010; Savickas, 2011). Savickas et al. (2009) described this period as follows:

> Individuals in the knowledge societies at the beginning of the 21st century must realize that career problems are only a piece of much broader concerns about how to live a life in a postmodern world shaped by a global economy and supported by information technology. (p. 241)

As corporations evolved in the 21st century, the locus of control of a person's career moved away from the organization (Hall, 1996a,b). Savickas (2011) stated that "(t)his shift in responsibility from the organization to the individual posed the new question of how individuals may negotiate a lifetime of job changes" (Savickas, 2011, p. 5). Savickas argued that the existing career theories from the vocational guidance and career education periods were inadequate for the monumental societal changes seen at the beginning of the 21st century. The new models and interventions of this period flow from constructivism and social constructionism.

Historical and Political Context

In the 1990s, the field of career counseling found itself being extended in a variety of new directions with an increasing societal focus on poverty and culture, the rapid advancement of technology, and the shortening of the economic boom and bust cycles.

Poverty and culture. One extension was into lower socioeconomic classes who were being required to go to work because of new governmental policies, such as Greater Avenues to Independence (GAIN), the Job Training Partnership Act (JTPA), Welfare to Work (WtW, 1997), and Workforce Investment Act of 1998 (WIA). The Welfare to Work Act of 1997 was the harshest of these laws because it set a five-year limit on any person in the US receiving economic support through a federally-administered economic support program called Temporary Assistance for Needy Families (TANF), which had replaced the federal program called Aid to Families with Dependent Children (AFDC).

The goal of these new policies was to get those who had experienced, or had characteristics associated with, long-term *welfare dependence* into lasting unsubsidized jobs, to get them into jobs first (called a *work first* service strategy) and, then, to train them post-employment for better positions which better matched their interests (which rarely happened). The role of counseling professionals was to assist in this process wherever they could, which varied from state to state and from local agency to local agency.

The focus of federal implementation monies was to help those who were most likely to have the greatest problems, such as individuals with disabilities, individuals who require substance abuse treatment, victims of domestic violence, individuals with limited English proficiency, and noncustodial parents. Unfortunately, with the focus on *work first* in this legislation, there was no provision for formal assessment and training as a precursor to finding a job that individuals would be more likely to maintain over their lifetime (Pope, 2000).

Workforce development. There was also a renewed interest and support for career counseling in other socioeconomic classes through the policies of the federal government. In fact, not since the 1960s had so many important laws affecting the career development of American citizens been passed by Congress and signed by a president. Beginning with President George Bush (1988-91) and carrying over to President Bill Clinton (1992-2000), there was resurgence in interest in the lifelong career development of the American people. Such federal legislation as the School-to-Work Opportunities Act (1994) and Workforce Investment Act (1998) were important initiatives in this national campaign (Pope, 2000).

The Workforce Investment Act (WIA) revamped all job-training programs in the country and reauthorized the Rehabilitation Act. Under WIA, all adults, regardless of income or employment status, became eligible for core services, including skills assessments, job search assistance, and information on educational and employment opportunities. WIA mandated that states and local governments establish and maintain networks of *one-stop centers* to provide citizens a single point of entry to federal job training and education programs, job market information, unemployment insurance, and other federal and state services and programs. These centers offered training referrals, career counseling, job listings, and similar employment-related services. Many states took advantage of this federal legislation to revamp and reorganize their antiquated state-run *unemployment* programs (Pope, 2000).

The role of schools. The School-to-Work Opportunities Act established partnerships among educators, businesses, and employers to facilitate the transition of students from high school to other education or work opportunities, including post-secondary education in technical or trade schools. The role of organized counseling professionals and federal agencies working together through the American Counseling Association (ACA), National Career Development Association (NCDA), American Vocational Association (AVA) (now the Association for Career and Technical Education [ACTE]), and American School Counselor Association (ASCA) was pivotal to the final legislation authorizing the School-to-Work Opportunities Act (NCDA, 1993). This legislation revolutionized the process of schooling in the US by refocusing the nation's educational resources on the very real, difficult, but under-attended transition that all students must make from schooling to jobs (Pope, 2000).

Three other bulwarks of career development legislation were reauthorized during this period: the Carl D. Perkins Vocational and Applied Technology Education Act Amendments of 1998 (formerly titled the Carl D. Perkins Vocational Education Act), the Higher Education Act (1998), and the Elementary and Secondary Education Act. The Elementary School Counseling Demonstration Act (1995) that allocated two million dollars in grant money for schools to develop comprehensive elementary school counseling programs also became law during this time (Pope, 2000).

Persons with disabilities. The Americans with Disabilities Act (ADA; 1990) was the single most important legislation protecting the right to employment of persons who experienced functional limitations (e.g., sensation and perception, ambulation, psychological well-being, and learning) across domains of life. The ADA prohibited job discrimination against people with disabilities and mandated that individuals with disabilities have the same access to goods, services, facilities, and accommodations afforded to all others. This law had far-reaching consequences for professional counselors, especially school, rehabilitation, and career counselors (Pope, 2012a).

Role of technology. Another aspect of this period was an increasing technological sophistication that has led to instant communication by Internet to anywhere in the world. Changes in the size and sophistication of such devices have contributed to ensuring their accessibility, portability, and use. Personal communication devices, such as mobile phones and smart phones, have made it possible to contact people wherever they are on the planet. Extensions of these changes for the career counselor were the provision of career services by phone and over the Internet.

With the opening of economic doors in China, dissolution of the former Soviet Union, the steady 7% annual economic growth in Southeast Asia, and technological advancements in connectivity and business communication, career counselors from the US have expanded their practices internationally. This expansion has included substantial energy and economic investment in taking career counseling to other countries. Career counselors from the US now do substantial contract work in Singapore, Russia, China, Hong Kong, Malaysia, Australia, Estonia, and Poland, to name but a few (Pope, 1995a,b; Pope, 1999). This is only the beginning of this trend as these technological advances continue to drive the worldwide dissemination of information and innovations in the delivery of career counseling services.

Work and worker issues. The world of work has changed drastically in the 21st century and not necessarily for the better for the individual worker. In the 20th century, secure employment and stable organizations predominated and were part of the social contract between workers and employers (Duarte, 2009). As part of this contract, organizations of that time and worker expectations were based on a promise that, if workers were loyal to the employer and performed well, they would have permanent employment for building their life and securing their future. In this new era, this has all changed. With its emphasis on nimbleness, flexibility, temporary assignments, quick profits, and time-limited project-driven processes, the digital/global era of the 21st century has, however, reneged on that contract, and left workers of this period more insecure and anxious (Kalleberg, 2009; Kalleberg, Reskin, & Hudson, 2000; Savickas, 2011).

This project-focused model has been the dominant model in certain occupations, such as construction, engineering, arts, and entertainment (especially movie making, theatre, music, and others) for much of their existence. The rise of large manufacturing and distribution companies as part of the more urbanized industrial era required, however, large stable groups of workers to perform their duties consistently in order for these companies to exist and be successful (Duarte, 2009). With changes in technology, shortened boom and bust economic cycles, and increasing population densities of highly skilled and educated workers in metropolitan areas, this project-focused model has overtaken the industrialized model and expanded its scope into many other organizations.

With such changes in organizations come changes in the structure of careers. Savickas (2011) noted this transition with data from several sources.

> For many workers, an assignment does not last even 2 years. More than half of the individuals born after 1980 left their first job within 5 months (Saratoga Institute, 2000). This was true not only with emerging adults, but also for those adults who, in previous times, had stabilized in jobs and families. Of the jobs started by workers between the ages of 33 and 38, 39% ended in less than a year and 70% ended in fewer than 5 years. One in four workers has been with his or her current employers for less than a year (Bureau of Labor Statistics, 2004). (p. 9)

The result of these changes is insecure and anxious workers. Savickas (2011) provided a list of the terms used to identify such workers in the popular and professional literature: "temporary, contingent, casual, contract, freelance, part-time, external, atypical, adjunct, consultant, and self-employed" (p. 10). Such previous benefits taken for granted as part of a job, including pensions, medical insurance, and others, might or might not be part of the contract. With the housing crash of the Great Recession (2008-2013), the dream of home ownership might be lost forever for many workers, and renting may be the better choice for jobs of short duration and individual careers that require geographic mobility.

Another loss due to the new project-driven model is the loyalty of workers, because employers who do not treat workers as long-term resources cannot expect workers to wait around for their next project or their next assignment. Workers have bills to pay and lives to lead. The individuals, who must now take control of their own careers, are no longer bound to an organization. Hall (1996a,b) discussed *protean* careers and Arthur (1994) wrote about *boundaryless careers*. Both are reflecting this new state of affairs for workers. As Savickas (2011) noted, "(r) ather than living a narrative conferred by a corporation, people must author their own stories as they navigate occupational transitions in the postmodern world" (p. 11).

Life Design Assessments

The emerging career assessments of this period had their foundations in Super's (1954) career pattern work and Tiedeman's (1961) reflective career consciousness ideas, and "the individual design perspective finds its paramount embodiment in Savickas's (2002) career construction theory and practice and its recent advancement within a comprehensive model of individual life designing (Savickas et al., 2009)" (Hartung, 2010, p. 7).

Informal qualitative assessment. The individual life design perspective uses informal qualitative assessment methods, such as the *Career Construction Interview* (Savickas, 1998; Savickas et al., 2009; Taber, Hartung, Briddick, Briddick, & Rehfuss, 2011), emphasizing subjective assessment of the individual's life story. "Practitioners apply career construction theory when they perform career counseling to (a) construct career through small stories, (b) deconstruct and reconstruct the small stories into a large story, and (c) co-construct the next episode in the story" (Savickas, 2011, p. 5). The central question that life design interventions address is: How can I use school and work to make my life more meaningful and complete in a way that matters to society? Life design interventions use both informal and formal assessments to evaluate and appreciate the rich tapestry of an individual's full life better, as told through the person's own story.

Occupational information. In 1997, the DOT was replaced by a preliminary version of the *Occupational Information Network* (O*NET), a free online database sponsored by the U.S. Department of Labor and developed through a grant to the North Carolina Employment Security Commission. "O*NET allows everyone to access data on job characteristics and worker attributes. It includes information on the knowledge, skills, abilities, interests, preparation, contexts, and tasks associated with 1,122 O*NET occupations" (Mariani, 1999, p. 2), and uses Holland's RIASEC model as its organizing schema.

The career exploration assessments that are available as part of O*NET include the *O*NET Ability Profiler*, *O*NET Interest Profiler*, *O*NET Computerized Interest Profiler*, *O*NET Interest Profiler Short Form*, *O*NET Work Importance Locator*, and the *O*NET Work Importance Profiler*. These self-directed inventories are available free electronically on O*NET and provide valuable career information.

Accurate and up-to-date occupational information is vitally important, especially at the third state of life design, that is, the co-construction of the next episode of the client's story, as the career counselor and the client work to identify what is next. The O*NET can be a useful tool in that it is a process to help illuminate vistas and career paths that would, otherwise, not be a part of a client's worldview. This is especially important for clients from lower socioeconomic communities and families and any individuals whose visions might have been more narrowly focused and circumscribed by life circumstances.

Rise of interest in cultural diversity and social justice. As part of this period, there has been a rise in interest and research on the role of cultural diversity and social justice in career development and counseling, broadening the social groups to which career counseling is now becoming more effective and relevant. Over a period of 30 years, Pope and his colleagues led an insurgent movement within the profession that began to look at the effects of culture on the career counseling process, including assessment, beginning with their work to establish and legitimize the study of career counseling with gays and lesbians (Pope, 1992, 1995a,b, 1996, 2008; Pope & Barret, 2002; Pope, Prince, & Mitchell, 2000; Pope et al., 2004, Pope et al., 2007); to expand the notions of career counseling with multiple diverse cultural groups in the US (Pope, 2010; Pope & Pangelinan, 2010) and internationally (Leong & Pope, 2002; Pope, 1999, 2003, 2012b; Pope, Musa, Singaravelu, Bringaze, & Russell, 2002; Pope, Singaravelu, Chang, Sullivan, & Murray, 2007; Puertas, Cinamon, Neault, Pope, & Rossier, 2012; Zhang, Hu, & Pope, 2002); to look at the special issues involved in using career assessment with culturally diverse clients (Pope, 1992; Pope & Barret, 2002; Pope & Pangelinan, 2010); to look at the social justice roots of career counseling (Pope, 2011, 2013; Pope, Briddick, & Wilson, 2013; Pope & Sveinsdottir, 2005); and to integrate issues of culture into the processes of career assessment in the career education period (Hartung et al., 1998).

This has led to the development of Pope's career counseling with underserved populations model (Pope, 2011, 2015b). Based on over 30 years of accumulated research, this model provides guidelines on how to proceed with conducting career counseling with clients from a culture or cultures different from the counselor's own, including assessment as a valuable piece of that process.

Conclusion

Career assessment has evolved over the past 100 years from the matching of an individual's traits with occupations of the vocational guidance period, with its focus on individual differences (Holland, 1997; Parsons, 1909; Strong, 1943); to the process-oriented approach to career decision-making and career development over the lifespan of the career education period, with its focus on individual development (Hartung et al., 1998; Super, 1953, 1954, 1957, 1990); and to individual construction of career through stories of the life design period, with its focus on individual design (Hartung, 2010; Maree, 2007; Savickas, 2011; Savickas et al., 2009). In doing so, career assessment has maintained consistency with the changing needs of individuals and the economy. What has developed is a rich tapestry of career assessment. As the career interventions of these three periods are conceptually additive, not mutually exclusive, each builds upon and supplements the work of the preceding period. Career counselors can choose an appropriate assessment from the total arsenal of career assessments that have arisen over these past 100 years, based on the specific career problems of their specific client.

References

Arthur, M. B. (1994). The boundaryless career [Special issue]. *Journal of Organizational Behavior, 15*(4), 295-306.

Aubrey, R. F. (1977). Historical development of guidance and counseling and implications for the future. *Personnel & Guidance Journal, 55*, 288–295. https://doi-org.ezproxy.una.edu/10.1002/j.2164-4918.1977.tb04991.x

Binet, A., & Simon, T. (1905). The development of intelligence in children (The Binet-Simon Scale). *L'Annee Psychologie, 12*, 182-273.

Bloomfield, M. (1915). *Readings in vocational guidance.* Boston: Ginn and Company.

Borow, H. (1964). Notable events in the history of vocational guidance. In H. Borow (Ed.), *Man in a world at work* (pp. 45-64). Washington, DC: Houghton Mifflin.

Brewer, J. M. (1919). *The vocational guidance movement.* New York: Macmillan.

Brewer, J. M. (1942). *History of vocational guidance.* New York: Harper & Brothers.

Briddick, W. C. (2009a). Frank findings: Frank Parsons and the Parson family. *Career Development Quarterly, 57*, 207-214.

Briddick, W. C. (2009b). Frank Parsons on interests. *Journal of Vocational Behavior, 74*, 230-233.

Bureau of Labor Statistics. (2004, August 25). *Number of jobs held, labor market activity, and earnings among younger baby boomers: Recent results from a longitudinal study.* Washington, DC: U.S. Department of Labor.

Crites, J. O. (1973). *The Career Maturity Inventory.* Monterey, CA: CTB/McGraw-Hill.

Crites, J. O., & Savickas, M. L. (1996). The revision of the Career Maturity Inventory. *Journal of Career Assessment, 4,* 131-138.

Darley, J. G., & Hagenah, T. (1955). *Vocational interest measurement.* Minneapolis, MN: University of Minnesota Press.

Davis, H. V. (1969). *Frank Parsons: Prophet, innovator, counselor.* Carbondale, IL: University of Southern Illinois Press.

Duarte, M. E. (2009). The psychology of life construction. *Journal of Vocational Behavior, 75,* 259-266.

Ginzberg, E. (1971). *Career guidance.* New York: McGraw-Hill.

Goldstein, H. (1999). The early history of the *Occupational Outlook Handbook. Monthly Labor Review, 5,* 3-7.

Hall, D. T. (Ed.) (1996a). *The career is dead–long live the career.* San Francisco, CA: Jossey-Bass.

Hall, D. T. (1996b). Protean careers of the 21st century. *Academy of Management Executives, 10,* 8-16.

Hartung, P. J. (2010). Career assessment: Using scores and stories in life designing. In K. Maree (Ed.), *Career counselling: Methods that work* (pp. 1-10). Cape Town, South Africa: Juta & Company.

Hartung, P. J., Vandiver, B. J., Leong, F. T. L., Pope, M., Niles, S. G., & Farrow, B. (1998). Appraising cultural identity in career-development assessment and counseling. *Career Development Quarterly, 46,* 276-293.

Hoyt, K. B. (1977). *A primer for career education* Washington, DC: U.S. Government Printing Office.

Hoyt, K. B. (2005). *Career education: History and future.* Broken Arrow, OK: National Career Development Association.

Hoyt, K. B., Evans, R., Mackin, E., & Magnum, G. L. (1972). *Career education: What is it and how to do it?* Salt Lake City, UT: Olympus Publishing.

Kalleberg, A. L. (2009). Precarious work, insecure workers: Employment relations in transition. *American Sociological Review, 74,* 1-22. doi:10.1177/000312240907400101

Kalleberg, A. L., Reskin, B. F., & Hudson, K. (2000). Bad jobs in America: Standard and nonstandard employment relations and job quality in the United States. *American Sociological Review, 65,* 256-278.

Layton, W. L. (Ed.). (1955). *The Strong Vocational Interest Blank: Research and uses.* Minneapolis, MN: University of Minnesota Press.

Leong, F. T. L., & Pope, M. (Eds.). (2002). Challenges for career counseling in Asia [Special section]. *Career Development Quarterly, 50*, 209-284. doi: http://onlinelibrary.wiley.com/doi/10.1002/cdq.2002.50.issue-3/issuetoc

Maree, J. G. (Ed.). (2007). *Shaping the story: A guide to facilitating narrative counselling.* Hatfield, South Africa: Van Schaik Publishers.

Mariani, M. (1999, Spring). Replace with a database: O*NET replaces the Dictionary of Occupational Titles. *Occupational Outlook Handbook*, pp. 1-9.

National Career Development Association. (1993). *A policy statement of the 1992-1993 Board of Directors.* Alexandria, VA: Author.

Nevill, D. D., & Super, D. E. (1986). *The Salience Inventory: Theory, application and research.* Palo Alto, CA: Consulting Psychologists Press.

Patton, W., & Lokan, J. (2001). Perspectives on Donald Super's construct of career maturity. *International Journal for Educational and Vocational Guidance, 1*, 31-48.

Pope, M. (1992). Bias in the interpretation of psychological tests. In S. Dworkin & F. Gutierrez (Eds.), *Counseling gay men and lesbians: Journey to the end of the rainbow* (pp. 277-291). Alexandria, VA: American Counseling Association.

Pope, M. (Ed.). (1995a). Gay/lesbian career development [Special section]. *Career Development Quarterly, 44*, 146-203. doi: http://onlinelibrary.wiley.com/doi/10.1002/cdq.1995.44.issue-2/issuetoc

Pope, M. (1995b). Career interventions for gay and lesbian clients: A synopsis of practice knowledge and research needs. *Career Development Quarterly, 44*, 191-203. doi: http://dx.doi.org/10.1002/j.2161-0045.1995.tb00685.x

Pope, M. (1996). Gay and lesbian career counseling: Special career counseling issues. *Journal of Gay and Lesbian Social Services, 4*(4), 91-105.

Pope, M. (1999). Applications of group career counseling techniques in Asian cultures. *Journal for Multicultural Counseling and Development, 27*, 18-30. doi:10.1002/j.2161-1912.1999.tb00209.x

Pope, M. (2000). A brief history of career counseling in the United States. *Career Development Quarterly, 48*, 194-211. doi: http://dx.doi.org/10.1002/j.2161-0045.2000.tb00286.x

Pope, M. (2003). Career counseling in the 21st century: Beyond cultural encapsulation. *Career Development Quarterly, 51*, 54-60. doi: http://dx.doi.org/10.1002/j.2161-0045.2003.tb00627.x

Pope, M. (2008). Culturally appropriate counseling considerations with lesbian and gay clients. In P. B. Pedersen, J. G. Draguns, W. J. Lonner, & J. E. Trimble (Eds.), *Counseling across cultures* (6th ed., pp. 201-222). Thousand Oaks, CA: Sage Publications.

Pope, M. (2010). Career counseling with diverse adults. In J. G. Ponterotto, J. M. Casas, L.A. Suzuki, & C. M. Alexander (Eds.), *Handbook of multicultural counseling* (3rd ed., pp. 731-744). Thousand Oaks, CA: Sage.

Pope, M. (2011). The career counseling with underserved populations model. *Journal of Employment Counseling, 48,* 153-156. doi: http://dx.doi.org/10.1002/j.2161-1920.2011. tb01100.x

Pope, M. (2012a). History and philosophy of the counseling profession. In V. F. Sangganjanavanich & C. A. Reynolds (Eds.), *Introduction to professional counseling* (pp. 25-46). Newbury Park, CA: Sage.

Pope, M. (2012b). Embracing and harnessing diversity in the US workforce: What have we learned. *International Journal for Educational and Vocational Guidance, 12,* 17-30. doi: http://dx.doi.org/10.1007/s10775-012-9215-x

Pope, M. (2013). Social justice. In M. Savickas (Ed.), *Ten essential ideas in the evolution of career intervention* (p. 9). Broken Arrow, OK: National Career Development Association.

Pope, M. (2015a). Career intervention: From the industrial to the digital age. In P. J. Hartung, M. L. Savickas, & W. B. Walsh (Eds.), *APA handbook of career intervention* (pp. 3-19). Washington, DC: American Psychological Association.

Pope, M. (2015b). Career counseling with underserved populations: The role of cultural diversity, social justice, and advocacy. In K. Maree & A. DiFabio (Eds.), *Exploring new horizons in career counseling: Turning challenges into opportunities* (pp. 297-312). Rotterdam, The Netherlands: Sense Publishers.

Pope, M., & Barret, B. (2002). Providing career counseling services to gay and lesbian clients. In S. G. Niles (Ed.), *Adult career development: Concepts, issues, and practices* (3rd ed., pp. 215-232). Broken Arrow, OK: National Career Development Association.

Pope, M., Barret, B., Szymanski, D. M., Chung, Y. B., McLean, R., Singaravelu, H., & Sanabria, S. (2004). Culturally appropriate career counseling with gay and lesbian clients. *Career Development Quarterly, 53,* 158-177. doi: http://dx.doi. org/10.1002/j.2161-0045.2004.tb00987.x

Pope, M., Briddick, W. C., & Wilson, F. (2013). The historical importance of social justice in the founding of the National Career Development Association. *Career Development Quarterly, 61,* 368-373. doi: http://dx.doi.org/10.1002/j.2161-0045.2013.00063.x

Pope, M., Musa, M., Singaravelu, H., Bringaze, T., & Russell, M. (2002). From colonialism to ultranationalism: History and development of career counseling in Malaysia. *Career Development Quarterly, 50,* 264-276. doi: http://dx.doi. org/10.1002/j.2161-0045.2002.tb00902.x

Pope, M., & Pangelinan, J. S. (2010). Using the ACA Advocacy Competencies in career counseling. In M. J. Ratts, R. L. Toporek, & J. A. Lewis. (Eds.), *ACA Advocacy Competencies: A social justice framework for counselors* (pp. 209-224). Alexandria, VA: American Counseling Association.

Pope, M., Prince, J. P., & Mitchell, K. (2000). Responsible career counseling with lesbian and gay students. In D. A. Luzzo (Ed.), *Career counseling of college students: An empirical guide to strategies that work* (pp. 267-284). Washington, DC: American Psychological Association.

Pope, M., Singaravelu, H. D., Chang, A., Sullivan, C., & Murray, S. (2007). Counseling gay, lesbian, bisexual and questioning international students. In H. D. Singaravelu & M. Pope (Eds.). *Handbook for counseling international students in the US* (pp. 57-86). Alexandria, VA: American Counseling Association.

Pope, M., & Sveinsdottir, M. (2005). Frank, we hardly knew ye: The very personal side of Frank Parsons. *Journal of Counseling & Development, 83*, 105-115. doi: http://dx.doi.org/10.1002/j.1556-6678.2005.tb00585.x

Puertas, A., Cinamon, R. G., Neault, R., Pope, M., & Rossier, J. (2012) Career development for diverse and underserved populations. In J. Trusty (Ed.), *Bridging international perspectives of career development* (pp. 33-46). Broken Arrow, OK: National Career Development Association.

Saratoga Institute. (2000). *Human capital benchmarking report.* Santa Clara, CA: Saratoga Institute.

Savickas, M. L. (1998). Career style assessment and counseling. In T. Sweeney (Ed.), *Adlerian counseling: A practitioner's approach* (4th ed., pp. 329-359). Philadelphia, PA: Accelerated Development.

Savickas, M. L. (2010). Foreword: Best practices in career intervention. In K. Maree (Ed.), *Career counselling: Methods that work* (pp. xi-xii). Cape Town, South Africa: Juta & Company.

Savickas, M. L. (2011). *Career counseling.* Washington, DC: American Psychological Association.

Savickas, M. L. (2012). Life design: A paradigm for career intervention in the 21st century. *Journal of Counseling & Development, 90*, 13-19.

Savickas, M. L., Nota, L., Rossier, J., Dauwalder, J. P., Duarte, M. E., Guichard, J., Soresi, S., Van Esbroeck, R., & van Vianen, A. E. M. (2009). Life designing: A paradigm for career construction in the 21st century. *Journal of Vocational Behavior, 79*, 239-250.

Strong, E. K. (1927). *Vocational Interest Blank.* Stanford, CA: Stanford University Press.

Strong, E. K. (1943). *Vocational interests of men and women.* Stanford, CA: Stanford University Press.

Strong, E. K. (1955). *Vocational interests eighteen years after college.* Minneapolis, MN: University of Minnesota Press.

Super, D. E. (1953). A theory of vocational development. *American Psychologist, 8*, 185–190.

Super, D. E. (1954). Career patterns as a basis for vocational counseling. *Journal of Counseling Psychology, 1*, 2-20.

Super, D. E. (1957). *The psychology of careers. An introduction to vocational development.* New York: Harper & Brothers.

Super, D. E. (1975). *Career education and the meaning of work.* Washington, DC: Office of Career Education.

Super, D. E. (1990). A life-span, life-space approach to career development. In D. Brown & L. Brooks (Eds.), *Career choice and development* (2nd ed., pp. 197–261). San Francisco, CA: Jossey-Bass.

Super, D. E., Thompson, A. S., & Lindeman, R. H. (1988). *Adult Career Concerns Inventory: Manual for research and exploratory use in counseling.* Palo Alto, CA: Consulting Psychologists Press.

Taber, B. J., Hartung, P. J., Briddick, H., Briddick, W. C., & Rehfuss, M. C. (2011). Career Style Interview: A contextualized approach to career counseling. *Career Development Quarterly, 59,* 274-287.

Terman, L. M., & Childs, H. G. (1912). A tentative revision and extension of the Binet-Simon measuring scale of intelligence. *Journal of Educational Psychology, 3*(2), 61-74.

Thorndike, E. L. (1912). The permanence of interests and their relation to abilities. *Popular Science Monthly, 81,* 449-456.

Tiedeman, D. V. (1961). Decisions and vocational development: A paradigm and implications. *Personnel and Guidance Journal, 40,* 15-20.

Whiteley, J. (1984). *Counseling psychology: A historical perspective.* Schenectady, NY: Character Research Press.

Wilensky, H. (1961). Careers, life-styles, and social integration. *International Social Science Journal, 12,* 553–558.

Zhang, W. Y., Hu, X. L, & Pope, M. (2002). The evolution of career guidance and counseling in the People's Republic of China. *Career Development Quarterly, 50,* 226-236.

CHAPTER 2

CAREER ASSESSMENT: PERSPECTIVES ON TRENDS AND ISSUES

Spencer G. Niles
College of William and Mary

Clayton V. Martin
Alverna University

Background

Since the earliest years of the twentieth century, policy makers, theorists, and counselors have viewed career assessments as important instruments for achieving social, economic, and political goals. Many perceive career assessment as an important sociopolitical instrument by which to achieve outcomes of significance to national aspirations. In oversimplified terms, goals to which career assessment is expected to contribute include (1) the prevention of long-term unemployment, the development of an effective workforce, and the matching of workers and employers; (2) the adjustment by potential or active workers to rapidly changing requirements for employment or for retention; (3) intervention programs for persons considered marginally employable due to poor academic or technical skills, functional disabilities, interpersonal or other social problems, or discrimination; and (4) the provision of assistance to those who are unemployed or underemployed as a result of industrial reorganization, outsourcing, or international economic competition.

A continuing stream of public policies and legislation reflect these national goals in both the United States and other nations, which, in turn, affect the form, substance, and purposes of career assessment and career interventions. Such policies and legislation are direct responses to changing conditions in society and tend to occur alongside issues pertaining to economic recession, national defense, civil rights, war, technological developments, or the consequences of the global economy that dominate the culture. This results in counselor assumptions about what types of assistance individuals need to develop the knowledge, skills, and attitudes for successful transitions through various stages of career development.

Goals, purposes, policies, and legislative actions related to the world of work catalyze the development, refinement, and implementation of career assessments and interventions. As career counselors respond to change and to the necessity of individual operation within shifting conditions of change, they must keep interventions relevant to the contextual factors within which workers and potential workers negotiate their career development, crystallize their career identity, and maximize their employability. This is true not only in the United States but, increasingly, throughout the world as nations come to terms with the reality that the major asset of any nation is not its wealth, raw material, and natural resources, but, rather, the literacy, the numeracy, the communications ability, technology skills, the teachability, and the flexibility of its work force.

Nations tend to share many of the same goals for career interventions regardless of their specific cultural traditions. Among them is helping persons function across the nation's occupational structure and supporting equal opportunities for access to work and educational opportunities. Thus, the efforts of career practitioners should lead to comprehensive services for persons and locales. The result is that, while accessibility to career services remains uneven across the globe, career assessment and career interventions are worldwide phenomena used to both actualize human potential and meet societal labor force needs.

These observations are not to suggest that the use of career assessments or other career interventions is the same from nation to nation. They are not. As discussed in the next section, there is an increase throughout the world of indigenous approaches to the delivery of career interventions that are compatible with the resources, cultural traditions, and policies of individual nations. The theories and practices of career assessment do not exist in a vacuum; they are affected by economic, political, and social events that spawn new needs and goals for career assessment. In a continuous progression, visionaries, theorists, researchers, and practitioners emerge who can help convert ideas related to career assessment into action.

Some Perspectives on Career Assessment

Career assessment originated in the United States, primarily as an adjunct to career counseling. Thus, in many cases, people viewed the scores and interpretations of career assessments as the ultimate result of career counseling. Many professionals in the US, and in other countries, continue to view career assessment as a part of the career counseling process, not as a separate intervention, even though the use of career assessments in self-directed, counselor-free, and computer-mediated career planning systems have demonstrated their unique contributions as interventions in their own right.

A further way to view career assessment is as a bridge from career development theory to practice, or as a method of operationalizing theoretical constructs by incorporating them into career interventions and, in particular, into tests and other measurements. This merger of theory and practice is apparent in Holland's theoretical constructs, for example, within assessments such as the *Vocational Preference Inventory* (Holland, 1985), *My Vocational Situation* (Holland, Daiger, & Power, 1980), and the *Self-Directed Search* (Holland & Messer, 2017). Additionally, Holland's theoretical framework (RIASEC) became the organizing and interpretive structure for the *Strong Interest Inventory* (Donnay, Morris, Schaubhut & Thompson, 2005), the *Career Key* (Jones, 1990), and for some of the informational and self-assessment components of Internet-based career planning systems, such as those developed by Kuder and the O*NET Interest Profiler.

Donald Super used assessments in a similar fashion to operationalize and evaluate his theoretical constructs (Super, 1990; 1994). Like Holland, he made his paradigm accessible to researchers and practitioners by bridging theory and practice with assessments. Examples of the instruments that evolved from his theoretical propositions include the *Career Development Inventory* (CDI; Super, Thompson, Lindeman, Jordaan, & Myers, 1979), the *Adult Career Concerns Inventory* (ACCI; Super, Thompson, & Lindeman, 1988), the *Work Values Inventory* (SWVI; Super, 1970), and the *Salience Inventory* (SI; Super & Nevill, 1985). These instruments assess constructs of career adaptability, career planning, knowledge and attitudes about career choice, intrinsic and extrinsic work values, and the relative importance of major life roles beyond those of occupation or career to the client. These instruments are useful in defining goals for career counseling and for explicating and assessing particular types of content of importance to the decision making of individual clients. Super developed the C-DAC Model (Osborne, Brown, Niles, & Miner, 1997), in which career assessment and counseling interact as interventions.

Utilizing assessments to connect theory and practice was continued by Krumboltz, whose work in behaviorism, social learning, and cognitive behavioral paradigms led to the development of several important theoretical concepts and innovative assessment devices. For instance, the *Career Beliefs Inventory* (CBI; Krumboltz, 1994) is a counseling tool linking theory and intervention by identifying negative thinking that has potential to block individuals from achieving career goals.

Using assessments to bridge theory and practice is a typical strategy for making theory useful to practitioners. Not surprisingly, therefore, assessments represent a primary tool for career practitioners as they address their clients' career concerns.

The Changing Context for Career Assessment

The preceding passages illustrate both the richness and the dynamic character of the history of career assessment. Obviously, the development of new career assessments and the refinement of older instruments continue as counselors address new contextual and measurement challenges. Indeed, several emerging trends will spawn new types of career assessments and catalyze updates and refinements to old instruments. In many cases, these trends include specific issues that require new career assessments or modified theoretical perspectives. An exhaustive investigation of such trends is beyond the scope of this chapter; however, several categories of trends and issues exemplify emerging pressures for new career assessments, new practices, and new theoretical perspectives. These categories include the changing nature of work, the international development or adaptation of career assessments, the widening use of technology and career assessment, and accountability, the last of which includes empirically supported treatments and evidence-based practice. We cover these trends and issues next.

The Changing Nature of Work

The function and organization of the world of work are changing rapidly. There are multiple factors that change and influence the types of career assessments that will be required in the future. Some of the most significant factors involve sustaining competition in the global economy, which includes the pervasive use of advanced technology in the workplace and a global labor surplus that involves many highly educated and skilled workers seeking opportunities in whatever nation offers employment and economic opportunity. As the migration of workers across national boundaries continues and the organization and implementation of jobs continue to shift rapidly, needs arise for new definitions of workplace skills, personal attributes, and career assessments of these competencies and behaviors.

The evolution of workplaces across the globe has led to an increased interest in assessing soft skills, including the ability to work in teams, the capacity to work across diverse cultural environments, the capability to make decisions across workplaces, the development of resilience in the face of constant change, the facility to adapt as new products and processes are generated in shorter intervals of time, and flexibility of thought regarding new ways of career planning that focus on short term horizons (e.g., five years) rather than decades. Furthermore, as lifespans increase and more people opt to delay retirement, workplaces are becoming places of generational diversity. In fact, Abrams and Von Frank (2014) identified at least four different generations as part of the contemporary workplace. Regardless of how individuals view work or career development in the twenty-first century, work and career development are no longer linear, and career stages are not easily separated into sequential life stages of growth, exploration, advancement, maintenance, and decline. Very few individuals remain in one job, with one firm, or in one occupation throughout their working life. Most workers transition across careers many times, and this continuum of change leaves them susceptible to mergers and consolidations of workplaces that eliminate redundant or outdated job functions. Furthermore, the use of technology to stimulate productivity and reduce costs of operations eradicates many occupations and leads to widespread termination of employment.

Knowledge Workers

In the US and a growing number of other countries, educational requirements for many forms of work are increasing as the workplace becomes more automated and replete with computer-driven lathes, robots, data analysis, 3-D printers, and design processes. The Internet, telecommunications, and global supply chains of products and services support many of these developments. Artificial intelligence programs are now performing some job processes, once handled by entire teams, in a fraction of the time (Koch, 2017). These changes increase the need for workers who possess different knowledge and who know how and why to implement specific work processes. Such workers, who compose 60% of the workforce, must be able to adapt to rapid changes in work processes and problems, troubleshoot solutions, solve problems, and apply new understandings, often within very fluid contexts. Morgan (2014) predicts that the ability to learn constantly and to apply and share new knowledge will be indispensable in the emergent workplace. Because of the need to link science and technology more fully to produce new products and services, more workplaces have become *learning organizations* (Senge, 1996) where assessing ideas and creativity are major elements in the continuous improvement of organizational production (Florida, 2004). Moreover, as technology increasingly emerges across workplaces, the need for maximizing effective human-automation interaction increases. Patterson (2017) noted that, historically, people tended to use only analytical cognition when engaging with technology. Analytical cognition involves thinking consciously, deliberating, and using logic to determine next steps. Patterson contended that a better model of human-automation interaction incorporates intuitive cognition (i.e., gut feelings). The model of human-interaction Patterson recommends, for example, might enhance further developments in technology related to smart cars and homes. Workers in such environments will need training to develop their capacity for logic and intuitive sensing. This is a different paradigm from the one that dominated the workforce in the 20th century.

Collectively, these trends, which are playing out in the global gig economy (Flanagan, 2017), result in changing workplaces where jobs once existed as clearly defined and fixed sets of tasks that are now giving way to new paradigms with concepts, including boundary-free careers and multitasking. Some observers have argued that the concept of jobs, as a way of organizing work, is a social artifact that has outlived its usefulness. Increasingly, employers expect workers to complete tasks that need to be done regardless of the artificial boundaries that separate specific sets of tasks (Bridges, 1994). In such contexts, it is likely that career assessments in the future will emphasize individual initiative, creativity, problem solving, flexibility, intuition, and the ability to multitask and tolerate stress (American Psychological Association [APA], 2017).

Lifelong Learning

Embedded in the emergent paradigm of knowledge, where continuous learning is essential, lifelong learning becomes a major part of workers' abilities to function effectively. For more and more workers, learning skills and achievements are major elements of individual career development. In a society of change, intense competition, creativity, and mastery of basic academic skills become a prerequisite for employability, lifelong learning, and gaining foundation skills for technical and occupational processes.

The World Bank (2003) suggested that the status quo for workers in a global economy is engagement in continuous learning and feeling constantly on edge and off balance due to an expectation of adaptation to the ongoing transformation of occupational organization. In response to such conditions, career assessments are becoming more likely to include attention to workers' coping skills for ambiguity and stress, and to the development of resilience. Examples of current instruments that gauge resilience and stress coping include the *Design My Future* scale (Santilli et al., 2017), which assesses middle school-aged children for future orientation and resilience, the *Career Decision Making Profile* (CDMP; Gati, Landman, Davidovitch, Asulin-Peretz, & Gadassi, 2010), which measures the adaptability of workers' career acquisition strategies, and the *Self-Efficacy for Work-Family Conflict Resolution* (SE-WFC; Cinamon, 2003, 2006), which investigates workers' beliefs about their ability to manage work-life conflicts.

Some Implications from the Changing Nature of Work for Career Assessment

Available perspectives about relevant skills necessary in the global economy suggest that the worker of the future must be his or her own career manager by keeping employability skills honed and attractive to employers, and by engaging in continuous learning and attention to trends that will affect his or her inventory of employable skills. Implicit in such perspectives is the view that, although many have cited constancy and stability (homeostasis) frequently in the psychological literature as desirable traits for individual development, career planning and choices in the future are likely to be more spontaneous, values oriented, and influenced by environmental and organizational flux, unpredictability, and turbulence.

The question relative to career assessment is: do our current instruments measure personal flexibility, commitment to continuous learning, comfort with cultural diversity, aptitude for teamwork, willingness to engage in multitasking, self-initiative, the ability to be creative, and the motivation to be responsible for one's own career development? These are among the major competencies seen as essential to functioning well in a global economy. Inventorying our current career assessment instruments to determine how well they measure such individual traits and abilities would seem useful. If these measures do not exist, constructing them will be necessary.

The Development or Adaptation of Career Assessment Cross-Nationally

Researchers and practitioners can identify career assessments that measure competencies salient to the changing world of work; furthermore, they can develop new assessments to measure such competencies. An ideal approach, however, would include the examination and revision of career assessments constructed across the globe. As career assessments and other career interventions take on global significance, developers tailor them, increasingly, to their own nations' characteristics and concerns. Until recently, the adaptation of career assessment instruments focused primarily on measurement instruments constructed in the US or Western Europe. Researchers translated these instruments into the language of a nation interested in validating the instrument's suitability for use in that nation. Though the adaptation of career assessments tends to flow largely from the US or Western Europe to other nations, future trends might focus more heavily on adapting assessments from across the globe. As the utility and comprehensiveness of career interventions from nations around the world becomes increasingly apparent and accessible, career assessments will feature more culturally sensitive content and high-quality procedures of relevance. The adaptation of indigenous instruments that measure skills, altitudes, or behaviors of interest to other nations will increase rapidly. Scholars who foresee this shift recently called for cross-cultural studies that focus on the generalizability of diverse instruments and a methodology for generating culture-specific career interventions (Duarte & Rossier, 2008). As the realm of career assessment becomes increasingly tied to technological platforms, the proliferation of cross-cultural career assessment is likely to accelerate. Osborn (2012) remarked on the restrictive and exclusionary manner in which career practitioners deliver career interventions and pointed to the importance of technological intervention delivery as a social justice concern for serving diverse and marginalized populations.

The importance of adapting accurately and validating thoroughly career assessments from another country is a growing issue. Minimally, this requires knowledge of the methodological processes that led to the instrument, its purposes, its psychometric properties in the country of origin, and the external and internal conditions that gave rise to the assessment instrument. An assessment under consideration for use in a new culture must be adapted, and then analyzed, for appropriate psychometric performance, culturally appropriate language, and local or national norms. In professional terms, adhering to copyright provisions during the adaptation of a test or assessment, obtaining the consent of the test's author and publisher, and observing the ethical standards that apply to test adaptation is important and should align with guidelines provided by counseling or psychological associations located in some 80 countries around the world, as well as by the International Test Commission (Bartram, 2001).

Rossier (2004) compared the cross-cultural equivalence of several personality inventories used frequently in career counseling (e.g., 16PF, NEO-PI, Internal-External Locus of Control Scale). His very strong point is that when counselors use a translated instrument, they must pay attention to its cultural validity or cultural replicability. Neglect to do so can result in erroneous conclusions about the meaning of the scale scores. In addition to linguistic, conceptual, and scale equivalence, there needs to be culture-specific normative equivalence if practitioners plan to use the scale in career counseling.

Duarte (2004) made the important point that adaptation of career assessment instruments from one nation to another is not simply a linguistic exercise. Rather, those who "translate" instruments from one language to another are obliged to do complete literature reviews related to the development of the instrument, as well as to the meanings of the constructs assessed by the instrument. In the case of indigenous instruments being adapted from other nations to the United States, this will require U.S. researchers to become familiar with the published work in European, Asian, and other national journals and with the languages in which they are published. To the degree that such a trend intensifies, there will likely be a greater sensitivity in the United States to excellent research occurring in other nations. This will bring researchers to greater cooperation transnationally as they fashion instruments that are truly international in their concepts and content or adapt career assessments that show reliability and validity across cultures and nations.

Technology and Career Assessment

One trend that will facilitate the cross-national development, adaptation, and use of career assessments is the pervasive use of computers and the Internet for research, statistical analyses, management of data banks, and other tasks associated with the construction of career assessment instruments. As computers and available software continue to become more user friendly, comprehensive in their content, and less expensive to purchase and use, these tools and the access to the Internet they provide will create pathways to new measurement instruments.

As the Internet achieved significant growth in web sites that provided career advice, career information, job placement, and career assessments (Harris-Bowlsbey, 2003), research indicated that career assessment instruments in these web sites varied from poorly constructed, locally used instruments to highly professional, standardized instruments with strong psychometric properties. Many of the latter were developed during the 1970s and 1980s when computer-based career guidance systems (e.g., DISCOVER [ACT, 2006], SIGI Plus) were being developed and used in state career information delivery systems, schools, colleges, employment counseling agencies, and some workplaces. In many of these systems, career assessments were prominent parts of the content as they helped users clarify the status of their interests, values, abilities, and career goals and the databases they should explore. As Internet-based career planning systems became increasingly common in their use over the past several decades, research has demonstrated the importance of career assessment as a complement to career counseling and other career interventions.

Whiston, Brecheisen, and Stephens (2003) found that counselor-free interventions were not as effective as were inventions that involved a counselor. In addition, they found that individuals who used a computer-assisted career guidance system, supplemented by counseling, attained better outcomes than persons who used a computer system not supplemented by counseling. As Internet web sites have grown rapidly in number and use, the National Board for Certified Counselors (NBCC), National Career Development Association (NCDA), and other groups have created ethical standards for the use of these interventions. Even so, there are still ethical problems occurring in the use of these interventions.

Thus, a number of observers note that the Internet provides a huge array of web sites, which, essentially, offer a "smorgasbord of disjointed" information that is available to the public free of charge and without consumer protection (Harris-Bowlsbey, 2003). At the same time, however, the Internet provides enormous possibilities for high-quality occupational information, video portrayals of work environments and occupations, online access to the best in professional literature, publications, summaries of research findings, cybercounseling, e-mail, chat rooms, text messaging, online discussion, e-learning, video conferencing, telephone help lines with replies online (Offer, 2005), and career assessments. What is at issue, to an increasing degree, is a research base that analyzes material on the Internet to identify those items that meet quality standards and those career interventions, including career assessments, that experts determine to be best practices, empirically supported, and evidence-based.

Evidence-Based Assessments, Empirically Supported Treatments, and Accountability

Use of terms, such as *best practices, empirically supported treatments,* and *evidence-based,* highlights, whether implicitly or explicitly, the role assessments play in achieving such outcomes. To an increasing degree, legislators, policy makers, and institutional administrators are questioning the whole range of interventions and the results assessments provide individually and collectively. These individuals and organizations are asking, "What are we receiving for our investment of resources in career services?" "How do we know what interventions or combinations of them are the most effective?" Do career services or interventions add value to the education of adolescents or college students, or to the purpose and productivity of adult workers?" "How do we know?" and "Why do we need counselors if counselor-free interventions are effective?" In one sense, the question is: can we create a matrix that identifies individual career presenting problems — stress, anxiety, indecision, indecisiveness, overcommitment to work, undercommitment to work, etc. — and the interventions and theories that researchers have found to affect these career concerns in positive and effective ways, for different subpopulations, under varying conditions. These questions raise the issue of how intervention A compares with the effects of intervention B or C or D vis-a-vis a particular presenting problem. What are the comparative costs of intervention A, B, C, or D in achieving the goals sought? How do we assure that the values achieved exceed the costs of the interventions? These are questions of accountability, of cost-benefit ratios, and of evidence-based or empirically supported practices.

There are now hundreds of career assessment instruments available, many of which researchers have studied at length in terms of their validity, reliability and other psychometric properties. One issue concerns which of these instruments measures the outcomes of most concern (career adaptability, information seeking, developmental status on necessary career tasks, personal flexibility) most directly and comprehensively when comparing the impact of different interventions on the outcomes chosen. A second issue is the need to reinvigorate career outcome research that assesses both single and comparative effects on the major career outcomes inherent in the most influential career theories in the field. Whiston et al. (2003) reported that there has been a decrease in career outcome research over the past 15 years, even though there have been new techniques, including the Internet, and new career outcomes needs assessments. Although some examples (Savickas, 2012) exist more recently to counter Whiston and her colleagues' contention, making the case that the situation has changed substantially from 2003 is difficult. A third issue has to do with the consistency of the instruments used to assess the effects of career interventions on career outcomes. If practitioners use different instruments to assess the same outcomes, unless it is clear that their contents are highly correlated, knowing what the obtained results mean becomes difficult. A further issue is that, unless career outcome research grows in its coverage and immediacy across a large spectrum of career interventions, whether used singly or in combination, editors, practitioners, and researchers might conclude that approaches to career counseling, career education, career guidance, and other career interventions are not empirically supported or evidence-based practices.

Although practitioners or researchers can argue persuasively that, in the broadest or aggregate sense, there is no longer a major question about the capacity of career counseling and other career interventions to improve or change career behavior (e.g., Brown & Ryan Krane, 2000; Oliver & Spokane, 1988; Rounds & Tinsley, 1984; Whiston, 2003; Whiston, Brecheisen, & Stephens, 2003; Whiston, Sexton, & Lasoff, 1998), the large array of available research has not addressed accountability, empirically supported treatments, or evidence-based practice questions systematically. Meta-analyses and other research techniques have permitted researchers to summarize large numbers of studies and to determine the collective effect of research studies of a specific process on different forms of behavior. But, in general, these studies have not compared the effects of intervention A to that of intervention B in relation to particular career-presenting problems. Nor have these studies contrasted, essentially, the utility of theory A versus theory B for understanding and intervening in specific career concerns. Increasingly, researchers and theorists are contending, as has Whiston (2003),

> there is not an established method or model for conducting career counseling that is consistently used in the field and evaluated by researchers. Hence, career counseling professionals do not have a clear understanding of precisely what is effective, nor has the field made great strides in comparing different approaches with different populations. (p. 40)

There does exist substantial evidence (Anderson & Niles, 2000; Masdonati, Massoui, & Rossier, 2009; Perdrix, de Roten, Kolly, & Rossier, 2010; Masdonati, Perdrix, Massoudi, & Rossier, 2014) pointing to the importance of the working alliance in career counseling. The consistent evidence is that this factor stands above others as the most critical variable in career counseling. When counselors establish the working alliance effectively, career counseling outcomes tend to be positive. With this in mind, career practitioners must consider how they integrate assessments into the career intervention process (Hartung, 2005).

Unlike some other mental health emphases (e.g., psychotherapy), career counseling protocols or treatment manuals have not been developed, typically, to assure that practices being evaluated are standardized so that those practices can be examined relative to their efficacy in promoting particular types of behavior, reframing irrational thoughts, facilitating counselee decision making, or obtaining other desired outcomes. Without such standardization of practices, comparing the implementation of theory A versus theory B is difficult. Nor can one deconstruct various approaches to career intervention into their components to assess which ingredients of that practice are essential and necessary or acceptable but not necessary (Wampold, 2001) as compared with other approaches. Though such research approaches might not occur in the foreseeable future, pursuit of such goals would enable the field to articulate differences better among its major theoretical and intervention processes; describe the importance of its contributions to societal goals to policy makers, legislators, and administrators; improve the training of practitioners; and address cost-benefit ratios of career interventions.

Cost-Benefit Analyses

One of the most important ways to examine accountability in the provision of career services for the future is cost-benefit analyses. Cost-benefit analyses tend to complete the circle from the creation, implementation, and evaluation of career assessments or other career interventions to their likely costs and benefits. A century ago, early career interventions, including career assessments, were largely philosophical and conceptual, not theoretical necessarily and rarely empirical. Early pioneers of career counseling created assessment instruments to serve such practical purposes as identifying interests and aptitudes. However, during the course of the twentieth century, a science of assessment, measurement, and evaluation evolved, largely, but not exclusively, as a complement to career counseling. The counseling profession, at large, has become increasingly accomplished in generating and presenting research evidence of the efficacy of career counseling and other career interventions for many purposes. Within such a context, practitioners have used career assessments as measures by which to determine the efficacy of career interventions in facilitating such outcomes or viability of specific theoretical propositions.

Researchers have studied career assessments as stand-alone or counselor-free career interventions in their own right, as portals by which counselees can identify and gain access to selected modules in Internet-based career planning systems, or as accountability monitors in such federal legislation as the Every Student Succeeds Act. At the same time that researchers have used career assessments as measures of dependent variables in research designs studying the effect sizes of different career interventions or as important adjunctive measures supporting career counseling and providing content for counselor-counselee dialogue, they have studied career assessment devices in terms of their validity, reliability, and utility for different purposes. In general, research has validated career assessments as effective for many purposes and that, as these purposes change and expand, researchers, theorists, and practitioners continue to create measurement methodologies and career assessments.

In spite of a clear set of philosophical assumptions about the value of career interventions and an enlarging research base that validates the importance of career interventions, suggesting that researchers and theorists in counseling, with the possible exception of those engaged in rehabilitation or in drug and alcohol research, have not taken the next systematic step of translating the available research findings into cost-benefit analyses is fair. Even though career professionals can make the oversimplified observation that every positive or negative correlation between a career intervention and a desired outcome carries economic costs and economic benefits with it, most theorists and researchers have not focused on these issues. There has not been systematic examination of the costs of providing counseling or assessment to various populations for specific purposes compared to the economic and social benefits derived from such services. Nor have analyses accrued that have focused on the added value to an entity (e.g., school, university, employer, government, or society at large) of providing career services or to the individual who participates in career services.

Given limited economic resources available for counseling and competing human services, and rising demands for such resources, a strategic issue for the future will be the need to train counselors, theorists, and researchers in the mentality and methodology of cost-benefit analyses. Assessment strategies will be critical as they produce relevant measures of the added value of career interventions and enhance the productivity of counselors in different settings. Such approaches will be effective tools, most likely, in advocating to legislators and administrators policies that incorporate career counseling, career assessment, measurement, and evaluation as important assets in addressing major social and individual career goals.

Summary

In this chapter, we demonstrated that career assessment, both as a stand-alone career intervention and as an adjunct to career counseling and other career interventions, has sunk its roots deep into U.S. policy, theory, and practice, as well as that of other nations. Clearly, the purposes for which legislators, policy makers, organizations, and those in the career counseling profession expect the career assessment process to be useful has expanded and taken on new content, formats, and venues. Career assessments are now available on the Internet as part of the growing presence of online career counseling and access to job information. Rather than adapting assessments developed in the U.S., nations around the globe are increasingly creating career assessment instruments with content and procedures that are indigenous to their goals for career services for those choosing, preparing for, making the transition to, and adjusting to work.

As important as current career assessments are, the organization and substance of work itself is changing rapidly and qualitatively, as are the expectations of workers. Workers need to become their own systematic career managers in the choices available to them. Because such career choices and career transitions will likely occur more often, workers will need to be flexible, able to cope with change, and engaged in continuous learning. The need to assess these types of competencies will broaden the content of career assessments yet to be developed.

The use of career assessments is worldwide; therefore, major trends will include the development or adaptation of career assessments cross-nationally. The use of technologies to administer and interpret career assessments as counselor-free interventions is becoming more prevalent. Each of these trends will rely increasingly on the creation of new career assessments that address the changing nature of work and its reflection in career theory, as well as provide measures of major dependent variables for purposes of accountability, empirically supported treatments, and evidence-based practices.

References

Abrams, F., & Von Frank, V. (2014). *The multigenerational workplace: Communicate, collaborate, and create community*. Thousand Oaks, CA: SAGE Publications.

ACT. (2006). *Research support for DISCOVER assessment components*. Iowa City, IA: Author.

American Psychological Association. (2017). *Coping with stress at work*. Retrieved from http://www.apa.org/helpcenter/work-stress.aspx

Anderson, W. P., Jr., & Niles, S. G. (2000). Important events in career counseling: Counselors and clients' perceptions. *The Career Development Quarterly, 48,* 251-263.

Bartram, D. (2001). The development of international guidelines on test use: The international test commission project. *International Journal of Testing, 1*(1), 33–54.

Bridges, W. (1994, September). The end of the job. *Fortune, 130,* 62–74.

Brown, S. D., & Ryan Krane, N. E. (2000). Four (or five) sessions and a cloud of dust: Old assumptions and new observations about career counseling. In S. D. Brown & R. W. Lent (Eds.), *Handbook of counseling psychology* (3rd ed., pp. 740–766). New York: Wiley.

Cinamon, R. G. (2003). *Work-family conflict self-efficacy and career plans of young adults.* Unpublished manuscript.

Cinamon, R. G. (2006). Anticipated work-family conflict: Effects of gender, self-efficacy, and family back-ground. *Career Development Quarterly, 54,* 202-215.

Donnay, D. A. C., Morris, M. L., Schaubhut, N. A., & Thompson, R. C. (2005). *Strong Interest Inventory® Manual.* Mountain View, CA: CPP, Inc.

Duarte, M. E. (2004, June). *Assessment and cultural riches: Adaptation of psychological instruments and the global research village.* Paper presented at the symposium on International Perspectives on Career Development, San Francisco, CA.

Duarte, M. E., & Rossier, J. (2008). Testing and assessment in an international context: Cross and multicultural issues. In J. A. Athanasou, & R. V. Esbroeck, (Eds.), *International handbook of career guidance* (pp. 489-510). Dordtrect, Netherlands: Springer.

Flanagan, F. (2017). Symposium on work in the 'gig' economy: Introduction. *The Economic and Labour Relations Review, 28*(3), 378-381.

Florida, R. (2004). *The rise of the creative class. And how it is transforming work, leisure, community and everyday life.* New York: Basic Books.

Gati, I., Landman, S., Davidovitch, S., Asulin-Peretz, L., & Gadassi, R. (2010). From career decision-making styles to career decision-making profiles: A multidimensional approach. *Journal of Vocational Behavior, 76*(2), 277-291.

Harris-Bowlsbey, J. (2003). A rich past and a future vision. *Career Development Quarterly, 52*(1), 19–25.

Hartung, P. J. (2005). Integrated career assessment and counseling: Mindsets, models, and methods. In W. B. Walsh & M. Savickas (Eds.), *Handbook of vocational psychology: Theory, research, and practice* (pp. 371-396). Mahwah, NJ : Erlbaum.

Holland, J. L., Daiger, D. C., & Power, P. G. (1980). *My Vocational Situation.* Retrieved from https://career.fsu.edu/sites/g/files/imported/storage/original/application/f3dd4d17aeae2f581fb9837fd16381f5.pdf

Holland, J. L., & Messer, M. (2017). *Professional manual, standard Self-Directed Search.* Lutz, FL: Psychological Assessment Resources.

Holland, J. L. (1985). *Manual for the Vocational Preference Inventory.* Odessa, FL: Psychological Assessment Resources.

Jones, L. K. (1990). The Career Key: An investigation of the reliability and validity of its scales and its helpfulness to college students. *Measurement and Evaluation in Counseling and Development, 23,* 67-76.

Koch, R. (2017). Will artificial intelligence eliminate my job? *Strategic Finance, 99*(3), 62-63.

Krumboltz, J. D. (1994). The Career Beliefs Inventory. *Journal of Counseling and Development, 72,* 424–428.

Masdonati, J., Massoudi, K., Rossier, J. (2009). Effectiveness of career counseling and the impact of the working alliance. *Journal of Career Development, 36,* 183-203. doi: 10.1177/894845309340798

Masdonati, J., Perdrix, S., Massdoudi, K., & Rossier, J. (2014). Working alliance as a moderator and a mediator of career counseling effectiveness. *Journal of Career Assessment, 22,* 3-17. doi: 10.1177/1069072713487489

Morgan, J. (2014, November 11). The 7 principles of the future employee. *Forbes.* Retrieved from: https://www.forbes.com/sites/jacobmorgan/2014/11/11/the-7-principles-of-the-future-employee/#6ec89e004cac

Osborn, D. (2012). An international discussion about cross-cultural career assessment. *International Journal for Educational and Vocational Guidance, 12*(1), 5-16.

Osborne, W. L., Brown, S., Niles, S. G., & Miner, C. (1997). *Career development assessment and counseling: Donald Super's C-DAC Model.* Alexandria, VA: American Counseling Association.

Offer, M. (2005, Summer). E-guidance: Can we deliver guidance by email and what issues does that raise? Recent research and evaluation in HE. *Career Research and Development, The NICEC Journal, 12,* 32–33.

Oliver, L. W., & Spokane, A. R. (1988). Career intervention outcome: What contributes to client gain? *Journal of Counseling Psychology, 35,* 447–462.

Patterson, R. E. (2017). Intuitive cognition and models of human–automation interaction, *Human Factors, 59*(1), 101-115. doi: 10.1177/0018720816659796

Perdrix, S., de Roten, Y., Kolly, S., & Rossier, J. (2010). The psychometric properties of the WAI in a career counseling setting: Comparison with a personal counseling sample. *Journal of Career Assessment, 18,* 409-419. doi: 10.1177/1069072710374583

Rossier, J. (2004, June). *An analysis of the cross-cultural equivalence of some frequently used personality inventories.* Paper presented at the Symposium on International Perspectives on Career Development, San Francisco, CA.

Rounds, J. B., Jr., & Tinsley, H. E. A. (1984). Diagnosis and treatment of vocational problems. In S. Brown & R. Lent (Eds.), *Handbook of counseling psychology* (pp.137 177). New York: Wiley.

Santilli, S., Ginevra, M., Sgaramella, T., Nota, L., Ferrari, L., & Soresi, S. (2017). Design My Future: An instrument to assess future orientation and resilience. *Journal of Career Assessment, 25*(2), 281-295.

Savickas, M. L. (2012). Life design: A paradigm for career intervention in the 21st century. *Journal of Counseling and Development, 90,* 13-19.

Senge, P. M. (1996). Leading learning organizations: The bold, the powerful, and the invisible. In F. Hesselbein, M. Goldsmith, & R. Beckhard (Eds.), *The leader of the future, new visions, strategies and practices for the next era* (pp.41–58). San Francisco, CA: Jossey-Bass.

Super, D. E. (1970). *Work Values Inventory manual.* Chicago: Riverside Publishing Company.

Super, D. E. (1990). A life-span, life-space approach to career development. In D. Brown & L. Brook (Eds.), *Career choice and development: Applying contemporary theories to practice* (pp.197–261). San Francisco, CA: Jossey-Bass.

Super, D. E. (1994). A life span, life space perspective on convergence. In M. L. Savickas & R. W. Lent (Eds.) *Convergence in career development theories: Implications for science and practice* (pp.63–74). Palo Alto, CA: CPP Books.

Super, D. E., & Nevill, D. D. (1985). *The Salience Inventory.* Palo Alto, CA: Consulting Psychologists Press.

Super, D. E., Thompson, A. S., & Lindeman, R. H. (1988). *The Adult Career Concerns Inventory.* Palo Alto, CA: Consulting Psychologists Press.

Super, D. E., Thompson, A. S., Lindeman, R. H., Jordaan, J. P., & Myers, R. A. (1979). *Career Development Inventory: School form.* Palo Alto, CA: Consulting Psychologists Press.

The World Bank. (2003). *Lifelong learning in the global knowledge economy: Challenges for developing countries.* Washington DC: Author.

Wampold, B. E. (2001). *The great psychotherapy debate: Models, methods, and findings.* Mahwah, NJ: Lawrence Erlbaum Associates.

Whiston, S. C. (2003). Career counseling: 90 years and yet still healthy and vital. *Career Development Quarterly, 52*(1), 35–42.

Whiston, S. C., Brecheisen, B. K., & Stephens, J. (2003). Does treatment modality affect career counseling effectiveness? *Journal of Vocational Behavior, 62*, 390–410.

Whiston, S. C., Sexton, T. L., & Lasoff, D. L. (1998). Career intervention outcome: A replication and extension. *Journal of Counseling Psychology, 45*, 150–165.

CHAPTER 3

COMPUTER-ASSISTED CAREER ASSESSMENT

Debra S. Osborn
Florida State University

Darrin L. Carr
Kansas State University

Mary-Catherine McClain Riner
Florida State University

Ryan D. Sides
Florida State University

Jill A. Lumsden
Zeiders Enterprises

James P. Sampson
Florida State University

Introduction

Computer-assisted career assessments (CACAs) have been available for decades and their use by career practitioners and career decision makers has only increased over time. Increases in quantity have not matched equally with increases in quality, however (Sampson et al., 2013). In the sections that follow, we seek to equip career practitioners with ethical considerations, as well as the knowledge of current trends and future possibilities, benefits and limitations, and counselor implications with respect to the use of CACAs.

Ethical Use of Computer-Assisted Career Assessment

When considering the ethical standards that apply to computer-assisted career assessments, career practitioners have several codes from various associations to reference. Career practitioners' primary code is the National Career Development Association's Code of Ethics (NCDA, 2015). In addition, nationally certified counselors must follow the Code of Ethics for the National Board of Certified Counselors (NBCC, 2016), which has 15 testing directives. Vocational psychologists must follow the Code of Fair Testing and Practices in Education (APA, n.d.), while career practitioners in other settings, such as mental health agencies or schools, must attend to the ethical standards set forth by those related professional associations. Within each of these standards, career practitioners must not only review standards relevant to assessment, but also review issues of confidentiality, privacy, diversity, research, and distance provision of services. In addition, career practitioners who are licensed must refer to state laws and insurance requirements, with respect to whether administering an assessment is seen as counseling, and to limits for reimbursements across state lines. Fortunately, despite the number of ethical standards and competencies that career practitioners should reference, there is reasonable consistency across the different resources. These general areas of concern focus on practitioner competency, client concerns and characteristics (e.g., informed consent and diversity issues), selection, administration, interpretation, and quality of assessments. Computer-assisted career assessments should meet the same psychometric properties as traditional assessments, and career practitioners using computer-assisted career assessments must apply the same standards, such as interpreting only those tests that fall within their boundaries of competence.

A fuzzy area within CACAs is defining what constitutes an assessment (Sampson et al., 2013). Some developers might argue that a ranking of personality or interests types or careers, or choosing a Holland type from a list of six descriptors, does not constitute an assessment. According to Sampson et al. (2013), "If it works like a scale, or a self-assessment of constructs, then it is assessment" (p. 40). There is also the issue of self-constructed assessments. When someone uses a social media site to create a board or collage of their interests, is this a self assessment, and more importantly, should a career practitioner attempt, ethically, to interpret this construction or link to potential occupations? We assert that career practitioners should not ignore self-generated information a client creates, but should use it in conjunction with validated measures and refer to the many non-standardized approaches and techniques reviewed in this book. In addition, we encourage career researchers to research the validity of these tools and, especially, interpretative suggestions to help inform about the ethical use of these tools. Whenever practitioners or researchers experience ethical dilemmas with respect to computer-assisted career assessments, Makela and Perlus (2017) suggested employing an ethical decision making model.

Current Trends in Computer-Assisted Career Assessment

Overall, technology has served as one means to remove potential barriers and limitations in connecting and delivering career services. Practitioners use CACAs, similar to other forms of innovative technology, more frequently to minimize costs while simultaneously providing more opportunities for self-learning and overall career growth (Perrotta, 2013). Likewise, Mayadas, Bourne, and Bacsich (2009) noted that traditional face-to-face career counseling is often expensive and unavailable to individuals in the workforce. Additionally, research demonstrates a positive relationship between online assessment, feedback, and engagement with respect to learning and user satisfaction (Ras, Whitelock, & Kalz, 2015).

Computer technology, web-based career support, and the Internet have each transformed the field and overall delivery of counseling and career assessment over the past 35 years (Betz & Turner, 2011). SIGI (Sampson, Reardon, & Rudd, 1998) and DISCOVER (ACT, 2006) were some of the first computer-assisted career guidance programs, while smaller web-based assessments have been developed to support all aspects of career exploration and decision-making. Additionally, these programs have the advantages of efficient scoring and profiling, are relatively easy to administer and use, and can provide current information to aid in decision-making (Betz & Borgen, 2009).

Larger assessment vendors appear to be implementing integrated, web-enabled delivery platforms through which they can deliver a variety of instruments from their portfolio of holdings using a common interface. Ultimately, such platforms allow for the centralized maintenance of client assessment records as well as easy purchase of additional test administrations. Khapova, Svennson, Wilderom, and Arthur (2006) reported that, often, these assessments include advising discussions, career planning forums, and online webinars for creating resumes. Figure 1 is an illustration of the relationships among access options, cost recovery, and quality for the development and delivery of Internet based career assessment. As shown by gray shading, such assessments have been self-help, historically, supported by indirect advertising and sponsors, and unvalidated. A current census of these assessments is required to confirm a continuation of this pattern.

During the past decade, technologies have become more sophisticated, users have expanded, and the number of online career assessments has increased significantly. Researchers have identified potential concerns, as well as several benefits. Common complaints, noted by Oliver and Whiston (2000), are that online websites and other Internet career programs might be difficult to navigate, lack security, require a referral fee, and/or encourage the purchase of additional products and services (e.g., book, online degree) in order to complete a "career test." However, present research provides evidence of well-established career assessments with strong psychometric properties (Sampson & Lumsden, 2000). Maintaining a critical eye is important for users, and equally important is that career assessment developers describe the reliability, validity, and standardization of assessments that are understandable to the general public. Similarly, developers should address potential biases, including cultural dimensions.

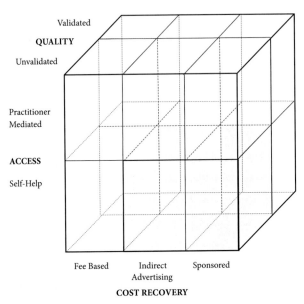

Figure 1: Organizational Schema for Internet-Based Career Assessment. As shown by gray shading, such assessments have been self-help, historically, supported by indirect advertising and sponsors, and unvalidated.

As mentioned earlier, CACAs, including career information delivery systems (CIDS), serve to reduce costs when delivering career information. The three components of CIDS include (1) assessment of varying combinations of values, interests, skills, and employment preferences; (2) use of assessment data to identify potentially appropriate occupational information (e.g., entry requirements for occupations, wage data) or educational options (e.g., description of educational programs and institutions); and (3) occupational and educational information delivery (Capuzzi & Stauffer, 2012). These three components integrate so that the information from one component is used in completing another component. Examples of integration include using assessment results to search for occupations or locating educational programs for an occupation under consideration. The three types of assessments used in CIDS include the following: standardized tests administered online, standardized tests administered offline (and then entered into CIDS), and the sorting of self-assessment of variables (e.g., a checklist of values, interests, and skills) in order to expand and/or narrow a client's occupational aspirations.

CIDS are available in almost all states and include occupational and educational information specific to location as well as on a national basis (Capuzzi & Stauffer, 2012; Zunker, 2011). Typically, state-based CIDS provide more specific and detailed local data (e.g., financial information, educational programs) and job information than national systems. In addition to self-help opportunities, CIDS are often available in most schools, colleges, and agencies. The Alliance of Career Resource Professionals (ACRP; 2016) established voluntary standards that guide the design and use of these systems.

Benefits of Computer-Assisted Career Assessment

Several benefits for computer-assisted career assessments exist, especially in areas of test design, administration, calculating scores, and interpretation of results. Advancements in modalities of digital technologies, including text, image, video, audio, and haptics (touch), allow for new designs in assessment that could be personalized for individuals to document their career learning in a variety of ways (Timmis, Broadfoot, Sutherland, & Oldfield, 2016). With respect to administration, these assessments are less cumbersome to store, often guide the client with step-by-step instructions, notify clients when they have missed an item or made an incorrect entry, and, through various scoring algorithms, can determine when a client has demonstrated mastery of an aptitude once a certain number of answers have been answered correctly (Betz & Turner, 2011). Calculation of results is also simplified, in that scores can be summed immediately, profiled, subscales, such as interest and values results, combined and linked to relevant information (Betz & Turner, 2011), such as O*NET, which is often of high quality due to maintenance by government agencies (Harris-Bowlsbey, 2012). Client access is improved, because assessments are available online or via mobile technology anytime and anywhere (Harris-Bowlsbey, 2012; Timmis et al., 2016), and use of CIDS can support collaborative learning and adaptive feedback to improve formative assessment and extend the decision making to include others in the assessment and discussion (Timmis et al., 2016).

Computer-based test interpretation (Sampson et al., 2013) is another benefit of CACAs and allows clients to receive "multimedia-based generalized test interpretations that review basic concepts and general test results before they receive a specific test interpretation from a counselor" (p. 36). This benefit allows clients to have a basic interpretation of their test results they can read prior to, during, or following their meeting with a career practitioner. This allows practitioners to spend more time on the specific applications of the test results for each client's unique situation. Research (Dozier, Sampson, & Reardon, 2013) that compared the online, individualized interpretive reports versus workbook versions of the *You and Your Career* (YYC; Holland, 1994b) and the *Education Opportunities Finder* (EOF; Rosen, Holmberg, & Holland, 1997) for the Self-Directed Search (SDS; Holland, 1994a) found that individuals with the individualized report were significantly more likely to recall their first and third letter summary codes accurately (but not the second letter) and more likely to increase their career options than those who received the workbook versions of YYC and EOF. However, no differences were found on time spent reviewing the information nor on their career decision state. The capability of computer-assisted career assessments to create individualized reports aligns with the recommendation from Brown and Ryan-Krane (2000) that the provision of individual, personalized feedback is an element of an effective career intervention.

Computer-assisted career guidance (CACG) systems also provide the opportunity for individualized reports, often combine several assessments and link those results to occupations, career information, educational and training information, and might provide crosswalks to various occupational databases or decision-making guides. Some CACG systems even allow for the creation of digital portfolios (Sultana, 2013). Highly interactive, CACG systems are transparent in that, as users change an answer, such as changing the rating of a value from "essential" to "desirable," their corresponding list of occupations changes (Maze, 2009). The design of these systems places users in control of which assessments and components they complete and in which order (Tirpak & Schlosser, 2013). In addition, research has shown that interacting with these systems leads to gains in decidedness and career decision-making self-efficacy, and clients usually report use of such systems as a positive experience (Betz & Turner, 2011).

Another major benefit of computer-assisted technology provides the possibility to aggregate assessment data. Career practitioners can build local norms through collecting, analyzing, and reporting assessment data for a body of clients. This could help career practitioners and individuals optimize learning by having more centralized control over assessment data and progress (Timmis et al., 2016). In addition, the aggregated assessment data can help career practitioners interpret results effectively. Computers can store large amounts of information, and statistical modeling optimizes judgmental accuracy (Youyou, Kosinski, & Stillwell, 2015), thus enabling career practitioners to analyze overall scores from multiple users, develop local norms, and conduct research based on aggregate data across users. Potentially, computers are accurate at predicting personality judgments and self-reported psychological health (see Youyou et al., 2015 and Ziemer & Korkmaz, 2017, respectively). There is room for improvement with these technologies, yet the assistance of computers could become a vital component in eliminating human bias while interpreting results.

Limitations of Computer-Assisted Career Assessment

Although several benefits exist for the use of CACAs, career practitioners need to be aware of potential limitations. Some of these include costs, design, determining psychometric properties of the assessments and accompanying test interpretations, confidentiality and privacy, client readiness, and appropriateness of use.

Costs of CACAs range from free (e.g., O*NET Interest Profiler) to thousands of dollars (for certain CACG systems). The extreme range of costs could present an access issue for many career practitioners and clients. A secondary limitation is that of design. Researchers (Greiff, Scherer, & Kirschner, 2017; Harris-Bowlsbey, 2012) suggested that computer-based assessment is lacking a theory to guide the design and use of digital instruments. Zunker (2016) advocated for the use of career theory to guide conceptualization of a client's career concerns, identifying key components that need addressing for successful career decision making, and determining appropriate interventions. Though a benefit of an a-theoretical assessment is that, by its very nature, that tool is not limited to a particular theory, one drawback is that the results might confuse a client who is taking the assessment as a stand-alone intervention. For example, a client might complete an interest inventory that results in either a handful or a plethora of options. Either situation can be problematic, and the next step might not be clear without a specific theory to guide the process. Another possibility is that negative career thinking might be affecting the client's results. Client results are likely to be a reflection of negative thinking and might not be accurate. Within cognitive information processing (CIP) theory (Sampson, Reardon, Peterson, & Lenz, 2004), the career practitioner would have recommended an assessment of negative thoughts prior to an interest assessment. Without a theory to guide the selection, use, and interpretation of computer-assisted career assessments, clients might end up discouraged by their results, not realizing that a more positive outcome might be possible if the practitioner would have addressed the negative thoughts further. To this point, Osborn and Zunker (2016) asserted that career practitioners should not view assessments as a standalone career intervention, but should conceptualize them as merely one step within the career counseling process.

Psychometric properties of computer-assisted career assessments are also a potential limitation. Because the technology of scoring and algorithms are hidden from the user and the practitioner, checking on scoring accuracy can be difficult, if not impossible. In addition, publishers of CACG systems tend not to have any reliability or validity data on the use of the individual assessments or integration of assessments, often giving the argument that "they do not need any because they simply help the respondent to sort occupations" (Maze, 2009, p. 47). Another rarely researched issue is the validity of test interpretations (i.e., does the test interpretation match the results?) (Sampson et al., 2013). For example, a report might provide a description of a particular Holland type and describe common characteristics of that type in terms of personality, interpersonal communication, strengths and weaknesses, values, and so forth. However, rarely is there research to support this information. Dozier et al. (2013) conducted research to determine equivalency of a computer-assisted career assessment with its paper and pencil version, but such research is the exception rather than the rule.

There are even some discrepancies between taking assessments on a computer versus taking them on a mobile device. Assessments designed for use on computers are not always optimized for mobile devices. This could cause poor usability resulting in submission errors and less data collected (Huff, 2015). Additionally, un-optimized assessments could strain working memory which could increase the time spent on a measure (Arthur, Doverspike, Muñoz, Taylor, & Carr, 2014; Huff, 2015; Illingworth, Morelli, Scott, & Boyd, 2014; Morelli, Mahan, & Illingworth, 2014). In longer assessments, fatigue on a mobile device becomes an issue, and the individual is at a higher risk of giving up when commitment is not sufficient (Huff, 2015).

Ethical issues include confidentiality and privacy, client readiness, and appropriateness of use for CACAs. Another primary concern is how and where practitioners store and use client data. If a client sits down to complete a CACA or is returning to complete a CACG system, and the previous client's information shows on the screen, this is an ethical violation. When an individual completes a career assessment online, how does the practitioner store and use that information, and is the client made aware and given the option to decline having their results used? Even if the client declines, how can a client be sure the information was not included? Many assessments available on social media publish the results onto their platform, which is another violation of privacy.

Client readiness and appropriateness for use are additional concerns. Unless a test developer or publisher puts measures in place to determine client readiness and appropriateness of the assessment, individuals completing an assessment that does not meet their needs is possible. Assessments utilize normative groups, but what if an individual, who was not represented by the norm group, takes the assessment? Without some training in measurement, they might misinterpret results as being a true representation of themselves. This is also true for international populations. The Internet provides access to CACAs around the world. However, generally, the assessments are not normed on all of these potential populations, and some of the occupations and career information might not exist or might not be accurate for other countries (Harris-Bowlsbey, 2012). In addition, clients who are confused about their career decision might actually become more confused or overwhelmed when presented with a large number of options and the "vast array of career information presented within the system" (Tirpak & Schlosser, 2013, p.

112). Lack of screening to determine the appropriateness of computer-assisted career assessments for clients remains a chief concern.

Future Innovations in Computer-Assisted Career Assessment

As anticipated by Harris-Bowlsby (2012), computer assisted career assessment systems, previously mediated by trained professionals, have become ubiquitous with the advent of broadband wireless communications and handheld computing devices (e.g., smart phones and tablets). While access to information has increased, so has the amount of information collected on users and their information consumption behaviors. A vendor-sponsored study suggests that by 2020, 44 zeta bytes (i.e., 10^{21} bytes or one billion, one terabyte hard drives) of stored information will exist but that only 37% of this information will be tagged and analyzed to allow for meaningful use (EMC, 2014). Such "big data" has the potential to inform the total process of career assessment, exploration, and decision-making.

Two areas of career assessment in which technology and resulting big data sets can make a significant contribution are in screening for career concerns and in describing person-environment fit. Social networks (e.g., Facebook and LinkedIn) provide a point of contact for identifying individuals who are facing career problems. A parallel example is seen in a collaboration by Google and the National Alliance on Mental Illness (NAMI), which offers smartphone users an opportunity to "Check if you're clinically depressed" by taking the Patient Health Questionnaire–9 (PHQ-9; Kroenke, Spitzer, & Williams, 2001) when they enter the phrase "clinical depression" into Google.com (Giliberti, 2017). This nine-item measure of depression severity offers interpretive feedback and referrals (e.g., National Suicide Prevention Lifeline) based upon user responses. An analogy in the domain of career assessment might be users posting "I've just been fired" to their Facebook account, which triggers an offer for a career readiness assessment and appropriate referrals (e.g., workforce centers, local qualified practitioners). These efforts should be guided by empirical evidence and comply with codes of ethical behavior.

Big data has demonstrated its ability to describe the personality traits of individuals based upon their history of online behavior. For example, Youyou et al. (2015) demonstrated that the sampling of individuals' Facebook "likes" described their five factor model personality traits more accurately than did ratings by friends or family (spouses performed only slightly better). Given that personality and vocational interests are somewhat interrelated (Larson, Rottinghaus, & Borgen, 2002; Mount, Barrick, Scullen, & Rounds, 2005), a quantitative, data mining approach would likely be successful as a method of career interest assessment. This approach could likely be adapted to measure other constructs as well (e.g., values, skills, self-efficacy, etc.).

Qualitative approaches, such as a career construction interview (Savickas, 2015), might be replicated, in part, by artificially intelligent (AI) agents that identify life narratives derived from users' choices across multiple internet services (e.g., movies watched in Netflix, books read in Amazon, and images posted to Pinterest). These agents are capable of "knowing" more about the users' choices *and* detailed information about the content of each choice (e.g., plot of the movie, thematic analysis of the book, content of the image) than a single counselor could. Although such agents suggest consumer purchases, currently, based on past browsing and buying behavior, what is unknown is whether they can, like counselors, transform many disparate pieces of data successfully into the information, knowledge and wisdom helpful to a specific career decision maker (Carr & Epstein, 2009). Furthermore, AI agents, themselves, can reflect the cultural biases inherent in the knowledge bases upon which they are built, including gender stereotypes of occupation (Caliskan, Bryson, & Narayanan, 2017). So far, such qualitative assessment and interpretation remain the domain of the career professional, but some are predicting that artificial intelligence might replace "white collar" positions, which execute "routine" procedures frequently requiring special content knowledge and skills (Ford, 2013).

As noted by Krumboltz and Jackson (1993), assessment taps into past learning and can shape future learning. In addition, technology enables more sophisticated design of assessments that incorporate learners' characteristics and emotional states. For example, Liu et al. (2015) found gender differences in student's emotional states (as measured by EEG) in response to positive feedback, in the form of applause, during computer-assisted self-assessment of a mathematics task. Their findings indicated that positive emotional feedback during assessment influenced males more than females, contributing to significantly lower post-task anxiety for males than females. Liu et al. interpreted this as evidence that males might be more responsive to environmental context than females, and they encouraged instructors to consider gender difference when designing learner feedback. Furthermore, Liu and colleagues (2015, p. 348), suggested "...that researchers explore gender differences in emotional reactions during computer-assisted self-assessment testing for different subjects and tasks." A cursory search of the computer assisted career assessment literature indicates this area needs further inquiry.

Simulation of occupational tasks has been used previously for career assessment, exploration, and decision-making in various delivery formats: paper and pencil (Lankard, 1981), CD-ROM (Krumboltz, Vidalakis, & Tyson, 2000), and live role-play simulations (National Life/Work Center, 2017). Virtual reality (VR), introduced with the microcomputer revolution of the 1980s, has been adapted less prominently for career assessment and exploration. In contrast to VR, in which all sensory information is computer generated, augmented reality (AR) overlays digital information (either text or graphical) over a view of the existing world (Kuo-Hung, Kuo-En, Chung-Hsien, Kinshuk, & Yao-Ting, 2016). Today, both VR and AR offer new promise in that they are relatively accessible through increasingly prevalent smartphone ownership.

An example of a low-cost entertainment-focused game that employs both VR and AR is *Job Simulator: The 2050 archives* (Owlchemy, 2017). Set in a future, where technology has eliminated the need for humans to work, this "tongue-in-cheek" simulation allows players to "...relive the glory days of work..." and tackle job tasks as a chef, clerical worker, store clerk, etc. (Owlchemy, 2017). Though the focus of this game is clearly not realism (fidelity) nor communication of accurate occupational information, it illustrates the potential of VR and AR for career assessment and exploration.

The use of these technologies in psychological assessment and learning activities is not without precedent. Parsons and Phillips (2016) have advocated for the inclusion of VR in neurocognitive assessments because it provides greater ecological validity (e.g., testing a client's attention in a virtual driving test or memory in a virtual apartment setting). Similarly, nursing educators have piloted AR to enhance fidelity in training simulations that could double as low-risk occupational exploratory activities for career decision makers (Vaughn, Lister, & Shaw, 2016). Both VR and AR offer the possibility of revising or reimagining existing career assessments and occupational information. Furthermore, they have the potential to make assessment and information accessible to individuals with differing learning styles and abilities.

In summation, a convergence of ubiquitous, relatively low cost data connectivity and handheld hardware, big data sets of user behavior, more complex insights into user experience, nascent artificially intelligent agents, and easily accessible virtual and augmented learning environments offer great challenges and opportunities to CACA. For over 50 years, career professionals have been at the forefront of leveraging advances in computer technology to help clients explore their options and make sound career decisions (Harris-Bowlsbey, 2012). The next 50 years offers a great deal of promise (and perhaps some peril) for career professionals as they continue to integrate new technologies into best practices and sustain our profession for the benefit of future generations of clients.

Career Practitioner Strategies for Computer-Assisted Career Assessment

Career assessment is a key element of the career counseling process, and CACA provides options for clients by removing potential barriers and limitations. Career practitioners can assist their clients in identifying career choice issues that are relevant using a variety of CACA tools (Maze, 2009). Although there are certainly many assessments available online that might not be reliable or valid, the career practitioner is key to helping clients understand, that even with the most highly respected instrument in our field, results should be viewed as providing suggestions for the client to explore further. The career practitioner helps the client utilize results of the career assessment better by knowing which questions to ask and applying the answers appropriately to the individual; these aspects of career counseling and career service delivery are not yet satisfied by computerized services alone (Maze, 2009).

Sampson (2008) recommended the following strategies when working with clients utilizing computer-assisted career assessment: screening, recommending, orienting, and follow-up. In addition to these recommendations, career practitioners should follow the ethical guidelines discussed earlier in this chapter, including taking the assessment themselves and having the results interpreted. Career practitioners might also consider how they might make use of local norms, as well as big data, to help with program evaluation of their career service delivery.

Suggested Resources for Further Reading

We suggest the following resources for further reference and reading:

- NCDA Code of Ethics: https://ncda.org/aws/NCDA/asset_manager/get_file/3395
- NCDA Competencies for Assessment: https://www.ncda.org/aws/NCDA/asset_manager/get_file/18143/aace-ncda_assmt_eval_competencies
- NBCC Code of Ethics: http://www.nbcc.org/Ethics/CodeOfEthics
- Ethical Use of Social Networking Technologies in Career Services: https://www.ncda.org/aws/NCDA/asset_manager/get_file/110167
- Code of Fair Testing and Practices in Education: https://www.apa.org/science/programs/testing/fair-testing.pdf
- Alliance of Career Resource Professionals: http://www.acrpro.org/aws/ACRP/pt/so/home_page
- O*NET Interest Profiler: https://www.onetcenter.org/IP.html
- Job Simulator: The 2050 archives: https://jobsimulatorgame.com/

Summary

The use of computer-assisted career assessments is likely to continue to increase. Career practitioners must consider part of their role to educate clients and potential consumers of these assessments on how to evaluate the appropriateness of these tools. Such appropriateness includes the quality of the instrument and the validity of the information provided within any report or results, as well as how to integrate the results in a meaningful way into their career decision-making process. The Internet not only expands the potential reach of career assessments, but also expands the career practitioners' responsibility to help clients to use these resources in a judicious manner.

References

ACRP. (2016). *Standards.* Retrieved from http://www.acrpro.org/aws/ACRP/pt/sp/standards

ACT. (2006). *Research support for DISCOVER assessment components.* Iowa City, IA: Author.

American Psychological Association. (n.d.). *Code of fair testing practices in education.* Retrieved from https://www.apa.org/science/programs/testing/fair-testing.pdf

Arthur, W., Doverspike, D., Muñoz, G. J., Taylor, J. E., & Carr, A. E. (2014). The use of mobile devices in high-stakes remotely delivered assessments and testing. *International Journal of Selection and Assessment, 22,* 113–123.

Betz, N. & Borgen, F. (2009). The CAPA integrative online systems for college major exploration. *Journal of Career Assessment, 18,* 317-327.

Betz, N., & Turner, B. (2011). Using item response theory and adaptive testing in online career assessment. *Journal of Career Assessment, 19,* 274-286.

Brown, S. D., & Ryan-Krane, N. E. (2000). Four (or five) sessions and a cloud of dust: Old assumptions and new observations about career counseling. In S. D. Brown, & R. W. Lent (Eds.), *Handbook of counseling psychology* (3rd ed., pp. 740–766). New York: Wiley.

Caliskan, A., Bryson, J. J., & Narayanan, A. (2017). Semantics derived automatically from language corpora contain human-like biases. *Science, 356,* 183-186.

Capuzzi, D., & Stauffer, M. D. (2012). *Career counseling: Foundations, perspectives, and applications* (2nd ed.). New York, NY: Routledge.

Carr, D. L., & Epstein, S. A. (2009). Information resources to enhance career advising. In K. Hughey, D. B. Nelson, J. Damminger, & E. McCalla-Wriggins (Eds.), *The handbook of career advising* (pp. 146-181). Manhattan, KS: National Academic Advising Association.

Dozier, V. C., Sampson, J. P., & Reardon, R. R. (2013). Using two different Self-Directed Search (SDS) interpretive materials: Implications for career assessment. *Professional Counselor, 3,* 67-72. doi:10.15241/vcd.3.2.67

EMC. (2014, April). *The digital universe of opportunities: Rich data and the increasing value of the internet of things.* Retrieved from: https://www.emc.com/leadership/digital-universe/2014iview/index.htm

Ford, M. (2013). Could artificial intelligence create an unemployment crisis? *Communications of the ACM, 56,* 37-39.

Giliberti, M. (2017, August 23). *Learning more about clinical depression with the PHQ-9 questionnaire.* Retrieved from: https://www.blog.google/products/search/learning-more-about-clinical-depression-phq-9-questionnaire/

Greiff, S., Scherer, R., & Kirschner, P. A. (2017). Some critical reflections on the special issue: Current innovations in computer-based assessments. *Computers in Human Behavior, 76*(C), 715-718. doi:10.1016/j.chb.2017.08.019

Harris-Bowlsbey, J. (2012). Computer-assisted career guidance systems: A part of NCDA history. *Career Development Quarterly, 61,* 181-185. doi:10.1002/j.2161-0045.2013.00047.x

Holland, J. L. (1994a). Self-Directed Search. Odessa, FL: Psychological Assessment Resources.

Holland, J. L. (1994b). You and your career. Odessa, FL: Psychological Assessment Resources.

Huff, K. C. (2015). The comparison of mobile devices to computers for web-based assessments. *Computers in Human Behavior, 49,* 208-212. doi:10.1016/j.chb.2015.03.008

Illingworth, A. J., Morelli, N. A., Scott, J. C., & Boyd, S. L. (2014). Internet-based, unproctored assessments on mobile and non-mobile devices: Usage, measurement equivalence, and outcomes. *Journal of Business and Psychology, 30,* 325-343.

Khapova, S. N., Svensson, J. S., Wilderom, C. P. M., & Arthur, M. B. (2006). Usage of internet-based career support. In M. Anandarajan, T. S. H. Teo, & C. A. Simmers (Eds.), *The internet and workplace transformation* (*Advances in Management Information Systems; No. 7;* pp. 162-176). Armonk, NY: M.E. Sharpe.

Kroenke, K., Spitzer, R., Williams, J., (2001). The PHQ 9: Validity of a brief depression severity measure. *Journal of General Internal Medicine, 16,* 606-613.

Krumboltz, J. D., & Jackson, M. A. (1993). Career assessment as a learning tool. *Journal of Career Assessment, 1,* 393-409.

Krumboltz, J. D., Vidalkis, N., & Tyson, J. (2000, April). Virtual job experience: Try before you choose. (ED 442 961). Paper presented at the annual meeting of the American Educational Research Association, New Orleans, LA.

Kuo-Hung, C., Kuo-En, C., Chung-Hsien, L., Kinshuk, & Yao-Ting, S. (2016). Integration of mobile AR technology in performance assessment. *Educational Technology & Society, 19,* 239 – 251.

Lankard, B. (1981). Career alert planning: Instructor guide. Columbus, OH: Ohio State University National Center for Research in Vocational Education. (ED214000). Retrieved from http://files.eric.ed.gov/fulltext/ED214000.pdf

Larson, L., Rottinghaus, P., & Borgen, F. (2002). Meta-analyses of big six interests and big five personality factors. *Journal of Vocational Behavior, 61*, 217-239.

Liu, C., Huang, C., Liu, M., Chien, Y., Lai, C., & Huan, Y. (2015). Does gender influence emotions resulting from positive applause feedback in self-assessment testing? Evidence from neuroscience. *Educational Technology & Society, 18*, 337-350.

Makela, J. P., & Perlus, J. (2017). *A case study approach to ethics in career development (2nd ed.)*. Broken Arrow, OK: National Career Development Association.

Mayadas, A. F., Bourne, J., & Bacsich, P. (2009). Online education today. *Science, 323*, 85-89.

Maze, M. (2009). Using computer assisted career guidance systems effectively. *Career Planning & Adult Development Journal, 25*, 46-53.

Morelli, N. A., Mahan, R. P., & Illingworth, A. J. (2014). Establishing the measurement equivalence of online selection assessments delivered on mobile versus nonmobile devices. *International Journal of Selection and Assessment, 22*, 124–138.

Mount, M., Barrick, M., Scullen, S., & Rounds, J. (2005). Higher-order dimensions of the big five personality traits and the big six vocational interest types. *Personnel Psychology, 58*, 447-478.

National Life/Work Center. (2017). *The real game series*. Retrieved from http://www.realgame.com

National Board of Certified Counselors. (2016). *Code of ethics*. Retrieved from http://www.nbcc.org/Assets/Ethics/NBCCCodeofEthics.pdf

National Career Development Association. (2015). *Code of ethics*. Retrieved from https://ncda.org/aws/NCDA/asset_manager/get_file/3395

National Center for O*NET Development. Interest Profiler (IP). O*NET Resource Center. Retrieved from https://www.onetcenter.org/IP.html?p=2

Oliver, L., W., & Whiston, S. C. (2000). Internet career assessment for the new millennium. *Journal of Career Assessment, 8*, 361-369.

Osborn, D. S., & Zunker, V. (2016). *Using Assessment Results for Career Development* (9th ed.). Boston, MA: Cengage Learning.

Owlchemy. (2017). *Job simulator: The 2050 archives*. Retrieved from https://jobsimulatorgame.com

Parsons, T., & Phillips, A. (2016). Virtual reality for psychological assessment in clinical practice. *Practice Innovations, 1*, 197-217.

Perrotta, C. (2013). Innovative technology-enhanced assessment in the UK and the USA: Future scenarios and critical considerations. *Technology, Pedagogy, & Education, 23*, 103-119.

Ras, E., Whitelock, D., & Kalz, M. (2015). The promise and potential of e-assessment for learning. In P. Reimann, S., Bull, M., Kickmeier-Rust, R., Vatrapu, & B. Wasson (Eds.), *Measuring and visualizing learning in the information-rich classroom* (pp. 21-40). New York: Routledge.

Rosen, D., Holmberg, K., & Holland, J. (1997). *Educational opportunities finder*. Odessa, FL: Psychological Assessment Resources.

Savickas, M. L. (2015). *Life design counseling manual*. Retrieved from: http://www.vocopher.com/LifeDesign/LifeDesign.pdf

Sampson, J. P., Jr. (2008). Designing and implementing career programs: A handbook for effective practice. Broken Arrow, OK: National Career Development Association

Sampson, J. P., & Lumsden, J. A. (2000). Ethical issues in the design and use of Internet-based career assessment. *Journal of Career Assessment, 8,* 21-35.

Sampson, J. P., McClain, M., Dozier, C., Carr, D. L., Lumsden, J. A., & Osborn, D. S. (2013). Computer-assisted career assessment. In C. Wood & D. G. Hayes (Ed.), *A counselor's guide to career assessment instruments* (6th ed.) (pp. 33-47). Broken Arrow, OK: National Career Development Association.

Sampson, J. P., Jr., Reardon, R. C., & Rudd, E. (1998). Computer-assisted career guidance: SIGI PLUS and SIGI bibliography. *The Center for the Study of Technology in Counseling and Career Development*. Retrieved from https://career.fsu.edu/sites/g/files/imported/storage/original/application/b7f759563f5c8bcce9796ca681197a83.pdf

Sampson, J. P., Jr., Reardon, R. C., Peterson, G. W., & Lenz, J. G. (2004). *Career counseling and services: A cognitive information processing approach*. Pacific Grove, CA: Brooks/Cole.

Sultana, R. G. (2013). Career management skills: Assessing for learning. *Australian Journal of Career Development, 22,* 82-90. doi:10.1177/1038416213496759

Timmis, S., Broadfoot, P., Sutherland, R., & Oldfield, A. (2016). Rethinking assessment in a digital age: Opportunities, challenges and risks. *British Educational Research Journal, 42,* 454-476. doi:10.1002/berj.3215

Tirpak, D. M., & Schlosser, L. Z. (2013). Evaluating FOCUS-2's effectiveness in enhancing first-year college students' social cognitive career development. *Career Development Quarterly, 61,* 110-123. 110. doi:10.1002/j.2161-0045.2013.00041.x.

Vaughn, J., Lister, M., & Shaw, R. (2016). Piloting augmented reality technology to enhance realism in clinical simulation. *Computers, Informatics, Nursing, 34,* 402 – 405.

Youyou, W., Kosinksi, M., & Stillwell, D. (2015). Computer-based personality judgments are more accurate than those made by humans. *Proceedings of the National Academy of Sciences, 112,* 1036-1040. doi:10.1073/pnas.1418680112

Ziemer, K. S., & Korkmaz, G. (2017). Using text to predict psychological and physical health: A comparison of human raters and computerized text analysis. *Computers in Human Behavior, 76,* 122-127. doi:10.1016/j.chb.2017.06.038

Zunker, V. G. (2011). *Career counseling: A holistic approach* (8th ed.). Independence, KY: Cengage Learning.

Zunker, V. G. (2016). *Career counseling: a holistic approach* (9th ed.). Boston, MA: Cengage Learning.

CHAPTER 4

MULTICULTURAL CONSIDERATIONS IN CAREER ASSESSMENT

Kerrie G. Wilkins-Yel
Indiana University Bloomington

Y. Barry Chung
San Diego State University

Jacks Cheng
Indiana University Bloomington

Yue Li
Indiana University Bloomington

Multicultural Considerations in Career Assessment

The United States is undergoing a rapidly changing cultural landscape. Never before has the population been comprised of such an abundant mix of multi-lingual, multi-racial, and multi-ethnic group of individuals. Given the increasing cultural diversity across institutions, such as workplaces, educational settings, and economic environments, it is imperative to equip career practitioners with appropriate skills to serve the complex needs of diverse client populations, particularly the use of career assessment tools (e.g., tests and inventories). According to Blustein and Ellis (2000), "the ethical and moral use of tests within a culturally diverse context offers perhaps the greatest challenge for career practitioners of the 21st century" (p. 380). Therefore, this chapter focuses on multicultural considerations that arise in career assessment. In this chapter, we use *assessment* as a global term that denotes the use of both quantitative and qualitative tools for assessing career-related constructs, and we refer to specific assessment tools as *career tests, measures, inventories,* or *instruments.* We outline common pitfalls in career assessments and offer ways in which career practitioners can augment career assessments to meet the needs of a diverse population.

Historical Context

Despite the clarion call for increased multicultural considerations in career assessment, notable scholars have indicated that, although ideal, this outcome will require a concerted effort. This is true especially because of the nearly 100-year career practice history of paying little to no attention to the experiences of culturally diverse clients. Career counseling was developed at a time, and as a result of, the social milieu of the early and mid-20th Century (Herr, 2001; Pope, 2000). The field was established by White scholars, namely pioneers such as Frank Parsons and Jesse Davis, and was based on a masculine and Western European ideal that foregrounds individualism, autonomy, affluence, and the stance that employment is accessible to all (Cook, Heppner, & O'Brien, 2002; Fouad & Bingham, 1995; Gysbers, Heppner, & Johnston, 2014). Given the Eurocentric framework that underscores the conceptualization of many career constructs and assessment tools, the applicability of career assessments to women, people of color, lesbian/gay/bisexual/transgender/queer (LGBTQ) persons, and other marginalized groups is questionable at best.

Scholars and researchers have risen to the challenge and devoted entire journal issues to advancing knowledge on multicultural considerations in career assessment. For example, the Fall 2000 special issue of the *Journal of Career Assessment* was focused on "Career Assessment in the New Millennium." Similarly, professional organizations have put forth guidelines and standards to address issues pertaining to practice and assessment with a diverse clientele. For example, Anderson (2000) published the *Guidelines on Multicultural Education, Training, Research, Practice, and Organizational Change for Psychologists*. Specifically, the *Guidelines* state that "multiculturally sensitive practitioners are encouraged to be aware of the limitations of assessment practices." Further, the American Counseling Association (ACA, 2014) Code of Ethics puts forth the expectation that counselors need to be culturally competent when conducting assessments with culturally diverse clients. This evidence shows that scholars and professional organizations (NCDA, 2009) have recognized the need for practitioners to be cognizant of the unique issues that arise when conducting assessments with culturally diverse clientele.

Culturally Competent Career Practitioner

To conduct culturally informed career assessments, practitioners must realize first that the career assessment tools (e.g., tests and inventories) are, in part, only as culturally sensitive as the test administrator and interpreter, whereas the other part is driven by the development of culturally informed career assessments. Consequently, embodying and engaging actively in a culturally competent practice is imperative for career practitioners. As stated by Sue, Arredondo, and McDavis (1992), counselors' multicultural competence includes three distinct components. These include, first, an awareness of counselors' own biases, understanding of their own cultural heritage including the status of their racial identity development, and recognition of the areas where they experience unearned privileges. Second, cultural competence includes knowledge of the historical context of marginalized groups and engagement in the process of understanding and informing oneself about a client's worldview. Third, cultural competence includes implementing the requisite counseling skills effectively, including, the effective implementation of microskills, ongoing establishment of culturally sensitive therapeutic alliance, and working with difficult client behaviors (Flores, Spanierman, & Obasi, 2003; Fouad & Bingham, 1995).

Successful multicultural career practice involves an awareness of, and attention to, an individual's entire lifespan, including life roles, sexual orientation status, disability status, gender constraints, racial/ethnic implications, and environmental opportunities and barriers. It also means utilizing the information gathered in interventions to support traditionally underrepresented clients in finding and maintaining satisfying work and coping with discriminatory workplace practices. In addition, cultural competence among career practitioners includes an awareness of the norming sample that was used to develop an instrument, and staying abreast of the empirical research pertaining to the career development of culturally diverse clientele. Failure to pay attention to a client's cultural context might heighten the use of inappropriate career assessments (Fouad, 1995), which then increases the risk of being irrelevant, or worse, harmful to clients (Blustein, 2006; Fouad & Bingham, 1995).

Career Assessment Considerations for Underrepresented Groups

There is a wealth of literature that demonstrates the effectiveness of career assessment tools in assisting individuals gain increased understanding about their interests, skills, and values. However, problems arise when the cultural applicability of these assessment tools are called into question. A number of researchers have shed light on these concerns, especially as it pertains to prominent career assessment tools and marginalized populations. In the following sections, we provide an overview of some widely used career instruments and the multicultural concerns that arise with each assessment tool.

Interests

Among the constructs assessed in career practice, a client's interests are, by far, the most commonly examined. Holland (1959, 1997) proposed that both individuals and their environments can be organized into six vocational types: Realistic, Investigative, Artistic, Social, Enterprising, and Conventional, collectively referred to as the RIASEC model. Since then, two of the most widely used and researched interest assessment tools are the Strong Interest Inventory (SII; Harmon, Hansen, Borgen, & Hammer, 1994) and the Self-Directed Search (SDS; Holland, Fritzsche, & Powell, 1994). The SII is a computer scored inventory that assesses career interests related to Holland's (1997) six interest domains. Holland developed the SDS to assess the six interest domains.

Researchers have examined the cultural applicability of the SII and SDS through a number of studies. Fouad, Harmon, and Borgen (1997) found that the order of interest domains differed between men and women such that women were less differentiated between *R* and *I* and between *E* and *S*. Additionally, the arrangement of interest for Asian American men was more triangular than circular, as indicated by the grouping of *C*, *E*, and *S* interests. The results also showed that the interests structure for Caucasian American and Latino-Hispanic American men resembled Holland's (1997) hexagon (versus circular arrangement) most closely.

The SII underwent an update in 2004 whereby the diversity within the norm sample was increased. Nonetheless, researchers continued to remark that the interest structure fit Caucasian samples the best, and that the norm sample of the updated version continues to lack diverse representation (Kelly, 2010).

In addition to racial/ethnic concerns, researchers have reported large differences in the vocational interests of men and women. As expected, women report interests that are consistent with traditional female gender roles, and men expressed interests that are in line with domains that society considers traditionally masculine (Betz & Fitzgerald, 1987; Hackett & Lonborg, 1994). Einarsdóttir and Rounds (2009) found that women scored higher on the *Social, Artistic,* and *Conventional* scales using the SII, whereas men scored higher on the *Realistic* and *Investigative* scales. Gender differences on career assessments can have unintended consequences on both the broader society and the individuals seeking career assistance. These differences can result in restrictive career options being suggested to clients based on their gender (e.g., women being encouraged to pursue the culinary arts versus engineering). Further, these differences maintain and perpetuate the status quo where only a limited range of occupations are deemed appropriate for men and women. Einarsdóttir and Rounds' (2009) research supported the argument that clients' responses to interest inventories are influenced by gendered barriers and opportunities present in the society, many of which are the result of internalized sex-role stereotypes.

Research examining gender and racial differences in the SDS reported similar findings as the SII. Rounds and Tracey (1996) reported poor structural fit among the Holland types within two U.S. African American samples. In addition, the SDS manual highlighted salient gender differences, even going as far as saying that these differences are much greater than racial and ethnic group differences.

Overall, the aforementioned research findings suggest the need for caution in assuming cultural applicability for the two most commonly used vocational interest inventories (i.e., SII and SDS).

Personality Assessment

Unlike clinicians who use personality assessments to diagnose psychopathology, career practitioners employ personality assessments to assist clients with gaining a better understanding of themselves. The most widely used personality assessments among career practitioners are the Myers-Briggs Type Indicator (MBTI; Myers, McCaulley, & Most, 1985; Sheperis, Perepiczka, & Limoges, 2011; Swanson & D'Achiardi, 2005; Whiston, 2012) and the Sixteen Personality Factor Questionnaire (16PF; Cattell, & Mead, 2008).

The MBTI is an extremely popular personality inventory designed to quantify non-psychopathological personality types using a Jungian framework (Boyle, 1995). Scholars have attributed its popularity to its ease in administration, comprehensibility, and its tendency to evoke a "feel good" response (Johnson, Mauzey, Johnson, Murphy, & Zimmerman, 2001). McCaulley and Moody (2008) regarded the MBTI effective in both domestic U.S. samples and cross-cultural samples. Nonetheless, Boyle (1995) lodged the complaint that "the MBTI types are not 'source traits' verified factor analytically (i.e., "causal" psychological dimensions), predictions based on these 'surface traits' (discontinuous types) are inevitably less powerful and remain somewhat speculative" (p. 6). Additional complaints include difficulty in retaining meanings of some idioms and concepts after translation into another language, and lack of criterion-related validity (McCaulley & Moody, 2008).

The 16PF is another popular personality assessment among career practitioners. It is a comprehensive measure of normal-range personality factors that allows clients to learn how they compare with others on these factors (Cattell & Mead, 2008). The 16PF was re-normed in 1994, at which time a reasoning test was added. This test resembled an intelligence test and was found to correlate highly with such tests as well. Similar to general intelligence tests, Conn and Rieke (1994) found that the reasoning test was biased towards the Caucasian sample. In the latest edition of the 16PF, the test developers improved the standardized test format and removed items that were reviewed for gender, cultural, and ethnic bias. Although research has shown some cross-cultural applicability of the revised 16PF (Rossier, 2005), further work is needed to examine the test's cultural applicability, particularly with domestic underrepresented minorities.

Career practitioners use the MBTI and 16PF extensively. The aforementioned results indicate that both inventories need additional work to be considered multiculturally applicable.

Values

Work value is another commonly assessed construct within career practice. More often than not, however, career practitioners conduct value assessments using idiosyncratic measures designed for particular projects. This approach can make cross-study comparisons difficult (Subich, 2005). The standardized measure used most commonly to assess work values is the Values Scale (VS; Super & Nevill, 1985). Super and Nevill developed the VS as part of the multinational Work Importance Project. As a result, this measure is thought to be more attuned to cultural factors (Subich, 2005). In their overview of the measure, Nevill and Kruse (1996) stated that practitioners can use the VS in both national and cross-national samples. Niles and Goodnough (1996) stated further that each version of the VS includes slightly different values to increase sensitivity to cultural differences.

Although Super and Nevill (1985) designed the VS with cultural sensitivity woven into its framework, Vacha-Haase et al. (2016) noted some differences in score patterns that were counter to the norm sample. Specifically, these researchers examined the VS responses in over 300 African American and Hispanic American high school and college students. They found that males, more so than females, reported a stronger value for people and aesthetically oriented pursuits. In addition, Vacha-Haase et al. found that both male and female minority students indicated a strong value for being able to express their cultural identity at work. These researchers noted that this result was stronger than in the norm sample. Further, they attributed these differences to cultural influences. Consequently, Subich (2005) recommended using caution when using the VS norms on groups other than White Americans.

Multicultural Pitfalls in Using Career Assessments

In examining cross-cultural issues in career assessment, scholars have identified three general areas of interconnected multicultural concerns. The first area is the presence of White ethnocentric bias in career practice as a legacy of its history. A White ethnocentric view shapes the lens through which culture and minority identities are conceptualized directly (Marsella & Leong, 1995; Sue, 2004). However, the reliance on the dominant culture as the standard could create false assumptions and operationalization of social constructs in assessments as equivalent between Caucasian and minority cultures, thus resulting in misinterpretation of assessment results (Marsella & Leong, 1995; Osborn, 2012). Consequently, researchers have highlighted the need to embrace cultural plurality in career assessments (Blustein & Ellis, 2000; Leong & Hartung, 2000; Marsella & Leong, 1995).

Second, there is a long history of overemphasizing person variables and neglecting environmental variables in research and practice of career assessment (Fitzgerald & Betz, 1994; Leong, 1997). This poses a significant threat to the cultural validity of the extant knowledge applied to people across cultural backgrounds (Leong, Hartung, & Pearce, 2014). Since Parsons' (1909) formulation of career choice, research has focused on examining the effect of personal factors such as interest, personality, and ability on career decision-making. Leong et al. (2014) proposed the Ecological-Identity Model which expanded multicultural consider-ations from a narrow focus on the microsystem to attending broadly to the meso-, exos-, macro-, and chronosystems when assessing influences on individuals' vo-cational situations.

The third area of multicultural concern is the role of language in career assess-ment instruments, particularly as it relates to the appropriateness of translations and multilingual abilities for interpreting the social construct in question (Fouad, 1993; Marsella & Leong, 1995; Watson, Duarte, & Glavin, 2005). To ensure accu-racy, the common practice is to have these assessment tools translated into other languages for use with different language groups. The process includes translating the instrument into the new language (forward translation), and then having the newly translated instrument re-translated into the original language (back trans-lation). However, the validity of back-translated instruments cannot always be guaranteed because this method assumes equivalence of cultural validity of social constructs and does not necessarily account for comparability, appropriateness, and connotations between cultures (Marsella & Leong, 1995).

Given the multicultural pitfalls evident in career assessments, we encourage career counselors, practitioners, and researchers to be vigilant in examining the biases that exist in both their training and the instruments they employ.

Improving and Expanding on Career Assessment Methods

There are a number of ways in which career practitioners and researchers can integrate cultural considerations into career assessments. We offer several recom-mendations for improvement and expansion below.

Strategies for Improvement

First, career counselors, practitioners, and researchers are encouraged to take responsibility for the extent to which their cultural identities and experiences in-fluence their selection, judgment, and interpretation of the assessment tools and the ensuing results. Career practitioners are also encouraged to actively mitigate the negative effects of White ethnocentric bias (Flores et al., 2003; Pope, 2009). One way to counteract biased training and instrumentation is to engage with the cultural narratives of the clients, including increasing knowledge of specific customs and issues for diverse cultural groups (Flores et al., 2003; Pope, 2009; Stead & Davis, 2015). Second, career counselors and practitioners are strongly encouraged to facilitate their clients' understanding of test items to minimize the impact of language and translation on test results. Third, we encourage career counselors and practitioners to take on the role of a multicultural advocate to both discuss and address issues of discrimination directly with clients, both in career intervention and in society. Practitioners are also encouraged to devise and utilize alternative career models and assessments, such as group and family-oriented interventions, to overcome societal stereotyping (Pope, 2009). Lastly, career counselors and practitioners should continue to increase their multicultural knowledge and seek other experienced counselors and practitioners for supervision or consultation (Flores et al., 2003).

Strategies for Expansion

Traditionally, career measures have been dominated by standardized quantitative instruments (e.g., the SII and SDS). These quantitative measures are useful in many ways, but the theoretical basis of the measurement, cultural lens of the test creator, scope of assessment items, and the normative samples can restrict their use. Consequently, standardized quantitative measures might have limited applicability to cultural minority groups, such as women, persons of color, immigrants, and LGBTQ persons.

We encourage the use of qualitative career instruments as a way to augment quantitative measures for career assessment with underrepresented groups. Qualitative instruments are open-ended and allow for the client to generate responses based on what is important and relevant to them, rather than being restricted by standardized items and response format. Culturally relevant themes might emerge naturally in qualitative assessments. Furthermore, when reviewing qualitative responses with clients, the career practitioner may engage clients in clarifying and giving meaning to their responses beyond their initial answers.

An example of a qualitative instrument is the use of sentence completion tests. Chung (1999) created a sentence completion test based on social cognitive career theory (SCCT; Lent, Brown, & Hackett, 1994). Chung chose SCCT as the theoretical basis because of its inclusion of contextual factors, self-efficacy and outcome expectations, and learning experiences. These are all important career development factors, particularly for persons of underrepresented groups. Other qualitative methods might include card sorts, value clarification exercises, and writing a career autobiography. Clients may reveal important themes in their educational and work history through these exercises, and the interviewer might make further inquiries based on these qualitative responses, so clients can clarify their life experiences, values, self-concepts, and meaning making further.

In addition to qualitative instruments, the interviewer is a critical element in the career assessment process. The interviewer can inquire about relevant contextual information and tap into cultural identities and experiences, economic needs and resources, important persons who might be barriers or supporters of the client, past coping experiences and outcomes, or current options available. These culturally based interviews are open and fluid. Interviewers build on information provided by clients in intake forms and initial interviews, and allow clients to identify relevant factors/persons and give meaning to their choices or behaviors. Combining qualitative methods and the interviewer, as an instrument, is a powerful assessment process.

Next, we discuss how career practitioners can incorporate quantitative and qualitative methods in multicultural career assessments.

Multicultural Career Assessment Models

To articulate the process of conducting multicultural career assessments using quantitative and qualitative methods, we apply Ridley, Li, and Hill's (1998) four-phase multicultural assessment model for the purpose of career assessments. In the first phase, the career practitioner identifies cultural data by using career interviews, questionnaires, and life/family history. This phase makes use of qualitative methods to tap into cultural information. In Phase 2, the career practitioner interprets cultural data and develops hypotheses by contrasting cultural factors with individual factors, dispositional stress with environmental stress, and important/relevant data with unimportant/irrelevant data. In Phase 3, the career practitioner incorporates cultural data when using standardized career assessments to test hypotheses generated from Phase 2. The final phase involves making career assessment decisions and conclusions using results of Phase 3.

Flores et al. (2003) proposed a Culturally Appropriate Career Assessment Model that also includes four steps. In Step 1, *Information Gathering*, practitioners use quantitative and/or qualitative methods to collect data about the client. Practitioners can use intake forms and questionnaires, career interviews, and other qualitative methods to understand the client's cultural identities, worldviews, cultural values, the salience and strength of various identities, and how these factors relate to the client's career development and concerns. In the second step, *Selection of Instruments*, the career professional identifies suitable career instruments based on relevance to the client's career concerns, the applicability of reliability and validity of the instrument to the client, and whether additional qualitative instruments could provide a more complete picture of the client. In Step 3, *Administration of Career Instruments*, career practitioners attempt to optimize testing conditions as specified in the test manual, as well as attend to contextual factors relevant to the client (e.g., having transportation to the test venue, cultural practice of being on-time, health and nutrition condition at the time of testing, understanding of language used in the test, and relationship with and trust in the test administrator). In the final step, *Interpretation of Career Assessment Results*, the career professional incorporates culturally relevant factors and integrates quantitative and qualitative methods to interpret all test results. Important to this process is taking into account language usage, applicability of the test to the client, and opportunities and resources available to the client. In addition, the client's learning experiences, and other contextual factors are important considerations in the interpretations of test results. Finally, career professionals cross-validate results by having a discussion with the client. See a case study applying this model by Evans (2013).

Relationship Cultural Career Assessment (RCCA) is another qualitative career assessment paradigm that centers on how individuals' relationships influence their career decision-making while acknowledging the adaptive function of interpersonal connection in the process of career development (Schultheiss, 2005; Pitre & Schultheiss, 2017). Cultural context and individuals' intersectional identities are central to the assessment of relational experience and meaning making. RCCA also expands the concept of work to include not only paid employment, but also unpaid work such as caregiving, volunteering, and community work. The goals of RCCA are to provide a thorough examination of the relational influence on one's life and career, and explore available relational resources. The Relationships and Career Interview (Schultheiss, 2003, 2005) can be used as a tool for career assessment. The RCCA steps are outlined as follows: explore client's socially constructed identities within relationships, inquire about client's perception of the influence of relational cultural experience on career development, identify relational themes, educate client on the role of systems in making career decisions, clarify important people in client's career development, and discuss past difficult career decision-making experiences.

The aforementioned models focus on somewhat different elements of multicultural assessments (e.g., the work of Flores et al. detailed a discussion of test administration), but all have strong emphases on gathering cultural data, selecting appropriate career instruments carefully, and incorporating cultural data in integrating and interpreting data from quantitative and qualitative assessment methods. This is a complex process. Effective multicultural career assessments require continuing education on different assessment methods and consultation with colleagues.

Summary

Career assessment rests on a longstanding history of demonstrated success and effectiveness. However, many of these models and tools were created and proliferated by predominantly masculine and Western European ideals that foregrounds individualism, autonomy, and affluence. This restrictive perspective has a host of multicultural implications on career assessment. As such, practitioners need to possess the knowledge, awareness, and skills necessary for conducting effective multicultural practice, as well as the skills needed to conduct culturally informed career assessment effectively with a diverse clientele. Failure to pay attention to a client's cultural context and the multicultural considerations pertinent to career assessment heightens the use of inappropriate assessments and may even increase the risk of being harmful to clients. Embracing cultural pluralism that is characteristic of the global context of the 21st century is no longer a luxury, but a critical necessity for culturally informed career practice and assessment.

References

American Counseling Association. (2014). *ACA code of ethics: As approved by the ACA Governing Council.* Alexandria, VA: Author.

Anderson, N. B. (2000). Guidelines on multicultural education, training, research, practice, and organizational change for psychologists. *American Psychologist, 58,* 377–402.

Betz, N. E., & Fitzgerald, L. F. (1987). *The career psychology of women.* Orlando, FL: Academic Press.

Bjork, R. A., & Druckman, D. (Eds). (1991). *In the mind's eye: Enhancing human performance.* Washington, DC: National Academies Press.

Blustein, D. L. (2006). *The psychology of working: A new perspective for career development, counseling, and public policy.* Mahwah, NJ: Erlbaum.

Blustein, D. L., & Ellis, M. V. (2000). The cultural context of career assessment. *Journal of Career Assessment, 8,* 379–390.

Boyle, G. J. (1995). Myers-Briggs Type Indicator (MBTI): Some psychometric limitations. *Australian Psychologist, 30*(1), 71–74. doi:10.1111/j.1742-9544.1995.tb01750.x

Cattell, H. E. P., & Mead, A. D. (2008). The Sixteen Personality Factor Questionnaire (16PF). In G. J. Boyle, G. Matthews, & D. H. Saklofske (Eds.), *The SAGE handbook of personality theory and assessment, Vol 2: Personality measurement and testing* (pp. 135–159). Thousand Oaks, CA: Sage Publications. https://doi.org/10.4135/9781849200479.n7

Chung, Y. B. (1999). *Chung Sentence Completion.* Unpublished career assessment instrument.

Conn, S. R., & Rieke, M. L. (1994). *The 16PF fifth edition technical manual.* Champaign, IL: Institute for Personality and Ability Testing.

Cook, E. P., Heppner, M. J., & O'Brien, K. M. (2002). Career development of women of color and White women: Assumptions, conceptualization, and interventions from an ecological perspective. *Career Development Quarterly, 50,* 291–305. doi:10.1002/j.2161-0045.2002.tb00574.x

Einarsdóttir, S., & Rounds, J. (2009). Gender bias and construct validity in vocational interest measurement: Differential item functioning in the Strong Interest Inventory. *Journal of Vocational Behavior, 74,* 295–307. doi:10.1016/j.jvb.2009.01.003

Evans, K. M. (2013). Multicultural considerations in career assessment. In C. Woods & D. G. Hays (Eds.), A counselor's guide to career assessment instruments (pp. 49-61). Broken Arrow, OK: National Career Development Association.

Fitzgerald, L. F., & Betz, N. E. (1994). Career development in cultural context: The role of gender, race, class, and sexual orientation. In M. L. Savickas & R. W. Lent (Eds.), *Convergence in career development theories: Implications for science and practice* (pp. 103-117). Palo Alto, CA: CPP Books.

Flores, L. Y., Spanierman, L. B., & Obasi, E. M. (2003). Ethical and professional issues in career assessment with diverse racial and ethnic groups. *Journal of Career Assessment, 11,* 76–95. doi:10.1177/106907202237461

Fouad, N. A. (1993). Cross-cultural vocational assessment. *Career Development Quarterly, 42,* 4-13.

Fouad, N. A. (1995). Balancing client and cultural specificity. *Counseling Psychologist, 23,* 63–67.

Fouad, N. A., & Bingham, R. (1995). Career counseling with racial/ethnic minorities. In W. B. Walsh & S. H. Osipow (Eds.), *Handbook of vocational psychology* (2nd ed., pp. 331–366). Hillsdale, NJ: Lawrence Erlbaum.

Fouad, N. A., Harmon, L. W., & Borgen, F. H. (1997). Structure of interests in employed male and female members of US racial-ethnic minority and nonminority groups. *Journal of Counseling Psychology, 44,* 339-345.

Gysbers, N. C., Heppner, M. J., & Johnston, J. A. (2014). *Career counseling: Holism, diversity, and strengths.* John Wiley & Sons.

Hackett, G., & Lonborg, S. D. (1994). Career assessment and counseling for women. In W. B. Walsh & S. H. Osipow (Eds.), *Career counseling for women* (pp. 43-86). Hillsdale, NJ: Lawrence Erlbaum.

Harmon, L. W., Hansen, J. C., Borgen, F. H., & Hammer, A. C. (1994). *Strong Interest Inventory applications and technical guide.* Stanford, CA: Stanford University Press.

Herr, E. L. (2001). Career development and its practice: A historical perspective. *Career Development Quarterly, 49,* 196–211. doi:10.1002/j.2161-0045.2001.tb00562.x

Holland, J. L. (1959). A theory of vocational choice. *Journal of Counseling Psychology, 6,* 35-45.

Holland, J. L. (1997). *Making vocational choices: A theory of vocational personalities and work environments* (3rd ed.). Odessa, FL: Psychological Assessment Resources.

Holland, J. L., Fritzche, B. A., & Powell, A. B. (1994). *Self-Directed Search technical manual.* Odessa, FL: Psychological Assessment Resources.

Johnson, W. L., Mauzey, E., Johnson, A. M., Murphy, S. D., & Zimmerman, K. J. (2001). A higher order analysis of the factor structure of the Myers-Briggs Type Indicator. *Measurement and Evaluation in Counseling and Development, 34,* 96-108.

Kelly, K. R. (2010). Strong Interest Inventory (newly revised). In R. A. Spies, J. F. Carlson, K. R. Geisinger (Eds.), *The eighteenth mental measurements yearbook.* Lincoln, NE: Buros Center for Testing.

Lent, R. W., Brown, S. D., & Hackett, G. (1994). Toward a unifying social cognitive theory of career and academic interest, choice, and performance. *Journal of Vocational Behavior, 45,* 79-122. doi:10.1006/jvbe.1994.1027

Leong, F. T. L. (1997). Cross-cultural career psychology: Comment on Fouad, Harmon and Borgen (1997) and Tracey, Watanabe, and Schneider (1997). *Journal of Counseling Psychology, 44,* 355–359. doi:10.1037/0022-0167.44.4.355

Leong, F. T., & Hartung, P. J. (2000). Cross-cultural career assessment: Review and prospects for the new millennium. *Journal of Career Assessment, 8,* 391–401.

Leong, F. T. L., Hartung P. J., Pearce, M. (2014). Work and career development: Theory and research. In F. T. L. Leong, L. Comas-Díaz, G. C. Nagayama Hall, V. C. McLoyd, & J. E. Trimble (Eds.), *APA handbook of multicultural psychology, Vol. 1: Theory and research* (pp. 451-469). Washington, DC: American Psychological Association.

Marsella, A. J., & Leong, F. T. (1995). Cross-cultural issues in personality and career assessment. *Journal of Career Assessment, 3,* 202–218.

McCaulley, M. H., & Moody, R. A. (2008). Multicultural applications of the Myers-Briggs Type Indicator. In L. A. Suzuki, J. G. Ponterotto, & P. J. Meller (Eds.), *Handbook of multicultural assessment: Clinical, psychological, and educational applications* (3rd ed., pp. 402-424). San Francisco, CA: Jossey-Bass.

Myers, I. B., McCaulley, M. H., & Most, R. (1985). *Manual: A guide to the development and use of the Myers-Briggs Type Indicator.* Palo Alto, CA: Consulting Psychologists Press.

National Career Development Association. (2009). *Minimum competencies for multicultural career counseling and development.* Broken Arrow, OK: Author.

Nevill, D. D., & Kruse, S. J. (1996). Career assessment and the values scale. *Journal of Career Assessment, 44,* 383-397. doi:10.1177/106907279600400403

Niles, S. G., & Goodnough, G. E. (1996). Life-role salience and values: A review of recent research. *Career Development Quarterly, 45,* 65–86. doi:10.1002/j.2161-0045.1996.tb00463.x

Osborn, D. S. (2012). An international discussion about cross-cultural career assessment. *International Journal for Educational and Vocational Guidance, 12*(1), 5–16. doi:10.1007/s10775-012-9220-0

Parsons, F. (1909). *Choosing a vocation.* Boston, MA: Houghton Mifflin.

Pitre, S., & Schultheiss, D. (2017). Relational cultural career assessment: The case of an Indian immigrant first-year college student. In L. A. Busacca & M. C. Rehfuss (Eds.), *Postmodern career counseling: A handbook of culture, context, and cases* (pp. 245-257). Alexandria, VA: American Counseling Association.

Pope, M. (2000). A brief history of career counseling in the United States. *Career Development Quarterly, 48,* 194–211. doi:10.1002/j.2161-0045.2000.tb00286.x

Pope, M. (2009). Jesse Buttrick Davis (1871–1955): Pioneer of vocational guidance in the schools. *Career Development Quarterly, 57,* 248–258. doi:10.1002/j.2161-0045.2009.tb00110.x

Ridley, C. R., Li, L. C., & Hill, C. L. (1998). Multicultural assessment: Reexamination, reconceptualization, and practical application. *Counseling Psychologist, 26,* 827-910. doi:10.1177/0011000098266001

Rossier, J. (2005). A review of the cross-cultural equivalence of frequently used personality inventories. *International Journal for Educational and Vocational Guidance, 5*(2), 175–188. doi:10.1007/s10775-005-8798-x

Rounds, J., & Tracey, T. J. (1996). Cross-cultural structural equivalence of RIASEC models and measures. *Journal of Counseling Psychology, 43,* 310–329. doi:10.1037/0022-0167.43.3.310

Schultheiss, D. E. P. (2003). A relational approach to career counseling: Theoretical integration and practical application. *Journal of Counseling and Development, 81,* 301-310. doi:10.1002/j.1556-6678.2003.tb00257.x

Schultheiss, D. E. P. (2005). Qualitative relational career assessment: A constructivist paradigm. *Journal of Career Assessment, 13,* 381–394. doi.org/10.1177/1069072705277912

Sheperis, D., Perepiczka, M., & Limoges, C. (2011). Individual and group assessment appraisal. In D. Capuzzi & M. D. Stauffer (Eds.), *Career counseling: Foundations, perspectives, and applications* (pp. 153-196). Upper Saddle River, NJ: Pearson.

Stead, G. B., & Davis, B. L. (2015). Qualitative career assessment: Research evidence. In M. McMahon, and M. Watson (Eds.), *Career assessment: Qualitative approaches* (pp. 21-30). The Netherlands: Sense Publishers.

Subich, L. M. (2005). Career assessment with culturally diverse individuals. In W. B. Walsh & M. L. Savickas (Eds.), *Handbook of vocational psychology* (3rd ed., pp. 397–421). Mahwah, NJ: Erlbaum.

Sue, D. W. (2004). Whiteness and ethnocentric monoculturalism: Making the "invisible" visible. *American Psychologist, 59,* 761-769.

Sue, D. W., Arredondo, P., & McDavis, R. J. (1992). Multicultural counseling competencies and standards: A call to the profession. *Journal of Counseling and Development, 70,* 477–486. doi:10.1002/j.1556-6676.1992.tb01642.x

Super, D. E., & Nevill, D. D. (1985). *The Values Scale.* Palo Alto, CA: Consulting Psychologists Press.

Swanson, J. L., & D'Achiardi, C. (2005). Beyond interests, needs/values, and abilities: Assessing other important career constructs over the life span. In S. D. Brown & R. W. Lent (Eds.), *Career development and counseling* (pp. 353-381). Hoboken, NJ: Wiley.

Vacha-Haase, T., Walsh, B. D., Kapes, J. T., Dresden, J. H., Thomson, W. A., Ochoa-Shargey, B., & Camacho, Z. (2016). Gender differences on the values scale for ethnic minority students. *Journal of Career Assessment, 2*, 408-421. doi:10.1177/106907279400200407

Watson, M., Duarte, M. E., & Glavin, K. (2005). Cross-cultural perspectives on career assessment. *Career Development Quarterly, 54*, 29–35. doi:10.1002/j.2161-0045.2005.tb00138.x

Whiston, S. C. (2012). *Principles and application of assessment in counseling* (4th ed.). Belmont, CA: Brooks/Cole.

CHAPTER 5

SELECTING AND UNDERSTANDING CAREER ASSESSMENTS

Kevin B. Stoltz
University of North Alabama

Stephanie Bell
Delta State University

Laith G. Mazahreh
Mississippi State University

Introduction

Career assessment is one of the most recognized and used processes in career counseling and development work. The practices of career counseling, student advising, workforce development, organizational consulting, and career developmental programing all include aspects of career assessment, which continues to evolve based on changes in the world of work (Niles & Martin 2019). Professionals can no longer rely on the assessment of interests, values, and abilities as the sole focus of career assessment.

Whiston (2013) divided career assessments into two broad categories: assessing individual differences (comparative testing) and assessing the career development process (e.g., identifying where people are in the career decision process). The practice of career assessment now includes various constructs that measure an individual's ability to adapt to work transitions (e.g., Planned Happenstance Career Inventory; Kim et al., 2014; Career Futures Inventory Revised; Rottinghaus, Buelow, Matyja, & Schneider, 2012; Career Adapt-Abilities Scale; Porfeli & Savickas, 2012), make continual decisions (e.g., Career Decision-Making Difficulties Questionnaire; Osipow & Gati, 1998), self-manage career planning and development (e.g., Protean & Boundaryless Career Attitudes Scales; Briscoe, Hall, & Frautchy DeMuth, 2006), cope with work stress (e.g., Work Well Index; Mauss, Li, & Angerer, 2017), and develop attitudes towards work engagement (e.g., Utrecht Work Engagement Scale; Schaufeli, Bakker, & Salanova, 2006).

In addition to instruments derived empirically, there is increased recognition of informal or qualitative assessment procedures spurred by constructivist theories of career counseling (McMahon & Patton, 2002; Palladino Schultheiss,

2005). These new assessment techniques are dependent on building a counseling relationship with the client and require practitioners to be engaged, active, and responsive in the assessment process (Goldman, 1990). Although many practitioners might use single experiential interventions for career development purposes (e.g., advising, consulting), often these assessments are embedded in and across the career counseling, advising, and consultation processes. The newer developments in career assessment require that career practitioners possess specialized skills and training for conducting career assessment.

The purpose of this chapter is to present fundamental development and evidentiary practices so practitioners can understand and select assessments for use in practice, research, and evaluation. First, we discuss the purpose and factors influencing the choice of assessments. Next, we provide a brief discussion of the psychometric tools used to demonstrate reliability and validity in tests. This is followed by presentation of concepts used to show credibility, consistency, and outcome in qualitative assessments. Finally, the chapter ends with ethical responsibilities.

Purpose for Career Assessment

Career assessment, like psychological and educational assessment in general (Whiston, 2013), is only one part of the counseling, advising, and developmental support processes that career practitioners provide for clients. Assessment is an ongoing and integrated part of these career development services. Integrating assessment throughout these career development processes is a focal point of providing services in the 21st century. The purposes of career assessment are varied and depend on the needs of the client. According to Schwiebert (2009), career assessment focuses on helping clients make career decisions. However, emerging theories include adaptive abilities, meaning making processes, work engagement, and attitudinal markers that go beyond career selection. These newer assessments measure and identify areas for growth or development and track developmental progress. Additionally, qualitative assessments are designed to evoke cognitive and affective responses from clients for helping them build continuity and meaning from life experiences (McMahon & Patton, 2002). Career assessments help clients learn and understand themselves and are described as "flexible and holistic" (p. 59). In addition, career assessments are used in evaluation and research as specified in chapter 11 (Lenz & Dozier, 2019) of this book.

With these various purposes in mind, we offer the following definition: career assessment is a set of tools, quantitative or qualitative, used to measure and describe aspects of the client's career identity, functioning, and development across the lifespan. In addition, practitioners use career assessments in any phase of counseling, advising, and developmental work to help clients learn about themselves holistically, demonstrate the effects of interventions, evaluate outcomes for programs, and inform public policy. Given the role of assessment in career counseling, advising, and career development work, having a thorough knowledge of how to review, understand, and select assessments is a necessary and ethical set of skills for career practitioners.

Factors to Consider in Selecting Career Assessments

The primary use of career assessment is to benefit the client. Thus, selecting assessments that will help elucidate the client's needs and assist the client with the identified problem or developmental transition is the central concern. More secondary uses of assessment include evaluating interventions, tracking progress, or informing public policy.

Client factors. When using career assessment, client factors are the first consideration. Using the same test or assessment for all individuals does not respect the diversity and variation in a pluralistic society (Wilkins-Yel, Chung, Cheng, & Li, 2019). For example, demographic aspects (e.g., race, sexual identity) can influence the outcome and results of the testing or assessment process. Additionally, client preferences toward formal (quantitative) or informal (qualitative) assessments might assist or hinder the retention and use of results. Associated mental and physical health factors (e.g., motivation, depression, physical disabilities) can influence aspects of the assessment process and lead to difficulties in interpretation and use of results.

The client's ability to understand the instructions and item content of a test or survey is critical to the results and interpretation. Most tests and surveys are prepared at the 5th to 7th grade reading levels so a wide variety of individuals can complete the instrument. For those clients who might have reading comprehension disabilities or English as a second language, alternate assessment techniques might be in order (e.g., pictorial tests, translated versions). Ensuring that clients are comfortable in the assessment environment and can respond to the assessment prompts completely, consistently, and accurately is an integral part of using career assessments appropriately.

Counselor factors. In addition to client factors, practitioner related factors influence the use and outcome of assessment results. Familiarity with a specific assessment can lead to overuse and reliance on results as true measures of the client. Alternately, using tests or informal assessments without appropriate training can lead to misuse of results and could be grounds for ethical and practice violations (American Counseling Association [ACA], 2014, National Career Development Association [NCDA], 2015). Practitioners must be aware of their reasons for suggesting, selecting, and using specific assessments. Additionally, appropriate training and supervision when learning about new or unfamiliar assessments is critical. Understanding the theory from which the assessment is derived, the purpose of the assessment, its application, and applicability to the client's needs are key aspects of using career assessments. The test manual or developmental literature concerning the test or assessment technique is an appropriate place to begin learning about the specifics of assessments.

In summary, knowing and addressing the factors in career assessment are critical processes. The assessment process is considered an intervention and, thus, having a specific need or developmental experience as the purpose for administering an assessment is vital. The practitioner must consider the abilities of the client, based on mental or physical factors, when selecting assessments. Additionally, practitioners need to use assessments for which they have received training and qualification. Selection of assessments focuses on serving the client's needs and is not a typical habit or requirement of assessment protocols required by the program, agency, or practitioner.

Reviewing Assessments for Use in Practice

In this section, we present the typical empirical information (psychometrics) that practitioners can review when considering a test for use in practice. First, we outline general steps used to build a quantitative career assessment (test or instrument). We follow this with a presentation of statistical procedures, definitions, and theoretical explanations used to support reliability and validity of tests. Next, we include a discussion of the links between quantitative assessments and specific career theories. Following quantitative forms of validity and reliability, we provide a review of methods for selection and use of qualitative assessments. Additionally, we provide suggestions for practitioners to support credibility in performing qualitative assessments.

Constructing Career Tests and Inventories

Building a career test is a complex and multistep process. The inclusion of these steps in the development of a test indicates the overall quality and scientific support for the test. Understanding and using this data to judge the quality and appropriateness of a test is an integral responsibility of career practitioners (ACA, 2014; NCDA, 2015). Generally, the test construction process begins with identifying a trait or behavior for measurement. In career assessment, traits are derived theoretically and called a *construct*. These constructs are usually descriptive of aspects of internal human social functioning and are not amenable to direct measurement. The indirect nature of the construct leads to question prompts (test items) that represent aspects of the variable called a *latent construct*.

Once the test developer identifies a latent construct, the developer will review the literature and consult with experts in the field who have knowledge of the construct. During this process, the developer might identify dimensions (e.g., academic self-concept, social self-concept, career self-concept) that represent specific aspects of the complete construct (e.g., self-concept). The developer might identify these dimensions as aspects to include in the measurement instrument. As test developers identify and narrow the constructs, they develop questions that assess aspects of the latent construct. Ultimately, the developer prepares many questions (test items or prompts), and, generally, many more than will be used in the actual assessment. Often, developers present these test items or prompts to other professionals for review and comment to assess how well the test items represent the latent construct. This is a primary aspect of *content validity*, and these procedures are usually presented in the original research describing the instrument development and might be included in a test manual. Understanding how the construct is measured and the theory from which the construct is derived is helpful in selecting assessments. Reviewing these procedures and understanding the initial development of a test is an integral part of selecting an instrument for use in ethical practice.

Following edits and changes, based on the content review, the next step entails testing the instrument for use with an intended population. This is completed by procuring a sample and administering the instrument. Generally, this first step includes collecting an adequate sample size to conduct statistical testing for reliability, validity, and item analysis.

Reliability. Commonly, the use of the term *reliability* indicates how consistent a person's score is on a test over time (Whiston, 2017). However, using classical test theory, Thorndike (2009) described reliability as an individual's true score plus the amount of error present. An individual's true score is the score earned on a given instrument if the individual were to complete the test repeatedly and without error (Aiken & Groth-Marnat, 2006). Classical test theory also purports that reliability is an estimate of true variance plus error variance. To be clear, error variance refers only to unsystematic or random error. Unsystematic errors are those that are inconsistent and can originate from many sources. For example, sources might include the conditions of the testing environment on a given day or conditions that might affect a test taker, such as illness or exhaustion (Whiston, 2017).

Reliability is most commonly reported using a coefficient. The coefficient of reliability is a numerical value calculated similarly to a correlation coefficient. Reliability coefficients are reported on a scale of 0.00 to 1.00, where a higher number indicates greater reliability results (Whiston, 2017). For example, a reliability coefficient of 0.85 would indicate high reliability. Reliability is demonstrated in several types of statistical analyses: test-retest, parallel or alternative forms, and internal consistency.

Test-Retest Reliability. What some call the coefficient of stability is now often referred to as test-retest reliability in many texts (Cronbach, 1951; Whiston, 2017). Test-retest reliability is a common way of calculating the reliability coefficient for a test by correlating individuals' scores from the first administration with their scores on a second administration (Thorndike, 1985). One important caveat worth noting is that this procedure is useful only to examine reliability if the trait or construct being measured is purported to be stable over defined periods.

Parallel Forms. In creating parallel or alternate forms of a test, researchers are able to examine the coefficient of stability and equivalence (Whiston, 2017). The coefficient of stability and equivalence is a statistic produced by calculating the correlation coefficient of the scores on two different forms of a test that assesses the same construct. However, this method can be more difficult because producing two equivalent forms of the same test is extremely hard. However, using parallel forms can reduce the practice effects that are a weakness of the test-retest method (Whiston, 2017).

Internal Consistency. A third way of measuring reliability involves using only one form of a test, called internal consistency (Whiston, 2017). Measuring internal consistency involves exploring the test inwardly, rather than testing multiple times or trying to create an equivalent form (Thorndike, 1985). One way to describe internal consistency is through split-half reliability. Using this method, once the test is administered, the number of items are split in half and scores from the first half of the test are correlated with the second half. The test or scale must be assessing the same construct to perform this analysis. When doing this, the Spearman-Brown formula is used to get an accurate approximation of what the reliability of the test would be in its original length (Whiston, 2017). Another set of formulas used to calculate internal consistency reliability are the Kuder-Richardson Formulas (KR-20 and KR-21). Finally, Cronbach's Alpha is used to calculate internal consistency reliability, but only when answer choices on items in the test are non-dichotomous (Cronbach, 1951; Whiston, 2017), such as items on a Likert scale rating job satisfaction.

Reliability is a key indicator of test quality. The more reliability analyses presented in a test manual or research report, the more rigorously the test has been subjected to scientific questioning. The rigorous nature of these analyses helps to build confidence in the use of the instrument. However, reliability is only one aspect of instrument functioning.

Validity. Before deciding to use any test with a client, a practitioner must examine whether there is evidence of validity for use in that situation. If not, then that test might not be the best option for that client (Whiston, 2017). A test must show reliability before it can have any evidence of validity (Aiken & Groth-Marnat, 2006; Whiston, 2017) because researchers theorize that a valid measure will assess the construct reliably, but the reverse is not true. Validity, in general, provides information concerning whether a test measures the construct for which the developers purported it to measure. Additionally, validity represents the individuals' scores as accurate representations of the construct being measured (Messick, 1989). Messick expanded the concept of validity to highlight the implications of test scores in interpretation and application.

Evidence gathered to assess validity of a given instrument could come from a variety of sources. When selecting assessments for career counseling, practitioners should begin by examining the reliability of an instrument to make sure it will measure consistently and, then, examine the validity evidence to ensure it will measure exactly what is intended and how accurately the test will measure the construct of interest (Whiston, 2017). There are several methods to examine validity evidence: content validity (mentioned above), criterion-related validity, and construct validity.

Content validity. One type of validity evidence is content validity. This type of validity addresses the issue of whether a specific test measures the content intended. For example, are there enough questions to cover the construct of interest thoroughly (Aiken & Groth-Marnat, 2006)? Also, do the questions represent the construct appropriately? Documentation of how the developers constructed the instrument and descriptions of all items and content are two ways of providing evidence of content validity (Whiston, 2017). Knowing the developers completed these procedures supports the overall quality and validity of the test.

Criterion-related validity. Criterion-related validity is an umbrella term that encompasses two additional types of validity. The processes use correlational methods to test hypotheses related to expected relationships between test scores and other measured variables.

Concurrent validity. Concurrent validity methods demonstrate the use of a test to predict scores or outcomes on a variable measured at the same time (Finch, Immekus, & French, 2016). For example, a researcher might be interested in measuring aptitudes as indicators of interests. High aptitudes for mechanical abilities might indicate high scores on an interest test in the *Realistic* code. High correlations indicate the construct in one test can predict traits or other outcomes. The important aspect is that the constructs are measured at the same time in concurrent validity.

Predictive validity. Predictive validity is a procedure focused on measuring a construct that is instrumental in predicting performance, scores, or other criteria in the future. For example, a researcher might predict that interest correspondence signals job satisfaction in the future. When an instrument can predict scores of future constructs, the instrument shows predictive validity.

Discriminant validity. Discriminant validity is an analysis related to criterion validity (Whiston, 2017). Discriminant validity procedures depend on group comparison rather than correlation. The key concept of discriminant validity is focused on showing differences between groups on the same construct or variable. Thus, a researcher might explore career decision-making self-efficacy. The researcher hypothesizes that groups high in self-efficacy will score higher on the instrument, and those lower in self-efficacy will score lower. The results help to differentiate the groups as described by theoretical propositions. This type of criterion validity is used to support overall validity of the instrument by showing the instrument can discriminate between groups.

Construct Validity. Construct validity is a term that encompasses additional types of validity evidence. Construct validity evidence informs whether a test assesses the construct being measured, while separating constructs not being measured (Whiston, 2017). Often, constructs in career counseling have multiple dimensions. For example, a test measuring job satisfaction might include satisfaction with work tasks, environment, and worker relationships. Items from each of these dimensions (scales) should show lower correlations with items from other (unrelated) scales but high correlations with items within each scale. This is the primary purpose of the group of analyses called *factor analysis* (Osborne, Costello, & Kellow, 2008). Both exploratory and confirmatory factor analysis are used to separate construct models mathematically to demonstrate how well items discriminate and correlate as scales in an instrument. Developers used exploratory factor analysis (EFA) to test the theoretical structure of the instrument. After original testing, the next standard for a test is to undergo confirmatory factor analysis (CFA). This procedure tests whether each item on a test is significant in producing the total score of a scale or construct. The process of CFA is a higher and more rigorous standard for test construction.

Two additional ways of examining construct validity is convergent and divergent validity. Each involves correlation procedures with existing instruments that are theorized to show relationships to the instrument being developed.

Convergent validity. Convergent validity refers to whether a person's score on one instrument would correlate highly with that same person's score on a different instrument measuring the same or similar construct. If the two scores correlate highly, the evidence supports convergent validity for the instrument. For example, in developing a new test to assess career maturity, a researcher might use an existing measure of career maturity to explore the performance of the new measure. The practitioner will administer both at the same time and will compare scores using correlational analyses. The value of the correlation represents the strength of the relationship between the two instruments, and higher values indicate the new test is measuring a similar construct to the existing test.

Divergent validity. Discriminant validity is essentially the opposite type of correlation. Thus, a person with high job satisfaction might show lower scores on a measure of work disengagement. The reverse or divergent correlations demonstrate the instrument measures a construct that diverges from theoretical constructs in predictable ways. This type of evidence is yet another quality marker in test development.

Test Norms

Another aspect of test selection is understanding the population upon which the test was normed. This is of critical importance as practitioners begin to explore use of the test with diverse clients. Questions that are important to consider include: *Will the items function with a different population in the same manner? Will the scores and interpretations be applicable to my diverse client?* The implications of test scores and interpretations are critical (Messick, 1989), and practitioners must exercise caution in understanding how the test results may misrepresent a client. Developers are using a newer procedure, called *metric invariance*, to compare test functioning based on demographic variables (e.g., gender, country of origin). Reporting of this evidence is another marker for quality in test construction and review.

In summary, test construction is a tedious and time-consuming process. Quality career tests undergo rigorous empirical development and analysis with a representation of multiple populations. These steps are quality markers for the assessment and should not be ignored or undervalued by career practitioners. Tests that do not display or offer access to this information could be suspect. Practitioners must explore and be able to consume this information in order to understand and apply test instructions and procedures in practice. Lack of exploring and understanding these concepts can lead to test misuse and client abuse.

Qualitative Assessments

Similar to quantitative assessment, qualitative assessment is developed from career theories. Knowing and understanding the constructs of the theory are important factors in selecting qualitative assessments for use in career counseling, advising, and developmental work (Gysbers, 2006; McMahon, Patton, & Watson, 2003). There are many advantages to using qualitative assessments. McMahon and Patton (2002) posited that qualitative assessments apply to a wide range of clients, respect the client's context, promote client involvement in the process, include subjective, affective, and cognitive data, provide support for holistic self-concept and worldview development, and bring client meaning to interpretation. Because of these distinct advantages and the idiographic nature of qualitative assessments, statistical testing of the constructs is not always possible. However, there are techniques for building credibility and consistency of these assessments (McMahon et al., 2003).

For example, using the career construction interview (CCI), researchers (Hartung & Vess, 2016; Lengelle, Meijers, & Hughes, 2016; Taylor, & Savickas, 2016; Vilhjálmsdóttir, & Tulinius, 2016) were able to demonstrate specific outcomes in behaviors, affect, and pictorial and dialogic representations. Others (Cardoso et al., 2016: Reid, Bimrose, & Brown, 2016) demonstrated processes at work during the CCI that led to reflexivity (client actions). These researchers used interpersonal process recall (IPR; Kagan, Schauble, Resnikoff, Danish, & Krathwohl (1969) and narrative research methods to demonstrate these outcomes and processes of the CCI. The IPR method involves interviewing clients after an intervention to determine what aspects of the intervention were memorable and might have had the most influence on the client. Additionally, using a quantitative approach to measure change, Barclay and Stoltz (2016) provided outcomes on various measures (e.g., career decision-making, career development) to investigate the effects of the CCI on group member participants. They showed gains in career decision-making, readiness for making academic and career decisions, and decreases in uncertainty, thereby, demonstrating that the CCI process supported change for these participants. In summary, studies, such as these, help support the credibility (validity) of the qualitative assessment.

Exploring the professional literature for studies supporting the use of qualitative assessment is a necessary step in preparing to use these assessment processes. Additionally, learning about the theory used to interpret the results is a critical step in using the assessment. Finally, developing an understanding of qualitative research processes and how the practitioner can use qualitative research methods and techniques in the course of counseling to enhance credibility (validity) is crucial. McMahon et al. (2003) suggested that the assessment process should include a focus on holism and integration of the person across roles. The processes should be clear and easily understandable to the practitioner and client. The assessment steps or tasks should be sequential and accomplished easily. The process should be focused, yet flexible enough, to accommodate different individuals and cultural worldviews. In the following paragraphs, we provide suggestions concerning qualitative methods for improving credibility of qualitative assessments.

Creswell and Miller (2000) provided the guidance for improving validity for qualitative research. We developed these suggestions based on Creswell and Miller. Although qualitative career assessment might end in a research report, many of the processes we present fit easily into career counseling sessions; some appear routinely in sessions already. Many practitioners look to use various sources of data to assist clients (Feller, 2019). Using quantitative assessments, along with qualitative assessment, and comparing results is one form triangulation (Denzin, 1989). These procedures assist in confirming interpretations and help both the counselor and the client have confidence in the results. Another aspect of this process is looking for disconfirming evidence (Creswell & Miller, 2000). Disconfirming evidence will help to expand the interpretation to include inconsistencies and various dimensions due to context, personal experience, or other factors that disrupt quantitative continuity. Disconfirming evidence signals the diverse experience and preferences of clients.

The next four methods involve the counseling process directly, which include *member checking, prolonged engagement,* an *audit trail,* and *peer debriefing.* Member checking is the process of reviewing the collected data with the client or clients to confirm the credibility of the data (Lincoln & Guba, 1985). This is an important aspect of validity and should occur often in counseling sessions. Allowing the client to examine the data (*collaboration* – another technique in qualitative research) assists the client in reviewing and offering feedback concerning the assessment process and results. Prolonged engagement (Fetterman, 2010) provides continuity to the counseling relationship and allows clients to feel comfortable discussing all aspects of the qualitative assessment. This is similar to building the therapeutic alliance and is an important component of career counseling (Masdonati, Massoudi, & Rossier, 2009).

Providing an audit trail (e.g., client notes, quantitative assessments) in career counseling is typical. Extending this into qualitative assessment includes artwork (e.g., pictorial narratives; Taylor & Savickas, 2016), recorded narratives (Hartung & Vess, 2016), or written assignments (Lengelle, Meijers, & Hughes, 2016). All these artifacts become the audit trail and provide validity evidence for the client and counselor alike. Included in many of these are thick rich descriptions (Denzin, 1989) of the events and narratives of the client. Also, the interpretations offered in stories and reflexive narratives help further the validity of qualitative career assessments. Finally, peer debriefing is a process similar to peer supervision. Reviewing all the data and interpretations with peers is an important element in supporting validity. Often, peers provide additional perspectives that might go unnoticed by the client and counselor. Also, peers can ask different questions or react differently to narratives, which provides more information for the counselor and client to consider.

In summary, career practitioners infuse qualitative assessments into the counseling process. Often, these assessments lack validity in quantitative terms. However, by using some of the qualitative research techniques mentioned above, career practitioners can enhance credibility of qualitative assessment, thereby, providing more holistic services to clients.

Ethical Aspects of Assessment Selection and Use

Due to the critical nature of using assessments in counseling, various professional organizations that govern the practices of counselors developed ethical codes that practitioners can use as guidelines when using assessments with clients. Generally, these guidelines focus on three main areas: first, the selection of the instruments used; second, the process of utilizing these instruments; and third, the distribution of tests results with third parties.

Concerning the selection of instruments, The National Career Development Association (NCDA, 2015) proposed that career counselors should use only career instruments that align with the training they received and the level of competence they have in administering these instruments. Additionally, NCDA's Code of Ethics (2015) highlights the need for counselors to utilize career instruments after careful examination of the psychometric qualities of these instruments (e.g., validity, reliability). We would add to this by suggesting that practitioners review the uses and support evidence for qualitative assessment as mentioned in the ACA Code of Ethics (ACA, 2014, Section, E.1.a).

The American Counseling Association (ACA, 2014) also discussed the use of assessments. Counselors are obligated to take the necessary steps to protect the welfare of clients. This might include providing clients with sufficient information concerning the nature of instruments or tests which the practitioner will use. Additionally, counselors are required to provide detailed descriptions of the procedures followed when administering these tests. Counselors are to inform clients about the rationale for selecting a specific instrument. Equally important after administering the instrument, is for counselors to provide interpretations of the results obtained from the instrument and discuss specific recommendations clients might follow as a result of the information obtained.

Counselors might receive requests to share test results with third parties (e.g., college students may have parents involved in career planning); therefore, awareness of the ethical guidelines that govern this process is essential for counselors. The code of ethics provided by both ACA (2014) and NCDA (2015) highlight the need for counselors to distribute client results only to individuals or organizations their clients identified and for whom clients provided sufficient consent. Additionally, to protect the welfare of clients, counselors are required to share results with individuals who are qualified to interpret the results obtained from these instruments.

Conclusion

Assessment in career counseling, advising, and other practitioner activities continues to be a central way of gathering data concerning the client. The purpose for use of career assessments is key to ethical practice. Establishing specific reasons for selecting career assessments that align with the client's needs and practitioner's training set the stage for both ethical and productive career counseling, advising, and other career development activities.

Knowing how to review assessment information, and choose assessments that are supported by rigorous development and evaluation procedures aids the practitioner in providing ethical, reliable, and valid assessment data. Understanding the quantitative (e.g., reliability, validity) and qualitative (e.g., credibility) concepts involved in the development and use of assessments help practitioners choose instrument and processes that meet the goals of the client. The steps and procedures contained in the chapter reflect the rigorous methods that practitioners need to understand for using quantitative and qualitative assessment in career counseling, advising, and other career development activities.

References

Aiken, L. R., & Groth-Marnat, G. (2006). *Psychological testing and assessment* (12th ed.). Boston, MA: Pearson Education Group.

American Counseling Association. (2014). *ACA code of ethics*. Alexandria, VA: Author. Retrieved from: https://www.counseling.org/knowledge-center/ethics

Barclay, S. R., & Stoltz, K. B. (2016). The life-design group: A case study assessment. *Career Development Quarterly, 64*, 83–96. https://doi.org/10.1002/cdq.12043

Briscoe, J. P., Hall, D. T., & Frautschy DeMuth, R. L. (2006). Protean and boundaryless careers: An empirical exploration. *Journal of Vocational Behavior, 69*, 30–47. https://doi.org/10.1016/j.jvb.2005.09.003

Cardoso, P., Duarte, M. E., Gaspar, R., Bernardo, F., Janeiro, I. N., & Santos, G. (2016). Life design counseling. A study on client's operations for meaning construction. *Journal of Vocational Behavior, 97*, 13-21.

Creswell, J. W., & Miller, D. L. (2000). Determining validity in qualitative inquiry. *Theory into Practice, 39*(3), 1-130.

Cronbach, L. J. (1951). Coefficient alpha and the internal structure of tests. *Psychometrika, 16* (3), 297-334.

Denzin, N. K. (1989). *The research act: A theoretical introduction to sociological methods.* New York: Routledge.

Feller, R. (2019). A menu based approach to using career assessments in private practice. In K. Stoltz & S. Barclay (Eds.), *A Comprehensive Guide to Career Assessment* [Online Companion]. Broken Arrow, OK: National Career Development Association. Retrieved from http://www.ncda.org

Fetterman, D. M. (2010). *Ethnography: Step by step* (3rd ed). Thousand Oaks, CA: Sage Publications.

Finch, W. H., Immekus, J. C., French, B. F. (2016). *Applied psychometrics using SPSS and AMOS*. Charlotte, NC: Information Age Publishing.

Goldman, L. (1990). Qualitative assessment. *The Counseling Psychologist, 18* (2), 205-213.

Gysbers, N. C., & Henderson, P. (2006). *Developing and managing your school guidance and counseling program* (4th ed.). Alexandria, VA: American Counseling Association.

Hartung, P. J., & Vess, L. (2016). Critical moments in career construction counseling. *Journal of Vocational Behavior, 97,* 31–39. https://doi.org/10.1016/j.jvb.2016.07.014

Kagan, N., Schauble, P., Resnikoff, A., Danish, S. J., & Krathwohl, D. R. (1969). Interpersonal process recall. *Journal of Nervous and Mental Disease,* 148, 365–374. doi: 10.1097/00005053-196904000-00004

Kim, B., Jung, S. H., Jang, S. H., Lee, B., Rhee, E., Cho, S. H., & Lee, S. M. (2014). Construction and initial validation of the Planned Happenstance Career Inventory. *Career Development Quarterly, 62,* 239–253. https://doi.org/10.1002/j.2161-0045.2014.00082.x

Lengelle, R., Meijers, F., & Hughes, D. (2016). Creative writing for life design: Reflexivity, metaphor and change processes through narrative. *Journal of Vocational Behavior, 97,* 60-67.

Lenz, J. G., & Dozier, V. C. (2019). Career assessment in research and program evaluation. In K. Stoltz & S. Barclay (Eds.), *A Comprehensive Guide to Career Assessment* [Online Companion]. Broken Arrow, OK: National Career Development Association. Retrieved from http://www.ncda.org

Lincoln, Y. S., & Guba, E. G. (1985). *Naturalistic inquiry.* Newbury Park, CA: Sage Publications.

Masdonati, J., Massoudi, K., & Rossier, J. (2009). Effectiveness of career counseling and the impact of the working alliance. *Journal of Career Development, 36,* 183-203. doi:10.1177/0894845309340798

Mauss, D., Li, J., & Angerer, P. (2017). Psychometric properties of the work well index: A short questionnaire for work-related stress. *Stress and Health: Journal of the International Society for the Investigation of Stress, 33,* 80-85. doi:10.1002/smi.2670.

McMahon, M., & Patton, W. (2002). Using qualitative assessment in career counselling. *International Journal of Educational and Vocational Guidance, 2,* 51–66

McMahon, M., Patton, W., & Watson, M. (2003). Developing qualitative career assessment processes. *Career Development Quarterly, 51,* 194–202. https://doi.org/10.1002/j.2161-0045.2003.tb00601.x

Messick, S. (1989). Validity. In R. L. Linn (Ed.), *Educational Measurement* (3rd ed., pp. 113-104). New York, NY: Macmillan.

National Career Development Association. (2015). *NCDA code of ethics.* Broken Arrow, OK: Author. Retrieved from https://associationdatabase.com/aws/NCDA/assetmanager/get_file/3395

Niles, S. G., & Martin, C. V., (2019). Career assessment: Perspectives on trends and issues. In K. Stoltz & S. Barclay (Eds.), *A comprehensive guide to career assessment* (pp. 25-41). Broken Arrow, OK: National Career Development Association.

Osborne, J. W., Costello, A. B., & Kellow, J. T. (2008). Best practices in exploratory factor analysis. In J. W. Osborne (Ed.), *Best practices in quantitative methods.* Thousand Oaks, CA: Sage Publications.

Osipow, S. H., & Gati, I. (1998). Construct and concurrent validity of the career deci-sion-making difficulties questionnaire. *Journal of Career Assessment, 6,* 347–364. https://doi.org/10.1177/106907279800600305

Palladino Schultheiss, D. E. (2005). Qualitative relational career assessment: A construc-tivist paradigm. *Journal of Career Assessment, 13,* 381-394.

Porfeli, E. J., & Savickas, M. L. (2012). Career Adapt-Abilities Scale-USA Form: Psycho-metric properties and relation to vocational identity. *Journal of Vocational Behavior, 80,* 748-753.

Reid, H., Bimrose, J., & Brown, A. (2016). Prompting reflection and learning in career construction. *Journal of Vocational Behavior, 97,* 51-59.

Rottinghaus, P. J., Buelow, K. L., Matyja, A., & Schneider, M. R. (2012). The Career Futures Inventory–Revised: Measuring dimensions of career adaptability. *Journal of Career Assessment, 20,* 123–139. https://doi.org/10.1177/1069072711420849

Schaufeli W. B., Bakker A. B., & Salanova, M. (2006). The measurement of work engage-ment with a short questionnaire: A cross-national study. *Educational and Psycholog-ical Measurement, 66,* 701-716. doi:10.1177/0013164405282471.

Schwiebert, V. L. (2009). Selecting a career assessment instrument. In E. A. Whitfield, R. W. Feller, & C. Wood. (Eds.). *A Counselor's Guide to Career Assessment Instruments* (5th ed.) (pp. 27-33). Broken Arrow, OK: National Career Development Associa-tion.

Taylor, J. M., & Savickas, S. (2016). Narrative career counseling: My story and pictorial narratives. *Journal of Vocational Behavior, 97,* 68–77.

Thorndike, R. M. (1985). Reliability. *Journal of Counseling and Development, 63,* 528-530.

Thorndike, R. M. (2009). *Measurement and evaluation in psychology and education* (8th ed.).Upper Saddle River, NJ: Pearson.

Vilhjálmsdóttir, G., & Tulinius, T. H. (2016). The career construction interview and literary analysis. Journal of *Vocational Behavior, 97,* 40–50. https://doi.org/10.1016/j.jvb.2016.07.011

Whiston, S. C. (2013). *Principles and applications of assessment in counseling* (4th ed.). Boston, MA: Cengage Learning.

Whiston, S. C. (2017). *Principles and applications of assessment in counseling* (5th ed.). Boston, MA: Cengage Learning.

Wilkins-Yel, K. G., Chung, Y. B., Chen, J., & Li, Y. (2019). Multicultural considerations in career assessment. In K. Stoltz & S. Barclay (Eds.), *A Comprehensive Guide to Career Assessment* (pp. 59-73). Broken Arrow, OK: National Career Development Association.

CHAPTER 6

TEST ADMINISTRATION, INTERPRETATION, AND COMMUNICATION OF RESULTS

Nikki A. Falk
University of Missouri - Columbia

Alec Eshelman
Southern Illinois University Carbondale

Patrick J. Rottinghaus
University of Missouri - Columbia

Introduction

The career assessment process is an integral aspect of career counseling that includes selection and administration of tests, and, then, the interpretation and communication of results. In this chapter, we locate this career assessment process within a sequential integrative career counseling model (Rottinghaus & Eshelman, 2015) and review major categories of career assessments along with broad multicultural considerations. Next, we discuss important aspects of the following career assessment stages: test selection and administration, scoring, interpretation, and communication of results. We utilize a quantitative and qualitative example to illustrate key points and multicultural considerations. The chapter concludes with a summary and recommended strategies. Throughout this chapter, *tests* or *testing* refers to the quantitative process that includes scores, scales, and measures. *Assessment* will be used as a broader term that includes both quantitative and qualitative processes.

Integrative Career Counseling Model

In their integrative model of career counseling, Rottinghaus and Eshelman (2015) noted that the use of assessments, both qualitative and quantitative, represent but only one facet of the broader counseling process. Moreover, they argued that practitioners should not administer assessments by default but should administer assessments as they relate to the specific goals of particular clients. As such, selecting and administering assessments occurs after key first steps, such as establishing rapport, orienting clients to the counseling process, and discussing their goals, life situations, and other important contextual variables. These initial steps might develop the context useful for a fuller understanding of the assessment process and a strong therapeutic alliance that facilitates open and fruitful discussion of outcomes. This enables clients to make better use of results by situating the assessment outcomes in the context of their lived experience.

Major Categories of Career Instruments

Before discussing processes, such as test administration and interpretation, reviewing major categories of career instruments is important. We do not mean for this list to be exhaustive, because the purposes and content of career instruments are diverse and varied (Zunker & Osborn, 2016). Most often, these tests are divided into two categories: assessing individual differences and assessing career development processes (Whiston, 2005).

Individual differences. Major career assessment constructs in this category include *interests, abilities, personality,* and *values.* The Strong Interest Inventory (SII; Donnay, Morris, Shaubhut, & Thompson, 2005) is a widely used interest inventory in career counseling. The profile report presents results of General Occupational Themes organized by Holland (1997) codes, Basic Interest Scales, Occupational Scales, and Personal Style Scales. An example of a qualitative interest assessment includes the Missouri Occupational Card Sort (Krieshok, Hansen, Johnston, Wong, & Shevde, 2008). Career specialists instruct clients to place cards into Like, Unsure, or Dislike groups, and the career specialist offers insights and facilitates interactive dialogue about these choices.

Abilities represent another key domain of individual differences (Whiston, 2005), and practitioners might want to consider the use of affiliated social cognitive variables, such as ability self-estimates and self-efficacy for occupationally relevant tasks. Ability tests, such as the Armed Services Vocational Aptitude Battery (ASVAB; U.S. Department of Defense, 2005), measure the physical and mental capacity to complete a task (Metz & Jones, 2013). Distinct from, but related to, abilities is self-efficacy, or an individual's beliefs in his or her capacity to organize, execute, and accomplish certain tasks. Often, practitioners use the Skills Confidence Inventory (SCI; Betz, Borgen, & Harmon, 1996), along with the SII. This 60-item instrument measures self-efficacy expectations in completing tasks and coursework successfully and also corresponds with Holland (1997) codes.

Personality tests measure the enduring set of individual styles of thinking, feeling, and overall tendencies, usually represented by the Big Five (Digman, 1990; Rottinghaus & Hauser, 2013). A widely researched example includes the

NEO Personality Inventory-Revised (NEO PI-R; Costa & McCrae, 1992), which includes six facet measures for each of the Big Five domains. Finally, practitioners assess values using instruments such as the Values Scale (Nevill & Super, 1989). The Values Scale measures both work-related and general values, producing scores for 21 values (e.g., Achievement, Economic Security).

Career development processes. We discuss two career assessment constructs in this category, including *career decision-making* and *career maturity/adaptability*. The Career Decision Scale (CDS; Osipow, 1987) is a widely used instrument that measures client certainty in making a career decision, as well as level of career indecision. Career specialists use the Career Decision-Making Difficulties Questionnaire (CDDQ; Gati, Krausz, & Osipow, 1996) to assess for barriers to the career decision-making process, including lack of readiness, lack of information, and inconsistent information. Clients with higher career choice readiness tend to engage in more exploratory activities following career assessment interpretation (Toman & Savickas, 1997). Another common measure is the Career Decision Self-Efficacy Scale (CDSE; Betz & Taylor, 2001), which specialists use to assess an individual's confidence in making career decisions. Subscales on the CDSE correspond to Crites' (1978) career choice competencies.

Driven by Super's (1955) early work on career maturity and, later, career adaptability (Super & Kidd, 1979), several measures and qualitative interventions have been developed to assess readiness to make informed and wise career decisions. Savickas and Porfeli's (2012) Career Adapt-Abilities Scale (CAAS) measures clients' perceived competence across four dimensions of career adaptability: concern, control, curiosity, and confidence. The Career Futures Inventory (CFI; Rottinghaus, Day, & Borgen, 2005) and Career Futures Inventory-Revised (CFI-R; Rottinghaus, Buelow, Matyja, & Schneider, 2012) offer additional insights on career adaptability by addressing related facets of career adaptability, including career optimism, career agency, support, work-life balance, and occupational awareness. These measures provide tools for examining how clients approach the career planning process and offer additional insights on intervention strategies.

Multicultural Considerations in Career Assessment

A critical topic to consider, prior to a discussion of test administration, interpretation, and communication, is multicultural considerations in career assessment. With the potential for cultural bias in mind, we urge career practitioners to utilize available frameworks to guide culturally appropriate career assessment (Fouad & Bingham, 1995). Leong (2010) reviewed the cultural formulation approach and offered recommendations for applying it to career assessment. He discussed the importance of acknowledging how cultural identity influences all components of career development, utilizing cultural conceptualizations of career problems unique to the client, and gaining awareness into cultural dynamics in the therapeutic relationship. For a more thorough discussion of multiculturalism in career assessment, see Chapter 4 of this text.

Guided by the integrative career counseling model (Rottinghaus & Eshelman, 2015) and frameworks for culturally appropriate career assessment (Leong, 2010), we review four stages of the career assessment process. Furthermore, we provide a case example that includes multicultural considerations and an example of integrating quantitative and qualitative results, specifically the Career Futures Inventory-Revised (Rottinghaus et al., 2012) and Career Construction Interview (Savickas, 2013, 2015; Savickas & Hartung, 2012; Taber, Hartung, Briddick, Briddick & Rehfuss, 2011).

Test Selection and Administration

The first step in the career assessment process is test selection and administration. As informed by the integrative career counseling model (Rottinghaus & Eshelman, 2015), we believe this assessment step works best when blended into the counseling process as opposed to being distinct from it. For example, conceptualizing this step as a beginning, with a discussion of ethics, informed consent, role induction, and building rapport with clients, could be helpful. Primarily, a clinician must abide by ethical guidelines for educational and psychological testing (American Counseling Association, 2014; American Psychological Association, 2017; NCDA, 2015). These guidelines outline the importance of ensuring test quality, counselor competence, and client welfare in the assessment and testing process.

Next, clinicians should pay special attention to building a strong working relationship with the client. During this rapport building process, the clinician can begin explaining the purposes of assessment in career counseling and what the client can expect. Providing the client with confidentiality and informed consent information not only serves an ethical purpose, but also can build rapport through establishing trust and putting the client at ease. Clinicians should invite clients to participate in the selection of assessments when appropriate. Empowering the client to learn about the purpose and nature of assessments can increase client motivation, utilization of results, and reduce overreliance on the career counselor.

During the collaborative assessment selection process, clients will provide information on the types of tests and assessment processes that might be useful. Career practitioners, then, can use this information to select a specific test or assessment that is appropriate. Clinicians should focus on the following factors when choosing a quantitative instrument: determining what information the clinician needs from the client, aligning the test purpose to clinical needs, instrument development details, the selection of norming group or criterion-referenced instruments, reliability, validity, bias, interpretation and scoring materials, user qualifications, and practical issues (Whiston, 2005). When choosing a qualitative assessment, such as a card sort or interview, clinicians should consider the client's willingness to engage in experiential exploration as well as his or her comfort with open-ended activities such as narrative approaches.

Once the clinician selects a test, the clinician can prepare for test administration. Both quantitative tests and qualitative assessments require various pretesting procedures, such as reading an administration manual, arranging the room in an appropriate way, and gathering materials. During the administration process, the counselor should adhere to the outlined methods and time limits, as well as note behavioral observations. Career counselors should also be aware of administrator effects, such as the influence on a strong examiner/examinee relationship (Masdonati, Massoudi, & Rossier, 2009) and race or culture of the examiner (Suzuki, Short, Pieterse, & Kugler, 2000).

Case Example

Bella is a 35-year-old Latina woman presenting to career counseling due to a career transition. She stated her company laid her off recently, and she is unsure which career choices to pursue next. Jenny, her career counselor, is a 28-year-old Euro-American woman with a master's degree. During the first session, Jenny provides information on confidentiality, informed consent, and what Bella can expect during career counseling. Jenny discusses her integrative style of utilizing verbal exploration, quantitative tests, and qualitative interventions. To build rapport, Jenny asks Bella what she hopes to gain from career counseling. Jenny provides Bella with education about career adaptability and explains this as her ability to adjust to the changing world of work. Together they decide that combining a narrative and a quantitative approach to assess for career adaptability would be beneficial.

Jenny selects the Career Futures Inventory-Revised (CFI-R; Rottinghaus et al. 2012) and the Career Construction Interview (CCI; Savickas, 2011, 2013, 2015) as appropriate tests for Bella. Jenny makes sure to familiarize herself with the psychometrics of the CFI-R, as well as relevant research on both instruments. Although she had previous training on administering the career construction interview, Jenny reads appropriate materials (Savickas, 2015) for administering this intervention. Prior to beginning the career construction interview, Jenny works to establish a trusting working alliance in which she honors Bella's cultural values and integrates those into the intervention and conceptualization process. Jenny is aware of her potential influence as a Euro-American clinician on Bella and remains alert to cultural dynamics within the therapeutic relationship.

95

Scoring

Due to their inherent differences, "scoring" quantitative versus qualitative tests will differ considerably. With respect to quantitative tests, *scoring* is an apt term that describes the process by which numerical results are derived. In contrast, *storying* is perhaps a better term for this process in qualitative assessment, because deriving results is more akin to developing a rich narrative than calculating a numerical result (Wood & Scully, 2017). As such, storying is understood as an interpretive process and is something we discuss in greater detail in a subsequent section.

Practitioners should follow the procedures recommended by test developers when scoring tests. Computer-based scoring provides accurate scores efficiently and minimizes errors in calculation. Simons, Goddard, and Patton (2002) noted that, often, clinicians assume, tacitly, that hand scoring will be error free despite evidence to the contrary. These authors observed that, as test complexity increased, so too did the number of errors made when hand scoring. Also, they found that these error rates were often serious. Consequently, especially when hand scoring complex tests, scorers should attend to test-scoring procedures with great care and check systematically for errors. For example, scorers can rescore previously scored tests regularly to check for scoring accuracy.

Interpretation

After scoring career tests, the career counselor must interpret the results. Although test interpretation has many definitions, in the context of career counseling, this most often involves the clinician helping the client ascertain meaning and implications from scores and profiles (Zytowski, 2015). This section will focus on the processes most relevant to the career counselor's role in this stage, and the final section will address best practices for communicating results to clients.

Several modes of test interpretation exist, including individual profile scores, computer-based or web-based interpretation, and group interpretation (Zytowski, 2015). A common profile interpretation approach involves displaying a client's scores across Holland's (1997) RIASEC codes. In computer-based interpretation, such as the online administration of the Self Directed Search (Psychological Assessment Resources, 2017), a 20-page report is delivered immediately that includes a description of the Holland (1997) types, a rank order of the codes based on the client's scores, occupations that correspond with each ranked code, and even suggestions for how test takers might utilize results. Practitioners might use group interpretation, such as with business or military groups, for instruments such as the Campbell Interest and Skill Survey (Campbell, Hyne, & Nilsen, 1992). Clinicians can direct participants to organize themselves in rank order, according to their percentile scores on a certain scale and, then, facilitate exploration questions, such as asking whether there are any surprises or reactions based on their positioning.

With regard to quantitative career assessment, a brief discussion of validity and interpreting test scores is warranted. Validity is a function of interpreting test scores for an intended purpose and the degree to which evidence supports these interpretations (American Educational Research Association, American Psychological Association, & National Council on Measurement in Education, 2014). Before interpreting the results, a counselor must have knowledge of the validation evidence. Often, this evidence is located in the instrument manual and includes information such as the test construction, how the instrument correlates with other constructs, and research support. The counselor must determine whether scores are norm-referenced (i.e., comparing an individual's scores to others who have taken the assessment) or criterion-referenced (i.e., comparing an individual's scores to a standard). Using norm-referenced instruments that were normed on a representative population to the client is an important multicultural consideration.

Many scholars (Brown, 2007; Hansen, 2013; Savickas, 2011, 2013, 2015) have suggested principles, guidelines, and skills to aid in assessment interpretation for career counselors. Although aimed specifically at interests, clinicians can apply Hansen's (2013) steps for interpretation to a variety of career constructs. These steps include using understandable language, gaining client participation, asking for client reactions, and summarizing results.

Groth-Marnat (2009a) discussed five crucial features that can improve psychological assessment reports and interpretations. Although Groth-Marnat developed these in the context of personality assessment, the clinicians can certainly apply these insights to career assessment. First, clinicians must improve the *readability* of reports. We encourage clinicians to minimize the use of difficult words, reduce jargon and acronyms, and increase subheadings. Next, counselors should be sure to *connect the report to the client's context.* For example, instead of simply reporting that the client has "high Realistic interest," we encourage clinicians to expand this description and offer more specifics relevant to the client's everyday life. In addition, clinicians should incorporate information on subcomponents (e.g., hands-on work versus outdoor work), observed behaviors in session (e.g., benefits of drawing genograms), and client-reported history (e.g., confidence while building a deck) and, then, relate this to future areas of life (e.g., possible careers in architecture).

Third, we recommend emphasizing *integrated,* as opposed to *fragmented interpretations.* Career practitioners might administer a variety of tests (e.g., interest, self-efficacy, values) and assessments, and we encourage clinicians to create a holistic meaning of these results as opposed to treating each as a separate entity. For example, instead of interpreting self-efficacy and interest results separately, a practitioner may blend these to foster a more in-depth understanding of careers possibilities. This process is illustrated further in our case example. Fourth, career counselors should focus on *client strengths* as opposed to weaknesses. This might involve closing an interpretation session with a summary of a client's strengths and relations to additional assessment data. Finally, counselors should *link the referral questions with referral question answers clearly*. When interpreting career assessment results, career counselors can link the client's expressed presenting concerns with insights from the results.

Many of the above recommendations also apply to qualitative assessment, but some additional observations are warranted. Because some qualitative assessments do not prescribe strict assessment protocols, clinicians should take care to administer and interpret such assessments in ways consistent with their theoretical underpinnings (Wood & Scully, 2017). Savickas's (2013) career construction approach offers a useful guide for qualitative/postmodern assessment interpretation. In this style, interpretation might focus less on test scores and more on co-creating meaning that yields a new purpose or life direction.

Additionally, although interpreting quantitative tests ideally entails client involvement, frequently, clinicians ask clients to be highly involved in the interpretive process of qualitative assessment (Wood & Scully, 2017). This involvement might include soliciting client feedback regarding the usefulness and applicability (or lack thereof) of the assessment, which can then be used to direct the assessment along more helpful lines. Whiston and Rahardja (2005) emphasized the importance of addressing clients' expectations, cultural values, and backgrounds. For instance, they noted that clients from certain cultures might assume counselors' views to be more valid than that of their own, which could lead such clients to "acquiesce to the counselor's analysis of meaning to avoid any type of dissonance" (p. 37). As such, maintaining awareness and working collaboratively to share power in qualitative assessment is important for clinicians.

Communication of Results

For many career assessments, particularly qualitative ones, the communication of results might be concurrent with the interpretive process. For example, when developing a client's career narrative collaboratively, the interpretive and communicative processes are mutually informative and overlapping. Nevertheless, addressing several points related specifically to the communication of assessment results is critical. Past approaches to vocational test interpretation emphasized testing and directive reporting of results—also known as "test 'em and tell 'em" (Rounds & Tracey, 1990). Super (1983) advocated for a broader and more collaborative approach that involves the client in the interpretation process. Savickas (2011, 2013) advanced this process further to suggest postmodern perspectives and narrative methods. These, and other authors, argued that an emphasis on scores alone, without context or client involvement, limits effectiveness (Toman & Savickas, 1997).

Groth-Marnat (2009b) observed that, optimally, the communication of assessment results would not merely be the communication of information but also a clinical intervention. Zytowski (2015) offered five principles of interest inventory interpretation and suggested ways clinicians could apply those principles more broadly to any career assessment interpretation. First, clinicians must prepare for the discussion of results. This includes emphasizing key points or finding inconsistencies in the profile. Second, counselors should involve clients in the communication of results. Clinicians should present results as hypotheses and check those against previous client experiences. For instance, clients might evaluate the accuracy of the results by describing previous experiences that fit with, or stand in contrast to, results (Groth-Marnat, 2009b).

Third, the communication must be simple and empathic. This includes matching client language, or even using creative modes of communication such as coloring. Fourth, clinicians should ask clients to summarize their results in their own words. This aids in the process of applying results to the individual's unique self-concept. Fifth and finally, counselors should help formulate next-steps and an action plan for the results. Counselors can suggest exploring options presented in assessment results, such as interviewing employees in selected lines of work.

Case Example

After obtaining Bella's initial CFI-R score and conducting the career construction interview, Jenny is ready to engage in assessment interpretation. Jenny prepares for the interpretation by searching for connections or inconsistencies that emerged during the assessment process. She notices Bella scored low on the *Career Agency* and *Occupational Awareness* scales of the CFI-R but that she had a moderately low score on the *Negative Career Outlook* scale. While reviewing her notes from the career construction interview, Jenny notices a general theme of optimism and hope in relation to Bella's favorite saying and identified role model. Jenny understands, clearly, that highlighting Bella's optimism as a strength might be significant in the assessment interpretation.

Taking a collaborative approach to interpretation, Jenny makes the observation to Bella that, despite scoring low on *Career Agency* and *Occupational Awareness*, Bella's scores on *Negative Career Outlook*, as well as her responses in the career construction interview, reflect a sense of optimism. Bella shares that her grandmother, who was a first-generation immigrant from Mexico, was a strong role model for her. Bella discloses that her grandmother experienced many difficulties over the course of her own life but, nevertheless, maintained a sense of hope. Bella recalls being impressed by this as a child and aspiring to maintain hope in her own life. Jenny and Bella discuss how this strength has helped Bella overcome challenges in the past, and Bella expresses a cautious sense of confidence that she will be able to overcome her present concerns. She discloses that she has a strong desire to honor the memory of her grandmother by maintaining optimism during trials in life. Jenny and Bella agree that Bella's recent layoff has likely affected her sense of *Career Agency*. Bella voices agreement with her low score on *Occupational Awareness*, and she and Jenny discuss ways that Bella can increase her knowledge of various occupations and the current occupational landscape. Bella leaves the session not only with a sense of optimism but also with a set of concrete goals. She shares that the formulation of a plan has already increased her sense of agency slightly.

Summary

In this chapter, we discussed the career assessment process through integrative (Rottinghaus & Eshelman, 2015) and multicultural (Leong, 2010) frameworks. Through the case of Bella, we illustrated how an integrative approach to career assessment can unfold, as well as how to embrace and explore cultural dynamics in session. In closing, we summarized the chapter content through recommending strategies for integrative and multicultural career assessment. First, we encourage counselors to involve their clients in the selection of career tests. Clinicians can accomplish this first through building a strong working alliance that values the clients' cultural identities. Incorporating both quantitative and qualitative tests allows for differing, but complementary, data that can provide in-depth and rich assessment results. When administering tests, being knowledgeable of the instrument protocol and following ethical guidelines is imperative. Second, counselors should follow scoring procedures provided in test manuals and should "story" their qualitative assessments in alignment with the appropriate postmodern theories. Third, counselors might benefit from gaining client participation in the interpretation process. Sharing power in this way acts as an influential multicultural intervention. Finally, clinicians should communicate assessment results in understandable language and in a collaborative fashion. Maintaining this collaboration through the final career assessment stage can poise clients to utilize and apply their results more effectively.

References

American Educational Research Association, American Psychological Association, & National Council on Measurement in Education. (2014). *Standards for educational and psychological testing.* Washington, DC: American Educational Research Association.

American Counseling Association. (2014). *ACA code of ethics.* Retrieved from https://www.counseling.org/resources/aca-code-of-ethics.pdf

American Psychological Association. (2017). Ethical principles of psychologists and code of conduct. Retrieved from https://www.apa.org/ethics/code/ethics-code-2017.pdf

Betz, N. E., Borgen, F. H., & Harmon, L. W. (1996). *Skills Confidence Inventory.* Palo Alto, CA: Consulting Psychologists Press.

Betz, N. E., & Taylor, K. M. (2001). *Manual for the Career Decision Self-Efficacy Scale and CDMSE-Short Form.* Columbus, OH: The Ohio State University.

Brown, D. (2007). *Career information, career counseling, and career development.* Boston, MA: Allyn & Bacon.

Campbell, D. P., Hyne, S. A., & Nilsen, D. L. (1992). *Manual for the Campbell Interest and Skill Survey: CISS.* Minneapolis, MN: National Computer Systems.

Costa, P. T., & McCrae, R. R. (1992). Normal personality assessment in clinical practice: The NEO personality inventory. *Psychological Assessment, 4*(1), 5-13.

Crites, J. O. (1978). *Career Maturity Inventory.* Monterey, CA: CTB/McGraw Hill.

Digman, J. M. (1990). Personality structure: Emergence of the five-factor model. *Annual Review of Psychology, 41*(1), 417-440.

Donnay, D. A. C., Morris, M. A., Shaubhut, N. A., & Thompson, R. C. (2005). *Strong Interest Inventory manual: Research, development and strategies for interpretation.* Palo Alto, CA: Consulting Psychologists Press.

Fouad, N. A. & Bingham, R. P. (1995). Career counseling with racial and ethnic minorities. In W. B. Walsh and S. H. Osipow (Eds.), *Handbook of vocational psychology: Theory, research, and practice* (2nd ed., pp. 331-365). Mahwah, NJ: Lawrence Erlbaum.

Gati, I., Krausz, M., & Osipow, S. H. (1996). A taxonomy of difficulties in career decision making. *Journal of Counseling Psychology, 43,* 510–526.

Groth-Marnat, G. (2009a). The five assessment issues you meet when you go to heaven. *Journal of Personality Assessment, 91*(4), 303-310.

Groth-Marnat, G. (2009b). *Handbook of psychological assessment* (5th ed.). Hoboken, NJ: John Wiley & Sons.

Hansen, J. C. (2013). Nature, importance, and assessment of interests. In S. D. Brown & R. W. Lent (Eds.), *Career development and counseling: Putting theory and research to work* (2nd ed., pp. 387-416). Hoboken, NJ: John Wiley & Sons.

Holland, J. L. (1997). *Making vocational choices: A theory of vocational personalities and work environments.* Odessa, FL: Psychological Assessment Resources.

Krieshok, T. S., Hansen, R. N., Johnston, J. A., Wong, S. C., & Shevde, E. (2008). *Missouri Occupational Card Sort* (4th ed.). Columbia, MO: University of Missouri Career Center.

Leong, F. T. (2010). A cultural formulation approach to career assessment and career counseling: Guest editor's introduction. *Journal of Career Development, 37,* 375-390.

Masdonati, J., Massoudi, K., & Rossier, J. (2009). Effectiveness of career counseling and the impact of the working alliance. *Journal of Career Development, 36,* 183-203.

Metz, A. J., & Jones, J. E. (2013). Ability and aptitude assessment in career counseling. In S. D. Brown & R.W. Lent (Eds.), *Career development and counseling: Putting theory and research to work* (pp. 449-476). Hoboken, N.J.: John Wiley & Sons, Inc.

National Career Development Association. (2015). NCDA code of ethics. Broken Arrow, OK: NCDA.

Nevill, D. D., & Super, D. E. (1989). *The Values Scale: Theory, application and research.* Palo Alto, CA: Consulting Psychologists Press.

Osipow, S. H. (1987). *Career Decision Scale manual.* Odessa, FL: Psychological Assessment Resources.

Psychological Assessment Resources. (2017). *Self-Directed Search.* Retrieved from http://www.self-directed-search.com/

Rottinghaus, P. J., Buelow, K., Matyja, A., & Schneider, M. (2012). The Career Futures Inventory-Revised: Assessing multiple dimensions of career adaptability. *Journal of Career Assessment, 20,* 123-139. doi 10.1177/1069072711420849

Rottinghaus, P. J., Day, S. X., & Borgen, F. H. (2005). The Career Futures Inventory: A measure of career-related adaptability and optimism. *Journal of Career Assessment, 13,* 3–24.

Rottinghaus, P. J., & Eshelman, A. (2015). Integrative approaches to career intervention. In P. J. Hartung, M. L. Savickas, & W. B. Walsh (Eds.), *American Psychological Association handbook of career intervention* (Vol. 2, pp. 25-39). Washington, DC: American Psychological Association.

Rottinghaus, P. J., & Hauser, P. M. (2013). Assessing additional constructs affecting career choice and development. In S. D. Brown & R. W. Lent (Eds.), *Career development and counseling: Putting theory and research to work* (pp. 477-506). Hoboken, N.J.: John Wiley & Sons, Inc.

Rounds, J. B., & Tracey, T. J. (1990). From trait-and-factor to person-environment fit counseling: Theory and process. In W. B. Walsh & S. J. Osipow (Eds.), *Career counseling: Contemporary topics in vocational psychology* (pp. 1- 44). Hillsdale, NJ: Erlbaum.

Savickas, M. L. (2011). *Career counseling.* Washington, DC: American Psychological Association.

Savickas, M. L. (2013). Career construction theory and practice. In R. W. Lent & S. D. Brown (Eds.) *Career development and counseling: Putting theory and research to work* (2nd ed., pp. 147-183). Hoboken, NJ: John Wiley & Sons.

Savickas, M. L. (2015). *Life-design counseling manual.* Rootstown, OH: Author.

Savickas, M. L., & Hartung, P. J. (2012). *My career story. An autobiographical workbook for life-career success.* Retrieved from: http://www.vocopher.com/CSI/CCI_workbook.pdf

Savickas, M. L., & Porfeli, E. J. (2012). The Career-Adapt-Abilities Scale: Construction, reliability, and measurement equivalence across 13 countries. *Journal of Vocational Behavior, 80,* 661-673. doi: 10.1016/j.jvb.2012.01.011

Simons, R., Goddard, R., & Patton, W. (2002). Hand-scoring error rates in psychological testing. *Assessment, 9*(3), 292-300.

Super, D. E. (1955). The dimensions and measurement of vocational maturity. *Teachers College Record, 57,* 151–163.

Super, D. E. (1983). Assessment in career guidance: Toward truly developmental counseling. *Personnel and Guidance Journal, 61,* 555-562.

Super, D. E., & Kidd, J. M. (1979). Vocational maturity in adulthood: Toward turning a model into a measure. *Journal of Vocational Behavior, 14,* 255–270.

Suzuki, L. A., Short, E. L., Pieterse, A., & Kugler, J. (2000). Multicultural issues and the assessment of aptitude. In L. A. Suzuki, J. G. Ponterotto, & P. J. Mellers (Eds.), *Handbook of multicultural assessment: Clinical, psychological, and educational applications* (2nd ed., pp. 359-382). San Francisco: Jossey-Bass.

Taber, B. J., Hartung, P. J., Briddick, H., Briddick, W. C., & Rehfuss, M. C. (2011). Career style interview: A contextualized approach to career counseling. *The Career Development Quarterly, 59*(3), 274-287.

Toman, S. M., & Savickas, M. L. (1997). Career choice readiness moderates the effects of interest inventory interpretation. *Journal of Career Assessment, 5*(3), 275-291.

U.S. Department of Defense. (2005). *ASVAB career exploration program: Counselor manual.* Washington, DC: Author.

Whiston, S. C. (2005). *Principles and applications of assessment in counseling.* Belmont, CA: Brooks/Cole.

Whiston, S. C., & Rahardja, D. (2005). Qualitative career assessment: An overview and analysis. *Journal of Career Assessment, 13,* 371-380.

Wood, C. & Scully, Z. (2017). Postmodern career assessment: Advantages and considerations. In L. A. Busacca & M. C. Rehfuss (Eds.), *Postmodern career counseling: A handbook of culture, context, and cases.* Alexandria, VA: America Counseling Association.

Zunker, V. G., & Osborn, D. S. (2016). *Using assessment results for career development* (9th ed.). Boston, MA: Cengage Learning.

Zytowski, D. G. (2015). Test interpretation: Talking with people about their results. In P. J. Hartung, M. L. Savickas, & W. B. Walsh (Eds.), *APA handbook of career intervention* (Vol. 2, pp. 3-10). Washington, DC: American Psychological Association.

PART II

APPLIED
CAREER
ASSESSMENT

ONLINE
ONLY

www.NCDA.org

PART III

GLOBAL PERSPECTIVES ON CAREER ASSESSMENT

ONLINE ONLY

www.NCDA.org

PART IV

CAREER ASSESSMENT INSTRUMENT REVIEWS

ABILITY EXPLORER, THIRD EDITION

Instrument Acronym or Preferred Short Name: AE

Instrument Authors: Joan C. Harrington, Thomas F. Harrington, Ph.D., and Janet E. Wall, Ed.D.

Publisher: JIST Career Solutions

Publisher Address: 875 Montreal Way, St. Paul, MN 55102
http://www.jist.com

Statement of Purpose: Ability Explorer (AE) ranks a person's strengths in the 12 abilities important in today's workplace. In less than 30 minutes, individuals learn their strongest abilities, plus related careers for developing and using these abilities. Written at an 8th-grade reading level, this 120-statement assessment raises self-awareness, provides practical insights and information, and creates a foundation for informed career and educational planning. Individuals are asked to read each statement and then indicate how good they are or would be at doing the activity. They then progress through steps that show the abilities they are best at and present career choices that match their abilities. Self-scoring and self-interpreting, AE is an ideal career exploration tool that can be used in any educational or workforce-related setting. AE aligns with National Career Development Guidelines and National Standards for School Counseling Programs.

Target Population: Middle school--adult

Norm Group(s) on which Scores are Based: (information not provided by publisher)

Titles of Subtests, Scales, Scores Provided: It covers these 12 abilities: Artistic, Clerical, Interpersonal, Language, Leadership/Persuasive, Manual/Technical, Musical/Dramatic, Numerical/Mathematical, Organizational, Scientific, Social, Spatial

Forms and Levels Available with Dates of Publication/Revision of Each: 2012

Date of Most Recent Edition of Manual, User's Guide, etc.: 2012

Available in which Languages: English Only

Actual Test Time: Average user completes the assessment in 30 minutes

Total Administration Time: 5 minutes for scoring

Required Level of Training and/or Credentials for Administrator: No special training needed.

Types of Scores: 12 ability score areas; the highest possible raw score for any ability is 60 and the lowest is 10; The Total Score chart eliminates the need for individuals to use norm tables. The numbers for each ability score represent raw scores that will be converted to percentiles and then the results are reported as high (67 to 99 percentile), medium (34 to 66 percentiles), or low (1 to 33 percentile).

Report Format/Content: After totaling the individuals will place their results in the chart on page 6 of the booklet. This helps users compare their results with those of other people. After recording all 12 ability scores, the user would then identify his or her top three abilities.

Report Format/Content for Group Summaries: N/A

Availability of Machine Scoring Service? No

Availability of Hand Scoring? Yes

If yes, time required for hand scoring? 5 minutes

If yes, who is it scored by? Individual Test Taker

Availability of Local Machine Scoring Service? N/A

Availability and Options for Computer Software? None Available

Link to webpage that specifies the costs of materials: http://jist.emcp.com/ability-explorer-third-edition-2774.html

Additional Comments of Interest to Users (e.g. forthcoming revisions, new material, etc): (information not provided by publisher)

Published Reviews of the Instrument in the Last 15 years: (information not provided by publisher)

ABILITY EXPLORER

Reviewed by
Kathy M. Evans
University of South Carolina

Introduction/Description

The Ability Explorer (Harrington, Harrington, & Wall, 2012a) is a self-report instrument designed to assist individuals in their career planning. The target population ranges from middle school students to college students and adults. Through use of this instrument, individuals can explore work-related abilities, some of which achievement and aptitude tests do not assess typically. The theoretical base for the Ability Explorer is Donald Super's (1957) developmental career theory and its 14 career propositions (Super, Savickas, & Super, 1996). The Ability Explorer operationalizes seven of the 14 propositions into 12 ability areas with 10 skill statements for each (120 in total) (Harrington, Harrington, & Wall,

2012b). Individuals rank the skill statements by indicating whether their ability in each area is above or below average. The Ability Explorer assesses ability in the areas of Artistic, Clerical, Interpersonal, Language, Leadership, Manual Technical, Musical and Dramatic, Numerical, Organizational, Scientific, Social and Spatial. Descriptions of these ability areas are as follows:

Artistic

The items in this area reflect abilities in drawing, sculpting, photography, and other creative pursuits. One sample item is *producing posters, scenery, or illustrations using paint, pen, charcoal, or colored markers.*

Clerical

The items in this area reflect abilities to perceive details accurately using the eyes, hands, and fingers at the same time. A sample item is *keeping accurate records of sales and purchases.*

Interpersonal

The items in this area reflect abilities to communicate with people individually and in groups. A sample item is *dealing with other people politely and with respect even in difficult situations.*

Language

The items in this area reflect abilities in writing and speaking clearly and using correct grammar. A sample item is *improving writing of other people by editing.*

Leadership/Persuasive

The items in this area reflect abilities in presenting ideas, convincing others to collaborate to reach a goal, and deciding on what is best for the group. A sample item is *persuading people to sign a petition for a cause.*

Manual/Technical

The items in this area reflect the ability to operate and repair machines using the hands, fingers, and eyes simultaneously. A sample item is *finding out what is wrong when something mechanical breaks down.*

Musical or Drama

The items in this area reflect abilities in performing with instruments or with one's voice. A sample item is *following musical symbols to express music properly.*

Numerical and Mathematical

The items in this area reflect abilities in using mathematical techniques to solve problems and exchange ideas. A sample item is *calculating your income tax.*

Organizational

The items in this area reflect abilities in prioritizing and the logical arrangement of information. A sample item is *working efficiently to get a project done.*

Scientific

The items in this area reflect abilities in using evidence to treat humans and animals with illness or injury. A sample item is *conducting a study with bacteria to learn about disease.*

Social

The items in this area reflect the ability solve problems people have and to work well with others either individually or in groups.

Spatial

The items in this area reflect abilities in visualizing how objects will appear if they are positioned differently or if there are missing parts. A sample item is *visualizing designs in three dimensions.*

Technical Considerations

The first edition of Ability Explorer was published in 1996. This review covers the third edition, which is the most recent version, and is the one JIST Career Solutions published in 2012. What follows is a discussion of the instrument's properties.

Item Development

Harrington et al. (2012b) based items for the Ability Explorer on the job descriptions developed by job analysts for the *Guide to Occupational Exploration*

(GOE; U.S. Department of Labor, Employment and Training Administration, 1979). The items included in the Ability Explorer were under the categories of educational development, aptitude, and knowledge in the GOE.

Although Harrington et al. (2012b) started with 550 skill statements, they reduced the number as they scrutinized items. They reviewed skill statements for readability and stated that they wrote the skill statements at the fifth grade level. However, they wrote the assessment booklet at the eighth grade level. Harrington et al. (2012b) stated the increased difficulty level was necessary because of the inclusion of occupational titles that use more complex language.

Harrington et al. (2012b) field-tested the statements with 8,100 students and reviewed for gender, grade, and cultural and racial bias. They tested the statements to determine whether each item correlated with its appropriate scale. Twenty-three statements resulted in "very poor" correlations and, thus, were eliminated. As a result, participant scores increased, regardless of gender or ethnicity. To provide further assurance there was no ethnic bias, the authors submitted the skill statements to a "panel of minority experts" (p. 26) who suggested revisions. Harrington et al. eliminated any statements considered biased.

Reliability

According to Harrington et al. (2012b), reliability analyses were conducted on the original version of the instrument using a normative sample of middle and high school children in 1995 (n=3,480). The median Cronbach's alpha for internal consistency was .87 and ranged from .84 - .89. Martinez (2002) conducted test-retest reliability analyses with 73 college students using an internet version of the Ability Explorer. Martinez found a .85 correlation between the two administrations, which supports reliability of the instrument with the sample. Finally, Harrington et al. (2012b) tested scorer reliability with 170 middle school children. The results indicated that, although there were strong correlations between participants' scores and the author's scores (.98), 8% of the students made significant scoring errors that would have changed their results.

Validity

Harrington et al. (2012b) presented results of three tests of validity: content, construct, and criterion from the original version of the Ability Explorer. The following sections relate the findings of these tests.

Content validity. Harrington et al. (2012b) gave a detailed accounting of the initial test construction and how the items created and selected represented the skills and abilities included in the GOE. Using the GOE, they chose skills and abilities that job analysts identified and described as meeting the criteria for the ability structure. Harrington et al. offered a solid rationale for how the skill statements met the seven ability-related propositions of Super's theoretic framework.

Construct validity. Harrington et al. (2012b) offered the intercorrelations among the Ability Explorer skill statements and stated the scales should be intercorrelated because they measure the same constructs, which is the self-perception of skills. However, they also stated that the items were different enough in that each subscale measures a different aspect of the construct. The developers did not use any other assessment of abilities to support construct validity with the items of this instrument

Criterion related validity. Harrington et al. (2012b) reported studies (e.g., Ramsey, 2004) that gave percentages of individuals whose self-reported ratings in the Ability Explorer matched with their occupational interests. When the Ability Explorer scores were compared with grade point averages (GPA) in specific content areas, there was a 69% discrepancy between self-report and GPA in males and 23% in females (Read, 2001). Harrington et al. provided results from a group of studies in which researchers used the Harrington O'Shea Decision-Making System (1993), which uses self-report of abilities according to the GOE, and compared those scores with achievement test results. Overall, the results of the various tests of validity are mixed. Content validity tests gave the strongest evidence that the Ability Explorer is a valid instrument that measures what it was intended to measure.

Norms

Harrington et al. (2012b) stated they used 4,837 cases as the normative group for the original version of the Ability Explorer. Within those cases, 49% were male (n=2,370) and 51% were female (n=2,467). Seventy-three percent (n=3,532) were middle/junior high school students, and 27% (n=1,305) were college students and adults. The group was ethnically diverse with 28% African American, 1% American Indians, 2% Asian and Pacific Islander, 15% Hispanic, and 54% other. Harrington et al. indicated that they over-sampled African Americans because Harrington and colleagues wanted to "examine whether young members of a culture/racial group had sufficient experience on which to base their evaluation items" (p. 27). The charts for the normative sample indicate information on the middle and high school populations only. The diversity of the normative sample, at first glance, appears to be excellent. However, the missing information about the percentage of White participants lessens its usefulness to those students because of a lack of information as to how relevant these results are to the White responders.

Use/Interpretation/Evaluation

The *Abilities Explorer* is a relatively inexpensive resource designed to assist counselors, teachers, psychologists, and job placement specialists with their clients' career exploration. The booklet takes individuals through four steps of rating their abilities, understanding their scores, identifying careers, and researching careers. The instrument is self-scored, and the total score chart makes interpretation easy, even without the use of norm tables. The addition of the career finder in the third edition not only enables clients to be active participants in their career exploration process, but also helps them increase awareness of their work skills. The Ability Explorer aligns with the information from O*Net and the Occupational Outlook Handbook which assists clients in this process.

In the third edition of the instrument, Harrington et al. (2012b) reduced the original 140 statements to 120 in response to feedback from users that they needed more time to devote to interpreting the results in a single session. However, the design of the instrument allows for those who have limited time with their clients (e.g., school counselors) to administer the instrument and interpret the results in two sessions. In addition, Harrington et al. reduced the number of ability areas from 14 to 12 to address reviewer feedback that there were too many categories for individuals to process cognitively.

The user's manual is brief and easy to read and outlines ideas on how to use the assessment with clients, including those with special needs. The professional manual (Harrington et al., 2012b) details the development of the instrument, reliability, and validity information, as well as other research conducted on the instrument.

Presentation and Interpretation

The Ability Explorer is contained in an attractive booklet where either the client or the practitioner can score the items. The ability areas are color-coded, which makes keeping track of scoring easy. The summary of scores at the end helps the individual understand his or her strengths and weaknesses. The instrument is forced choice in that there is no neutral position—a client must choose between being very good, good, a little above average, a little below average, poor or very poor for each item. Color-coding helps the client add the appropriate scores for each area, and the isolated check box for each item helps the client mark the response for that statement. The occupations finder gets clients involved in the career exploration process immediately. The occupations finder includes the names of occupations and the number of years of education those occupations require before individuals decide to do any further research. However, only a limited number of occupations can be included to maintain a booklet of a manageable size. Consequently, there is an absence of some ability combinations.

To aid in interpretation, the professional manual contains activity worksheets that practitioners can duplicate for clients. The worksheets can help individuals identify activities in which they might want to engage if they want to increase their skills.

Evaluation

The strengths of the Ability Explorer include its relative affordability, its attractive appearance and easy to follow steps, and its strong theoretical foundation. The instrument includes motivational components that might serve to boost client self-esteem. A further strength is its alignment with O*NET and the *Occupational Outlook Handbook*—two free resources. The fact that the Career Finder and subsequent steps keep clients engaged in the work of career exploration is commendable at a time when getting a computer-generated printout with all the information already available is common. The Ability Explorer is a good instrument for individual and group career exploration, especially in a school situation in which each of the four steps could take place in different sessions.

In terms of weakness, the reading level might be a problem for some students. Harrington et al. (2012b) wrote the instrument at the eighth-grade level yet declared the instrument is appropriate for middle school students, the majority of whom are in the sixth and seventh grades. Administering the instrument to these students could require more involvement from the practitioner because of having to read the information to students. In addition, individuals must be able to calculate their scores and transfer the numbers, and this might require more assistance from the administrator.

Another serious weakness in the newer version is the lack of additional analysis concerning the reliability, validity, and normative information. Although the original version went through rigorous testing and analysis, the newer version lacks this type of evidence. Additional empirical research developing this evidence is needed to insure the assessment still functions as expected.

The Career Finder is an excellent addition to the instrument but, as Harrington et al. (2012b) admitted, there are some combinations of abilities not found on the list. Adding instructions in the booklet might have been helpful to clients who encounter issues like this. In addition, having the worksheets incorporated into the professional manual rather than the user guide is counter intuitive. Practitioners are more likely to use the user guide when working with their clients.

Although reliability and content validity evidences are strong, the other forms of validity (i.e., construct, criterion) cited in the professional manual are less compelling. As Mau (2013) suggested, the Ability Explorer might be more useful "for personal awareness and self-efficacy intervention rather than for prediction of occupational obtainment or job satisfaction" (p. 119).

Cultural Considerations and Implications

Harrington et al. (2012b) were diligent in their quest to eliminate gender and cultural bias from the language in the Ability Explorer. They stated firmly that the norm group was non-gender specific and that listed abilities were gender neutral. The question is whether Harrington et al. went far enough to ensure that the instrument measures everyone equally. Avoiding language bias is not the only issue in test bias. The fact that an occupation does not have a gender or culture attached to it does not mean that women, men, and all cultures have an equal opportunity to develop the skills needed for that job. In fact, some researchers have found gender differences in the ability self-assessments of men and women (Betz et al., 2003; Hansen & Bubany, 2008) and cultural differences between African Americans and other ethnic minority groups (Tracey & Hopkins, 2001; Westbrook, Buck, Wynne, and Sanford 1994). These topics warrant additional research.

Research and Evaluation: Assessment Uses

Almost all the research on the Ability Explorer was completed on the previous edition of the instrument. That research supported the breakdown of the skill areas (Harrington & Harrington, 2001; Langlier, 2003; Ramsey, 2004; Watson, Harrington & Morrison, 1996) and demonstrated the relationship between the Ability Explorer and preferred learning styles, the discrepancy between self-perception of abilities and grades, and how much high school faculty know about their students' skills outside their own classrooms. A search of the recent literature does not reveal any new studies on the third edition of the Ability Explorer.

References

Betz, N., Borgen, F., Rottinghaus, P., Paulsen, A., Halper, C., & Harmon, L. (2003). The expanded skills confidence inventory: Measuring basic dimensions of vocational activity. *Journal of Vocational Behavior, 62*, 76-100. doi:10.1016/S0001=-8791(02)00034-9

Hansen, J., & Bubany, S. (2008). Do self-efficacy and ability self-estimate scores reflect distinct facets of ability judgments? *Measurement and Evaluation in Counseling and Development, 41*, 66-88.

Harrington, T., & Harrington, J. (2001). A new generation of self-report methodology and validity evidence of the ability explorer. *Journal of Career Development, 9*(1), 41-48.

119

Harrington, J. C., Harrington, T. F., & Wall, J. E. (2012a). *Ability Explorer, Third Edition.* St. Paul, MN: JIST Publishing.

Harrington, J. C., Harrington, T. F., & Wall, J. E. (2012b). *Ability Explorer professional manual, Third Edition.* St. Paul, MN: JIST Publishing.

Harrington, T. & O'Shea. A. (1993). *The Harrington-O'Shea Career Decision-Making System revised manual.* Circle Pines, MN: American Guidance Service.

Langlier, C. (2003). Teachers' knowledge of student abilities. Unpublished study, Pinkerton Academy, Bow, New Hampshire.

Martinez, L. (2002). Internet-based vs. paper-pencil test administration: An equivalency study using the Ability Explorer. Unpublished dissertation. Texas A & M University, College Station.

Mau, W. (2013). Ability Explorer [Test Review]. In C. Wood & D. G. Hays (Eds.), *A counselor's guide to career assessment instruments* (6th ed., pp. 116-124). Broken Arrow, OK: National Career Development Association.

Ramsey, R. (2004). *Interventions to try to improve the success rate of students completing the alternative school.* Unpublished dissertation. Nova Southeastern University, North Miami Beach, Florida.

Read, R. (2001). Self-estimates of vocational abilities as a measure of school and career motivation. Unpublished study. Davers Public School, Davers, MA.

Super. D. (1957). *The psychology of careers.* New York, NY: Harper & Row.

Super, D., Savickas, M. & Super, C., (1996). The life-span, life-space approach to careers. In D. Brown, L. Brooks & Associates (Eds.), *Career choice and development* (3rd. ed.). San Francisco: Jossey-Bass.

Tracey, T., & Hopkins, N. (2001). Correspondence of interests and abilities with occupational choice. *Journal of Counseling Psychology, 48,* 178-189. doi:10.1037//0022-0167.48.2.178

U.S. Department of Labor, Employment, and Training Administration. (1979). *Guide for occupational exploration.* Washington, DC: U.S. Government Printing Office.

Watson, M., Harrington, T., & Morrison, R. (1996). The self-reported values and abilities of respiratory therapy students. *Respiratory Care Education Annual, 5,* 3-17.

Westbrook, B., Buck, R., Wynne, C., & Sanford, E. (1994). Career maturity in adolescence: Reliability and validity of self-ratings of abilities by gender and ethnicity. *Journal of Career Assessment, 2,* 125-161.

Ashland Interest Assessment

Instrument Acronym or Preferred Short Name: AIA

Instrument Authors: Douglas N. Jackson, Ph.D., & Connie W. Marshall, M.A.

Publisher: Sigma Assessment Systems

Publisher Address: P.O. Box 3292, Station B London, ON, N6A 4K3

http://www.sigmaassessmentsystems.com/assessments/ashland-interest-assessment

Statement of Purpose: Counseling, educational, and career planning

Target Population: 15+, individuals with limited abilities

Norm Group(s) on which Scores are based: 725 females, 725 males

Titles of Subtests, Scales, Scores Provided: Arts and Crafts, Food Service, Sales, Protective Service, Mechanical, Plant or Animal Care, Personal Service, Clerical, General Service, Health Care, Construction, Transportation

Forms and Levels Available with Dates of Publication/Revision of Each: 1997

Date of Most Recent Edition of Manual, User's Guide, etc.: 1997

Available in which Languages: English, French

Actual Test Time: 35 minutes

Total Administration Time: 45 minutes

Required Level of Training and/or Credentials for Administrator: Bachelor's degree in psychology

Types of Scores: Standard, percentile, verbal

Report Format/Content: Narrative text, scales, charts and figures

Report Format/Content for Group Summaries: (information not provided by publisher)

Availability of Machine Scoring Service? Yes, Mail-in scoring

If yes, maximum time required for machine scoring and return: 48 hours

Availability of Hand Scoring? Yes

If yes, time required for hand scoring? (information not provided by publisher)

If yes, who is it scored by? Test Administrator

Availability of Local Machine Scoring Service? (information not provided by publisher)

> **If yes, provisions/conditions/equipment required for local machine scoring:** (information not provided by publisher)
>
> **Availability and Options for Computer Software?** Computer Software Available; Standard administration online
>
> **If available, describe the ways in which computer/online version differs:** (information not provided by publisher)
>
> **Link to webpage that specifies the costs of materials:** http://www.sigmaassessmentsystems.com/assessments/ashland-interest-assessment/#heading-pricing
>
> **Additional Comments of Interest to Users (e.g. forthcoming revisions, new material, etc):** (information not provided by publisher)
>
> **Published Reviews of the Instrument in the Last 15 years:** (information not provided by publisher)

ASHLAND INTEREST ASSESSMENT

Reviewed by

Darrin L. Carr
Indiana University – Purdue University Columbus

Pamela McCoy
Milestones Clinical & Health Resources

Alyssa West
Insights Consulting

Introduction/Description

Jackson and Marshall (1997) created the Ashland Interest Assessment (AIA) in response to similar measures either not meeting the career exploration needs of clients with disabilities or having technical limitations, such as limited reliability and validity, lack of normative data, or biased pictorial prompts. The authors noted that differentiating features of the AIA include its use of simpler language (all items are at or below a third-grade reading level), larger type fonts, and a focus on target populations typically not holding a high school diploma or any postsecondary education. The AIA contains 144 forced-choice items distributed equally among 12 basic interest scales, which include arts & crafts, sales, clerical, protective service, food service, personal service, health care, general service, plant or animal care, construction, transportation, and mechanical. For each item, the respondent chooses between two familiar activities of interest (e.g., keep office records vs. drive a tractor). Jackson and Marshall excluded occupational titles from these items intentionally to make them as widely understood as possible. Validity indices created include a percentage of failed (omitted or double scored) responses and a response consistency index across all scales.

Technical Considerations

The technical manual describes a four-phase developmental process for the AIA clearly, including steps taken to develop the items pool, refine the item presentation format, test a final version of the instrument, and obtain a national standardized sample. The developers enhanced content validity by developing items from standard references of Canadian occupational information, structured interviews with agencies serving targeted populations, and factor analyses of the *Career Directions Inventory* (CDI, Jackson, 1986) and the *Jackson Vocational Interest Survey* (JVIS, Jackson, 1985). These analyses formed a framework for the 12 basic interest areas within, which allowed the developers to author entirely new items. Jackson and Marshall (1997) retained items based on inspection of p-values and efficiency indices for male, female, and combined groups. After an empirical comparison of item presentation formats, the developers selected a forced choice format, over a single item "like – dislike" format, to reduce response bias and enhance the instrument's construct validity. Jackson and Marshall found acceptable internal consistencies (Cronbach alphas from .79 to .91) across the instrument's 12 basic interest scales after a trial study of the final draft of the AIA with 88 individuals from agencies serving the target population.

To create a normative group, Jackson and Marshall (1997) administered the final version of the AIA to 1,450 participants (725 female, 725 male) 15 to 64 years of age in 10 of 12 Canadian provinces. Participants ages 45 to 64 are underrepresented, which the authors noted is consistent with past findings about lower rates of work participation among older adults with disabilities. Jackson and Marshall recruited individuals living with various disabilities through employment agencies, schools, psychiatric services, and mental health associations. Notably, 65.4% of the sample reported one or more disabilities with almost half (48%) endorsing either mental health or learning disabilities. In addition, the authors gathered occupational group data by surveying workers or trainees for occupations within each of the 12 basic interest categories, thereby enabling a comparison of individual respondent profiles against a typical profile for each occupational group. For the final norm group, Cronbach's alphas for the 12 basic interest scales ranged from .72 to .90 for the combined sample, .69 to .88 for males, and .73 to .87 for females. The authors did not report test-retest or alternate forms reliabilities. Although the authors hoped the AIA would predict client occupational satisfaction, and not aptitude or performance, they did not provide any studies examining either the concurrent, predictive, convergent, or divergent validities of the instrument.

Perhaps in an effort to provide further evidence of construct validity, Jackson and Marshall (1997) conducted a final principal components analysis with varimax rotation by gender. Only eight of the 12 scales loaded on a factor for the male sample. Their four unipolar factors represented practical outdoor activities, attention to detail (conscientious adherence to rules), arts & crafts, and serving others. In contrast, the factor analysis of responses by the female sample captured all 12 scales. Furthermore, each of their four factor loadings was bipolar in nature. The first factor was composed of positive loadings on construction and mechanical activities versus negative loadings on personal service and health care. The second factor comprised positive loadings on mechanical activities and protective services versus negative loadings on food service and sales. The third factor included positive loadings on transportation and arts and crafts versus negative loadings on general services. The fourth factor captured positive loadings on clerical and protective services versus negative loadings on plant or animal care, arts and crafts, and construction. The authors interpreted these findings as evidence that women in the sample have more broadly defined, but mutually exclusive, interests compared to men, who have more clearly defined interests and a preference for "so-called blue-collar occupations" (Jackson & Marshall, 1997, p. 67).

Use/Interpretation/Evaluation

The AIA is available in print for use with either hand scored templates or mailed-in scoring by the publisher, who will accommodate practitioners' requests for special handling (e.g., maintaining groupings of instruments). Computer-based and web-based versions of the assessment are available also, though these were not accessible for consideration in this review. Both assessment materials and reports are available in English and French. Normed originally in Canada, AIA interpretive reports are available for clients seeking employment in either Canada or the United States. These reports seem to differ mostly in terms of referenced occupational information systems (e.g., Canada's National Occupational Classification [NOC] system vs. O*NET used in the United States), but they are both based on the original Canadian norm group. Each report contains a bar chart of gender-based percentile scores for each of the 12 basic interest scales, descriptions of these scales, similarity indices for each of 12 corresponding occupational groups, and lists of example occupations and NOC and O*NET codes for each of the client's top three occupational groups. The report includes a counselor's summary report that repeats the occupational group similarity indices and reports validity indices.

A strength of the AIA is that Jackson and Marshall (1997) created the AIA for individuals living with a variety of disabilities and a wide range of functioning. Professionals working with persons who have varying degrees of intellectual ability are likely to find the AIA easier for clients to understand than other interest assessments. Furthermore, the forced choice format (versus multi-point scale format) might make responding to items less overwhelming for many clients. The professional manual provides detailed directions which the practitioner might read aloud to orient respondents. These emphasize that the AIA is measuring interests, not abilities, to help respondents approach the task in the desired frame of mind. The manual includes tips on avoiding common errors and a discussion of how to handle "difficult cases," when interpreting results.

Based on our previous clinical experiences, we suggest that administering the AIA to persons with intellectual disabilities, including those on the autism spectrum, could present some challenges. Such clients vary widely in their cognitive and physical abilities, and many live with comorbid conditions (e.g., obsessive compulsive disorder, attention deficit hyperactivity disorder) which can complicate the completion of any lengthy questionnaire. For example, as emphasized in the technical manual, communicating that the assessment does not consider respondents' ability to complete certain jobs and is only a guide to areas of interest is important. Although an individual might score very high in transportation as an interest, entry into a specific occupation (e.g., taxi driver) might not be feasible due to difficulties operating a motor vehicle. The AIA is an appropriate tool to help clients determine their interests, but a skillful, individualized orientation and interpretation by a counselor is required to avoid client frustration during administration and in the possible event that client interests and abilities do not align.

Research and Evaluation/Assessment Uses

Although the Ashland Interest Assessment has been reviewed on at least four previous occasions (McCowan & McCowan, 2001; Roznowski, 2001; Herman & Schaff, 2009; Ellison, 2013), it does not appear to have been employed significantly in research activities related to career assessment and counseling. At the very least, there is a need for continued evaluation of the AIA with respect to test-rest reliability and predictive, convergent, and divergent validities. Furthermore, a current norm group that crosses national and cultural boundaries would be desirable. The item content of the AIA, now two decades old, might also require some minimal revision. Though the items meet the authors' goal of being "familiar, easy to understand, and … realistically accomplished by the target population"

125

(Jackson & Marshall, 1997, p. 7), some might reference technology (e.g., an adding machine) or work tasks (e.g., replace oven clocks) encountered less frequently in contemporary workplaces.

The AIA serves the needs of individuals whose career development is neglected often due to perceived limitations on their education or abilities. Similarly apparent is that, though reviewed frequently and available commercially, the further development and application of the AIA is relatively idle in the research and practice literature. This is unfortunate, because this measure has many strengths, including a systematic design and development process, robust content validity, overall good internal consistency of scales, and a thorough manual, which addresses important issues of practice thoughtfully. Perhaps the next review of the Ashland Interest Assessment will report new findings that advance both this helpful measure and the careers of people with disabilities.

References

Ellison, L. (2013). Ashland Interest Assessment [Test Review]. In C. Wood & D. Hays (Eds.), *A counselor's guide to career assessment instruments* (6th ed., pp 416 - 419). Broken Arrow, OK: National Career Development Association.

Herman, A., & Schaff, C. (2009). Ashland Interest Assessment [Test Review]. In E. A. Whitfield, R. W. Feller, & C. Wood (Eds.), *A counselor's guide to career assessment instruments* (5th ed., pp. 422 - 427). Broken Arrow, OK: National Career Development Association.

Jackson, D. N., & Marshall, C. W. (1997). *Ashland Interest Assessment manual*. Port Huron, MI: Sigma Assessment Systems.

Jackson, D. N. (1985). *Jackson Vocational Interest Survey Manual*. Port Huron, MI: SIGMA Assessment Systems.

Jackson, D. N. (1986). *Career Directions Inventory Manual*. Port Huron, MI: SIGMA Assessment Systems.

McCowan, R. J., & McCowan, S. C. (2001). Ashland Interest Assessment [Test Review]. In B. S. Plake & J. C. Impara (Eds.), *The fourteenth mental measurements yearbook*. Retrieved from http://marketplace.unl.edu/buros/

Roznowski, M. (2001). Ashland Interest Assessment [Test Review]. In B. S. Plake & J. C. Impara (Eds.), *The fourteenth mental measurements yearbook*. Retrieved from http://marketplace.unl.edu/buros/

QUANTITATIVE

ASVAB CAREER EXPLORATION PROGRAM

Instrument Acronym or Preferred Short Name: ASVAB CEP; ASVAB, CEP iCAT, FYI

Instrument Author: U.S. Department of Defense

Publisher: U.S. Department of Defense

Publisher Address: 400 Gigling Rd, Seaside, CA 93955

www.asvabprogram.com

Statement of Purpose: The ASVAB is a heavily researched and well-respected aptitude test that measures developed abilities and helps predict future academic and occupational success in the military. The ASVAB is offered to high school and post-secondary students as part of the ASVAB Career Exploration Program. The program provides tools to help students learn more about career exploration and planning, in both the civilian and military worlds of work. The FYI is a 90-item measure of career and vocational interests designed by the Department of Defense specifically for the ASVAB Career Exploration Program. The FYI is designed to help students learn about their career-related interests. Based on John Holland's well-accepted theory of career choice, the FYI assesses an individual's resemblance to each of the six RIASEC (Realistic, Investigative, Artistic, Social, Enterprising, and Conventional) types described by Holland (1997). The results of these assessments are used to guide career exploration activities at asvabprogram. com and careersinthemilitary.com. These resources help students gather and understand all the facts about themselves and the world of work so they can make informed career decisions.

Target Population: The ASVAB CEP is offered to students in grades 10-12 and first and second-year post-secondary students, and for career exploration purposes at job corps centers and correctional facilities.

Norm Group(s) on which Scores are Based: National norming studies for the ASVAB Testing Program are typically conducted every 15-20 years. The need for new norms is evaluated regularly, and new norms are introduced when the evaluations suggest the current norms no longer adequately represent the testing population. The current national norms for the ASVAB were implemented in 2004. A nationally representative sample consisting of approximately 4,700 youth expected to be enrolled in grades 10, 11, and 12 as of fall 1997 was utilized in the creation of the norms.

The FYI norming sample included 1,958 high school students across 28 states. The sample consisted of approximately equal numbers of female adolescents

(52%; n = 1,013) and male adolescents (48%; n = 945). Most students were sophomores (44%; n = 849), juniors (42%, n = 825) or seniors (14%; n = 277). The mean age was 15.9 years (SD = 0.9 years.) Ethnically, the sample consisted mostly of Caucasian students (86%; n = 1,682), with relatively small numbers of American Indians (4%; n = 75), African Americans (6%; n = 112), Hispanic Americans (11%; n = 206), Asian Americans (2%; n = 43), Native Hawaiian/ Pacific Islanders (1%; n = 18), and students from other racial/ethnic descents or who declined to provide information about their racial/ethnic descent (1%; n = 13). Because participants could elect to self-identify as a member of several different ethnic/racial categories, these numbers and percentages should be viewed accordingly. Geographically, the sample evidenced considerable diversity, with well over a third (45%; n = 889) from rural schools and from urban schools (44%; n = 858), and about one-tenth (11%; n = 211) from suburban schools. There was considerable regional diversity as well, with about one-sixth of the students each from the New England (13%; n = 264), Mid-Atlantic (14%; n = 275), Southeastern (17%; n = 329), South Central (13%; n = 245), and Western states (15%; n = 298), and about one quarter from the North Central states (27%, n = 528). Very few students were from the Northwest Central states (1%, n = 19). Participants were primarily enrolled in public (89%; n = 1,746) rather than private (11%; n = 212) schools.

Titles of Subtests, Scales, Scores Provided: The paper and pencil (P&P) ASVAB consists of eight subtests: General Science, Arithmetic Reasoning, Word Knowledge, Paragraph Comprehension, Mathematics Knowledge, Electronics Information, Auto and Shop Information, and Mechanical Comprehension. The computer adaptive ASVAB (CEP iCAT) consists of 10 subtests: General Science, Arithmetic Reasoning, Word Knowledge, Paragraph Comprehension, Mathematics Knowledge, Electronics Information, Auto Information, Shop Information, Mechanical Comprehension, and Assembling Objects. Scores on the individual ASVAB subtests are reported as Standard and Percentile Scores. Standard Scores are scores that have a meaning relative to a national sample of youth in grades 10-12. About half the population scores at or above a Standard Score of 50. Percentile Scores indicate the percentage of examinees in a reference group that scored at or below that particular score. A Percentile Score of 50 indicates that the examinee scored as well as or better than 50% of the nationally-representative sample ASVAB subtest scores are combined to yield three Career Exploration Scores: Verbal Skills, Math Skills, and Science/ Technical Skills. Each of these scores is made up of a combination of some of the individual ASVAB subtests for career exploration purposes. Examinees also receive a score on what is called the Armed Forces Qualification Test (AFQT). AFQT scores are computed using the Standard Scores from four ASVAB subtests: Arithmetic Reasoning (AR), Mathematics Knowledge (MK), Paragraph Comprehension (PC), and Word Knowledge (WK). They are reported as percentiles between 1-99. ASVAB scores are statistically linked across different forms and administration modes through a process called "equating." As a result of equating, ASVAB scores have the same meaning regardless of which form or administration mode the examinee receives. FYI Scales: Realistic (R), Investigative (I), Artistic (A), Social (S), Enterprising (E), and Conventional (C). Scores are provided for each scale. Results are self-scored.

Forms and Levels Available with Dates of Publication/Revision of Each: The ASVAB forms, their publication and revision dates are proprietary. This information is not published for test security purposes. There is one FYI form currently available. It was published in 2010. Available both in paper and pencil and online (www.asvabprogram.com).

Date of Most Recent Edition of Manual, User's Guide, etc.: There are various forms of user guides. The guide developed for students was updated in 2017. Similarly, the guide developed for counselors was developed in 2012 and is currently being updated. Both guides are available for download at www.asvabprogram.com/general-resources

Available in which Languages: English Only

Actual Test Time: The P&P ASVAB is a traditional test and takes about three hours to complete. The CEP iCAT is self-paced and generally takes about 1.5 hours to complete. The FYI takes 15-20 minutes for Paper and Pencil (includes scoring) and 10 minutes for online version (results generated).

Total Administration Time: The P&P ASVAB is a traditional test, which means that everyone takes the same set of questions at the same pace. This version consists of eight subtests (a total of 200 items) and takes about three hours to complete. The CEP iCAT is self-paced and generally takes about 1.5 hours to complete. Because CEP iCAT tests are catered to each individual, extra time is allotted for each subtest. The FYI takes 15-20 minutes for Paper and Pencil (includes scoring) and 10 minutes for online version (results generated) The Post-Test Interpretation session can be completed in as little as one 45-minute class period.

Required Level of Training and/or Credentials for Administrator: Administrator training requirements include ASVAB security, accountability, administration, and CAT-ASVAB stand-alone testing procedures. The FYI does not require training. It is self-administered and scored.

Types of Scores: The ASVAB Summary Results Sheet reflects percentile and standard scores for Career Exploration Scores and each of the individual ASVAB Subtests. Examinees also receive a score on the AFQT (reported as a percentile score). The FYI results are raw scores (for each scale), percentile scores, and gender-based percentile scores (online). For paper and pencil version, students are provided instructions on how to interpret their scores on specific scales based on their gender.

Report Format/Content: All ASVAB scores (Career Exploration Scores, Subtest Scores and AFQT) are reported on the ASVAB Summary Results Sheet. Participants can also access their score report online. FYI assessments are self-scored. Scores are presented with descriptions of each RIASEC code, descriptions of percentile scores, and descriptions/explanations of gender-based scores. Please see Exploring Careers: The ASVAB Career Exploration Guide for samples of these explanations. Users who have taken the ASVAB test can log onto the website and receive the explanations with their scores as well.

Report Format/Content for Group Summaries: n/a

Availability of Machine Scoring Service? Yes

If yes, maximum time required for machine scoring and return: CEP iCAT and FYI results can be generated immediately.

Availability of Hand Scoring? Yes

If yes, time required for hand scoring? Paper and pencil FYI results can also be hand scored.

If yes, who is it scored by? Individual Test Taker

Availability of Local Machine Scoring Service? No

Availability and Options for Computer Software? Computer Software Available; Standard administration online

If other, please describe: The CEP iCAT is a computer adaptive test. The CEP iCAT software is developed using Java. The FYI can be administered online. The online FYI is developed using Angular JS.

If available, describe the ways in which computer/online version differs (if any): The P&P ASVAB consists of eight subtests, a total of 200 items. The CEP iCAT is computer-adaptive. The CEP iCAT consists of 10 subtests, a total of 145 items. The questions on both version of the FYI are identical on both the paper and online version. The only difference is that students self-score the paper and pencil version and the online is automatically scored for them.

Link to webpage that specifies the costs of materials: The ASVAB CEP is provided at no cost to participating schools. Program website: www. asvabprogram.com

Additional Comments of Interest to Users (e.g. forthcoming revisions, new material, etc): Related to these assessments are career planning resources. The ASVAB is one component of the ASVAB CEP. The FYI is another. The third component of the ASVAB CEP is the career exploration activities available at asvabprogram.com and careersinthemilitary.com.

In 2016, the ASVAB CEP website was completely revamped. Users can now search thousands of occupations that match their skills (as measured by the ASVAB) and their interests (as measured by the FYI) in the OCCU-Find, a catalog of careers packed with information including job summary information, education requirements, salary outlook, military opportunities and more from the U.S. Department of Labor, Employment and Training Administration, the Bureau of Labor Statistics, National Center of Education Statistics, CareerOneStop, and Defense Manpower Data Center.

In 2017, careersinthemilitary.com was revamped to link directly to occupations in the OCCU-Find and provide detailed information on 266 military career fields. Users can move seamlessly between these sites and find related jobs in the military and civilian sectors, document aspirations and achievements in the shared portfolio, and apply what they are learning in the classroom to the real-world using the in-class activities.

Published Reviews of the Instrument in the Last 15 years:

Patrick, J., Blosel, C.W., & Gross, C. L. (2009). Review of Armed Services Vocational Aptitude Battery/Career Exploration Program. In E. A. Whitfield, R. Feller, and C. Wood (Eds.), *A counselor's guide to career assessment instruments* (5th ed., pp. 97 – 103). Broken Arrow, OK: National Career Development Association.

Note: This review covers the entire ASVAB CEP program, not the FYI instrument.

Armed Services Vocational Aptitude Battery Career Exploration Program

Reviewed By
Laith G. Mazahreh
Mississippi State University

Introduction/Description

The Armed Service Vocational Aptitude Battery Career Exploration Program (ASVAB-CEP) is an expansive print and web-based package that the developers designed to assist high school and post-secondary students in becoming aware of their capacities and interests, explore the world of work, and plan for their future careers. Furthermore, the U.S. Armed Services utilizes the ASVAB-CEP to identify potential U.S. military recruits based on both the participants' interests as well as other qualifications examined by this instrument. Due to the flexible design of the ASVAB-CEP, professionals can use it as an independent tool for career exploration and educational programs, or program developers can incorporate the instrument into an established career counseling program (Baker, 2002). The primary purpose of the ASVAB-CEP is to provide students with an opportunity to learn more about themselves and the world of work. In addition, the ASVAB-CEP acts a valuable career exploration tool to assist students in discovering a post-secondary career pathway that aligns with their skills, motivations, and interests. Career professionals administer the ASVAB-CEP to high school and post-secondary students at no cost. The instrument, located on the program website, includes three major components: The Armed Service Vocational Aptitude Battery (ASVAB), the Find Your Interests Inventory (FYI), and the OCCU-Find feature.

The first component of the ASVAB-CEP is the Armed Service Vocational Aptitude Battery (ASVAB). The ASVAB is one of the most widely utilized multiple-aptitude battery tests in the world and is administered to approximately 800,000 high school and post-secondary students nationwide annually (Baker, 2002). The ASVAB is appropriate for students in the 10th, 11th, and 12th grades, as well as students enrolled in post-secondary educational programs. Currently, career professionals can administer the ASVAB by two different means: a printed copy, which can be administered as a paper-and-pencil test (P&P- ASVAB), and an electronic module (CAT-ASVAB), which can be administered electronically.

The P&P ASVAB has undergone numerous updates that led to the development of different forms. Forms 25 and 26 are the most current updated versions of the P&P AVSAB. The P&P ASVAB comprises 225 items and takes approximately three hours to complete. Specifically, the test requires 149 minutes of actual test time and 36 minutes of administration time. The instrument measures participants' scores on nine different subtests. The first subtest is General Science (GS), which consists of 25 items. GS measures knowledge in the areas of biological and physical sciences. Arithmetic Reasoning (AR) is the second subtest and encompasses 30 items. AR assesses individuals' ability to solve basic arithmetic word problems. The Word Knowledge (WK) subtest includes the largest number of items (35 items). The WK subtest evaluates students' abilities to understand the meaning of words through synonyms. The fourth scale is Paragraph Comprehension (PC), which contains 15 items and measures respondents' ability to obtain information through written material. Mathematics Knowledge (MK) is the fifth subtest and consists of 25 items. This subtest assesses respondents' knowledge and understanding of mathematical concepts. The Electronics Information (EI) subtest includes 20 items measuring knowledge of electrical current, circuits, devices, and electronic systems. Auto and Shop Information (AS) is the seventh subtest and measures respondents' knowledge of automotive maintenance and repair, and wood and metal shop practices. The total number of items in this subtest is 25. The Mechanical Comprehension (MC) subtest consists of 25 items and measures individuals' knowledge of the principles of mechanical devices, structural support, and properties of materials. Finally, the Assembling Objects (AO) subtest includes 25 items measuring the individual's ability to determine the way an object will look after it is assembled (ASVAB, 2012a).

Although the CAT-ASVAB and the P&P ASVAB measure similar abilities, there are differences between the two scales. One important difference is that the seventh subtest on the P&P ASVAB, AS, was divided into two separate subtests on the CAT-ASVAB [i.e., Auto Information (AI) and Shop Information (SI)]. The AI and SI are administered as two separate tests on the CAT-ASVAB, however, scores on the combined test, AS, are reported for both the CAT-ASVAB and P&P-ASVAB. Additionally, there are differences between the CAT-ASVAB and P&P ASVAB in terms of the number of items included in every subtest. The CAT-ASVAB consists of only 145 items, GS (16 items, AR (16 items) WK (16 items), PC (11 items), MK (16 items), EI (16 items), AI (11 items), SI (11 items), MC (16 questions) AO (16 items) compared o the P&P ASVAB which has 225 items. Finally, although every individual subtest on the CAT-ASVAB has a time limit, respondents can move at their own pace through the test. Therefore, if a respondent finishes a subtest prior to reaching the designated time limit, he or she moves automatically to the next subtest, which may aid in reducing the testing time.

In addition to the previous eight subtests, the ASVAB provides five individuals scores. The first four scores represent four main skills: Verbal Skills, Math Skills, Science and Technical Skills, and Spatial Skills. The military uses the fifth score, known as the Military Entrance score or the Armed Forces Qualification Test (AFQT), to select and classify enlisted military personnel. The respondents' scores on one or more of the ASVAB's subtests described above contain each of the five scores. Following is a description of the five composites scores (ASVAB, 2012b).

Verbal Skills is the first score obtained by the ASVAB-CEP. Respondents' Verbal Skills score indicates their vocabulary and reading skills. Respondents' Verbal Skills score is a combination of their scores on the WK and PC subtests of the ASVAB. Higher scores on Verbal Skills reflects individuals' who can perform successfully on assignments that require adequate vocabulary and reading skills (ASVAB, 2012b).

Math Skills is the second score. This score indicates a person's mathematical capacities. Students' math capabilities are combination of their scores on both the AR and the MK subtests of the ASVAB. Respondents with higher scores tend to accomplish successfully tasks that require knowledge in the field of math (ASVAB, 2012b).

The third score, Science and Technical Skills, is a measure of science and technical related skills. This composite scale is a combination of students' scores on three different subtests of the ASVAB. The three subtests are: GS, EI, and MC. Candidates with higher scores have a strong tendency to perform well on tasks that require scientific thinking or technical skills (ASVAB, 2012b).

The fourth score is Spatial Skills which assesses respondents' abilities to conclude the way an object may look after all parts are being collected. This is the only non-composite score, meaning that a participant's Spatial Skills score is obtained only from calculating the score on the AO subtest. Respondents' with higher scores have more understanding of basic construction concepts and principles.

The military uses the Military Entrance score, or AFQT, which is the fifth score, to identify the specific military career fields for a respondent. Respondents' scores on four subtests: AR, MK, PC, and WK combine to create the AFQT.

The ASVAB summary results Sheet, available to both students and counselors, contains a display of respondents' scores on all eight subtests and four composite scores (ASVAB, 2012b).

Scores are usually reported as standard scores and percentile ranks. The standard scores, range from 30 to 70, are displayed using gray bands. Standard scores indicate a student's performance in contrast to the average scores of other students who took the test. In addition to standard scores, the report contains three percentile ranks that indicate a student's level of performance in comparison to all students in the same grade level, students from the same sex within the same grade level, and students from the opposite sex among the same grade level.

The Find Your Interests (FYI) inventory is the second component of the ASVAB-CP. The FYI is an instrument used to assess individuals' interests. The FYI was developed based on Career Choice Theory (Holland, 1985). In Career Choice Theory, Holland (1985) presented six types of interest known as the six RIASEC interest codes, [i.e., Realistic (R), Investigative (I), Artistic (A), Social (S), Enterprising (E), and Conventional (C)]. Respondents' answers on the FYI generate six RIASEC scores that correspond to the different types of interests' codes proposed by Holland. The FYI includes 90 items on both the printed copy and electronic forms. Completing and scoring the FYI printed copy takes approximately in 15 minutes; however, students who use the electronic version are able to see their scores immediately after completing the instrument. Each item on the FYI represents a specific activity. Using a three-point–scale, respondents' answer each item indicating their preference (like, indifferent, and dislike) for the individual activity. In scoring the FYI, items students answer with a *Like* receive the highest score (2), whereas, items answered with a *Dislike* receive the lowest score (0). An *Indifferent* response receives a score of (1). Raw scores on the FYI range from 0 to 30. Higher scores on the instrument reflect higher interest in a specific activity or occupation domain.

The third component of the ASVAB-CEP is the OCCU-Find. The OCCU-Find, provided electronically only, is a unique tool that assists individuals in exploring their career choices. The OCCU-Find allows students to view occupational videos and participate in interactive exploration experiences. The OCCU-Find provides a list of approximately 500 occupational titles, from the O*NET taxonomy, which are organized in a way that correspond to the six interest codes postulated by Holland (1985). Thus, after students identify their top career interest codes obtained from their scores on the FYI, they can use the OCCU-Find to explore the occupations that correspond to their interest codes. Additionally, the OCCU-Find equips students with information concerning the characteristics of workers in each occupation, as well as the skills necessary for performing the duties of each career. Thus, using the OCCU-Find, students can find careers that match their interests, skills, and work values.

Technical Considerations

The ASVAB is one of the most developed career exploration aptitude assessments in the world (Baker 2002). The ASVAB Forms 23 and 24 are the two forms administered currently to high school and post-secondary students. Because there are different forms of the ASVAB, ensuring consistency in score interpretations is essential regardless of the form used. Therefore, the developers of the ASVAB equated the results obtained from the current forms with earlier versions of the ASVAB, thus, indicating that consistency in results interpretation is valid.

After obtaining a student's scores on the ASVAB test, the student can compare performance on the tests to a national representative sample. The Defense Manpower Data Center conducted the most updated national norming for the ASVAB in 2004. The Defense Manpower Data Center used data that was collected from youths who participated in the Profile of American Youth Project in 1997 (PAY97). Specifically, two samples of American youths were included in the (PAY97). Participants in the first sample included 6,000 participants between the ages of 18 to 23. To ensure adequate representation of participants from diverse ethnic backgrounds, the developers of the ASVAB oversampled Hispanics and Non-Hispanic black participants. The second national sample that was used comprised of high school students (10th, 11th, and 12th grades). A total of 4,700 high school students were included in this sample. Both samples were obtained based on clustered random sampling procedures to ensure general representation of the U.S. youth population (Sims & Hiatt, 2004).

Grounded in the principles of item response theory, several researchers (Avila, Boccanfuso, & Metcalfe, 2011; Ree & Wegner, 1990; Talboy, 2011) conducted studies to measure the reliability of the ASVAB. Research findings indicated good reliability coefficients of the ASVAB. Researchers conducted the reliabilities estimates using Cronbach Alpha coefficients. The findings indicated the reliability estimates for the eight subtests ranged from .69 to .88, whereas, the reliability coefficients for the three composite scores ranged from .88 to .91. Researchers presented reliability coefficients for both male and female students between grades 10th-12th.

Because use of the ASVAB is mainly for military screening and recruiting purposes, research findings indicated that the ASVAB is a valid predictor of individuals' level of success as future military personnel (Carey, 1994; Earles & Ree, 1992; Sperl, Ree, & Steuck, 1992; Welsh, Kucinkas, & Curran, 1990). Although an additional use of the ASVAB is to assist students' exploration of civilian occupations, few researchers examined the validity of the ASVAB outside the military sector. Holmgren and Dalldorf (1993) tested the validity of scores obtained by the ASVAB in determining participants' success in 11 civilian occupations. They found significant correlations between the ASVAB composite scores and individuals' measure of success with a total of eight occupations. Due to the lack of comprehensive findings on the validity of the ASVAB in predicting individuals' success in civilian occupations, practitioners need to use caution when using the ASVAB as a sole instrument for predicting individuals' success in non-military occupations. Therefore, career counselors should use scores obtained from the ASVAB-CEP as a holistic approach, rather than relying solely on the ASVAB test, for assisting students in exploring the world of work and planning for future careers, especially for individuals interested in occupations outside the military sector.

The other testing instrument included in the ASVAB-CEP is the FYI inventory. The development of the FYI took place in three phases. In the first phase, the focus was on developing items that would assess the construct of the RIASEC domains. Developers created more than 1,000 items. A panel of experts reviewed the items and selected 515 items. In the second phase, developers administered the 515 items to more than 5,000 high school students. Afterwards, the developers tested the psychometric qualities of the items and selected 120 items to administer to a second national group of high school students (N =1,958). The gender distribution of the participants in the second national sample was approximately equal. Additionally, the second sample comprised an adequate representation of students from diverse ethnic backgrounds. Developers analyzed the responses on the 120 items to identify the best 90 items that they included in the final form of the FYI.

The psychometric qualities of the FYI are very promising. All six domains of the FYI have exceptional reliability alpha coefficients, with .92 for both the A & E domains and .94 for the R, I, S, & C domains. Furthermore, the developers measured the stability of scores obtained from the FYI using test-retest procedures on two occasions over a two to two-and-a half week period. Findings ranged from .89 to .93.

Based on examination of the item and scale relationship, developers found the FYI had an adequate goodness of fit. Additionally, examination of the item-level, using factor analysis procedures, supported the six domains structure of the FYI, with each factor distinguishing the corresponding RIASEC domain. Furthermore, the FYI findings exhibited a hexagonal shape and structure similar to the one obtained from different interest inventories developed according to Holland's model. Finally, results indicated positive and significant relationships between students' scores on the FYI domains and their scores on the 1994 version of the Strong Interest Inventory (SII; Harmon, Hansen, Borgen, & Hammer, 1994). Thus, the FYI is a valid indicator for measuring high school students' interests.

Use/Interpretation/Evaluation

The ASVAB-CEP materials are easy to read and designed thoughtfully. The accompanying user manual provides adequate information concerning the content of the tests, reliability, validity, and test administration and interpretation procedures. The program provides a wealth of strengths to both the administrator and the test taker. School counselors can use the program to help students understand their strengths and career interests. The program provides insight to help school counselors as they direct students to select courses that might increase their knowledge in relation to their career preferences. Additionally, school counselors can use the activities provided by the program to engage students in experiences that enhance their skills and nurture their readiness for post-secondary education and future occupations. With the results obtained from the ASVAB-CEP, counselors can aid students in taking more ownership of their development and use the results as a navigation tool in post-graduation decision-making. In addition, the program provides comprehensive electronic tools that school counselors and students can use via the program's website. The website provides graphs and illustrations that are appealing and easy to follow for both students and school counselors.

Students can obtain their scores for the ASVAB via the ASVAB's Summary Results Sheet. The result sheet, available to school counselors, includes score bands for all eight subtests. Additionally, this report provides students and counselors with four percentiles, the first three concerning career exploration and the fourth one representing military entrance requirements. An important benefit of using the ASVAB's summary result sheet is providing each participant with score bands and percentiles that he or she can compare to a national norm. Students can compare their scores to their peers based on both grade level (10th, 11th, and 12th) and gender. Additionally, participants can compare their band scores and percentiles to an overall aggregated national score. For the FYI, students can choose to take the test electronically, which concludes with immediate results, or use the paper-and-pencil version. Both the paper and the electronic version of the FYI provide students with a detailed RIASEC profile that is very beneficial for career-exploration.

The ASVAB-CEP is an exceptional method that school counselors can use when providing career counseling to students. In addition, the ASVAB-CEP provides a pathway to exploration for career interests and the world of work. Developers and researchers found that the program had good reliability and validity coefficients. The program includes a manual that provides school counselors with sufficient information about the instruments, as well as the procedure of administering the instruments. Finally, the manual includes scores based on national samples to help students understand more about their performance on the test.

Despite gender and cultural concerns regarding previous forms of the ASVAB and FYI, developers administered the current forms to large national samples that included high school students from diverse cultural backgrounds. Additionally, developers improved female representation in the current sample significantly. The statistical procedures researchers followed to develop the ASVAB-CEP led to the selection of items that minimized bias based on the student's gender or ethnic background (U.S. Military Entrance Processing Command, 2005).

In conclusion, the ASVAB-CEP is a state of the art instrument in terms of career aptitude and interests. The military uses the program widely to recruit and screen for prospective successful military personnel. Additionally, activities included in the ASVAB-CEP allow enormous opportunities for student engagement in exercises aimed at enhancing a student's self-knowledge, exploration of the world of work, and understanding the skills and cognitive capacities required for each occupation. Thus, using the ASVAB-CEP contributes to promoting students' ability to find future occupations that match their skills and values, which is the heart of effective career decision-making process.

Research and Evaluation/Assessment Uses

Career and school counselors can use the ASVAB-CEP either as an instructive strategy to promote students' career development or as an intervention with students who struggle with career uncertainty. Career counselors focus on assisting students' career development by providing them with opportunities to learn more about themselves, explore the world of work, and make career decisions based on understanding the self, personal motivations, and aptitude. School counselors can use the ASVAB to facilitate students' career development, career decision-making process, and career transition. The ASVAB-CEP is a comprehensive program suitable for administering to high school students and postsecondary students to help them make effective decisions by providing inventories and career exploration activities to enhance both professional and self-discovery. Once students enroll in

10th grade, school counselors might administer the test on students on multiple occasions. The multiple use of the ASVAB-CEP allows school counselors to track and nurture students' career development. Furthermore, using the ASVAB-CEP assists school counselors in preparing high school students as they transition to post-secondary education. In addition, career counselors can use the ASVAB-CEP as an intervention with students who experience career indecisiveness. One of the most prominent contributing elements to career indecisiveness is the lack of knowledge about the self and the unawareness of the variety of occupational opportunities that exist. This makes matching their interest to future career options nearly impossible. Due to the flexible nature of the ASVAB-CEP, career counselors might use the program as a sole career counseling tool or in combination with other career counseling interventions to assist clients who experience career uncertainty. In summary, school counselors can use the ASVAB-CEP to track the career development of high school students, assist them as they transition to post-secondary education, and intervene when they have difficulties making a career decision.

References

ASVAB. (2012a). *Career Exploration Program: Counselor guide: Empower you students.* Retrieved from https://www.asvabprogram.com/pdf/ASVAB_CEP_Counselor_Manual.pdf

ASVAB. (2012b). *Career Exploration Program: Technical summary.* Retrieved from https://www.asvabprogram.com/pdf/ASVAB_CEP_Technical_Chapter.pdf

Avila, R., Boccanfuso, V., & Metcalfe, S. (2011). *The Armed Services Vocation Aptitude Battery.* Retrieved from: http://www.drmillslmu.com/Testing/SPR2000/asvab.htm

Baker, H. E. (2002). Reducing adolescent career indecision: The ASVAB career exploration program. *Career Development Quarterly, 50,* 359-370.

Carey, N. B. (1994). Computer predictors of mechanical job performance: Marine corps findings. *Military Psychology, 6,* 1-30.

Earles, J. A., & Ree, M. J. (1992). The predictive validity of the ASVAB for training grades. *Educational and Psychological Measurement, 52,* 721-725.

Harmon, L.W., Hansen, J. C., Borgen, F. H., & Hammer, A. L. (1994). *Strong Interest Inventory: Applications and technical guide.* Palo Alto, CA: Consulting Psychologists Press.

Holland, J. L. (1985). *Making vocational choices: A theory of vocational personalities and work environments* (2nd ed.). Englewood Cliffs, NJ: Prentice-Hall.

Holmgren, R. L., & Dalldorf, M. R. (1993). *A validation of the ASVAB against supervisors' ratings in the General Aptitude Test Battery (GATB).* Washington, DC: United States Employment Service.

Ree, M. J., & Wegner, T. G. (1990). Correcting differences in answer sheets for the 1980 armed services vocational aptitude battery reference population. *Military Psychology 2*, 157-169.

Sims, W. H., & Hiatt, C. M. (2004). *Description of student testing program norms.* Alexandria, VA: CAN Corporation.

Sperl, T. C., Ree, M. J., & Steuck, K. W. (1992). Armed Services Vocational Aptitude Battery and Air Force Officer Qualifying Test: Analyses of common attributes. *Military Psychology, 4*, 175-188

Talboy, A. (2011). A brief evaluation of the Armed Services Vocational Aptitude Battery (ASVAB). *Journal of Young Investigators, 22*, 81-84.

U.S. Military Entrance Processing Command. (2005). *ASVAB career exploration program counselor manual* (DD Form 1304-SCM). North Chicago, IL: Author.

Welsh, J. R., Kucinkas, S. K., & Curran, L. T. (1990). Armed Services Vocational Aptitude Battery (ASVAB): Integrative review of validity studies (AFHRL-TR-90-22). Brooks Air Force Base, TX: Air Force Human Resources Laboratory.

CALIFORNIA PSYCHOLOGICAL INVENTORY

Instrument Acronym or Preferred Short Name: CPI 260

Instrument Author: Harrison G. Gough

Publisher: The Myers-Briggs Company

Publisher Address: 185 North Wolfe Road Sunnyvale, CA 94086
www.themyersbriggs.com

Statement of Purpose: The California Psychological Inventory (CPI 260) assessment is a powerful tool for helping individuals improve their performance. Using a sophisticated technique to extract detailed personality insights, they summarize and explain how other people see a person and judge his or her leadership style. The CPI 260 assessment enables organizations to find and develop high-potential employees, making it an essential tool for your investment in employee training and development. The CPI assessment helps people gain a clearer picture of their personal and work-related characteristics, motivations, and thinking style. They use an empirical measure, comparing an individual's responses to data on 5,600 managers and executives who participated in the Leadership Development Program at the Center for Creative Leadership (CCL). The CPI assessments indicate which of four different ways of living, or lifestyles, best describe the respondent. They offer a unique perspective on how people manage themselves and deal with others, indicating strengths and developmental opportunities.

Target Population: Anyone over the age of 13.

Norm Group(s) on which Scores are Based: The primary norm group for the CPI 260 (on which standard scores are based) consists of a U.S. national sample of 3,000 males and 3,000 females. The Coaching Report for Leaders utilizes a norm group of 5,610 Executives and Managers from the Leadership Development Program offered at the Center for Creative Leadership. Additional norms reflecting the U.S. workforce and its component industries are available from CPP.

Titles of Subtests, Scales, Scores Provided: The CPI 260 contains a total of 29 scales, categorized as follows: Client Feedback Report: Dealing with Others: 1.Dominance 2.Capacity for Status 3.Sociability 4.Social Presence 5.Self-Acceptance 6.Independence 7.Empathy; Self-Management 1.Responsibility 2.Social Conformity 3.Self-Control 4.Good Impression 5.Communality 6.Well-Being 7.Tolerance; Motivations and Thinking Style: 1.Achievement via Conformance 2.Achievement via Independence 3.Conceptual Fluency; Personal Characteristics: 1.Insightfulness 2.Flexibility 3.Sensitivity; Work-Related Measures: 1.Managerial Potential 2.Work Orientation 3.Creative

Temperament 4.Leadership 5.Amicability 6.Law Enforcement Orientation; Higher-Order Measures: 1.Vector 1 (Orientation Toward Others) 2.Vector 2 (Orientation Toward Societal Values) 3.Vector 3 (Orientation Toward Self). Scores Provided: Scores are reported on a T-scale. That is, they are presented as standard scores based on a mean (normative) score of 50 and standard deviation of 10. Coaching Report for Leaders The Coaching Report for Leaders utilizes the same scales indicated above, but combines them into 18 Competencies. This is a narrative report that also offers three categorizations of scores. One designation indicates that the client is typical to other executives or managers for that competency. A second designation indicates that the client may need to develop that particular competency, and a third designation indicates that a client may or may not need to focus developmental attention on that competency (e.g., it may be a strength in some cases and a weakness in others). The competencies contained in the Coaching Report for Leaders include: 1.Self-Awareness 2.Self-Control 3.Resilience 4.Use of Power and Authority 5.Comfort with Organizational Structures 6.Responsibility and Accountability 7.Decisiveness 8.Interpersonal Skill 9.Understanding Others 10.Capacity for Collaboration 11.Working with and Through Others 12.Creativity 13.Handling Sensitive Problems 14.Action Orientation 15.Self-Confidence 16.Managing Change 17.Influence 18.Comfort with Visibility The CPI 260 also contains a Configural Analysis Report which presents narrative descriptions based on scores on combinations of various scales.

Forms and Levels Available with Dates of Publication/Revision of Each: The original version of the assessment was published in 1954 and has undergone several revisions throughout its history. The CPI 260 was published in 2002.

Date of Most Recent Edition of Manual, User's Guide, etc.: 2005

Available in which Languages: English Only

Actual Test Time: 45 minutes

Total Administration Time: 60-90 minutes

Required Level of Training and/or Credentials for Administrator: CPI Certification or masters or doctoral degree in psychology or a related field and/or hold a specific state license or national or state certification (in the United States only). For a full list, go to https://www.themyersbriggs.com/en-US/Support/Educational-Eligibility.

Types of Scores: The client feedback report provides T scores (e.g., standardized scores). The Coaching Report for Leaders provides narrative feedback as well as a visual marker indicating a strength, developmental opportunity, or a competency that may serve as either, depending on context.

Report Format/Content: CPI 260 Client Feedback Report provides a detailed profile of their scores and descriptive information in a graphic format. Provides results on three vector scales assessing three basic orientations:

toward others, toward societal values, and toward self. Indicates how clients perceive their placement in one of the four lifestyles displayed in a grid/quadrant diagram. Includes an additional page solely for the administrator that plots clients' raw scores to clearly indicate their particular lifestyle (does not print out on the client's report). CPI 260 Coaching Report for Leaders: This highly intuitive 17-page report enables your clients to identify their strengths and blind spots and capitalize on the strengths, target areas for development, and plan action steps to increase their leadership effectiveness. (Note: While scales and scores drive the narrative, they are not presented in this report.) Can be used in combination with the CPI 260 Client Feedback Report or as a stand-alone solution CPI 260 Configural Report: This advanced interpretive report builds on the CPI 260 Client Feedback Report by providing helpful and deeper insights into a client's personality. This lengthy report provides screening of the client's results, classification for CPI type and level, client's CPI 260 profile, interpretive comments on the folk scales and additional work-related measures, analysis of the meaning of select configurations of scores, and highly individualized description based on the Interpersonal Q-sort (IQS). The configurations and Q-sorts are totally unique to this report. The Scale Configuration section combines designated scales into configurations and then states the percentages of the basic norm sample manifesting this combination, followed by adjectival descriptions of men and women in whose CPI profiles these configurations appear. The CPI 260 Configural Report is intended for use by psychologists and others qualified to administer and interpret multivariate instruments, and who have knowledge of basic psychometrics, supervised experience in the interpretation of personality assessment data, and familiarity with major sources of information on the CPI instrument. It is not meant to be shared with clients, and the gender of the client is required to generate the report.

Report Format/Content for Group Summaries: Our general practice is to not encourage group summaries of CPI scores considering that the instrument provides potentially sensitive (and possibly negative) personal information. Nonetheless, we have created customized group reports for specific clients using scores from the Client Feedback Report and Designations from the Coaching Report for Leaders.

Availability of Machine Scoring Service? No

Availability of Hand Scoring? No

Availability of Local Machine Scoring Service? No

Availability and Options for Computer Software? Computer Software Available, Computerized adaptive administration

If available, describe the ways in which computer/online version differs (if any): (information not provided by publisher)

Link to webpage that specifies the costs of materials: https://www.cpp.com/en-US/Products-and-Services/Popular-Products#CPI https://www.cpp.com/en-US/Products-and-Services/Sample-Reports#cpi

Additional Comments of Interest to Users (e.g. forthcoming revisions, new material, etc): While occupationally specific norm groups have not been incorporated directly into CPI 260 reports, such data is available from Research upon request.

Published Reviews of the Instrument in the Last 15 years: Dean, G. J & Freeman, S. J. (2010). Test review of the CPI 260. In Spies, R. A., Carlson, J. F., & Geisinger, K. F. (Eds.), *The eighteenth mental measurements yearbook* [electronic version]. Retrieved from the Burros Institute's Mental Measurements Yearbook online database.

CALIFORNIA PSYCHOLOGICAL INVENTORY

Reviewed by
Rebekah Reysen
University of Mississippi

Introduction

The California Psychological Inventory (CPI) provides valuable insight into how leadership style can influence the workplace. Drawing from research on personality theory, those who take the CPI will learn more about their key attributes, drives, motivations, values, and thought processes, as well as how others might view these characteristics (Gough & Bradley, 2005). The first version of the CPI was released in 1954 and contained 548 items. After several iterations, this assessment now has 260 items and is known as the CPI 260 (Gough, 1957, 1987; Gough & Bradley, 1996/2002, 2005). A significant portion of the previous versions of the CPI were derived from several other well-known psychological assessments, including the Minnesota Multiphasic Personality Inventory versions I and II (Butcher, Dahlstrom, Graham, Tellegan, & Kaemmer, 1989; Hathaway & McKinley, 1943).

The CPI 260 is a self-reporting tool that assesses everyday folk concepts, or "concepts that arise from and are linked to the processes of interpersonal life, and that are to be found everywhere that humans congregate into groups and establish societal functions" (Gough & Bradley, 1996/2002, p. 1). Self-directedness, flexibility, dominance, and amiability are just a few examples of folk concepts. Assessing such concepts is ideal because they are universal to many different social realms and continue to be referenced from generation to generation (Gough & Bradley, 1996/2002, 2005).

Two reports are accessible to those who take the CPI 260. The first is the CPI 260 *Coaching Report for Leaders*, which provides information on leadership type, as well as the strengths and weaknesses of each type. The interpretive report corresponds to the user's guide published by Manoogian (2005). The second report is the CPI 260 *Client Feedback Report*, with corresponding manual by Devine (2005). These guides provide valuable information that is helpful for assessment interpretation. To be able to administer and interpret the CPI, the practitioner must have at least a master's or doctorate in psychology or a related field, as well as hold the appropriate state certification. Case studies are helpful in putting CPI interpretations into context, and resources such as Meyer and Davis' (1992) book on use of the CPI in Industrial-Organizational contexts, as well as Craig's (1999) and Groth-Marnat's (1996) texts serve as valuable supplemental guides.

Subscales

The CPI 260 includes 260 true/false statements, whereby participants categorize whether they agree or disagree with each statement presented. The instrument contains 29 subscales, including three structural scales, six used for special purposes, and 20 folk concept scales (CPP, 2002; Gough & Bradley, 2005).

The folk concept scales contain four categories or classes. The first category was constructed to measure interpersonal characteristics like self-assurance and influence. This scale is known as *Dealing with Others* and includes subscales of *Capacity for Status, Sociability, Social Presence, Self-Acceptance, Independence,* and *Empathy*. The second category, known as *Self-Management*, displays values related to social norms, such as taking responsibility and self-discipline. Subscales in this category include *Responsibility, Social Conformity, Self-control, Good Impression, Communality, Well-being,* and *Tolerance*. The third classification, known as *Motivations and Thinking Style* reports an individual's orderliness and grit. This scale includes subscales of *Achievement via Conformance, Achievement via Independence, and Conceptual Fluency*. The final folk class, known as the *Personal Characteristics* scale, assesses constructs such as perceptiveness and empathy and includes subscales of *Insightfulness, Flexibility, and Sensitivity* (CPP, 2002; Gough & Bradley, 2005).

Next, three scales form the cuboid model foundation of the CPI. These scales include Vector 1, *Orientation Towards Others*, Vector 2, *Orientation Towards*

Societal Values, and Vector 3, *Orientation Towards Self* (CPP, 2002; Gough & Bradley, 2005). Gough and Bradley report that cut scores were established at the middle of both vectors 1 and 2, creating four separate categories of personality. Participants fall into one of these four personality types based on their vector score, with types including the *Visualizer* (Delta), *Supporter* (Beta), *Innovator* (Gamma), and *Implementer* (Delta).

Last, several purpose scales are included in the assessment in order to evaluate constructs that might be helpful for investigating: *Managerial Potential, Work Orientation, Creative Temperament, Leadership, Amicability,* and *Law Enforcement Orientation* (CPP, 2002; Gough & Bradley, 2005).

Report Results - Managerial Style

Each CPI 260 report contains a description of the participant's dominant managerial style. Essentially, this style is the way in which people engage in the workplace and is based on their values, desires, the types of initiatives for which they advocate, how others might perceive them, and how they tend to respond to being alerted to or discovering their mistakes (Gough & Bradley, 2005).

Alpha personalities are the *Implementer Managers* in that they are goal-directed and skillful in planning. They prefer solving problems by taking a step back to view the big picture of the given issue instead of focusing only on minutiae. Alphas make goals clear to their colleagues and supervisees and place importance on accountability in the workplace with their preference for adhering to social rules and norms. On their best days, Alphas can be inspiring, take-charge leaders; on their worst days, their Machiavellian nature can prove to be contentious, forceful, aggressive, and unsavory (Gough & Bradley, 2005).

Beta managers are the *Supporter Managers* because they are strong leaders whom others view as genuine, peaceful, composed, and supportive of others. They are very private individuals and will rarely show their vulnerability by disclosing personal feelings. Other strengths include their ability to cultivate a harmonious workplace, adhere to social rules and axioms, and exemplify a strong moral compass. Beta's major areas for growth, however, include struggles with low self-esteem and not being outspoken enough for others to pay attention to their ideas (Gough & Bradley, 2005).

Gammas are *Innovator* managerial types because they are ingenious, inventive, creative, like to think "outside the box," and view progress as key, whether that follows the status quo or not. They enjoy assuming new projects but can get overwhelmed by taking on too many. Gammas are not fond of organizational "red-tape," and they derive their energy from spending time with others. Significant areas of growth for Gammas would be recognizing and considering their tendency to be stubborn, as well as their obstreperous and overbearing personalities (Gough & Bradley, 2005).

Last but not least, Deltas are the *Visualizer* managers who are usually contemplative, sensitive, and creative individuals. They are introverted leaders who enjoy working either by themselves or in small groups, and they tend not to seek the limelight in their leadership role. They appreciate diversity, which can be helpful for developing new approaches and projects. Two significant weaknesses of this type, however, are the tendency to be unrealistic in their pursuits and being less willing to share key information with others (Gough & Bradley, 2005).

Technical Considerations

The CPI, in its various forms, has undergone 40 different translations, minimally, and has been cited over 2,000 times (Gough & Bradley, 2005). The multiple revisions conducted on the CPI have retained specific key items yet make the process easier for participants to complete due to reduced test time. Each of the scales on the most recent version can be rated on both the original (Gough, 1957) and the 462-item assessments (Gough, 1987), although four of the original scales were renamed for the CPI 260 (Gough & Bradley, 2005).

The CPI 260 scales are strongly correlated with the CPI 434 instrument, with medians equaling .95 for women, men, and total overall samples (Gough & Bradley, 1996/2002, 2005). Because of this high degree of correlation, practitioners can interpret scores with confidence on the CPI 260 instrument based on normative data acquired from the CPI 434 (Gough & Bradley, 2005). Practitioners can use the CPI 260 Manual (Gough & Bradley, 2005) to interpret the CPI 260, because it contains both reliability and validity data taken from the previous manual on the CPI 434 by Gough and Bradley (1996/2002).

In their various CPI Manuals, Gough and Bradley (1996/2002, 2005) discuss the research that was conducted on the CPI 260 and 434. In one study for example, Gough and Bradley (1996/2002) report a poll of 6,000 individuals (50% male and 50% female), with individuals representing all walks of life and ranging from full-time employees to students. Reliability scores fell within a range from .36 (Law Enforcement Orientation) to .86 (Dominance), and .72 was the average reliability score for all the scales.

Oxford Psychologists Press (Cook, McHenry, & Leigh, 1998) conducted additional testing using the CPI 434 on samples from the United Kingdom (n=2001), while Gough (1987) discusses the additional testing that was done in France (n=1,424) and in Italy (n=1,362) (Gough, 1959) using the CPI 480. Considering each of these three samples, along with the United States sample of 6,000 individuals (Gough & Bradley, 1996/2002), median internal consistency coefficients ranged from .70-.76, with individual scales ranging from .39-.87 (Gough & Bradley, 1996/2002, 2005).

Helson began a study of personality over the lifespan in 1958, and continued to study this construct over the course of several decades (Helson, Jones, & Kwan, 2002; Helson, Stewart, & Ostrove, 1995). She and her colleagues calculated five-year test-retest reliability statistics for women ($n=91$) as part of their investigation. After an initial testing of participants in their senior year of high school, Helson conducted a second administration five years later and found a .58 median test-retest correlation (as cited in Gough & Bradley, 1996/2002, 2005).

In a separate study, researchers at the University of California at Berkeley conducted testing of participants ($n=460$) when they were in their 30s and, then, a second time ten years later when they were in their 40s. Median scores for test-retest reliability were .77 overall, with men scoring slightly higher than women (Eichorn, Clausen, Haan, Honzik, & Mussen, 1981; Gough & Bradley, 1996/2002, 2005). Each of these seminal studies indicate that the CPI 260, and its predecessors, demonstrate strong reliable evidence of managerial style.

In addition to its high reliability evidence, Gough and Bradley (2005) conceptualized the CPI 260 to control for four kinds of validity, including issues pertaining to when participants: a) leave items blank or do not answer all assessment items; b) attempt to look meritorious (known as the "fake-good" effect); c) answer in a manner that emphasizes negative qualities (known as the "fake-bad" effect); and d) complete questions randomly due to either poor reading skills, mistakes in marking the appropriate answer, or refusing to be honest. When individuals complete the CPI and receive their results in the CPI 260 Client Feedback Report, the report indicates whether responses fall into any of those categories. If that is the case, practitioners can discuss the influence on respondent scores, and in some cases, practitioners might advise clients to take the assessment a second time (Gough & Bradley, 2005).

To establish convergent and divergent validity, Gough and Bradley (2005) reported that researchers demonstrated significant correlations between the CPI 260 scales and scales from other well-known psychological inventories, such as the NEO-AC inventory (Costa & McCrae, 1992), Barron-Welsh Art Scale (Barron & Welsh, 1952), Fundamental Interpersonal Relations Orientation-Behavior inventory (FIRO-B; Schutz, 1958), and Holland's occupational theme scales derived from the Strong Interest Inventory (Harmon, Hansen, Borgen, & Hammer, 1994)

Additionally, CPI subscales have been shown to have strong predictive validity. For example, a wide variety of researchers found that CPI scores can predict academic performance successfully (Gough & Lanning, 1986; Rosenberg, McHenry, Rosenberg, & Nichols, 1962), as well as leadership performance in specific occupations (Blake, Potter, & Slimak, 1993).

Use/Interpretation/Evaluation

There are a variety of reasons why practitioners utilize the CPI 260 for career development purposes. First, the strength of the CPI 260 lies in its ability to help clients, and the professionals who assist them, with identifying their leadership style and with exploring potential reasons why their work performance is either working well or failing to work as effectively as it could. Learning how personality contributes to work, the work environment, and ultimately, work performance, can be motivating for clients. The CPI 260 highlights client's strengths and areas for development, thus, helping clients to strategize ways to develop and enhance their personal style.

Next, the CPI 260 results can help managers recruit strong employees by understanding which candidates are most qualified to meet the needs of the organization. Does a given organization need an employee that is a take-charge, big picture type, like the Alpha? Or, would the company benefit more from having additional employees who are low-key and take a behind-the-scenes approach, like the Beta? Furthermore, discussing each lifestyle might be helpful during team building exercises, where participants can discuss both strengths and areas for growth for the various types within the team.

The instrument is efficient in that completion takes only 45 minutes, and users can access the assessment online from any location with internet access. The CPI 260 is a valuable tool not only for adults, but also for teens or anyone seeking to know more about their leadership style. With the true/false item presentation, respondents can categorize their thoughts and values easily with each test item.

The *Client Feedback Report* is an easy document to navigate and makes interpretation of each scale straightforward to the reader. As questions arise, practitioners can access manuals, such as the CPI 260 Manual (Gough & Bradley, 2005). This manual provides a thorough overview of the instrument in areas such as its history, development, normative data, and reliability and validity measures, yet unlike the Gough and Bradley (1996/2002) 400 plus page manual, is concise enough in its 85 pages so as not to be too overwhelming for the interpreter.

Practitioners must place importance in considering the cultural implications of using this instrument. Developers and researchers have created CPI manuals for various populations and translated them into a number of languages, including German (Weinert, 1998), Mandarin Chinese (Yang & Gong, 1993), Romanian (Pitariu, 1995), Spanish (Gough & Seisdedos, 1992), and Russian (Tarabrina & Grafinina, 1998). However, research is needed using different cultural samples, especially Hispanic/Latino and Asian samples. Given that Gough and Bradley

(2005) acquired much of the normative data using White/Caucasian participants, conducting future research that includes diverse populations (Gough & Bradley, 2005) seems prudent.

Research and Evaluation/Assessment Uses

Researchers and practitioners would be wise to consider utilizing this instrument to evaluate client career development and choice. Test scores from the CPI 260 can help clients navigate the next steps of their career development in a variety of ways. If they are unsure about which career path to take, their scores might help them achieve a greater understanding as to how their personality type might be satisfied most in specific occupations or roles. For example, if a client scores as a highly introverted Beta, she or he might want to consider positions where the supervisor values autonomy. Likewise, supervisors might want to consider using this assessment to provide workers with a greater understanding as to why some employees behave the way that they do in the workplace, based on their unique personality. Having a solid understanding of employees can help pave the way for open lines of communication and expectations.

Finally, researchers can expand upon previous studies by exploring further as to how administrators of the CPI 260 can use the results to predict outcomes and behaviors of students, employees, and supervisors, and for diverse populations. One potential avenue for exploration could be predicting academic success for various generations of students (e.g., Generation Z, adult learners) or for those of specialized populations (e.g., first generation students, honors students, those with disabilities). Fortunately, there are still many opportunities available to exploring the CPI 260 and its utility further.

References

Barron, F., & Welsh, G. S. (1952). Artistic perception as a factor in personality style and its measurement by a figure-preference test. *Journal of Psychology, 33,* 193-203.

Blake, R. J., Potter, E. H., & Slimak, R. E. (1993). *Journal of Business Psychology, 7,* 431-448.

Butcher, J. N., Dahlstrom, W. G., Graham, J. R., Tellegan, A., & Kaemmer, B. (1989). *Manual for the restandardized Minnesota Multiphasic Personality Inventory: MMPI-2. An administrative and interpretive guide.* Minneapolis, MN: University of Minnesota Press.

Consulting Psychologists Press (CPP). (2002, February). *Technical brief for the CPI 260 instrument.* Retrieved from https://shop.themyersbriggs.com/Pdfs/CPI260_Technical_Brief.pdf

Cook, M., McHenry, R., & Leigh, V. (1998). The decision to retrain: A serendipitous finding. *Oxford Psychometric Forum* (pp. 1-9). Oxford: Oxford Psychologists Press.

Costa, P. T., Jr., & McCrae, R. R. (1992). *The revised NEO Personality Inventory (NEO-PI-R) and NEO Five Factor Inventory.* Odessa, FL: Psychological Assessment Resources.

Craig, R. J. (1999). *Interpreting personality tests: A clinical manual for the MMPI-2, MCMI-III, CPI-R, and 16PF.* New York: John Wiley & Sons.

Devine, R. (2005). *CPI 260 Client Feedback Report guide for interpretation: Strategies for use in business and organizations.* Sunnyvale, CA: CPP.

Eichorn, D. H., Clausen, J. A., Haan, N., Honzik, M. P., & Mussen, P. H. (1981). *Present and past in middle life.* New York: Academic Press.

Gough, H. G. (1957). *Manual for the California Psychological Inventory.* Sunnyvale, CA: CPP.

Gough, H. G. (1959). *California Psychological Inventory manuale.* [California Psychological Inventory Manual]. Firenze, Italy: Edizioni Organizzazioni Speciali.

Gough, H. G. (1987). *California Psychological Inventory administrator's guide.* Sunnyvale, CA: CPP.

Gough, H. G., & Bradley, P. (1996/2002). *CPI manual* (3rd ed.). Sunnyvale, CA: CPP.

Gough, H. G., & Bradley, P. (2005). *CPI 260 manual.* Mountain View, CA: CPP.

Gough, H. G., & Lanning, K. (1986). Predicting grades in college from the California Psychological Inventory. *Educational and Psychological Measurement 46*(1), 205-213. doi: 10.1177/0013164486461024

Gough, H. G., & Seisdedos, N. (1992). *CPI: Inventario Psicologico de California* [CPI: California Psychological Inventory]. Madrid, Spain: TEA Ediciones, S. A.

Groth-Marnat, G. (1996). *Handbook of psychological assessment* (3rd ed.). New York: John Wiley & Sons.

Harmon, L. W., Hansen, J. C., Borgen, F. H., & Hammer, A. L. (1994). *Strong Interest Inventory applications and technical guide.* Sunnyvale, CA: CPP.

Hathaway, S. R., & McKinley, J. C. (1943). *Minnesota Multiphasic Personality Inventory.* Minneapolis, MN: University of Minnesota Press.

Helson, R., Jones, C., & Kwan, V. S. Y. (2002). Personality change over 40 years of adulthood: Hierarchical linear modeling analysis of two longitudinal samples. *Journal of Personality and Social Psychology, 83,* 752-766.

Helson, R., Stewart, A. J., & Ostrove, J. (1995). Identity in three cohorts of midlife women. *Journal of Personality and Social Psychology, 69,* 544-557.

Manoogian, S. (2005). *CPI 260 Coaching Report for Leaders user's guide.* Sunnyvale, CA: CPP.

Meyer, P., & Davis, S. (1992). *The CPI applications guide: An essential tool for individual, group, and organizational development.* Sunnyvale, CA: CPP.

Pitariu, H. (1995). *CPI Manual Inventarul Psihological California* [Manual for the California Psychological Inventory]. Cluj-Napoca, Romania: Universitatea Babes-Bolyai.

Rosenberg, L. A., McHenry, T. B., Rosenberg, A. M., & Nichols, R. C. (1962). The prediction of academic achievement with the California Psychological Inventory. *Journal of Applied Psychology, 46,* 385-388.

Schutz, W. C. (1958). *FIRO: A three-dimensional theory of interpersonal behavior.* New York: Holt, Rinehart & Winston.

Tarabrina, N., & Grafinina, N. (1998). *Handbook for the Russian language edition of the CPI.* Moscow: Institute of Psychology, Russian Academy of Science.

Yang, J., & Gong, Y. (1993). The revising of the California Psychological Inventory in China. *Chinese Journal of Clinical Psychology, 1,* 11-15.

Weinert, A. B. (1998). *Deutscher CPI: Manual (Revidierte Version 462)* [Germany's California Psychological Inventory Manual]. Hamburg, Germany: Universitat der Bundeswehr Hamburg.

QUANTITATIVE

CAREER DECISION SELF-EFFICACY SCALE

Instrument Acronym or Preferred Short Name: CDSE

Instrument Authors: Nancy E. Betz and Karen M. Taylor

Publisher: Mind Garden, Inc.

Publisher Address: 855 Oak Grove Ave Suite #215, Menlo Park, CA 94025
http://www.mindgarden.com

Statement of Purpose: To measure an individual's degree of belief that he/she can successfully complete tasks necessary to making career decisions.

Target Population: High school, university, and adults facing career decisions

Norm Group(s) on which Scores are Based: Ohio Wesleyan University Undergraduates Ohio State University Undergraduates

Titles of Subtests, Scales, Scores Provided: Self-Appraisal Occupational Information Goal Selection Planning Problem Solving

Forms and Levels Available with Dates of Publication/Revision of Each: Career Decision Self-Efficacy Scale, copyright 1993 Career Decision Self-Efficacy Scale Short Form, copyright 1993

Date of Most Recent Edition of Manual, User's Guide, etc.: 2012

Available in which Languages: In addition to English: Chinese (Cantonese - Traditional) - Short Form only Chinese (Mandarin - Simplified) - Short Form only Greek - Short Form only Hungarian - Short Form only Indonesian - Short Form only Khmer (Cambodia) - Short Form only Slovak - Short Form only

Actual Test Time: 15 minutes, 10 minutes for the short form

Total Administration Time: 15 minutes

Required Level of Training and/or Credentials for Administrator: none

Types of Scores: raw score percentile score

Report Format/Content: Individual Report and Group Report sections are: Introduction Career Decision Self-Efficacy Scales Getting the Most Out of Your Report Your CDSE Scores Your CDSE Scores Comparison to Norms All Items by Scale Individual Planning and Development Tracking Progress Reflection: do these scores feel accurate?

Report Format/Content for Group Summaries: individual report above, group report sections below: Introduction Career Decision Self-Efficacy Scales Making Sense of Your Results This Group's CDSE Scores Group Agreement This Group's CDSE Scores Compared to Norms All Items by Scale Reflection: do these scores feel accurate?

Availability of Machine Scoring Service? No

Availability of Hand Scoring? Yes

If yes, time required for hand scoring? a few minutes

If yes, who is it scored by? Test Administrator

Availability of Local Machine Scoring Service? Not Available

Availability and Options for Computer Software? Computer Software Available, Standard administration on-line

If available, describe the ways in which computer/online version differs (if any): no difference

Link to webpage that specifies the costs of materials:

http://www.mindgarden.com/79-career-decision-self-efficacy-scale

http://www.mindgarden.com/career-decision-self-efficacy-scale/440-cdse-manual.html

http://www.mindgarden.com/career-decision-self-efficacy-scale/437-cdse-individual-report.html

http://www.mindgarden.com/career-decision-self-efficcy-scale/439-cdse-group-report.html

http://www.mindgarden.com/career-decision-self-efficacy-scale/433-cdse-original-transform-survey-hosting.html

http://www.mindgarden.com/career-decision-self-efficacy-scale/436-cdse-license-to-reproduce.html

Additional Comments of Interest to Users (e.g. forthcoming revisions, new material, etc): (information not provided by publisher)

Published Reviews of the Instrument in the Last 15 years: (information not provided by publisher)

CAREER DECISION SELF-EFFICACY SCALE

Reviewed by
Joshua C. Watson
Texas A&M University-Corpus Christi

Description

The Career Decision Self-Efficacy Scale (CDSE; Taylor & Betz, 2012) is the most frequently used assessment tool concerning career decision self-efficacy in the field of career counseling and vocational guidance (Chaney, Hammond, Betz, & Multon, 2007; Lo Presti et al., 2013). Based on Bandura's (1977, 1997) social cognitive theory of self-efficacy, practitioners use the CDSE to assess how confident individuals are in their ability to complete the necessary tasks associated with making career decisions successfully (Betz, Hammond, & Multon, 2005; Taylor & Betz, 1983). The CDSE is a self-report instrument consisting of 50 items measuring the five career competencies identified in Crites' (1978) model of career maturity: accurate self-appraisal, gathering occupational information, goal selection, planning, and problem solving. Betz and colleagues reviewed the definitions of each competency to determine specific behaviors relevant to each and to create the initial item pool. Each subscale includes 10 items to be addressed utilizing a 10-point Likert-type response continuum with values ranging from 0 (*no confidence at all*) to 9 (*complete confidence*). Per the authors, higher scores are indicative of higher degrees of general self-efficacy for career decision making.

The *self-appraisal* subscale assesses how well individuals know themselves. Sample items on this scale include "list several majors that you are interested in" and "accurately assess your abilities." The *occupational information* subscale assesses an individual's ability to gather information about specific jobs and the duties associated with those jobs. Sample items on this scale include "use the internet to find information about occupations that interest you" and "find information about companies who employ people with college majors in English." The *goal selection* subscale assesses how confident individuals feel in their ability to choose a job appropriate for them and that they would enjoy. Sample items on this scale include "select one major from a list of potential majors you are considering" and "select one occupation from a list of occupations you are considering." The *planning* subscale assesses both how individuals look ahead and their confidence in their ability to begin taking the steps necessary to meet their career goals. Sample items on this scale include "make a plan of your goals for the next five years" and "determine the steps you need to take to successfully complete your chosen major." The *problem-solving* subscale assesses how confident individuals feel in their ability to know what they should do to succeed in their chosen career. Sample items on this scale include "determine the steps to take if you are having academic trouble with an aspect of your chosen major" and "persistently work at your major or career goal even when you get frustrated."

In 1996, Betz, Klein, and Taylor introduced an abbreviated version of the CDSE, the CDSE-SF (short form). The CDSE-SF assesses the same five career competencies but includes only 25 of the original items spread equally across each competency. The items retained were those that met a set of interpretive and statistical criteria established by the authors (Betz & Luzzo, 1996). In addition to a reduction in items, Betz and Luzzo revised the CDSE-SF further to feature a new response continuum. Based on results gathered in a study including three samples of college students (n = 1832), Betz, Hammond and Multon (2005) found that a condensed 5-point Likert-type response format was at least as valid and reliable as the 10-point response format when used for norming the original version of the CDSE two decades earlier. Using this new scale, individuals respond to each item using a scale with values ranging from 1 (*no confidence at all*) to 5 (*complete confidence*). Considering these findings, as well as the short form's relative ease of administration, Betz and Taylor (2012) recommended use of the revised 5-point response continuum for both clinical and research purposes.

Both the CDSE and CDSE-SF yield six scores: a full-scale score and five sub-scale scores. Subscales include either 10 (CDSE) or five (CDSE-SF) items, and scoring is cumulative. Across each subscale, instrument administrators sum the response values and divide the sum by the number of items represented on each scale. Using the recommended five-point response continuum, full-scale scores on the CDSE range between 50 and 250, with scores on the CDSE-SF ranging between 25 and 125. For the subscales, ranges of 10 to 50 and 5 to 25 are noted for the CDSE and CDSE-SF respectively. Averages for both the full-scale and subscale scores should range between one and five. The test manual provides guidelines that inform the interpretation of scores. According to Betz and Taylor (2012), full-scale and subscale scores between 1 and 2.5 describe an individual with low to little confidence who might be in need of intervention; scores between 2.5 and 3.5 describe an individual with moderate confidence who might be comfortable exploring or might need some help; and scores between 3.5 and 5 describe an individual with high confidence who is comfortable with this skill set. For the normative sample used to develop the CDSE, the highest mean score was obtained on the *self-appraisal scale* (M = 7.1), while the lowest mean was on the *problem-solving scale* (M = 6.3). Means and standard deviations for each of the subscales appear to be similar across various ethnic groups studied (Betz et al., 2005; Chaney, Hammond, Betz, & Multon, 2007).

Technical Considerations

Hackett and Betz (1981) were the first to introduce the construct of career decision self-efficacy. The CDSE and CDSE-SF represent the most widely used instruments in assessing this context-specific self-efficacy (Makransky, Rogers, & Creed, 2015). The normative sample for the CDSE included 346 college students attending schools in the Midwest who received course credit for their participation in the study. Within the normative sample, 156 students (68 males, 88 females) attended a small private liberal arts college while the remaining 190 students (60 males and 130 females) were enrolled at a large public state university. The average age of students in the normative sample was 19.1 years, with most of the students (79%) identifying as freshmen (Taylor & Betz, 1983). The authors did not provide information pertaining to the ethnic and cultural backgrounds of these participants.

Psychometric properties of the CDSE and the CDSE-SF are strong. Initial reliability estimates reported by the authors support the instrument's ability to produce consistent and stable scores. For the original norming sample, Taylor and Betz (1983) computed an internal consistency alpha coefficient of .97 for the full-scale and values between .86 and .89 for each of the five subscales. Six-week test-retest reliability of the CDSE was found to be .83 (Luzzo, 1993). For the 25-item CDSE-SF using the original 10-point response continuum, Betz, Klein, and Taylor (1996) computed an internal consistency alpha coefficient of .94 for the full-scale and alpha coefficients ranging between .73 and .83 for each of the five subscales. Using the revised 5-point response continuum, Betz et al. (2005) found an internal consistency alpha coefficient of .95 for full-scale and values ranging from .78 to .87 for each of the five subscales. Finally, previous researchers have found the data obtained from the CDSE-SF to be reliable across different language versions and within different populations (Betz & Klein, 1996; Betz, Klein, & Taylor, 1996; Buyukgoze-Kavas, 2014; Chung, 2002; Creed, Patton, & Watson, 2002; Lo Presti et al., 2013; Miguel, Silva, & Prieto, 2013; Nam, Yang, Lee, Lee, & Seol, 2011; Nilsson, Schmidt, & Meek, 2002).

Both the CDSE and the CDSE-SF have been validated across multiple studies using multiple methodologies. Both criterion-related and construct validity have been established by comparing scores on the CDSE with several other indices of adaptive career development (Betz et al., 2005). In a recent study utilizing a sample of 534 Australian high school students, Makransky et al. (2015) found strong support for the content, structural, and substantive aspects of validity for the CDSE-SF and its five subscales. Though researchers have assessed the psychometric properties of the CDSE and CDSE-SF across cultural groups, gender differences in levels of career decision self-efficacy (Betz & Klein, 1996; Betz et al, 1996; Chung, 2002; Creed et al., 2002; Taylor & Popma, 1990) remain largely unreported. Further information related to the validity of these instruments can be found in the most recent test manual (Betz & Taylor, 2012).

General Utility and Evaluation

Over the years, the CDSE and CDSE-SF have proven to be two of the most frequently used instruments to assess individual levels of career-related self-efficacy (Chaney et al., 2007). The test manual provides a wealth of information on the development, administration, scoring, interpretation, and functionality of the instrument. Additionally, the authors included a narrative overview of self-efficacy and career maturity theory because these serve as the theoretical foundation of the instrument. In terms of administration, the manual simply states that test users should adhere to all local and national ethical standards and best practices for use of standardized tests when using either the CDSE or CDSE-SF (Betz & Taylor, 2012). The manual provides no information in terms of the amount of time in which individuals should be able to complete the instruments, nor whether it is preferable to administer the instrument individually or in a group.

The authors also do not provide age norms in the test manual. Although Taylor and Betz initially developed the CDSE using a normative sample of college students, the possibility exists that instrument administrators can use the instrument effectively with a younger population. In fact, previous researchers have adapted the instrument for use with both middle school (Gibbons & Borders, 2010) and high school students (Hampton, 2006; Jones, 1992; Lo Presti et al., 2013). However, the wording of the original test items, and their focus on traditional college-level career exploration activities, suggest the instrument is used best with a college student population. Although not stated specifically in the test manual, both the CDSE and CDSE-SF appear to be written at a fifth-grade reading level using the Flesch-Kincaid method.

Overall, the CDSE-SF and its predecessor, the CDSE, are well-developed instruments with sound psychometric properties. Over 30 years of research studies are reported in the test manual, indicating the constructs of career decision-making assessed by these instruments are evidence-based. Despite recent findings supporting various factor structures of the CDSE-SF (see Makransky et al., 2015), it remains a widely-used instrument with great utility. The instrument is easy to both administer and score and should take relatively little time for students to complete. As such, Betz and Taylor (2012) recommend using the CDSE or CDSE-SF as tools to assess individuals' confidence in approaching the variety of behaviors associated with the career decision-making process. Specifically, they mention the instruments' ability to produce pre-post dependent measures of the effectiveness of career exploration interventions utilized with a student as a strength. Based on the supporting literature, the CDSE and CDSE-SF instruments appear to be useful career exploration assessment tools.

References

Bandura, A. (1977). Self-efficacy: Toward a unifying theory of behavioral change. *Psychological Review, 84,* 191-215.

Bandura, A. (1997). *Self-efficacy: The exercise of control.* New York, NY: Freeman.

Betz, N. E., Hammond, M. S., & Multon, K. D. (2005). Reliability and validity of five-level response continua for the Career Decision Self-Efficacy Scale. *Journal of Career Assessment, 13,* 131-149. doi:10.1177/106907279600400103

Betz, N. E., & Klein, K. (1996). Relationships among measures of career self-efficacy, generalized self-efficacy, and global self-esteem. *Journal of Career Assessment, 4,* 285-298. doi:10.1177/106907279600400304

Betz, N. E., Klein, K., & Taylor, K. M. (1996). Evaluation of a short form of the Career Decision-Making Self-Efficacy Scale. *Journal of Career Assessment, 4,* 47-57. doi:10.1177/106907279600400103

Betz, N. E., & Luzzo, D. A. (1996). Career assessment and the Career Decision-Making Self-Efficacy Scale. *Journal of Career Assessment, 4*(4), 413-428.

Betz, N. E., & Taylor, K. M. (2012). *Career Decision Self-Efficacy Scale and short form and manual.* Menlo Park, CA: Mind Garden, Inc.

Buyukgoze-Kavas, A. (2014). A psychometric evaluation of the Career Decision Self-Efficacy Scale-Short Form with Turkish university students. *Journal of Career Assessment, 22*(2), 386-397. doi:10.1177/1069072713484561

Chaney, D., Hammond, M. S., Betz, N. E., & Multon, K. D. (2007). The reliability and factor structure of the Career Decision Self-Efficacy Scale-Short Form with African Americans. *Journal of Career Assessment, 15,* 194-205. doi:10.1177/1069072706298020

Chung, B. Y. (2002). Career decision-making self-efficacy and career commitment: Gender and ethnic differences among college students. *Journal of Career Development, 28,* 277-284. doi:10.1023/A:1015146122546

Creed, P. A., Patton, W., & Watson, M. B. (2002). Cross-cultural equivalence of the Career Decision-Making Self-Efficacy Scale-Short Form: An Australian and South African comparison. *Journal of Career Assessment, 10,* 327-342. doi:10.1177/10672702010003004

Crites, J. O. (1978). *Career Maturity Inventory.* Monterey, CA: CTB/McGraw Hill.

Gibbons, M. M., & Borders, L. (2010). A measure of college-going self-efficacy for middle school students. *Professional School Counseling, 13*(4), 234-243.

Hackett, G., & Betz, N. E. (1981). A self-efficacy approach to the career development of women. *Journal of Vocational Behavior, 18,* 326-339. doi:10.1016/0001-8791(81)90019-1

Hampton, N. Z. (2006). A psychometric evaluation of the Career Decision Self-Efficacy Scale-Short Form in Chinese high school students. *Journal of Career Development, 33*(2), 142-155. doi:10.1177/0894845306293540

Jones, L. (1992). Career Decision-Making Self-Efficacy Scale-High School Version. Unpublished scale.

Lo Presti, A., Pace, F., Mondo, M., Nota, L., Casarubia, P., Ferrari, L., & Betz, N. E. (2013). An examination of the structure of the Career Decision Self-Efficacy Scale (Short Form) among Italian high school students. *Journal of Career Assessment, 21*(2), 337-347. doi:10.1177/1069072712471506

Luzzo, D. A. (1993). Reliability and validity testing of the Career Decision-Making Self-Efficacy Scale. *Measurement and Evaluation in Counseling and Development, 26,* 137-142.

Makransky, G., Rogers, M. E., & Creed, P. A. (2015). Analysis of the construct validity and measurement invariance of the Career Decision Self-Efficacy Scale:
A Rasch model approach. *Journal of Career Assessment, 23*(4), 645-660.
doi:10.1177/1069072714553555

Miguel, J. P., Silva, J. T., & Prieto, G. (2013). Career Decision Self-Efficacy Scale-Short
Form: A Rasch analysis of the Portuguese version. *Journal of Vocational Behavior,
82*(2), 116-123. doi:10.1016/j.jvb.2012.12.001

Nam, S. K., Yang, E., Lee, S. M., Lee, S. H., & Seol, H. (2011). A psychometric evaluation of the
Career-Decision Self-Efficacy Scale with Korean students: A Rasch model approach.
Journal of Career Development, 38(2), 147-166. doi:10.1177/089485310371374

Nilsson, J. E., Schmidt, C. K., & Meek, W. D. (2002). Reliability generalization: An examination of the Career Decision-Making Self-Efficacy Scale. *Educational and Psychological Measurement, 62*, 647-658. doi:10.1177/0013164402062004007

Taylor, K. M., & Betz, N. E. (1983). Applications of self-efficacy theory to the understanding and treatment of career indecision. *Journal of Vocational Behavior, 22*, 63-81.
doi:10.1016/0001-8791(83)90006-4

Taylor, K. M., & Popma, J. (1990). An examination of the relationships among career
decision making self-efficacy, career salience, locus of control, and vocational indecision. *Journal of Vocational Behavior, 37*, 17-31.

QUANTITATIVE

Copsystem Career Guidance Program

Instrument Acronym or Preferred Short Name: COPSystem
Instrument Authors: Knapp, L., Knapp, R., & Knapp-Lee, L.
Publisher: EdITS LLC
Publisher Address: PO Box 7234, San Diego CA 92167
http://www.edits.net

Statement of Purpose: The COPSystem assessments (Career Occupational Preference System Interest Inventory [COPS], Career Ability Placement Survey [CAPS], and Career Orientation Placement and Evaluation Survey [COPES]) are designed to provide individuals with coordinated measures of interest, abilities, and work values in terms of eight career clusters that are divided into professional and skilled levels. Scores on the combined profile provide a starting point for career exploration and eventual occupational choice and satisfaction.

Target Population: Middle School, High School, College students and Adults; grade 4 and up.

Norm Group(s) on which Scores are Based: Junior high, high school, and community college/college/adult norms

Titles of Subtests, Scales, Scores Provided: All assessments are keyed to the COPSystem career clusters which consist of eight major career clusters, five of which are divided into professional and skilled clusters. COPSystem Interest Inventory measures interests in terms of: Science Professional Science Skilled Technology Professional Technology Skilled Consumer Economics Outdoor Business Professional Business Skilled Clerical Communication Arts Professional Arts Skilled Service Professional Service Skilled. The CAPS ability battery measures abilities in terms of eight separate ability tests that are also all related to the COPSystem Career Clusters. CAPS ability tests are: Mechanical Reasoning Spatial Relations Verbal Reasoning Numerical Ability Language Usage Word Knowledge Perceptual Speed and Accuracy Manual Speed and Dexterity. The COPES work values survey measures eight work values dimensions, all related to the COPSystem Career Clusters. The COPES work values dimensions are: Investigative vs. Accepting Practical vs. Carefree, Independence vs. Conformity Leadership vs. Supportive Orderliness vs. Flexibility Recognition vs. Privacy Aesthetic vs Realistic Social vs. Reserved

Forms and Levels Available with Dates of Publication/Revision of Each: COPS (2015), COPS Professional Level (COPS-P, 2002), COPS Intermediate Inventory (COPS II, 2011), COPS Picture Inventory (COPS-PIC, 2013), Spanish COPSystem (2017), Career Ability Placement Survey (CAPS, 1976, version 2017) and Career Orientation Placement

Date of Most Recent Edition of Manual, User's Guide, etc.: Test Manuals and users guides are accompanied by various short technical publications updating information as available. Dates vary.

Available in which Languages: English, Spanish, Non-reading, Screen Reader adaptation, Some translations of directions for the COPS-PIC, CAPS and COPES are available in Spanish, Hmong, Russian, Croatian, Laotian, and Vietnamese.

Actual Test Time: COPS: 15-20 minutes, CAPS 50 minutes, COPES 15-20 minutes

Total Administration Time: 1.5 to 2.0 hours

Required Level of Training and/or Credentials for Administrator: Some testing and counseling background required or affiliation with an accredited institution.

Types of Scores: Raw scores, Percentiles, Stanines, and Verbal Labels are included for the assessments. All scores are related to the COPSystem career clusters and are described in the interpretive information which is available online and in printed format. Interpretive information provides a definition of each career cluster, related courses of study, sample occupations related college majors, necessary skills and abilities, activities for experience, career planning worksheet, educational planning worksheet, and local job interview sheet. Online format includes database of 1,389 job descriptions, salary information, educational requirements and links to occupational data sources and job postings.

Report Format/Content: Results pages include complete career exploration information and a summary of results specific to each examinee.

Report Format/Content for Group Summaries: Group summary information available for online version depending on request of administrator. Summary of Interests provides the number of times one of the 14 career clusters was chosen by examinees as one of their top three areas of interest. Needs assessment summary provides data summary of student responses to a career planning questionnaire.

Availability of Machine Scoring Service? Yes

If yes, maximum time required for machine scoring and return: 10 day turnaround

Availability of Hand Scoring? Yes

If yes, time required for hand scoring? Hand scored by examinee, clerk, or counselor in approximately 15-20 minutes

If yes, who is it scored by? Individual Test Taker

Availability of Local Machine Scoring Service? Yes

If yes, provisions/conditions/equipment required for local machine scoring: Local machine scoring with optical mark read scanner. Limited support available.

Availability and Options for Computer Software? Computer Software Available, Standard administration on-line

If available, describe the ways in which computer/online version differs (if any): Online version contains links to occupational database of over 1,300 job descriptions

Link to webpage that specifies the costs of materials: http://www.edits.net

Additional Comments of Interest to Users (e.g. forthcoming revisions, new material, etc): Screen Reader adaptation available. A summary of the predictive usefulness of CAPS in technology occupations is in publication. A long term follow up of examinees taking the COPS will also be released Fall 2017.

Published Reviews of the Instrument in the Last 15 years:

Bullock, E.E., & Madson, M.B. (2009). [COPSystem Career Guidance Program (COPS, CAPS, and COPES.)] In E.A. Whitfield, R.W. Feller, & C. Wood (Eds.), *A counselor's guide to career assessment instruments* (5th ed., pp. 119-125). Broken Arrow, OK: National Career Development Association.

Bullock-Yowell, E. & Osborne, L.K. (2013). COPSystem Career Guidance Program: Career Occupational Preference System Interest Inventory Career Ability Placement Survey Career Orientation Placement and Evaluation Survey. In C. Wood & D.G. Hays (Eds.), *A counselor's guide to career assessment instruments* (6th ed., pp 177-182). Broken Arrow, OK: National Career Development Association.

CAREER OCCUPATIONAL PREFERENCE SYSTEM

Reviewed by
Jenna Crabb
University of New Mexico

The Educational and Industrial Testing Service (EdITS) published the Career Occupational Preference System (COPSystem), written by Robert Knapp and Lila Knapp, in 1974 with revisions completed in 1995 and 2018. The COPSystem consists of three assessments: The Career Occupational Preference System Interest Inventory (COPS), the Career Ability Placement Survey (CAPS), and the Career Orientation Placement and Evaluation Survey (COPES). These three assessments measure interests, abilities, and work values with the overarching goal of assisting individuals, specifically high school students, college students, and adults, in their career decision-making. The results focus on interests within 14 occupational clusters (Science Professional, Science Skilled, Technology Professional, Technology Skilled, Consumer Economics, Outdoor, Service Professional, Service Skilled, Business Professional, Business Skilled, Clerical, Communication, Arts Professional, Arts Skilled) that represent possible career, educational, and training opportunities.

Career specialists administer the three assessments by either paper and pencil or electronically online. Clients or students may complete the assessments individually or in a group setting. Upon completion, individuals receive a comprehensive report detailing the results of their three assessments measuring their interests (COPS), abilities (CAPS), and values (COPES) to help them with their career decision-making.

The COPS Interest Inventory (COPS)

The COPS Interest Inventory (COPS) consists of 126 work activity questions in relation to the 14 occupational clusters. The assessment does not have a specific time limit; however, most respondents finish in 30 minutes or less (Knapp, Knapp, & Knapp-Lee, 2009). Individuals respond to questions using answer choices (i.e., like very much, like moderately, dislike moderately, or dislike very much). Questions focus on work activities, such as helping a dentist make fillings for teeth or arranging flower displays. There are different age levels offered within the COPS: COPS-PIC - Grades 7-12 (adults and non-readers), COPS II - Grades 6-12 (4th grade reading level), COPS-P – College and Adult. The results include percentile ranks for the 14 occupation clusters with comparisons to others at the user's educational level or normative sample.

The Career Ability Placement Survey (CAPS)

This assessment consists of eight five-minute ability tests. The assessment is unique in that researchers developed the assessment to measure abilities in a quick and easy-to-complete format (Knapp et al., 2009). Completion of the CAPS takes place in less than one hour. The eight ability tests within this assessment are *Mechanical Reasoning, Spatial Relations, Verbal Reasoning, Numerical Ability, Language Usage, Word Knowledge, Perceptual Speed and Accuracy,* and *Manual Speed and Dexterity.* The examinee has five minutes to complete each section. The number of questions vary for each section.

The results display as comparisons to national norms for the specific ability within the occupational cluster. The interpretive report presents estimates of the examinee's currently measured abilities in relation to the occupational clusters.

Practitioners interpret the results using national norms in two ways: plotted on the CAPS Ability profile in the form of stanines and national norming, or through various combinations matched to the occupational family clusters (Knapp & Knapp, 1985, Knapp, Knapp, & Knapp-Lee, 1992, Knapp et al., 2009).

The Career Orientation Placement and Evaluation Survey (COPES)

This assessment consists of 80 value questions, generally completed within 30 minutes. The questions connote values individuals consider important in their professional and personal worlds. The assessment contains two value statements per question, and users choose the one that best describes their value. Instructions clarify that each examinee should pose the statement: "I value activities or jobs in which (I)… or …" to choose the one that best describes his or her value. The assessment measures eight work value dimensions: *Investigative vs. Accepting, Practical vs. Carefree, Independence vs. Conformity, Leadership vs. Supportive, Orderliness vs. Flexibility, Recognition vs. Privacy, Aesthetic vs. Realistic,* and *Social vs. Reserved.* The individual report presents results with a bar graph comparison to a normative sample. The results identify the user's top three highest values.

The COPSystem

Upon completion of the three assessments, the user can enter the answers into the Comprehensive Career Guide (if self-administered, paper and pen) or receive the Career Occupational Preference System Summary (if administered online). Each report summary helps organize and focus the collected career information (Knapp-Lee, 1995). The results center on the 14 COPSystem occupational clusters. The guide allows for future homework and research concerning the occupational clusters. Time to score and interpret the assessments is dependent on the counselor and the individual and whether the assessment is online or paper and pen.

Technical Considerations

COPSystem Reliability and Validity

According to the EdIT's website, updated data was gathered from five geographical areas (Midwest, Northeast, Southeast, Southwest, and West) from January 2012 through June 2015 (Educational and Industrial Testing Service, n.d. -d). The sample included 17,128 seventh through twelfth grade students. They analyzed gender, grade, and region comparisons.

Career Occupational Preference System Interest Inventory (COPS).
Reliability coefficients ranged from .83 to .91 for the scales (Educational and Industrial Testing Service, n.d. -a). There are many studies supporting the validity of the COPS Interest Inventory (Knapp, Knapp, & Knapp-Lee, 1990). When comparing the Kuder scales to the COPS, correlations ranged from .21 to .49. The comparisons indicated that 89% of participants had one of the same interest areas for both the COPS and the Kuder. In addition, a comparison with the Holland based Vocational Preference Inventory (VPI) yielded correlations ranging from .50 and .70 (Educational and Industrial Testing Service, n.d. -a).

According to the Educational and Industrial Testing Service website, researchers measured construct validity of the COPS with freshmen declaring their major as participants (Educational and Industrial Testing Service, n.d. -a). Seventy-one percent matched to one of their top three measured interests. In addition, "a long-term predictive validity study showed that 64% of students were in a job or college major that matched one of their three highest interest areas from one to seven years after taking the COPS" (Educational and Industrial Testing Service, n.d. -a, paragraph 3).

Within another page of the Educational and Industrial Testing Service website, *Stability of the COPS Interest Inventory Scores Between Eighth and Twelfth Grades*, researchers also explored the longitudinal validity data for COPS regarding the stability of interests from eighth to twelfth grade (Educational and Industrial Testing Service, n.d. -e). Students (807 female, 668 male) were administered the assessment in eighth grade and again in twelfth grade. In that study, 87% of the students had one of the same interest areas emerge from 8th grade to 12th grade.

Career Ability Placement Survey (CAPS). Test-retest reliability coefficients ranged from .70 to .95 for the CAPS (Educational and Industrial Testing Service, n.d. -a). Researchers measured concurrent validity with the Differential Aptitude Tests (DAT). These correlations ranged from .65 to .81. In addition, researchers obtained correlations between .30 and .60 between CAPs tests and specific subject areas (e.g., numerical ability correlation to grades in math).

Career Orientation Placement and Evaluation Survey (COPES). Alpha reliabilities ranged from .60 to .85 for the COPES (Educational and Industrial Testing Service, n.d. -a). Researchers compared the COPES (values) scores to the COPS (interests) scores resulting in an 89% match of work values to career choice or college major.

Norms. Researchers gathered data from five geographical areas (Midwest, Northeast, Southeast, Southwest, and West) in the United States from 2012 through 2015 for a sample of 17,128 sixth through twelfth grade students (Educational and Industrial Testing Service, n.d. -d). Analysis included comparisons across gender, grade level, and region to explore possible differences based on these variables.

Only gender showed differences in mean scores and thus, separate normative data are available by gender as noted in previous COPS analyses. CAPS norms analysis revealed differences between the grade levels. Therefore, the authors grouped the normative measurement into two distinctions: 8-9 grade and 9-12 grade. These results were consistent with 2004 through 2007 data.

Use/Interpretation/Evaluation

General Utility. The COPSystem is a set of three assessments encompassing interests, abilities, and values to help inform and direct individuals when making career related decisions. Career development decisions are difficult to make, and, often, individuals struggle with where to start and how to begin. These assessments offer very concrete ways to begin a search for a career, an academic major, or an educational pursuit. The COPSystem starts with the interests assessment (COPS). This interests assessment aligns career interests with the 14 occupational clusters, which seems to set the stage for the career decision-making process. The assessment organizes the 14 clusters into eight major career areas, each is distinguished by skilled versus professional occupations. The 14 clusters represent aspects of the early works of Thurstone, Kuder, and Roe (Knapp-Lee, 1995).

Next, the system incorporates the abilities assessment (CAPS) and the values assessment (COPES). CAPS is a unique measurement of abilities that helps solidify this aspect within the career development process. Often, measuring abilities uses self-declared measures that can lead to inaccurate results. The CAPS is a quick way of assessing actual performance abilities in relation to career. The user can gain knowledge to understand educational opportunities, growth, and development options, as well as general ability strengths. The COPES (values) completes the process by aligning what the individual values in relation to work tasks and places. Utilizing the values component can help users understand the importance of values within a work context.

Supplemental Tools: Presentation and Interpretation

Career specialists can administer the instruments through self-scoring, or web-based (through the Educational and Industrial Testing Service website) processes. The self-scoring is more complicated and outdated in appearance. The online version is appealing and easy to use from a user and counselor perspective.

There are a variety of supplemental tools available for the COPSystem and the three assessments. These are available through both hard copies and online versions. Pocket charts, wall charts, booklets, kits, handbooks, and other visual aids assist the administrator and user. The publisher offers *Career Briefs* (Educational and Industrial Testing Service, n.d. -b) online, which describes the occupational clusters. These Career Briefs link to information on 1,389 job titles that include information such as skills, abilities, salary, job outlook, and general information on the career.

The Comprehensive Career Guide for the paper version serves as a step-by-step process that individual users can utilize to create a type of career portfolio. This guide takes the user through the system and ends with a career planning page, a program planning guide, and a local job interview form (Educational and Industrial Testing Service, 2004). The career cluster information, embedded within the guide, provides links to the Occupational Outlook Handbook (U.S. Department of Labor, 2017) along with related courses of study, skills, and abilities needed for these jobs and college majors. The career guide instructions might be lengthy and complex for some users.

The online COPSystem web-based tutorial (Educational and Industrial Testing Service, n.d. -c) provides a summary and visual interpretation of the career guide. The tutorial is colorful and easy to read and understand. The test scores are easy to understand and present the opportunity to learn and read more about what each assessment means and ways to use the results. For example, the CAPS (abilities) assessment explains how to use the results as options for study and training. Lastly, the online version provides a summary section, which combines the scores from the COPS, CAPS and COPES assessments. From the online version, the user can download the Comprehensive Career Guide or a Canadian Career Guide. The online version is easy to follow, easy to read, and links to related information concerning the occupational clusters (e.g., definitions, tasks, job titles, skills, college majors). In addition, there are links to resources such as O*NET and Indeed.com.

The Technical Manual (Knapp, Knapp, & Knapp-Lee, 1990) provides detailed information on each of the assessments along with ways to use the assessments appropriately. Also, the manual provides information on how to use the system in schools, teaching, early career awareness, and employment settings. In addition, the authors included case studies, and explained and outlined administrative and interpretation suggestions in the manual.

Cultural Considerations and Implications

When reviewing any assessment, including a multicultural perspective is important. The COPSystem has many great options for being inclusive regarding language and reading levels. Researchers have translated many of the assessments into multiple languages, although most are in English and Spanish. However, there are no data concerning the reliability, validity, and norms of using the system with diverse populations. Large print (14-20-point font) is available for those individuals with sight impairments.

The developers wrote the COPS Intermediate Inventory (COPS II) at a fourth-grade reading level, and practitioners can administer the assessment to small groups and individually. Practitioners might use the assessment with elementary aged, special education, and older individuals who have difficulty reading. COPS Picture Inventory of Careers (COPS-PIC) is for non-readers and offers a non-verbal occupational interest assessment.

Research, Evaluation, and Assessment Uses

Although designed to assist with career exploration in middle school, high school, and college, career specialists might use the assessments to assist with general career exploration concerning transition, displacement, retirement, and general career counseling in private practice settings. The CAPS (ability) assessment results might assist with training and continued educational options for individuals in multiple settings. Practitioners might consider using the new web-based interest inventory, COPS-P for those individuals in transition and for high school and college students exploring career paths and majors.

Future research opportunities exist for exploring multicultural dimensions and use of this system. Another area for consideration would be the changing nature of the world of work and the career options available. Updating careers and occupations to meet the current labor market demands would be important. Research does not exist on how often the publisher updates the career paths, occupational clusters, and general skills and abilities to meet the needs of the current workforce.

Evaluation

The COPSystem is a well-researched career decision-making assessment system focused on interests, abilities, and values. If used as a system, it provides a comprehensive picture of where to begin in the career exploration process. Practitioners might use individual assessments, within the system, for client exploration or as part of the decision-making activities.

Each specific assessment in the COPS system is unique and can be used separately. However, the combined system represents a comprehensive system of assessments. Taking each assessment separately, in the online system, organizes the information and makes more sense to the user. Each assessment is available independently or as a complete battery of assessments (interests, abilities, and values). The online version is easy to use and links to relevant resources. The online resources available to both user and counselor are visually appealing.

The updated print version (paper and pen) is available. The technical manual, along with supplemental manuals for each assessment, might appear outdated in style and visual appeal, as well.

Overall, the COPSystem provides a strong tool for assisting individuals in exploring their career decisions through a series of assessments that encompass important aspects of the career decision-making process. This tool provides a comprehensive framework for exploration in schools, colleges, and workforce and professional settings.

References and Resources

Educational and Industrial Testing Service. (n.d. -a). *Brief summary of the reliability and validity of the COPSystem assessments.* Retrieved from https://blog.edits.net/a-brief-summary-of-the-reliability-and-validity-of-the-copsystem-assessments/

Educational and Industrial Testing Service. (n.d. -b). *Career briefs.* Retrieved from https://www.edits.net/via/career-briefs/

Educational and Industrial Testing Service. (n.d. -c). *COPSystem web-based tutorial.* Retrieved from https://www.edits.net/support/eap-interpretation/

Educational and Industrial Testing Service. (n.d. -d). *Norms for the COPS System Assessment.* Retrieved from https://blog.edits.net/the-journey-begins/

Educational and Industrial Testing Service. (n.d. -e). *Stability of the COPS interest inventory scores between eight and twelfth grades.* Retrieved from https://blog.edits.net/stability-of-the-cops-interest-inventory-scores-between-eighth-and-twelfth-grades/

Educational and Industrial Testing Service. (2004). *COPSystem Comprehensive Career Guide* (2015 Revision). San Diego, CA: Author.

Educational and Industrial Testing Service. (2009). *CAPS examiner's manual.* San Diego, CA: Author.

Knapp, L., Knapp, R. R., & Knapp-Lee, L. (1992). *CAPS technical manual.* San Diego, CA: Author.

Knapp, R. R., & Knapp, L. (1985). Occupational interest measurement and subsequent career decisions: A predictive follow-up study of the COPSystem interest inventory. *Journal of Counseling Psychology, 32,* 348-354.

Knapp, R. R., Knapp, L. & Knapp-Lee, L. (1990). *COPSystem technical manual.* San Diego, CA: Author.

Knapp, R. R., Knapp, L. & Knapp-Lee, L. (2009). *COPSystem examiners guide.* San Diego, CA: Author.

Knapp-Lee, L. (1995). Use of the COPSystem in career assessment. *Journal of Career Assessment, 3,* 411-428.

U.S. Department of Labor, Bureau of Labor Statistics. (2017). *Occupational outlook handbook, 2014-15.* Retrieved from https://www.bls.gov/ooh/

QUANTITATIVE

CAREER THOUGHTS INVENTORY

Instrument Acronym or Preferred Short Name: CTI

Instrument Authors: James P Sampson, Jr., PhD, Gary W. Peterson, PhD, Janet G. Lenz, PhD, Robert C. Reardon, PhD, and Denise E. Saunders, MS

Publisher: PAR, Inc.

Publisher Address: 16204 N. Florida Ave   Lutz, FL 33549

http://www4.parinc.com/Products/Product.aspx?ProductID=CTI

Statement of Purpose: The CTI is a self-administered, objectively scored measure of dysfunctional thinking in career problem solving and decision making. It is designed to identify individuals who would benefit from counseling assistance and pinpoint the nature of their career problems. The CTI helps identify, challenge, and alter negative career thoughts that interfere with effective career decision making.

Target Population: Ages 17 to 83 years

Norm Group(s) on which Scores are based: Three demographic groups are included in the normative sample: adult (n = 571), college (n = 595), and high school (n = 396).

Titles of Subtests, Scales, Scores Provided: Total score (a single global indicator of negative thinking in career problem solving and decision making), and three construct scales: Decision-Making Confusion, Commitment Anxiety, and External Conflict.

Forms and Levels Available with Dates of Publication/Revision of Each: Workbook and Test booklets. All versions published in 1996.

Date of Most Recent Edition of Manual, User's Guide, etc.: 1996

Available in which Languages: In addition to English: Bulgarian Farsi Finnish Greek Icelandic Korean Latvian Malay Turkish Urdu

Actual Test Time: 7-15 minutes

Total Administration Time: 12-23 minutes (including scoring)

Required Level of Training and/or Credentials for Administrator: Counselors, psychologists, vocational rehabilitation specialists, human resource specialists, psychiatrists, nurses, social workers, and marriage and family therapists, who are qualified to provide services within the limits of their training and experience. Professionals-in-training can use the CTI under the supervision of a qualified practitioner.

Types of Scores: Raw Scores, Percentiles, and T Scores.

Report Format/Content: Reports include: A summary profile with percentiles and T-scores; plus responses to Highly rated items and a summary of item responses.

Report Format/Content for Group Summaries: Not Available

Availability of Machine Scoring Service? No

Availability of Hand Scoring? Yes

If yes, time required for hand scoring? 5-8 minutes

If yes, who is it scored by? Test Administrator

Availability of Local Machine Scoring Service? Not Available

Availability and Options for Computer Software? Computer Software Available; Standard administration online

If available, describe the ways in which computer/online version differs: (information not provided by publisher)

Link to webpage that specifies the costs of materials: http://www4.parinc.com/ Products/Product.aspx?ProductID=CTI#

Additional Comments of Interest to Users (e.g. forthcoming revisions, new material, etc): (information not provided by publisher)

Published Reviews of the Instrument in the Last 15 years: (information not provided by publisher)

CAREER THOUGHTS INVENTORY

Reviewed by
Brian M. Calhoun
Wake Forest University

Introduction/Description

The Career Thought Inventory (CTI; Sampson, Peterson, Lenz, Reardon, & Saunders, 1996a) is a self-report inventory created to help with career decision-making processes for high school and college students and adults. The professional manual provides a theoretical basis for the CTI, a rationale and use of the CTI Professional Manual & Workbook, and descriptions regarding CTI materials, administration, and scoring.

Sampson et al. (1996b) developed the CTI Professional Manual, test booklet, and CTI workbook to help career professionals assist clients with learning about negative thoughts that affect career decision-making. The authors developed the CTI to partner the tasks of assessment and intervention within the context of career service delivery. Career specialists can use the CTI for clients, research, evaluation, and theory development. The ultimate goal of the developers was to provide career clients with a time efficient tool to incorporate the assessment concepts into change interventions. After completing the assessment, the client can use the CTI workbook to complete such change interventions as action planning, cognitive restructuring, and problem and decision-making exercises. Career practitioners have the traditional assessment components (i.e., Professional Manual and CTI Test booklet) and a CTI workbook to prompt client learning with homework and interventions. The CTI has many applications for career counseling professionals, including screening, needs assessment, and as a learning resource.

The CTI Professional Manual describes the *cognitive information processing* (CIP) model as the theoretical approach used for career development and career services (Peterson, Sampson, & Reardon, 1991). Sampson et al. (1996e) selected CIP theory as a basis for developing the CTI using three perspectives: (a) coverage of a broad range of relevant aspects of problem solving and decision-making; (b) an explanation of the positive and negative influence of metacognitions (i.e., self-talk, control and monitoring, and self-awareness) on career problem solving and decision-making; and (c) a conceptual basis for instruction designed to enhance skills in career problem solving and decision-making. There are two principal components in the CIP approach – the CASVE cycle (which includes stages of communication, analysis, synthesis, valuing, and execution) and the pyramid of information processing domains. Combined, these components explain the process of career information coding and retention and demonstrate the model highlighting the effect of metacognition on career decision-making.

The *Pyramid of Information* begins with the base of the domains of both occupational knowledge and self-knowledge (Peterson et al., 1991). The next level uses the process of problem solving and decision-making illustrated with the CASVE cycle. Sampson et al. (1996e) described the CASVE cycle as a relatively simple schema to describe a career decision-making process that can often be very complex. A single career decision that evolves overtime might involve numerous iterations of the CASVE cycle (Sampson et al., 1996b). The top of the Pyramid of Information contains the *Executive Procession Domain* with metacognitions influencing the function and content of all lower domains.

Technical Considerations

The CTI consists of 48 questions. There are three empirically derived factors or scales. The first scale pertains to *Decision-Making Confusion* (DMC) and contains 14 items; the second scale is related to *Commitment Anxiety* (CA) and contains 10 items; and the third scale is focused on *External Conflict* (EC) and contains five items (Sampson et al., 1996b). The DMC scale measures a person's inability to begin and maintain decision-making processes. Commitment anxiety represents the anxiety an individual experiences when attempting to commit to a career decision. The EC scale assesses an individual's conflict with decisions concerning external input from others and personal desires. The total CTI score represents a single measure of dysfunctional thinking. All four scores are relevant for client interpretation. Respondents use a four-point Likert scale (SD = *Strongly Disagree*, D = *Disagree*, A = *Agree*, and SA = *Strongly Agree*) to respond to the 48 items. Completion time is less than 15 minutes. Hand scoring is convenient, and practitioners can accomplish scoring in session. After scoring, the practitioner can transfer scores to the profile sheet (i.e., adult, college student, or high school student) that converts raw scores to *t*-scores and percentile ranks for easy interpretation and comparison of scales.

High CTI scores show negative correlations with career certainty, vocational identity, and knowledge about occupations and training. Additionally, Sampson et al. (1996b) found the total score for the CTI correlated positively with vulnerability, neuroticism, and indecision. A 200-word sample from the CTI workbook assessment received a 7.7 grade level for readability (Harris & Jacobson, 1982). The authors noted in the CTI manual that readability measures are extremely critical when working with clients who have low reading levels.

Sampson et al. (1996b) provided a detailed explanation of reliability and content validity in the professional manual. The internal consistency of the CTI was considered high (M α = .86) (Sampson et al., 1996b). Test re-test reliability was .77 for the total score. In addition, Sampson et al. (1996b) provided sufficient criterion-related validity in the professional manual. The CTI discriminates accurately between persons seeking career services (clients) and those who are not seeking career services (non-clients). Sampson et al. (1996b) mentioned that a group of 199 clients and 149 non-clients completed a demographic form and the CTI. A MANOVA showed significant differences in CTI scores of clients and non-clients. Clients always scored above non-clients. The data provided in the study of 348 subjects indicated that the CTI discriminates non-clients and clients accurately. The developers considered other psychometric properties as reasonable; those details are available for review in the test manual.

Administration and Interpretation

The CTI assessment form and workbook are relatively easy to use and score. The practitioner can transfer self-reported scores with little effort. The CTI workbook contains case studies and separate example profiles (including *t*-scores and percentiles) for high school, college, and adult clients (Sampson et al., 1996c). In the future, researchers and counselors will need to cooperate in order to ensure that career assessments like pen-and-pencil CTI assessment are available online as well (Gati & Noa, 2001).

Sampson et al. (1996c) suggested the following four-step approach to the CTI in counseling:

1. Begin by selecting two or three highly rated items (i.e., rated *Strongly Agree* or *Agree*) either across the entire instrument or related to a specific construct scale or content dimension.

2. Ask the individual to verbalize thoughts and feelings associated with each item. Using this elaborative approach, the individual provides data to aid in understanding specific career problem-solving difficulties.

3. Review the corresponding reframing stimulus statements for cognitive restructuring using the portion of Section 3 of the CTI Workbook entitled, *Challenging and Altering Your Negative Career Thoughts*.

4. Review additional highly rated items and either assign corresponding reframing stimulus statements as homework or discuss reframing statements in a future session.

The authors described the utility of the CTI in the professional manual. Practitioners can administer the CTI to clients quickly (7 to 15 minutes). Rapid scoring can occur within 5 to 8 minutes. In addition, practitioners can interpret the CTI with clients quickly. The CTI workbook has examples and interpretive information for all four levels of intervention (e.g., text, illustrations, metaphors for facilitation). Sampson et al. (1996d) developed the CTI to match the levels of intervention with the levels of dysfunctional thinking as measured by the CTI. Level one displays as a *t*-score of less than 40. Level two displays as a *t*-score of 40-50. Level three displays as a *t*-score of 51 to 60, and Level four displays as a *t*-score of greater than 60. The authors stated that practitioners can integrate the CTI into counseling homework easily and that the CTI is a relatively low cost assessment to use with clients.

Sampson et al. (1996b) did not provide much information regarding cultural considerations related to the CTI other than to state that individuals define *career thoughts*. The influence of diversity factors relating to age, ethnicity, gender, socioeconomic status, disability, and sexual orientation on career thoughts can be an important environmental factor in career choice. Additional research in this area could expand the use of the CTI with diverse clients.

Evaluation

The manual identifies four levels of interventions based on the client's assessment results. Level one requires the least intensive intervention, and level four requires the most intensive intervention. Level one intervention might be merely the career counselor highlighting the dysfunctional thought and making the client aware of it. For a client requiring a level four intervention, the counselor might need to seek referral for the client to have additional mental health counseling. A *t*-score of greater than 60 (level 4) might indicate the client has a significant career problem and might require immediate mental health counseling.

In summary, Sampson et al., (1996e) mentioned that level one might include only an item-level analysis. Level two consists of item-level analysis plus cognitive restricting. Level three is an item-level analysis, cognitive restructuring, and rehearsal and practice. Level four includes things such as item-level analysis, cognitive restructuring, rehearsal and practice, progressive relaxation, and guided imagery.

In addition, the authors described specific intervention techniques:

1. Initial interview – In this interview, a practitioner gains qualitative information about the context of the client's career problem.
2. Preliminary assessment – The client completes the CTI to give the practitioner quantitative information about the client's problem.
3. Define the problem and analyze causes – The practitioner and client come to a mutual understanding of the problem, defined in terms of a gap between current and desired state. Together, they develop hypotheses regarding the causes of an identified gap.
4. Formulate goals – The practitioner and client develop attainable counseling goals to eliminate the gap.
5. Develop Individual Learning Plan (ILP) – The practitioner assists client with developing an ILP, identifying a sequence of resources and activities necessary in attaining the counseling goals. (The CTI Workbook uses an Individual Action Plan, or IAP, which is similar to an ILP.)
6. Execute Individual Learning Plan – The client engages the ILP or IAP with the practitioner providing encouragement, information, clarification, reinforcement, and future planning.

7. Summative review and generalization – Upon completion of the ILP or IAP, the client discusses progress toward reaching the counseling goals. If needed, the practitioner and client create additional plans using the same approach to career problem solving.

Finally, the authors suggested that consideration for future research include exploring: 1) the relationship between dysfunctional thinking and verbal ability, 2) the relationship between dysfunctional thinking and verbal thinking, 3) the influence of personality on CTI scores, 4) relationships between career variables and the CTI (e.g., career maturity, interests, career beliefs, subjective career distress), 5) clients' expectations about career services delivery and the CTI scores, 6) whether completing the CTI workbook influences dysfunctional thinking, 7) whether completing the CTI workbook influences a client's ability to learn the skill of cognitive restructuring, and 8) whether practitioners' use of the CTI influences their ability to work capably to reduce clients' dysfunctional career thinking.

The CTI is an excellent consideration for program evaluation. Program evaluators can use the instrument in pre-test, post-test, and repeated measures evaluation designs to track a client's progress in restricting dysfunctional thinking and mitigating anxiety related to career decision-making. Additionally, the use of individual intervention scales might help illuminate program areas that practitioners can enhance to assist clients (Sampson et al., 1996e). Career practitioners should not just assess client information, but be active in helping clients modify their emotions consistent with their personal strengths and weaknesses (Barak, 2001).

The CTI has a vast and growing literature supporting its use, empirical support, and positive effects with clients. The instrument and accompanying materials are efficient for use in counseling and other career services. Career practitioners and researchers can use the assessment with clients in high school, college, and adulthood. The authors suggested that adults who are seeking employment change, are facing unemployment or underemployment, or are re-entering the labor market (e.g., life event) might find the CTI useful in their career search. Though research has shown that the CTI has high reliability and validity, there are still areas for career-focused research regarding the use of CTI and high school students with learning disabilities (Dipeolu, 2007). Career practitioners will need to determine the appropriateness of the CTI when administering career assessments to college students (Carson & Davis, 2000). When working with incarcerated clients, use of the CTI might help reduce recidivism by going beyond basic career interests and examining problems with career decision making (Meyer et al., 2015). Overall, the CTI is appropriate for use in research and program evaluation.

References

Barak, A. (2001). A cognitive view of the nature of vocational interests: Implications for career assessment, counseling, and research. In F.T.L. Leong (Ed.), *Contemporary models in vocational psychology: A volume in honor of Samuel H. Osipow* (pp.97-131). Mahwah, NJ: Lawrence Erlbaum Associates.

Carson, A. D., & Davis, R. V. (2000). Determining the appropriateness of career choice assessment. In D. A. Luzzo (Ed.), *Career counseling of college students: An empirical guide to strategies that work* (pp. 95-120). Washington, DC: American Psychological Association. doi: 10.1037/10362-005

Dipeolu, A. O. (2007). Career instruments and high school students with learning disabilities: Support for the utility of three vocational measures. *Journal of Career Development, 34*, 59-78. doi: 10.1177/0894845307304065

Gati, I., & Noa, S. (2001). Internet-based versus paper-and-pencil assessment: Measuring career decision-making difficulties. *Journal of Career Assessment, 9*, 397-416. doi: 10.1177/106907270100900406

Harris, A. J., & Jacobson, M. D. (1982). *Basic reading vocabularies*. New York: Macmillan.

Meyer, J. M., & Shippen, M. E. (2015). The Career Thoughts Inventory and incarcerated males: A preliminary psychometric review. *American Journal of Criminal Justice, 41*(2), 340-358. doi: 10.1007/s12103-015-9303-9.

Peterson, G. W., Sampson, J. P., Jr., & Reardon, R. C. (1991). *Career development and services: A cognitive approach*. Pacific Grove, CA: Brooks/Cole.

Sampson, J. P., Jr., Peterson, G. W., Lenz, J. G., Reardon, R. C. & Saunders, D. E. (1996a). *The Career Thoughts Inventory*. Odessa, FL: Psychological Assessment Resources.

Sampson, J. P., Jr., Peterson, G. W., Lenz, J. G., Reardon, R. C. & Saunders, D. E. (1996b). *The Career Thoughts Inventory: Professional manual*. Odessa, FL: Psychological Assessment Resources.

Sampson, J. P., Jr., Peterson, G. W., Lenz, J. G., Reardon, R. C. & Saunders, D. E. (1996c). *Improving your career thoughts: A workbook for the Career Thoughts Inventory*. Odessa, FL: Psychological Assessment Resources.

Sampson, J. P., Jr., Peterson, G. W., Lenz, J. G., Reardon, R. C., & Saunders, D. E. (1996d). Negative thinking and career choice. In R. Feller & G. Walz (Eds.), *Optimizing life transitions in turbulent times: Exploring work, learning and careers* (pp. 323-330). Greensboro, NC: University of North Carolina at Greensboro, ERIC Clearinghouse on Counseling and Student Services.

Sampson, J. P., Jr., Peterson, G. W., Lenz, J. G., Reardon, R. C., & Saunders, D. E. (1996e). *The use and development of the Career Thoughts Inventory*. Odessa, FL: Psychological Assessment Resources.

Sampson, J. P., Jr., Peterson, G. W., Lenz, J. G., Reardon, R. C., & Saunders, D. E. (1998). The design and use of a measure of dysfunctional career thoughts among adults, college students, and high school students: The Career Thoughts Inventory. *Journal of Career Assessment, 6*, 115-134.doi:10.1177/106907279800600201

QUANTITATIVE

JACKSON CAREER EXPLORER

Instrument Acronym or Preferred Short Name: JCE

Instrument Authors: Julie Aitken Schermer, PhD, Robyn MacDougall, MSc, & Douglas N. Jackson, PhD

Publisher: SIGMA Assessment Systems, Inc.

Publisher Address: PO Box 3292, Stn. B, London, ON, N6A 4K3

www.JacksonCareer.com

www.SigmaAssessmentSystems.com

Statement of Purpose: To guide individuals toward satisfying and fulfilling careers.

Target Population: Students & career changers, ages 15+

Norm Group(s) on which Scores are Based: 527 individuals (234 males, 293 females), average age of 18.2. 40% attended high school, 43% enrolled in post-secondary education, and 13% did not provide their current educational setting.

Titles of Subtests, Scales, Scores Provided: Academic Achievement Accountability Adventure Authoritarian Leadership Author-Journalism Business Consulting Creative Arts Elementary Education Endurance Engineering Family Activity Finance Independence Interpersonal Confidence Job Security Law Life Science Mathematics Mediation and Persuasion Medical Service Nature-Agriculture Office Work Organization Performing Arts Personal Service Physical Science Sales Skilled Trades Social Science Social Service Supervising Others Teaching Technical Writing

Forms and Levels Available with Dates of Publication/Revision of Each: Publication date of the test: 2012

Date of Most Recent Edition of Manual, User's Guide, etc.: 2017

Available in which Languages: English, French

Actual Test Time: 20 minutes

Total Administration Time: 25 minutes

Required Level of Training and/or Credentials for Administrator: Level A Qualifications Level

Types of Scores: Percentile scores are presented on the report.

Report Format/Content: The report includes scores for 34 basic interest, 10 work personality scores, 17 educational groups, 30 job groups, administrative indices, and a narrative summary of the top 3 job clusters as well as an Exploring my Options section.

Availability of Machine Scoring Service? No

Availability of Hand Scoring? No

Availability of Local Machine Scoring Service? Not Available

Availability and Options for Computer Software? Computer Software Available, Standard administration on-line

If available, describe the ways in which computer/online version differs (if any): The JCE is available for online testing at www.SigmaTesting.com or www.JacksonCareer.com.

Link to webpage that specifies the costs of materials:
http://www.sigmaassessmentsystems.com/assessments/jackson-career-explorer/
http://www.sigmaassessmentsystems.com/wp-content/uploads/2017/03/JCE-Pricing.pdf

Additional Comments of Interest to Users (e.g. forthcoming revisions, new material, etc): The website JacksonCareer.com is a licensing model specifically created for schools. Schools can use the site for unlimited use for a fee of $425.

Published Reviews of the Instrument in the Last 15 years: (information not provided by the publisher)

JACKSON CAREER EXPLORER

Reviewed by
Justin R. Fields
Denton High School

Description

The Jackson Career Explorer (JCE; Schermer & Vernon, 2008) is an interest inventory that provides results to individuals about careers and work sectors. Using the Jackson Vocational Interest Survey (JVIS; Jackson, 1977, 2000), researchers developed the JCE with the goals of making the instrument shorter and providing gradient amounts of interests rather than the forced choice response system used in the JVIS (Schermer & Vernon, 2008). Developers intended the JCE to be easier for people to use. The JCE is a level A test instrument, and users can interpret their score reports individually or with the help of a qualified practitioner. The intended population of this instrument is high school and college students; however, practitioners can use the JCE with individuals seeking post-secondary options or career changes.

The foundation of the JCE is the 34 *Basic Interest Scales* that consist of 27

Work Roles and seven Work Styles (Schermer, MacDougall, & Jackson, 2017). The purpose of these scales is to provide feedback to individuals about preferences for certain work activities (Work Roles) and work environments (Work Styles). The developers define Work Roles as categories of activities related to an occupation, (e.g., consulting, social service, and life science). For example, a person interested in consulting might enjoy surveying, consulting, and providing professional recommendations. Work Styles represent qualities of a work environment for which an individual might demonstrate preferences (e.g., accountability, organization, or independence). For example, a person with a preference for organization might seek situations that encourage routine work assignments (Schermer et al., 2017).

The JCE contains 170 items. Individuals respond using a five-point Likert scale. The inventory includes two sections. Section 1 (Work Roles) contains 135 items and describes occupational activities that assess work behaviors (Schermer et.al, 2017). Example items include "teaching students to read" or "buying business securities for a large bank," and individuals indicate degrees of preference (i.e., 1 = Strongly Dislike, 2 = Dislike, 3 = Neutral, 4 = Like, 5 = Strongly Like). Section 2 (Work Styles) contains 35 items and describes work environments. Individuals respond to each item by indicating the extent to which they agree with each statement (i.e., 1 = Strongly Disagree, 2 = Disagree, 3 = Neutral, 4 = Agree, 5 = Strongly Agree). Examples of items include "I like going to academic lectures" and "I would prefer a job where I could be my own boss." Within each section of the JCE, five items are associated with each Basic Interest Scale, so scores for each scale can range from 5 (indicating the least preferred) to 25 (indicating the most preferred).

Technical Considerations

To create the JCE, developers selected JVIS items that demonstrated the highest correlation with specific categories of the 34 Basic Interest Scales (Schermer et al., 2017). Items demonstrating a strong statistical relationship to the specific basic interest scale of the JVIS were included in the final version. After selecting the initial pool of items, Schermer et al. (2017) developed and tested 60 additional items, with a sample of 481 subjects, to ensure thorough representation of each Basic Interest Scale using modern examples. The developers analyzed items for statistical qualities (e.g., mean, variance, distribution, item-total correlation, corrected-item total correlation, and internal reliability). The analysis aided in reducing the item pool to 170 items.

Schermer (2012) assessed the internal consistency of the JCE by exploring the average inter-item correlations and Cronbach's alphas for each scale. Data from the normative sample yielded average inter-item correlations for the Basic

Interest Scales and Work Styles Scales, ranging from .33 (Accountability) to .73 (Mathematics and Medical Service) with a median of .55 (Schermer et al., 2017). The Cronbach's alpha values ranged from .70 (Accountability) to .93 (Mathematics and Medical Service) with a median of .87 (Schermer et.al, 2017). Schermer and Vernon (2008) completed a follow-up study with a sample of 742 adults that yielded median Cronbach's alpha (α = .77).

Schermer and Vernon (2008) assessed convergent validity by analyzing the correlations between the scales of the JCE and JVIS. The average correlation between the scales was .53, with a range of .24 to .81. Schermer et al. (2017) studied similar correlations for the *Job Group* (range .56 - .85) and *Educational Group* (range .54 - .85) scales for the JCE and JVIS. The average correlation between the scales of the two instruments was .80. Schermer and MacDougall (2011) assessed convergent validity of the JCE by comparing results with the Career Directions Inventory (CDI; Jackson, 2003). The results yielded high correlations between 11 similar Basic Interest scales of the two instruments, thereby, building support for convergent validity. In another study (Schermer et al., 2017), the JCE predicted chosen college major accurately for 71.1% of male participants and 68.9% of female participants. Similar to many interest inventories, there were specific sex differences in scores (e.g., males scored higher in math and science based interests, and women scored higher in art and social professions) (Schermer, 2012).

The normative sample for the JCE was 527 people. Of that sample, 55% identified as females, and 44% identified as males, with an average age of 18.2 years (Schermer et al., 2017). The sample consisted of 40% high school students and 43% in some form of post-secondary education. The racial ethnic demographics were Caucasian (64%), Asian (11%), multi-racial (4%), African-American (2%), and Hispanic (2%).

General Utility and Evaluation

The intended application of the JCE is with high school, college, or university aged individuals. School counselors working with high school students considering options beyond post-secondary education might use the JCE to help students explore vocational opportunities or college majors. The publisher posits practitioners can use the JCE with adults considering career changes; however, the normative sample represents an average age of 18.

Administration of the JCE is electronic using two web portals: http://www. jacksoncareer.com and http://www.sigmatesting.com. With clear and concise instructions, the time required to move from the initial web page to the assessment is brief. Users can complete the JCE in approximately 20 minutes.

Instructions on the Work Roles section inform individuals they are not to focus on their current level of skill when responding, but should focus on how much they would enjoy doing a particular work activity. On the Work Styles section, instructions encourage individuals to consider their preferences; however, their ability to actualize a style might influence the score. For example, an individual might express a preference for organization, but the individual really does not practice organizational skills. Adolescent users without much personal insight might drift frequently towards responses of "unsure" or "neutral" on the five-point scale, which can yield vague or directionless summary reports.

The JCE provides a lengthy and thorough score report. First, the 34 Basic Interest Scales are presented with percentile ranks, so individuals can see their preferences in the Work Roles and Work Styles easily. Scores are arranged into color-coded groups (green = high, blue = average, red = low) so individuals can focus on different work categories for interpretation.

Next, the presentation of *Work Personality* preferences allows an individual to review the types of preferences and learn about personal styles of approaching work. Examples of work personalities include "Structured: …may indicate that you tend to be a responsible, stable, and disciplined person who may prefer structured work to that which involves a great deal of creativity" (Schermer et al., 2017, p. 46) and "Practical: …likely enjoy activities requiring physical or mechanical skill; you tend to seek satisfaction from the quality of the work you produce" (p. 45).

The JCE score report includes information about 17 *Education Groups*. The groups represent potential education programs that match the interest profiles for an individual's highest scores. Examples of Education Groups include education, engineering, and computer science. Individuals should interpret Education Group matches as an indication that their interests are similar to those of students enrolled in a university program corresponding to those Education Groups (Schermer et al., 2017). In addition, this section of the score report includes examples of potential academic programs for the top three Education Group matches.

To provide further direction, the JCE score report provides *Job Group* suggestions. The JCE matches individuals' scores with those of people across 30 Job Groups using a positive or negative indicator. A higher positive number indicates a stronger match between the individual and the Job Group (e.g., music, social sciences and research, and medical diagnosis and treatment). To be clear, the Job Group matches suggest an individual has similar interests to those who occupy a job in a particular job group but not necessarily the job itself (Schermer et al., 2017). Further, included in the score report are three separate pages of careers within each Job Group that are organized by the level of education (i.e., vocational school training or Associate's Degree, Bachelor's Degree, or Graduate Degree) required to attain that respective job. Each sample career is matched with its O*NET Code (National Center for O*NET Development, n.d.) so individuals can refer to that resource.

The *Exploring My Options* section of the score report includes general career advice. This section provides suggestions, such as researching common job tasks, shadowing professionals, and visiting useful internet resources. Although the suggestions are very basic, the JCE provides ample information by referring individuals to O*NET and professional association web sites to explore additional information.

The score report for the JCE is thorough. The score report includes lists and definitions of terms, such as Work Roles, Work Styles, and Job Groups for clarity. The referring practitioner can elect to have the score report sent to the client directly. Although the score report is informative and the client can use the report independently, a practitioner can provide a venue for questions, reflection, and planning next steps through an interpretation experience. The publisher recommends printing the entire document to navigate the report and the appendices. The appendices provide additional support in the form of definitions of terms.

The JCE report provides insightful career-related information to an individual, particularly in tandem with career counseling. The developers wrote the JCE at an eighth grade reading level and do not recommend use of this assessment with individuals under the age of 13. Similarly, because the average age of the normative sample is 18 years, practitioners should consider carefully the use of this instrument with individuals beyond high school age. No research has verified the assessment's utility with diverse groups. This is an important limitation to consider when using of the instrument with diverse clients.

Conclusion

The JCE has many applications for high school students. Adolescents require support and education connecting their interests, life goals, and educational aspirations to career options. Furthermore, many adolescents might have ideas about what careers they want to pursue but might not have a clear understanding of how to actualize those goals. The JCE can help students who require assistance generating career aspirations while also helping them understand the type of education required to pursue specific careers. The JCE is most useful as a starting point in career counseling. The JCE can help provide a framework for counseling and help guide a young person through meaningful and relevant exploratory experiences. A primary avenue for continued research with the JCE is to assess its utility with different racial and ethnic groups. Furthermore, additional research is required to assess how practitioners might use this tool with older clients who are making career transitions.

References

Jackson, D. N. (1977). *Jackson Vocational Interest Survey manual.* Port Huron, MI: Research Psychologists Press.

Jackson, D. N. (2000). *Jackson Vocational Interest Survey manual* (2nd ed.). Port Huron, MI: Research Psychologists Press.

Jackson, D. N. (2003). *Career Directions Inventory manual* (2nd ed.). Port Huron, MI: Research Psychologists Press.

National Center for O*NET Development. (n.d.) *O*NET Online.* Retrieved from https://www.onetonline.org/

Schermer, J. A. (2012). The Jackson Career Explorer: Two further validity studies. *Journal of Career Assessment, 20,* 507-519.

Schermer, J. A., & MacDougall, R. (2011). The Jackson Career Explorer in relation to the Career Directions Inventory. *Journal of Career Assessment, 19,* 442-451.

Schermer, J. A., MacDougall, R., & Jackson, D. N. (2017) *Jackson Career Explorer: Technical manual.* Port Huron, MI: SIGMA Assessment Systems.

Schermer, J. A., & Vernon, P. A. (2008). A behavior genetic analysis of vocational interests using a modified version of the Jackson Vocational Interest Survey. *Personality and Individual Differences, 45,* 103-109. doi:10.1016/j.paid.2008.03.009

QUANTITATIVE

Jackson Vocational Interest Survey

Instrument Acronym or Preferred Short Name: JVIS

Instrument Authors: Douglas N. Jackson, Ph.D

Publisher: Sigma Assessment Systems

Publisher Address: P.O. Box 610757, Port Huron, MI, 48061-0757

http://www.sigmaassessmentsystems.com/assessments/jackson-vocational-interest-survey/

http://www.jvis.com/

Statement of Purpose: Career planning, counseling, high school, college, university, outplacement

Target Population: Age 14

Norm Group(s) on which Scores are Based: 1750 males and 1750 females from Canada and the U.S.

Titles of Subtests, Scales, Scores Provided: Creative Arts, Life Science, Personal Service, Stamina, Finance, Law, Independence, Performing Arts, Social Science, Family Activity, Accountability, Business, Professional Advising, Planfulness, Mathematics, Adventure, Medical Service, Teaching, Office Work, Author-Journalism, Interpersonal Confidence, Physical Science, Nature-Agriculture, Dominant Leadership, Social Service, Sales, Academic Achievement, Human Relations Mgmt, Engineering, Skilled Trades, Job Security, Elementary Education, Supervision, Technical Writing

Forms and Levels Available with Dates of Publication/Revision of Each: 1977, 2000

Date of Most Recent Edition of Manual, User's Guide, etc.: 2000

Available in which Languages: English, French

Actual Test Time: 45 minutes

Total Administration Time: 45 minutes

Required Level of Training and/or Credentials for Administrator: Bachelor's degree in psychology

Types of Scores: Percentile ranks

Report Format/Content: Narrative text, percentile graphs

Report Format/Content for Group Summaries: Not available

Availability of Machine Scoring Service? Yes, Mail-in scoring

If yes, maximum time required for machine scoring and return: 24-48hrs

Availability of Hand Scoring? Yes

If yes, time required for hand scoring? 15mins

If yes, who is it scored by? Test Administrator

Availability of Local Machine Scoring Service? Yes

If yes, provisions/conditions/equipment required for local machine scoring:
Computer, Windows OS

Availability and Options for Computer Software? Computer Software Available,
Standard administration on-line

If available, describe the ways in which computer/online version differs (if any):
None

Link to webpage that specifies the costs of materials:
http://www.sigmaassessmentsystems.com/assessments/jackson-vocational-
interest-survey/

**Additional Comments of Interest to Users (e.g. forthcoming revisions, new
material, etc):** (information not provided by publisher)

Published Reviews of the Instrument in the Last 15 years: Not applicable

JACKSON VOCATIONAL INTEREST SURVEY

Reviewed by
Julie Aitken Schermer
The University of Western Ontario

The Jackson Vocational Interest Survey (JVIS; Jackson, 2000) is an extensive measure of 34 vocational interests based on the construct validity approach to test construction (Juni & Koenig, 1982). The JVIS was constructed to be similar to the Strong Vocational Interest Blank, which fits Holland's six factor hexagon model (Campbell & Borgen, 1999), but to be more general in nature (Jackson & Williams, 1975) and to represent a balance of masculine and feminine interests. The JVIS was developed to aid in the vocational guidance of high school and college students, assist adults who might be out of school and making career decisions, be used in employment testing (for example in selection settings), and be used for research purposes (Thomas, 1985). The measure was designed to be administered either individually or in group settings with statements written at a grade seven level of understanding or for individuals 14 years of age or older.

The JVIS consists of 289 pairs of statements (e.g., 2 A. Becoming a recording star or 2 B. Discussing better teaching methods at a professional teachers' meeting; 39 A. Learning a new branch of mathematics, or 39 B. Doing extra reading for a project.) with each statement referring to a behavior that might occur in the workplace. Table 1 provides a sample of item statements from the JVIS. Test takers are instructed to choose one of the two behavioral item options as the action they prefer or is most characteristic of them. Test takers choose option A or B making the JVIS a forced choice measure. Completion of the test requires approximately 45 minutes.

When constructing the JVIS, a distinction was made between work roles, or actions performed while in a particular job, and work styles, which represent a preference for a certain occupational environment. Of the 34 scales, 27 scales represent work behaviors or roles, and the remaining seven reflect work styles. In grouping the scales, Jackson (2000) presented the JVIS in two different formats. The first grouping of the scales, a *conceptual* grouping, reflects nine work role groups and two work style groups. The second grouping presented in the manual is the *factor analytic* results which suggest a 10 factor (or group) solution. Presented in Table 2 is a list demonstrating how the JVIS scales are grouped together for each of the two models, the conceptual and the factor analytic. Of interest in this table are the differences in the two grouping methods. The conceptual model includes all 34 scales without overlap. The factor analytic results are less distinct. Seven of the scales load onto more than one factor, and the adventure scale is not included at all (denoted with a question mark in the table). The ten JVIS factors might reflect the difficulty that is inherent in conducting multivariate statistics, such as factor analysis with ipsative measures (Baron, 1996). These differences in grouping styles suggest that the JVIS scales might be excellent for career counselling situations with respect to the breadth of scales, but that the measure may not be ideal for multivariate research purposes.

Technical Considerations

Reliability of the JVIS scales, as presented in the manual, was assessed with respect to temporal stability (test-retest correlations) as well as internal consistency. Two temporal studies are reviewed in the manual. University students ($N = 172$) completed the JVIS again one week after initially taking the scale, and the test scores were found to correlate highly with values ranging from .72 for the *Independence* scale to .91 for the *Social Service* scale (Jackson, 2000). The second temporal stability results reported are from an unpublished Master's thesis by Berk (1988, as cited in Jackson, 2000) of 95 university students who completed the JVIS between four and six weeks apart. Test-retest correlations reported for that study ranged from .69 for the *Independence* scale to .92 for the *Social Service* scale. In general, these values suggest that the JVIS scales are fairly consistent, but users should note that the time periods between first and second administrations were fairly short and the samples were university students only.

Table 1. Sample Items from the JVIS

Scale	Sample item
Creative Arts	Creating unusual dishware on a pottery wheel
Performing Arts	Becoming a recording star
Mathematics	Expressing the mathematical relationship between two objects
Physical Science	Investigating the characteristics of electrons in the upper atmosphere
Engineering	Coordinating facilities for transmitting electrical power to consumers
Life Science	Investigating cell division in microscopic organisms
Social Science	Investigating the causes of social unrest in cities
Adventure	Test flying new airplanes
Nature-Agriculture	Raising berries for commercial use
Skilled Trades	Servicing television sets
Personal Service	Arranging transportation and accommodation for groups of tourists
Family Activity	Painting a room in bright colours for a child
Medical Service	Sewing up a skin wound with surgical stitches
Dominant Leadership	Giving orders to employees
Job Security	Working for a large, stable organization rather than one with an uncertain future
Stamina	Working overtime to complete a project
Accountability	Being polite to those with whom I have contact
Teaching	Discussing better teaching methods at a professional teachers meeting
Social Service	Helping ex-patients of a mental hospital gain employment
Elementary Education	Teaching children how to write
Finance	Buying and selling stocks for a client
Business	Managing a municipal fruit and vegetable market
Office Work	Running a photocopier in an office
Sales	Selling magazine subscriptions in different cities
Supervision	Deciding about salary increases for employees
Human Relations Management	Convincing a company board of directors not to dismiss an executive
Law	Representing a client against an insurance company seeking a settlement
Professional Advising	Managing the sales campaign of a cosmetics company
Author-Journalism	Writing scripts for television dramas
Academic Achievement	Putting forth the best effort possible in studies
Technical Writing	Writing historical introductions for books by famous authors
Independence	Organizing my work projects on my own
Planfulness	Always putting tools back in place after use
Interpersonal Confidence	Feeling confident in unfamiliar surroundings

Note. Reproduced with permission from Sigma Assessment and adapted from Schermer & MacDougall, 2011.

Table 2. JVIS Scales

JVIS Scale Title	Conceptual Title	Factor(s)
Creative Arts	The Arts	II and VI
Performing Arts	The Arts	II
Mathematics	Science and Mathematics	VII
Physical Science	Science and Mathematics	VII
Engineering	Science and Mathematics	VII
Life Science	Science and Mathematics	IV
Social Science	Science and Mathematics	IV
Adventure	Practical, Outdoor Activities	?
Nature-Agriculture	Practical, Outdoor Activities	VI
Skilled Trades	Practical, Outdoor Activities	VI
Personal Service	Service Activities	VI
Family Activity	Service Activities	VI
Medical Service	Medicine and Health	IV
Dominant Leadership	Interpersonal and Job-related Work Styles	X
Job Security	Interpersonal and Job-related Work Styles	VIII
Stamina	Interpersonal and Job-related Work Styles	VIII
Accountability	Interpersonal and Job-related Work Styles	VIII
Teaching	Teaching and Social Welfare Activities	IX
Social Service	Teaching and Social Welfare Activities	IX
Elementary Education	Teaching and Social Welfare Activities	IX
Finance	Business, Administrative, and Related Activities	I
Business	Business, Administrative, and Related Activities	I and III
Office Work	Business, Administrative, and Related Activities	III
Sales	Business, Administrative, and Related Activities	I and III
Supervision	Business, Administrative, and Related Activities	I and III
Human Relations Management	Legal, Professional, Persuasive Work Roles	I
Law	Legal, Professional, Persuasive Work Roles	I
Professional Advising	Legal, Professional, Persuasive Work Roles	I
Author-Journalism	Literary, Academic	II and V
Academic Achievement	Literary, Academic	V
Technical Writing	Literary, Academic	V
Independence	Work Styles Related to Job Activities	X
Planfulness	Work Styles Related to Job Activities	VIII
Interpersonal Confidence	Work Styles Related to Job Activities	I and X

Note. Reproduced with permission from Sigma Assessment and adapted from Schermer & MacDougall, 2011.

With respect to internal consistency, the JVIS demonstrates moderately-high to high internal consistency for both high school ($N = 1573$) and university ($N = 3500$) samples (Jackson, 2000). Cronbach's coefficient alpha values, which represent the average of all possible split-half correlations, ranged from .54 for the *Professional Advising* scale to .88 for both the *Mathematics* and *Medical Service* scales. These values suggest that responses within scales are fairly consistent.

Validity studies with the JVIS have focused on convergent and predictive validity. With respect to convergent validity, two studies are highlighted in the manual that demonstrate evidence of convergence. In the first study, high school students in their final year completed the JVIS, as well as rated their interest in the scale titles (following brief descriptions). Rated interest and scale totals correlated significantly, suggesting convergence in constructs using the two methods of assessment (Jackson, 2000). The JVIS scales were also correlated with the Strong Vocational Interest Blank and the results demonstrated convergence for scales measuring similar interest areas (Jackson, 2000). Also included in the validity studies highlighted by Jackson (2000) is a large-scale unpublished study by Locklin and Marks from Pennsylvania State University in which JVIS scores were used to assess their predictive power in distinguishing students studying in various fields. Approximately 60% of the students were classified correctly in specific academic areas using the JVIS and an intelligence test. In general, the results of these studies provide construct validity support for the JVIS scales.

Scoring and Normative Information

As with most commercially available vocational interest measures, the JVIS can be either hand scored or machine scored. Because the response page is formatted as a matrix, hand scoring the responses simply requires counting "A" or "B" responses for the individual scales. In addition, hand scoring packages come with a graph for plotting responses such that the test taker can observe the pattern of their interests. Machine scoring provides this graph (the basis of the JVIS "Basic Report") also. The test publishers, Sigma Assessment Systems, provide a JVIS "Extended Report," which is an individualized report demonstrating the differences and similarities of the response profile against the normative university student groups and 32 occupational groups.

As stated in the manual, normative data was last collected with the JVIS in 1999 suggesting that some of the information might be dated and might not reflect more contemporary, younger generations. For example, according to the World Bank, in 1999, only 8.14% of the population had a mobile cellular subscription (World Bank, n.d.). In 2015 (most recent data reported), the percentage rose to 98.33%. For another example, according to the 2001 census, Statistics Canada (n.d.) reported that 22.6% of the Canadian population had a university degree. By the next census in 2011, the percentage had increased to 25.9%. These examples of cohort differences suggest there might be differences in the degree of exposure to information pertaining to possible careers and work related behaviours between those assessed in 1999 and present day. Because of these possible differences, ideally, more recent normative data would be an asset.

Of the normative data provided in the JVIS manual, data is provided on large samples of males and females entering an American college, high school students, and Canadian adults. In addition to the mean, standard deviation, and normality data (skewness and kurtosis), percentiles are provided for easy comparison of raw scores. Also of interest, the manual provides the JVIS profiles for groups of employees from 32 job groups including medical sciences, computer careers, police, entertainment, teaching, mechanics, religion, and even sports. These reference groups are of use for career counsellors examining the JVIS profile of a client.

Evaluation

The JVIS is a broad vocational interest measure assessing 34 dimensions. The strengths of the JVIS are found in the method of scale construction and item creation and selection. Items were constructed carefully to balance male and female behaviours and to reflect actions an individual in a certain career may engage in on a daily basis. Items were then rigorously analyzed statistically to ensure a moderate to high level of scale discrimination and to reflect construct validity. These strengths are possibly the reason why Paunonen (2005) estimated that the JVIS has been administered to over 500,000 individuals.

Possible weaknesses of the JVIS include the fact that the normative data, which itself may be slightly out of date, is based specifically on American and Canadian samples (ethnic group information is not provided). Although the JVIS has been translated from English into both French and Spanish, cross cultural studies using the JVIS are missing from the literature. One possible reason for the lack of research with the JVIS, in general, could be due to the ipsative nature of the scale. As stated earlier, forced choice scales tend to be reliable but are not ideal for factor analytic analyses which may reduce the use of the JVIS in multivariate studies. Researchers choosing a vocational interest measure might opt for a continuous scale. An alternative for research could be the Jackson Career Explorer (Schermer, MacDougall, & Jackson, 2012), which is based on the top five JVIS items, with respect to item-scale total correlations, resulting in a total of 170 individual items assessing the 34 dimensions, which are responded to with a five-point continuous scale.

References

Baron, H. (1996). Strengths and limitations of ipsative measurement. *Journal of Occupational and Organizational Psychology, 69*(1), 49-56.

Campbell, D. P., & Borgen, F. H. (1999). Holland's theory and development of interest inventories. *Journal of Vocational Behavior, 55*, 86-101.

Jackson, D. N. (2000). *Jackson Vocational Interest Survey manual (second edition)*. Port Huron, MI: Research Psychologists Press.

Jackson, D. N., & Williams, D. R. (1975). Occupational classification in terms of interest patterns. *Journal of Vocational Behavior, 6*, 269-280.

Juni, S., & Koenig, E. J. (1982). Contingency validity as a requirement in forced-choice item construction: A critique of the Jackson Vocational Interest Survey. *Measurement and Evaluation in Guidance, 14*(4), 202-208.

Paunonen, S. V. (2005). Obituaries – Douglas N. Jackson. *American Psychologist, 60*(4), 335.

Schermer, J. A. & MacDougall, R. (2011). The Jackson Career Explorer in relation to the Career Directions Inventory. *Journal of Career Assessment, 19*(4), 442-451.

Schermer, J. A., MacDougall, R., & Jackson, D. N. (2012). *Jackson Career Explorer*. London, Canada: SIGMA Assessment Systems.

Statistics Canada (n.d.). *Distribution of the population aged 25 to 64, by highest certificate, diploma and degree and age group*. Retrieved from http://www.statcan.gc.ca/eng/start

Thomas, R. G. (1985). Review of Jackson Vocational Interest Survey. In J. V. Mitchell, Jr. (Ed.), *The ninth mental measurements yearbook* (Vol. 1, pp. 740-742). Lincoln, NE: Buros Institute of Mental Measurement of the University of Nebraska-Lincoln.

World Bank. (n.d.). *Mobile cellular subscriptions (per 100 people)*. Retrieved from http://data.worldbank.org/indicator/IT.CEL.SETS.P2/

QUANTITATIVE

Kuder Career Planning System: Kuder Skills Confidence Assessment and Kuder Skills Confidence Assessment-Adult

Instrument Acronym or Preferred Short Name: KSCA-R and KSCA-A

Instrument Authors: Hoi Suen, JoAnn Harris-Bowlsbey, Spencer Niles, Jack Rayman, and Jerry Trusty

Publisher: Kuder, Inc.

Publisher Address: 302 Visions Parkway, Adel, IA 50003

https://navigator.kuder.com

https://journey.kuder.com

Statement of Purpose: The Kuder Skills Confidence Assessment (KSCA-R and KSCA-A) is designed to be optimally efficient, while meeting or exceeding the latest technical standards of reliability, validity, and fairness set forth by the Joint Committee of the American Psychological Association, the American Educational Research Association, and the National Council on Measurement in Education (AERA/APA/NCME, 1999, 2014). The aim of the KSCA-R and KSCA-A is to determine the relative self-efficacy of the respondent in each of the six areas of the respondent's Holland profile. These self-efficacy scores are then used to identify the clusters and pathways of the National Career Clusters Framework as well as O*NET occupations that best match the respondent's self-efficacy, based on the combined value of a Euclidean distance similarity index and a measure of congruence. [Kuder Career Interests Assessment is a registered trademark of Kuder, Inc.; O*NET is a registered trademark of the U.S. Department of Labor, Employment and Training Administration; National Career Clusters is a registered trademark of Advance CTE.]

Target Population: Students (grades 7 through 12) for the Kuder Skills Confidence Assessment (KSCA-R); young adults and adults ages 18 and older for the Kuder Skills Confidence Assessment-Adult (KSCA-A).

Norm Group(s) on which Scores are Based: To ensure that the KSCA-R scores reliably and validly reflect self-efficacy in the six Holland areas, with efficiency and without bias, a number of psychometric research and development activities were undertaken prior to its release. These activities involved the use of a) an initial pool of 175 potential Likert-type items aimed at measuring self-efficacy in the six Holland areas; b) a panel of five incontrovertible national leaders in career counseling and guidance for various formal judgmental exercises; and c) item by item response data from a national sample of 2,100 respondents for various statistical analyses. Similarly, for the KSCA-A, activities involved the use of a) an initial pool of 170 potential Likert-type items aimed at measuring self-efficacy in the six Holland areas; b) a panel of five incontrovertible international leaders in career counseling and guidance for various formal judgmental exercises; and c) item-by-item response data from a national sample of 2,000 respondents for various statistical analyses. The result of these R&D activities is the final versions of the KSCA-R and KSCA-A. For the KSCA-R, 72 of the best items from the initial pool of 175 are included. For the KSCA-A, 67 of the best items from is initial pool of 170 are included. From the final items, the level of self-efficacy of a respondent in the six Holland areas are measured with high levels of reliability, strong evidence of validity based on content, strong evidence of validity based on internal structure, strong evidence of freedom from gender or race/ethnic bias, and strong evidence of freedom from biased, insensitive, stereotypic, or offensive content, context, or language.

Titles of Subtests, Scales, Scores Provided: The KSCA-R presents scores primarily by occupational scales of the clusters and pathways of the National Career Clusters Framework. The KSCA-A presents scores primarily by occupational scales of Holland (RIASEC) work environments. In addition, Kuder provides scores for both versions on other career cluster systems as requested by customers both domestically and internationally.

Forms and Levels Available with Dates of Publication/Revision of Each: The KSCA-R /KSCA-A is one of three assessments included in the Kuder Career Planning System. It is Internet based and featured in the products Kuder Navigator, Kuder Journey, and Kuder Atlas. These products are career planning systems that provide research based assessments, occupational and school databases, and job-seeking tools. Some editions of these products include tools for education plans, college planning, scholarships and other financial assistance, and connections to parents and administrators.

Date of Most Recent Edition of Manual, User's Guide, etc.: The KSCA-R and KSCA-A assessments are revised on a five-year cycle. During 2017, selected assessment items are being evaluated for revision or replacement in updated versions of the assessments with anticipated publication by the end of the year.

Available in which Languages: English (American and British forms), Spanish (United States and Latin America forms), Portuguese, Arabic, Kinyarwandan, and Chinese (Simplified).

Actual Test Time: 4-10 minutes

Total Administration Time: 15-25 minutes

Required Level of Training and/or Credentials for Administrator: N/A; the assessment is self-administered.

Types of Scores: Bar graphs with Low, Medium, High scales as well as verbal labels of top five pathway results are provided.

Report Format/Content: Kuder provides a skills confidence results report as well as a composite report comparing results from the interests and skills confidence assessments. Scoring of the KSCA-R and KSCA-A is immediate on completion of the last item.

Report Format/Content for Group Summaries: Group summaries are sorted on several variables that may be accessed at the administrator's site.

Availability of Machine Scoring Service? No

Availability of Hand Scoring? No

Availability of Local Machine Scoring Service? Not Available

Availability and Options for Computer Software? Computer Software Available, Standard administration on-line

If other, please describe: The KSCA-R is offered within Kuder Navigator; the KSCA-A is offered within Kuder Journey. For Kuder Atlas, either the KSCA-R (for youth and students younger than age 18) or KSCA-A (for ages 18 and older) is automatically selected based on the user's age. Immediate online scoring for both KSCA-R and KSCA-A after completion of the assessment.

Link to webpage that specifies the costs of materials: An annual site license for Kuder Navigator (for secondary students) and/or Kuder Journey (for postsecondary students and adults) can be purchased by an organization for a number of licensed uses. Site license purchases include access to all three Kuder assessments as well as the Kuder Administrative Database Management System (ADMS), in which counselors and administrators can view individual and aggregate assessment results and run reports. Individual user accounts for both Navigator and Journey, as well as special packages and volume discounts are available for purchase. Please contact Kuder for a quote.

Additional Comments of Interest to Users (e.g. forthcoming revisions, new material, etc): Internationally, the KSCA-R and KSCA-A have been used to present skills confidence results aligned to occupational classifications beyond O*NET as used in the United States. To date, these skills confidence result alignments have included the International Standard Classification of Occupations (ISCO-08), the Arab Standard Occupation Classification (ASOC), the Australia/New Zealand Standard Classification of Occupations (ANZSCO), and Mexico's Sistema Nacional de Clasificacion de Ocupaciones (SINCO 2011).

Published Reviews of the Instrument in the Last 15 years: (information not provided by publisher)

KUDER CAREER INTERESTS ASSESSMENT-LIKERT

Instrument Acronym or Preferred Short Name: KCIA-L

Instrument Authors: Hoi Suen, JoAnn Harris-Bowlsbey, Spencer Niles, Jack Rayman, and Jerry Trusty

Publisher: Kuder, Inc.

Publisher Address: 302 Visions Parkway, Adel, IA 50003

https://navigator.kuder.com

https://journey.kuder.com

Statement of Purpose: The Kuder Careers Interests Assessment-Likert (KCIA-L) is designed to be optimally efficient, while meeting or exceeding the latest technical standards of reliability, validity, and fairness set forth by the Joint Committee of the American Psychological Association, the American Educational Research Association, and the National Council on Measurement in Education (AERA/APA/NCME, 1999, 2014). The aim of the KCIA-L is to determine the relative level of interest a respondent has in each of the six Holland work environments. In the United States, these six interest scores are then used to identify the pathways and clusters of the National Career Clusters Framework as well as O*NET occupations that best match the respondent's Holland interest profile, based on the combined value of a Euclidean distance similarity index and a measure of congruence. [Kuder Career Interests Assessment is a registered trademark of Kuder, Inc.; O*NET is a registered trademark of the U.S. Department of Labor, Employment and Training Administration; National Career Clusters is a registered trademark of Advance CTE.]

Target Population: Students (grades 7 and higher), young adults, and adults.

Norm Group(s) on which Scores are Based: The KCIA-L does not use norms. Rather, scores are self-referenced in that raw scores for each respondent are compared directly to one another. To ensure that KCIA-L scores reliably and validly reflect interests in the six Holland areas, with efficiency and without bias, a number of psychometric research and development activities were undertaken prior to its release. These activities involved the use of a) an initial pool of 168 items; b) a panel of five incontrovertible international leaders in career counseling and guidance for various formal judgmental exercises; and c) item-by-item response data from a national representation of 5,871 U.S. respondents. The result of these and other R&D activities is the final version of the KCIA-L that includes only the best 66 items from the initial pool of 168. From these 66 items, the levels of interest of a respondent in the six Holland areas are measured with high levels of reliability, strong evidence of validity based on content, strong evidence of validity based on internal structure, strong evidence of freedom from gender or race/ethnic bias, and strong evidence of freedom from biased, insensitive, stereotypic, or offensive content, context, or language. In addition, multidimensional scaling (MDS) analysis (proxscal method) results show that the interrelations among the six KCIA-L Holland scores display the characteristic hexagonal configuration of Holland vocational interest theory.

Titles of Subtests, Scales, Scores Provided: The KCIA-L presents scores primarily in two manners; either by the pathways and clusters of the National Career Clusters Framework or by Holland personality types (RIASEC codes). In addition, Kuder provides scores on other career cluster systems as requested by customers both domestically and internationally.

Forms and Levels Available with Dates of Publication/Revision of Each: The KCIA-L is one of three assessments included in the Kuder Career Planning System. The assessment is available for middle school through adult levels. It is Internet-based and featured in the products Kuder Navigator, Kuder Journey, and Kuder Atlas. These products are career planning systems that provide research based assessments, occupational and school databases, and job-seeking tools. Some editions of these products include tools for education plans, college planning, scholarships and other financial assistance, and connections to parents and administrators.

Date of Most Recent Edition of Manual, User's Guide, etc.: 2012. The KCIA-L is revised on a five-year cycle. During 2017, selected assessment items are being evaluated for revision or replacement in an updated version of the assessment to be published by the end of the year.

Available in which Languages: English (American and British forms), Spanish (United States and Latin America forms), Portuguese, Arabic, Kinyarwandan, and Chinese (Simplified).

Actual Test Time: 4-10 minutes

Total Administration Time: 15-25 minutes

Required Level of Training and/or Credentials for Administrator: N/A; the assessment is self-administered.

Types of Scores: Bar graphs with Low, Medium, and High scales, as well as verbal labels of the top five pathway results or Holland codes are provided.

Report Format/Content: Kuder provides an interest results report aligned to career interest areas and occupations as well as a composite report comparing results from interest and skills-confidence assessments. Scoring of the KCIA-L is immediate on completion of the last item.

Report Format/Content for Group Summaries: Group summaries are sorted on several variables that may be accessed at the administrator's site.

Availability of Machine Scoring Service? No

Availability of Hand Scoring? No

Availability of Local Machine Scoring Service? Not Available

Availability and Options for Computer Software? Computer Software Available, Standard administration on-line

If available, describe the ways in which computer/online version differs (if any): (information not provided by publisher)

Link to webpage that specifies the costs of materials: An annual site license for Kuder Navigator (for secondary students) and/or Kuder Journey (for postsecondary students and adults) can be purchased by an organization for a number of licensed uses. Site license purchases include access to all three Kuder assessments as well as the Kuder Administrative Database Management System (ADMS), in which counselors and administrators can view individual and aggregate assessment results and run reports. Individual user accounts for both Navigator and Journey, as well as special packages and volume discounts are available for purchase. Please contact Kuder for a quote.

Additional Comments of Interest to Users (e.g. forthcoming revisions, new material, etc): Internationally, the KCIA-L has been used to present interest results aligned to occupational classifications beyond O*NET as used in the United States. To date, these interest result alignments have included the International Standard Classification of Occupations (ISCO-08), the Arab Standard Occupation Classification (ASOC), the Australia/New Zealand Standard Classification of Occupations (ANZSCO), and Mexico's Sistema Nacional de Clasificacion de Ocupaciones (SINCO 2011).

Published Reviews of the Instrument in the Last 15 years: (information not provided by publisher)

Kuder Career Planning System

Reviewed by

Melinda M. Gibbons
Charmayne R. Adams
University of Tennessee, Knoxville

Description

Kuder, Inc. based the newly revised Kuder Planning System (2017) on original career assessments created by Frederic Kuder in 1938. According to the Kuder website, their mission is "to be the global authority in career guidance and education by providing evidence-based and proven tools to navigate life's journey" (Kuder, n.d.). The Kuder Career Planning System offers developmentally linked career and educational information based on interests, skills, and work values assessments. System users create personal portfolios that save their test scores and other information on the website. Kuder provides multiple levels of career programming, including the Kuder Galaxy for Pre-K and elementary school, Kuder Navigator for middle and high school, and Kuder Journey for postsecondary students and adults. Although the Kuder platform was revised in 2018 to increase mobile-compatibility, include an updated design, and improve search tools, the actual surveys did not change and are reviewed below. The three main assessments, Super's Work Values Inventory- Revised (Super & Zytowski, 2015), Kuder Skills Confidence Assessment (2015), and Kuder Interest Assessment (2015), are available through the Navigator and Journey sections.

Kuder Career Interest Assessment

The Kuder Career Interest Assessment – Likert (KCIA-L; Kuder, Inc., 2015), formerly referred to as the Kuder Career Interest Assessment-32 and the Kuder Career Search, is an updated interest inventory. The inventory is short, requiring 4-10 minutes to complete (Suen, 2015a). It includes 60 Likert-type questions that require test takers to decide whether they strongly dislike, dislike, are neutral, like, or strongly like, the described task. Users can indicate each ranking only once per question. The same version of the assessment, in both English and Spanish, is available for both Navigator and Journey. Sample items include, "operate heavy machinery" and "take charge of a failing business." A bar graph appears on the screen above the assessment questions, visually and via percent completed, to indicate how much of the assessment a user has completed. At the bottom right of the assessment is the option to start over and finish later if test takers are not able to finish in one sitting or need to clear all their answers and start over.

In both Navigator and Journey, the KCIA-L reports interest results based on the National Career Clusters Framework, which the National Association of State Directors of Career Technical Education Consortium (Advance CTE, n.d.) created. The 16 broad clusters represent a range of career options designed to help people identify specific career pathways linked to interest areas. On the Kuder systems, the results display interest ratings for both the clusters and the pathways. There are additional tabs for related careers and related majors, which users can sort by educational level and person matches, which link to interviews of people with various careers who have similar interests to those the test taker has indicated. Participants can learn more about specific careers that match their interests via hyperlinks to O*NET information.

Kuder Skills Confidence Assessment

The Kuder Skills Confidence Assessment (KSCA; Kuder, Inc., 2012), formerly known as the Kuder Skills Assessment, is available in two versions: KSCA-R for Navigator and the KSCA- A for Journey. Kuder revises the KSCA-R and KSCA-A assessments on a five-year cycle. Kuder planned revisions for 2017; however, revisions were incomplete at the time of this review (Suen, 2012). The KSCA-R includes 72 different skills, and 67 skills are in the KSCA-A. Both versions are available in English or Spanish, and each takes approximately 4-10 minutes to complete. Items include skills such as "read for someone who is blind" and "build a dog house."

The KSCA-R is targeted for 7th-12th graders and asks test takers to estimate their current confidence (self-efficacy) for each of the tasks, which correspond with Holland RIASEC codes (Suen, 2012). Students respond to each item on a 5-point Likert-type scale (*cannot do at all, slightly certain can do, moderately certain can do, very certain can do, and completely certain can do*) by indicating the level to which they can do the task currently. Each page includes eight items. As with the KCIA-L, results present as career pathways based on the 16 national career clusters. There are additional tabs for related occupations and sample education plans that align with the top national cluster.

The KSCA-A is similar; test takers rate their current level of confidence (self-efficacy) for each of the tasks and, again, on a 5-point scale (*cannot do at all* to *completely certain can do*). Results present in a similar way with the top five careers from the interest inventory and their respective national career, but the additional tabs include related occupations and related majors in contrast to the KSCA-R's sample education plans.

Super's Work Values Inventory- Revised

Seventy-two work-related values make up the Super's Work Values Inventory- revised (SWVI-r; Suen, 2015b), formally known as the Kuder Work Values Assessment (KWVA). The SWVI-r takes approximately 4-10 minutes to complete, and test takers rate the level of importance of different occupational features and characteristics on a 5-point Likert-like scale (*not important at all- not a factor in my job selection; somewhat important- I would take this into account, but could do without it; important- I would like it, but other things are more important; very important- need to have it, but not the most important; crucial- I would not consider a job without it*). Some of the values include independence and variety, and items that help identify these include, "can try out new ideas" and "can get a raise if I want." The SWVI-r is available in both English and Spanish, and a bar graph helps test takers identify how much of the instrument they have completed in a visual presentation and in a displayed percent. The results page provides a list of the 12 values with a bar indicating, low, medium, or high, for each value. The site includes a related occupations tab containing the results. The SWVI-r is identical for Kuder Journey and Kuder Navigator.

Technical Considerations

Kuder, Inc. reviews all three instruments associated with the Kuder Career Planning System every five years, with the most recent revision for the KCIA in 2015 and the others in 2012. Kuder, Inc. designs and reviews KCIA and KSCA for efficiency, reliability, validity, and cultural fairness based on standards from the leading psychological research standards. The SWVI is an updated version of Super's original values scale, but with a much broader norm group to increase cultural sensitivity (Suen, 2012).

Instrument Development and Soundness

KCIA-L. Kuder transitioned from the KCIA-32 to the KCIA-L in 2015. The purpose of the instrument is to identify interests based on the six Holland codes and, then, relate them to the 16 career clusters (Suen, 2015a). The KCIA-L began with an initial pool of 168 items, which a panel of five experts in career counseling and guidance reviewed for content validity, prior to undergoing an item-by-item response analysis by 5,871 participants. Reviewers kept items from the content validity review with higher than 80% consensus, and they eliminated items if more than one reviewer identified potential bias. To accomplish efficiency, reviewers completed item analysis and reliability assessment and kept only those items with very high item discrimination (.62 to .76) and overall coefficient alphas (.89 to .94; Suen, 2015a). Finally, reviewers completed additional analyses, including factor analysis, differential item functioning, and multidimensional scaling, to demonstrate evidence of consistency with the six-factor Holland model. Reviewers shortened the KCIA-L, based on the collective results of these validity and reliability activities, from the initial pool of 168 to 60 items (Suen, 2015a). They made modifications to the KCIA-L for use in Singapore and in Rwanda, in addition to the norming to populations in the U.S. Results of these adaptations demonstrate similar levels of soundness.

KSCA-A and KSCA-R. As stated previously, Kuder revises the KSCA-A and the KSCA-R on a five-year cycle and, during late 2017, will have selected assessment items evaluated for revision or replacement in the updated version. The purpose of the KSCA is to identify levels of self-efficacy for various work-related tasks based on the six Holland codes and 16 career pathways (Suen, 2012). Both versions began with an initial pool of 175 items, which five experts reviewed for content validity and cultural fairness, and then reviewed with an item-by-item response analysis from the results of 2,000 U.S. participants. Based on these analyses, 72 items were kept for the KSCA-R and 67 for the KSCA-A (Kuder Inc., 2017). Specific reliability coefficients could not be found for the two new versions of the KSCA, but reliability coefficients for the 2012 KSCA for the final items ranged from .74 to .91 (Suen, 2012). The two instruments are available in Spanish, Portuguese, Arabic, Chinese, and Kinyarwandan (Kuder Inc., 2017).

SWVI-r. SWVI-r is a revision of the original 1970 edition (Super, 1970) of the SWVI. The overall purpose of the SWVI-r is to determine the importance of values related to work. Revisions, over time, have resulted in dropping three of the original 15 values, thus, leaving 12 values measured in this most recent version. The information provided by the publisher indicates the scale scores are norm referenced based on a national stratified sample of 8,785 participants. Reliability coefficients from a group of 426 college students indicate sufficient alpha values ranging from .72 to .88 (Suen, 2015b). Like the KCIA-L, the SWVA-r has been normed for international use in Rwanda, Singapore, and Australia, in addition to other regions not specified by the publisher (Kuder Inc., 2017).

Use, Interpretation, and Evaluation

General Utility

Administering, scoring, and saving Kuder assessments takes place in the online platform. These online systems provide an organized way for clients and clinicians to access information and connect to resources that align with clients' individualized results. This organization and ease of access create a user-friendly way for clients to self-direct their educational and/or vocational exploration. Even though the ease of access allows clients to complete the assessments and view results without a clinician, support from a professional would aid in the expansion of the results and offer an understanding as to how to maximize the resources offered through the platform and the assessment results. Kuder assessment results are organized and connected by the client's name, so clients can access their results at any time. Clinicians can recommend that clients take the assessment prior to meeting with them, offer the assessments as a task completed during a session due to their short administration time, or recommend the assessment as a supplement to additional face-to-face vocational counseling services offered. The manual that accompanies the assessments is extremely brief with minimal information beyond general reliability and validity information; however, the system itself is easy to use without an extensive manual.

Presentation and Interpretation

The Kuder online platform is attractive and easy to navigate. The site includes a task bar on the left side to access various functions, including the assessments and a task-list on the right side with a suggested order in which clients use resources. Clients create their personal portfolio, where they are able to track and compare their test results, explore occupations, plan for education and work, and find a job. Each of the assessments has a standardized format that enhances functionality and ease of use. Test results are available immediately and saved in a portfolio. Users can explore careers by career clusters or by assessment results, and career information links to O*NET information. Education and work planning includes a variety of options, based on desired education level and activities needed to apply for a job successfully. Users can interpret much of the information without a professional counselor, but for maximum results, clients should work with a school or career counselor as they proceed through the website. One of the challenges the standardized format might present is clients forgetting which of the assessments they are completing. Users can rectify this challenge easily by referencing the question prompt at the top of the screen. Clinicians could provide this simple directive to clients prior to clients beginning the assessments.

Cultural Considerations and Implications

The researchers attempted to address cultural considerations in several ways. They surveyed a national sample of participants for all of the instruments and had career counseling experts review all potential items for cultural bias. Kuder Inc. has begun the process of adapting the KCIA and KSCA for participants in other countries, using similarly rigorous activities to ensure reliability and validity. One negative aspect we noted was the lack of specific demographic information about validation study participants. Without this information, knowing cultural representation in the norming group is impossible. For example, we could not locate any information regarding response differences by ethnicity, gender, or socioeconomic status. As such, counselors working with culturally diverse groups need to engage in cautious interpretation to help increase cultural sensitivity. Counselors should be aware of the unique needs of diverse groups and incorporate this knowledge into the use of the Kuder.

Evaluation

The Kuder Career Planning System is a useful, interactive, online program that provides career planning for clients from ages four and older. Each of the Navigator and Journey systems include three career assessments to help clients learn more about themselves as they plan for their future. Navigator focuses on middle and high school students, and Journey targets college students and adults. Kuder paid careful attention to providing valid instruments with the least amount of items necessary. The assessment platform is user friendly, with continuity across all three assessments on both Navigator and Journey. In addition, the extensive research conducted for each assessment demonstrates strong evidence of reliability, validity, and attempts at cultural fairness. These assessments are a great tool for career and school counselors to use with clients in exploring educational and vocational opportunities that align with skills, values, and interests.

Research and Evaluation

The Kuder assessments appear to demonstrate soundness of validity and reliability. The developers update and reevaluate the instruments consistently on a five-year cycle, demonstrating a strong attempt to remain updated and current. Practitioners can use the assessments to help students and clients explore a variety of career-related beliefs in a one-stop location. The system's ease of use, instant results, and ability to repeat assessments, as needed, make it easy for practitioners to access and review client results. Both clients and counselors can review results through the client portfolio, and, then, use the results to work through the suggested next steps to identify potential majors, careers, or educational pursuits. Kuder provides limited information regarding the use of the assessments for research purposes, but it appears that clinicians could use the assessments for project and program evaluation or to consider differences across cultural or demographic groups. The Kuder Systems' short, yet comprehensive, assessments seem to represent a useful, valid, and reliable way for practitioners to assist their clients as they determine their career plans.

References

Advance CTE. (n.d.). *Career Clusters.* Retrieved from https://careertech.org/career-clusters

Kuder, Inc. (n.d.). *Kuder.* Retrieved from https://www.kuder.com/about/

Kuder, Inc. (n.d.). *Kuder Interest Assessment-Likert.* Adel, IA: Author.

Kuder, Inc. (n.d.). *Kuder Skills Confidence Assessment.* Adel, IA: Author.

Kuder, Inc. (2017). *Kuder planning system.* Adel, IA: Author.

Suen, H. K. (2012). *Technical brief: Kuder Skills Confidence Assessment 2012.* Adel, IA: Kuder, Inc.

Suen, H. K. (2015a). *Technical brief: Kuder Career Interest Assessment – Likert 2015.* Adel, IA: Kuder, Inc.

Suen, H. K. (2015b). *Technical brief: Super's Work Values Inventory – revised.* Adel, IA: Kuder, Inc.

Super, D. E. (1970). *Work values inventory.* Boston, MA: Houghton Mifflin.

Super, D. E., & Zytowski, D. G. (2015). *Super's Work Values Inventory – Revised.* Adel, IA: Kuder.

QUANTITATIVE

NEO PERSONALITY INVENTORY

Instrument Acronym or Preferred Short Name: NEO-PI

Instrument Authors: Paul T. Costa, Jr., PhD, and Robert R. McCrae, PhD

Publisher: PAR, Inc.

Publisher Address: 16204 N Florida Ave, Lutz, FL 33549

https://www.parinc.com/Products/Pkey/273

Statement of Purpose: Obtain a detailed assessment of general personality in adolescents and adults. The NEO PI-3 measures the five major domains (Neuroticism, Extraversion, Openness, Agreeableness, and Conscientiousness) and gives insight into the six facets that define each domain. The 192 NEO-4 questionnaire items and the scoring keys are identical to those of the E, O, A, and C factors of the NEO PI-R™. Norms for the NEO-4 are based on the NEO PI-R combined-gender normative sample.

Target Population: Adolescents (12-20 years) and adults (21-99 years)

Norm Group(s) on which Scores are Based: Male and Female Adolescents (12-20 years) and Male and Female Adults (21-99 years)

Titles of Subtests, Scales, Scores Provided: Five major domains of personality and six facets defining each domain: - Neurotocism: Anxiety, Angry Hostility, Depression, Self-Consciousness, Impulsiveness, Vulnerability - Extraversion: Warmth, Gregariousness, Assertiveness, Activity, Excitement-Seeking, Positive Emotions - Openness: Fantasy, Aesthetics, Feelings, Actions, Ideas, Values - Agreeableness: Trust, Straightforwardness, Altruism, Compliance, Modesty, Tender-Mindedness - Conscientiousness: Competence, Order, Dutifulness, Achievement Striving, Self-Discipline, Deliberation

Forms and Levels Available with Dates of Publication/Revision of Each: Item Booklet, Answer Sheet, Profile Forms, Summary Feedback Sheets, Style Graph Booklets, Problems in Living Checklists, Job Profiler Booklets. All published in 2010.

Date of Most Recent Edition of Manual, User's Guide, etc.: 2010

Available in which Languages: In addition to English: Publications: Czech Danish Dutch Finnish French French-Canadian German Italian Korean Norwegian Romanian Russian Slovak Spanish Swedish Turkish UK English Translations: Albanian Chinese (Traditional) Estonian Greek Hungarian Lithuanian Macedonian Marathi Spanish Urdu Vietnamese

Actual Test Time: 30-40 minutes

Total Administration Time: 45-55 minutes (including scoring)

Required Level of Training and/or Credentials for Administrator: The NEO PI-3 is essentially a self-administered instrument, and thus can be administered and scored by individuals who do not have formal training in clinical psychology, personality, or related fields. The interpretation of the results, however, should be performed by professionals with training in psychological testing and measurement (e.g., reliability and validity, use of norms), in addition to familiarity with the materials and procedures presented in the Professional Manual.

Types of Scores: T-scores; Range descriptors

Report Format/Content: Basic Score Report includes Validity Indices; T-Score Profile; Data Table including Raw Scores, T-Scores, and corresponding Range descriptor; Summary of Item Responses; Validity Items. Interpretive/Narrative option includes all Score Report contents plus a Global Description of the client's personality; Detailed Interpretation of each Factor and its Facets; Possible Implications of Personality Correlates; Stability of Profile; Personality Style Graphs; Problems in Living Checklist. A Summary Report may be generated to provide the client with a description of their personality based on the five factors. Professional Development Planning (PDR) Reports are available as well. The Management Planning Report helps the administrator better understand the client to assist him/her in their current career situation as well as future opportunities. The Individual Planning Report is directed toward the client themselves. Both provide a summary of the client's most distinctive characteristics and how those may work to the client's advantage/disadvantage. Profile Graphs are provided for: Emotional Reactions; Interpersonal Patterns; Openness to Change; Agreeableness; Work Ethic; All Domains. The reports also review the client's: Problem Solving Skills; Planning, Organizing, and Implementation Skills; Style of Relating to Others; Personal Style.

Report Format/Content for Group Summaries: Not available

Availability of Machine Scoring Service? Yes

If yes, maximum time required for machine scoring and return: Once received, reports are processed and returned within 24 hours or on the next business day.

Availability of Hand Scoring? Yes

If yes, time required for hand scoring? 15 minutes

If yes, who is it scored by? Test Administrator

Availability of Local Machine Scoring Service? Yes

If yes, provisions/conditions/equipment required for local machine scoring: Windows XP, Vista, 7, 8, 10 (32-bit only). NEO SoftwareC_x0002_B version 3.01; NEO-PI-3 and NEO PI-R modules (PDR module optional); Compatible OMR scanner (iNSIGHT 2, 4/4ES, 20, 30, 70, 150; OpScan 2, 3, 4/4U/4ES, 5/6, 7/8, 10, 15, 21, 9010M/9020M); CD-RO

Availability and Options for Computer Software? Computer Software Available, Standard administration on-line

If available, describe the ways in which computer/online version differs (if any): Computer software provides a single-user license with unlimited scoring/ report generation when keying in response data from a completed print form. Must purchase Comprehensive Software System to generate PDR reports. On-screen administration usages are available for purchase. Online administration and/or scoring is available via PARiConnect. Accessible from supported devices that have internet access. This option is ideal when working from multiple locations or with multiple clinicians. Administrations are priced per use as are reports. Online administration can be performed on-screen with the client present or by e-mailing a link to the assessment for the client to complete remotely.

Link to webpage that specifies the costs of materials: https://www.parinc.com/Products/Pkey/273

Additional Comments of Interest to Users (e.g. forthcoming revisions, new material, etc): (information not provided by publisher)

Published Reviews of the Instrument in the Last 15 years:

Benson, N. F., & Kluck, A. S. (2017). [Test review of the NEO Personality Inventory-3]. In J. F. Carlson, K. F. Geisinger, & J. L. Jonson (Eds.), *The nineteenth mental measurements yearbook*. Lincoln, NE: Buros Center for Testing.

NEO-4

Reviewed by
Brian J. Taber
Oakland University

Description

The NEO-4 is a personality inventory that was modified from the NEO-PI-R and is intended for use in career counseling, career development, employee training, and personal growth. The NEO-PI-R assesses the big five personality traits of Neuroticism, Extraversion, Openness to Experience, Agreeableness, and Conscientiousness. The NEO-4 measures all but the trait of Neuroticism, or the tendency to experience negative affect, such as anxiety, sadness, anger, and guilt. The rationale for a measure focusing on the other four traits and excluding Neuroticism pertains to the appropriateness of use under certain contexts. More specifically, there might be instances in group contexts when people might be more comfortable talking about their personality profiles when information regarding emotional stability is not discussed (Costa & McCrae, 1998). Also, given that the NEO-4 is intended for use in career counseling, research has shown that Neuroticism tends not to be related to vocational interests and, therefore, adds little to this aspect of vocational guidance (Costa, McCrae, & Holland, 1984). As such, the NEO-4 assesses the remaining four personality domains.

There are two forms of the NEO-4. Form S is for self-report assessment and Form R is for completion by a third party observer. The test is available only through paper and pencil administration and is hand scored. Test instructions are clear, and scoring is easy, which makes results available quickly. Both forms contain 192-items and use a Likert response format from *strongly disagree* to *strongly agree*. Both measure across four dimensional trait domains, and each domain contains six specific facets. Extraversion (E) refers to the degree to which a person is outgoing, sociable, and active. The Extraversion facets include *warmth, gregariousness, assertiveness, activity, excitement-seeking,* and *positive emotions.* Openness to Experience (O) refers to the degree a person possesses broad interests, imagination, and creativity. The Openness to Experience facets include: *fantasy, aesthetics, feelings, actions, ideas,* and *values.* Agreeableness (A) refers to the degree a person is compassionate, cooperative, and avoids conflict. The Agreeableness facets include *trust, straightforwardness, altruism, compliance, modesty,* and *tender-mindedness.* Conscientiousness (C) refers to the degree a person is well organized, dependable, and methodical. Conscientiousness facets include *competence, order, dutifulness, achievement striving, self-discipline,* and *deliberation.* Three questions at the bottom of the answer sheet serve as validity checks. The questions encompass whether the respondent answered questions honestly, whether all statements were answered, and whether the responses were recorded in the appropriate area. Additionally, instructions encourage test administrators to review the responses (i.e. acquiescent, nay-saying, random responding etc.) on the entire measure and use clinical judgment about whether the pattern of responses merit discarding the results. The test administrator removes the top page of the answer sheet and simply adds values related to the marked responses across each row to produce a facet score. After calculating each facet score, the scorer summates the facets to yield a total raw score for each respective trait domain.

There are two ways to present results to respondents. The first is to plot the raw scores on the profile form for each of the four trait domains and the respective facets. Once plotted, the raw scores will align with the corresponding T-score to indicate where the respondent falls within each trait and each facet relative to the norm reference group. Respondents receive a summary sheet that includes a brief interpretive description of their traits based on whether they were high, average, or below average on a trait. The second way to give results is through the presentation of six personality styles. These are derived through the intersection of two personality traits along horizontal and vertical axes forming a circumplex.

The six styles encompass Interests, Interactions, Activity, Attitudes, Learning, and Character. The *Style of Interests* is created through the combination of Openness and Extraversion and refers to preferences for the novel versus the familiar and solitary versus social activities. The *Style of Interactions* is formed through the intersection of Extraversion and Agreeableness and refers to preferences regarding social interaction and friendliness. The *Style of Activity* is comprised of the combination of Extraversion and Conscientiousness and refers to style of orientation with respect to energy and focus in pursuing goals. The *Style of Attitudes* is the combination of Openness and Agreeableness and refers to the degree to which people are open to new perspectives and opinions in relation to the viewpoints of others. The *Style of Learning* is comprised of the combination of Openness and Conscientiousness and reflects orientations with respect to openness to new ideas and use of imagination and a corresponding need for structure. *Style of Character* is the combination of Agreeableness and Conscientiousness and reflects the degree of orientation concerning being cooperative and hardworking. The resulting intersection of the combined traits divides high and low scores on the traits into quadrants that represent personality tendencies within the context of each style. For example, regarding a respondent's *Style of Learning,* if the person scores on the higher end of Openness and scores on the lower end of Conscientiousness, this would place that person in the quadrant labeled *Dreamers.* Falling in this quadrant would indicate that this person has a tendency to be attracted to new ideas, start innovative projects, and tolerate ambiguity, but might have difficulty staying focused and completing projects successfully.

Technical Considerations

Psychometric and normative information provided for the NEO-4 are based on the NEO-PI-R. As mentioned previously, the notable difference between the NEO-4 and the NEO PI-R is the removal of the Neuroticism scale; otherwise, all the items are the same between the two inventories. The supplemental manual for the NEO-4 refers the test user to the manual for the other NEO inventories (McCrae & Costa, 2010) for technical information. Because the manual provides information on the NEO-PI-3, NEO-FFI-3, and the NEO PI-R, practitioners using the NEO-4 should focus on NEO PI-R technical information and exclude the information specific to the other two inventories.

The manual reports test-retest and internal consistency reliability estimates for the trait domains and facets. For the trait domains assessed on the NEO-4, the test-retest reliability over a one-week interval ranged from .92 for Extraversion to .93 for Openness to Experience. For the facets over the same period, reliability ranged from .70 to .91. Test-retest reliability over a 10-year period for domains and facets show remarkable stability as would be expected for a personality assessment (Terracciano, Costa, & McCrae, 2006). Estimates of internal consistency reliability for the domains range from .86 for Agreeableness to .90 for Conscientiousness.

The supplemental manual for the NEO-4 does not present any unique validity evidence for the measure. Instead, the manual references validity evidence from other NEO PI measures deemed appropriate for the contextual use of the NEO-4. For instance, criterion validity evidence, in relation to vocational interests, demonstrated trait domains correlating significantly in the theoretically expected direction with Holland's RIASEC types (e.g. Schinka, Dye, & Curtiss, 1997). Also, the manual highlights the predictive validity of the NEO PI scales in relation to job performance (Cellar, Miller, Doverspike, & Klawsky, 1997) and academic performance (Schmitt, Ryan, Stierwalt, & Powell, 1995). As for convergent validity, Furnham (1996) reported that the E, O, A, and C trait domains correlated with the theoretically corresponding preferences on the Myers-Briggs Type Indicator.

Regarding norms, the NEO-4 does not have a separate norm reference group and uses data collected for the NEO PI-R for this purpose. The normative sample consisted of 1,000 people (500 men and 500 women), whom the developers selected to match the 1995 U.S. Census projections for age and race. The normative sample has slightly higher educational attainment than the general population. Although separate norms refer to men and women, instructions encourage users of the NEO-4 to use the combined gender norms due to potential legal implications of using gender-based norms in employment settings.

Uses in Counseling

The NEO-4 is intended for use for career counseling and in employment settings. However, neither manual provided with the test materials presents specific information on how to use the NEO-4 results in these settings. A NEO bibliography is available through the publisher's website and contains a section for *Industrial/Organizational and Career Psychology*. There is a significant body of scholarship on the Five Factor Model of personality assessment and application in regards to enhancing person-environment fit, career choice, motivation, workplace interpersonal behavior, and training (e.g. Hammond, 2001; Lee, Johnston, & Dougherty, 2000). Much of this scholarship encompasses the inclusion of the Neuroticism domain, which shows the contextual relevance for career counseling. For instance, while the scale of Neuroticism may not be strongly related to vocational interests, the construct of neuroticism is linked to other important career related variables, such as decision-making and employability (Di Fabio & Bucci, 2016). Also, in the context of career counseling, discussing emotional distress and vulnerability with career clients and how those might impact work life and influence choices is important. Accordingly, for career counselors using one of the other NEO PI assessments might be more advantageous.

Evaluation

With the absence of the Neuroticism scale, the NEO-4 is essentially a shorter version of the NEO PI-R. The rationale for excluding the Neuroticism scale does have some merit, particularly in relation for use in employment settings. If employers were to use personality assessment as part of group employee training, for instance, exploring the emotional vulnerability of employees publicly and dealing with the resulting concomitant issues that may arise in the workplace as a consequence of such disclosure might not be necessary nor desirable. Therefore, the NEO-4 does have potential utility in certain circumstances. The NEO-4 scales have good reliability and the NEO PI-R, on which the NEO-4 is based, has accumulated much validity evidence over the years. In fact, the Five Factor Model of personality has received much research attention in relation to career counseling and industrial/organizational psychology. Accordingly, there is a significant body of literature from which career counselors, human resource personnel, and trainers can draw to make use of results and, in particular, as scores pertain to the E, O, A, and C domains.

Although the NEO-4 is intended for use for career counseling and in employment settings, there is too much reliance on validity evidence from other versions of the NEO PI. Thus, users should note that the NEO PI-R has accrued a substantial amount of construct and criterion validity evidence. However, whether the removal of Neuroticism has any effect on any of the other scales or their interpretation is unknown. This, of course, warrants investigation. Another area that requires further investigation regards the six personality styles. A long-standing criticism of the NEO-4 has been the lack of research supporting the use of the six personality styles (Henington, 2001). For instance, future research should examine the utility of the personality styles in vocational guidance, job performance, work engagement, training, job satisfaction, and team building. Results from such research would be useful and, potentially, provide counselors, human resource personnel, and trainers better information on how to use the personality style results effectively. In a related vein, the interpretive material presented to test respondents is rather brief and does not provide a comprehensive overview of what the facet scores mean. Computer scoring and a narrative report that provides more details about personality domains and facets would be useful. These are available for the other NEO PI assessments.

Another shortcoming of the NEO-4 is that it relies on what appears to be a dated norm reference group that was intended to reflect the U.S. in general over 20 years ago. Further, these individuals were volunteers that likely did not feel the need to engage in impression management when completing the assessment. However, in an employment setting, this might not be the case. The NEO-4 could benefit from having a specific norm group that conforms to the contexts for the intended use.

The NEO-4 does have potential utility in the context of public organizational settings where discussing emotional vulnerability might not be necessary nor warranted. However, the NEO-4 does need more research as a separate inventory rather than reliance on inferences from the NEO PI-R. Also, providing more comprehensive interpretation of results would be useful for both test administrators and respondents. Addressing these shortcomings could help distinguish it from the other NEO PI assessments and might provide those conducting personality appraisal in employment settings a contextually sound assessment.

References

Cellar, D. F., Miller, M. L., Doverspike, D. D. & Klawsky, J. D. (1997). Comparison of factor structures and criterion-related validity coefficients for two measures of personality based on the five factor model. *Journal of Applied Psychology, 81,* 694-704.

Costa, P. T., & McCrae, R. R. (1998). *Manual supplement for the NEO-4.* Lutz, FL: PAR, Inc.

Costa, P. T., McCrae, R. R., & Holland, J. L. (1984). Personality and vocational interests in an adult sample. *Journal of Applied Psychology, 69*(3), 390-400.

Di Fabio, A., & Bucci, O. (2016). Neuroticism and career outcomes: An empirical study from a preventive perspective. In A. Di Fabio (Ed.), *Neuroticism: Characteristics, impact on job performance and health outcomes* (pp. 147-159). Hauppauge, NY: Nova Science Publishers.

Furnham, A., (1996). The big five versus the big four: The relationship between the Myers-Briggs Type Indicator (MBTI) and the NEO-PI five factor model of personality. *Personality and Individual Differences, 21,* 303-307.

Hammond, M. S. (2001). The use of the five-factor model of personality as a therapeutic tool in career counseling. *Journal of Career Development, 27,* 153-165. doi:http://dx.doi.org/10.1023/A:1007878824517

Henington, C., (2001). NEO-4 [Review]. In B. S. Plake & J. C. Impara (Eds.), *The fourteenth mental measurements yearbook.* Lincoln, NE: Buros Institute of Mental Measurements.

Lee, F. K., Johnston, J. A., & Dougherty, T. W. (2000). Using the five-factor model of personality to enhance career development and organizational functioning in the workplace. *Journal of Career Assessment, 8,* 419-427. doi:http://dx.doi.org/10.1177/106907270000800411

McCrae, R. R., & Costa, P. T. (2010). *NEO inventories professional manual.* Lutz, FL: PAR, Inc.

Schinka, J. A., Dye, D. A., & Curtiss, G. (1997). Correspondence between five-factor and RIASEC models of personality. *Journal of Personality Assessment, 36,* 355-368.

Schmitt, M. J., Ryan, A. M., Stierwalt, S. L., & Powell, A. B. (1995). Frame-of-reference effects on personality scale scores and criterion-related validity. *Journal of Applied Psychology, 80,* 607-620.

Terracciano, A., Costa, P. T., & McCrae, R. R. (2006). Personality plasticity after age 30. *Personality and Social Psychology Bulletin, 32,* 999-1009.

QUANTITATIVE

Occupational Aptitude Survey and Interest Schedule – Third Edition: Interest Survey and Aptitude Survey

Instrument Acronym or Preferred Short Name: OASIS-3: IS and OASIS-3: AS (two separate kits)

Instrument Author: Randall M. Parker

Publisher: Hammill Institute, a division of PRO-ED, Inc.

Publisher Address: 8640 Shoal Creek Blvd. Austin, TX 78757
www.proedinc.com

Statement of Purpose: To assist individuals in 8th grade through post-secondary settings in their career search by providing them with information regarding their vocational interests related to the world of work.

Target Population: 8th grade through 12th grade and adult

Norm Group(s) on which Scores are Based: Norming population: 2,005 students in 8th grade through post-secondary education settings, and 500 adults in post-secondary educational settings. Normative data was gathered from four regions of the United States.

Titles of Subtests, Scales, Scores Provided: Scales: Artistic, Scientific, Nature, Protective, Mechanical, Industrial, Business Detail, Selling, Accommodating, Humanitarian, Leading-Influencing, and Physical Performing.

Scores provided: raw scores, percentiles, stanines.

Forms and Levels Available with Dates of Publication/Revision of Each: Forms available: Student Test Booklet, Student Answer Sheet, Student Profile, Scoring Forms (2001)

Date of Most Recent Edition of Manual, User's Guide, etc.: 2001

Available in which Languages: English Only

Actual Test Time: 30-45 minutes

Total Administration Time: 45-60 minutes

Required Level of Training and/or Credentials for Administrator: Level A: no special qualifications are necessary for the administration of the OASIS-3: IS or AS. To make valid interpretations of scores and data, users must have appropriate knowledge and skill in tests and measurements.

Types of Scores: Raw scores, percentiles, Stanines are generated for each of the scales.

Report Format/Content: A narrative report format is not provided. Examiner's Manual recommends reviewing results with examinee verbally and in person.

Report Format/Content for Group Summaries: Not available

Availability of Machine Scoring Service? Yes

If yes, maximum time required for machine scoring and return: 2-3 days. Protocols are returned to PRO-ED for scoring.

Availability of Hand Scoring? Yes

If yes, time required for hand scoring? Estimated 15-20 minutes

If yes, who is it scored by? Test Administrator

Availability of Local Machine Scoring Service? Not Available

Availability and Options for Computer Software? None Available

Link to webpage that specifies the costs of materials: www.proedinc.com

Additional Comments of Interest to Users (e.g. forthcoming revisions, new material, etc): (information not provided by publisher)

Published Reviews of the Instrument in the Last 15 years:

Venn, J. J. (2014). *Assessing Students With Special Needs*, Fifth Edition., pps. 227-228, Pearson, Inc.

OASIS-3

Reviewed by
Amanda G. Flora
The University of Virginia

Introduction/Description

The Occupational Aptitude Survey and Interest Schedule, 3rd edition (OASIS-3) is an enduring career assessment developed to provide individuals with information about their abilities and interests to aid in the career search (Parker 2002a; 2002b). The overall purpose of the OASIS-3 is to help individuals, eighth grade-level students through adult, in the self-awareness and vocational exploration stages of career development by providing them with more information about themselves. Ideally, the information gleaned through the assessment process will assist in further stages of the career development process, such as decision-making. This third edition included an expanded sample of postsecondary adults from the initial 8th to 12th grade age norming group from the OASIS-2.

As expected from the title, the OASIS-3 measures two distinct areas, aptitude and interest, and contains two separate instruments for administration, scoring, and interpretation. Moving forward, I provide the majority of this review based on the individual scales - Aptitude Scale (AS) or Interest Inventory (IS).

Utility - Aptitude Survey (AS)

Parker (2002a) developed the AS to assist individuals in identifying strengths during career exploration. He acknowledged the debate over the term *aptitude*, with support to differentiate it from *achievement*. After he provided viewpoints on whether aptitude is innate or learned, Parker asserted that aptitude would fall in the middle of these two. Test-takers complete the instrument manually, after receiving a Student Booklet, Student Answer Sheet, pencils, and scratch paper. The AS contains five subtests of varying lengths and time limits:

- Vocabulary: 40 items, in which respondents choose two of the four words as synonyms or antonyms in 9 minutes; Vocabulary items include sets, such as "Winter, Extreme, Near, Summer" and "Empty, Civil, Void, Utter";

- Computation: 30 items containing arithmetic and algebra problems with a 12 minute time limit;

- Spatial Relations: 20 items for which respondents select, within 8 minutes, one three-dimensional image based on the image of a two-dimensional object;

- Word Comparison: 100 items in which respondents select whether two sets of words, numbers, or nonsense symbols are the same or different in 5 minutes. Sample items from Word Comparison include "Richard B. Jones" and "Richard B. Jones" (same) or "Edith's Interior Design" and "Edyth's Interior Design (different)";

- Making Marks: respondents must draw three lines, in the form of an asterisk, into 160 boxes divided into two sections within 30 seconds per section.

Utility - Interest Schedule (IS)

The IS provides individuals in educational settings, in 8th grade and beyond, with information about career interests related to the world of work (Parker, 2002b). Test-takers receive a Student Booklet and Student Answer Sheet during

221

administration and an Interpretation Booklet with their results. As with the AS, students complete the instrument manually. The Student Booklet contains 240 items organized into two lists: 120-item Occupations and 120-item Job Activities. Each item represents an occupation or task along one of the twelve interest areas: Artistic (ART); Scientific (SCI); Nature (NAT); Protective (PRO); Mechanical, (MEC); Industrial (IND); Business Detail (BUS); Selling (SEL); Accommodating (ACC); Humanitarian (HUM); Leading-Influencing (LEA);   and, Physical Performing (PHY). Items on the Occupation list offer a range of vocational options, including musician, astronomer, and police officer. Examples of Job Activities are draw and paint, develop new chemical products, and organize and oversee office works. Respondents use the Student Answer Sheet to record *Like*, *Neutral*, or *Dislike* for each of the 240 items. There is no time limit, though students finish in about 30 minutes typically (Osborn & Zunker, 2015).

Technical Considerations

Both the AS and IS Examiner's manuals contain comprehensive and detailed psychometric information. Like the prior utility section, I separate the parametric data of the OASIS-3 by AS and IS in the following paragraphs and provide an overview of the reliability, validity, and norming information of each. Combined AS and IS reliability and validity does not appear to be available.

Instrument Development Processes and Procedures

Parker (2002a) provided ample information on the development of the AS scale. In an effort to establish validity, he employed factor analysis procedures used for the development of, and in comparison with, the General Aptitude Test Battery (GATB; U.S. Department of Defense, 1993). Factor loading varied slightly on some subtests among the five factors (Manual Dexterity, Perceptual Aptitude; Numerical Aptitude; Spatial Aptitude, and Verbal Aptitude), though the overall analysis revealed 73% variance with nine factors on the GATB. This finding indicated that an aptitude test, shorter than the GATB, was warranted, but additional analysis regarding validity continued to ensure replicability of the five factors (or subtests) using a rotated factor structure matrix, which yielded additional support for the five factors of the AS (87.2% match compared to GATB).

Development of the IS derived from a factor analysis procedure as well (Parker, 2002b). The twelve interest areas derived directly from the *Guide for Occupational Education* (Farr, Ludden, & Shatkin, 2001) and *The Enhanced Guide for Occupational Exploration* (Mayall & Maze, 1995). Construction of the instrument was iterative and produced favorable validity measures for all 12 scales included in the IS.

Reliability - AS

Parker (2002a) provided information about the AS using four types of reliability for the 8th-12th grade population and two types of reliability for the post-secondary population. Alpha coefficients ranged from .70 to .94, with a median of .86 for all five AS scales across the five grade levels using a sample of 357 students. Citing McGee (1979), Parker reported split-half reliabilities for the Spatial Relations subtest because they have two factors (spatial visualization and spatial orientation) typically, which could impact overall alpha negatively. For the Spatial Relations subtest, split-half reliabilities of .70 to .92, with an estimated median of .78, substantiated the reliability.

Alternate forms reliability information is available for two subtests: Word Comparison and Making Marks. Initially, the Word Comparison subtest included two separate sections, which allowed for alternate-forms, although developers included only one form in the final version of the AS. Reliability coefficients ranged from .85 to .94, with a median of approximately .90. Making Marks had similar coefficients of .86 to .93 (median approximately .89). Similar to other reliability coefficients, available alternate forms reliability continue to support sound reliability for the AS.

Reliability - IS

Parker (2002b) reported reliability based on the populations for 8th-12th grade students and post-secondary students. For the IS, Parker (2002b) provided information on internal consistency (alpha) and test-re-test reliability.

For grades 8 to 12, alpha coefficients ranged from .78 to .95 on all 12 scales, indicating suitable reliability that the items in the assessment relate to conversations about career exploration based on interest. Developers used Structural Equation Models (SEMs) to determine the confidence (intervals) for the stanines with +/- 1 and revealed percentages ranging from 84% (Leading-Influencing) to 97% (Protective). The 81% for Leading-Influencing derived from another sampling group of post-secondary students so the lower confidence percentage shows in the Scoring Profile is important to note.

Test-retest coefficients provide additional support for the overall reliability of the OASIS-3: IS. Fifty-four 8th to 12th grade students responded to the assessment, within a two-week interval, resulting in a range of coefficients .66 (Selling) to .91 (Artistic), with a majority of the scales having a reliability coefficient in the .70 to .80 range. These results indicate an acceptable level of stability for the OASIS-3: IS over time.

223

Validity - AS

Construct-related validity for the AS was low, which Parker (2002a) expected, because aptitude factors of the subtests are independent. Further analysis revealed high factor loading for Vocabulary and Computing subtests for the General Ability Factor, which resulted in the decision to use only those two subtests for the composite General Ability score. In an effort to establish strong internal consistency item analysis on initial versions of the AS, developers eliminated any item with correlations below .20. Parker noted that developers do not use item analysis for speed tests, typically (Word Comparison & Making the Mark subtests), so he did not provide any information on those.

Convergent and discriminant validity emerged through a multitrait-multimethod matrix and, compared with the other prevalent aptitude assessments, yielded hardy coefficients (Parker, 2002b). For example, when correlated with the aforementioned GATB, coefficients (Pearson's r) were as high as .84 (Verbal Aptitude) with a .60 correlation for at least six of the nine total subtests of the AS.

Validity – IS

Regarding construct validity for the IS, factor analysis followed by varimax rotations (Parker, 2002b) identified all 12 factors using an initial sample of 8th to 12th grade males and females. Additionally, measures for both internal consistency (via item-total score correlations), as well as correlations between existing, popular inventories (such as the Self Directed Search, Holland, Fritzche, & Powell, 1994) indicated acceptable validity for the IS items and overall construction. Continued replications, comparisons with other instruments, and unpublished studies produced similar results, reinforcing the IS's consistency in construction and measurement.

Parker (2002b) addressed how, although the Mechanical and Industrial scales are "highly related" (p. 27) based on item content, each scale has its own primary loading factor (terminology): Mechanical (81); Industrial (91). Continued replications produced similar results.

Norms (AS/IS)

Sample norming information is the same for both the AS and the IS. Parker (2002a; 2002b) referenced his 1991 OASIS manual's sample size information as a basis for the standardization and normative data for the OASIS-3 manual. Parker based the IS norms on 2,005 students, ranging from 8th grade to 12th grade (n = 1505) and those in post-secondary educational settings (n = 500). Parker made efforts to create a sample representative of the larger population based on the

U.S. Census and U.S. Department of Education data. Parker used the normative data, gleaned from this sample, to establish percentiles and stanine scores. Characteristics collected included region (of the United States), gender, race, and residence (e.g. urban, suburban, and rural). Parker (2002b, citing Anastasi & Urbina, 1997) suggested the collection and use of local norms for interpreting scores between similar students.

Parker (2002b) reported the inherent gender bias associated with interest assessments and responded to the standards for gender equality, enacted by the National Institute of Education (NIE), and the related laws and acts, such as Affirmative Action and Title IX. Developers designed this third edition with gender-neutral language throughout. I provide more information on gender, as well as other cultural norming issues, in the following section.

Uses: Interpretation and Evaluation

The OASIS-3 provides individuals and career practitioners with aptitude and interest information during vocational exploration (Parker 2002a; Parker 2002b). The administration of both instruments of the OASIS-3 requires "appropriate knowledge and skills obtained through training and supervised of experience" (2002a, p. 5; 2002b, p. 5). In conjunction with the National Career Development Association (NCDA) Code of Ethics (2015) and assessment administration guidelines in Niles and Harris-Bowlsbey (2013), Parker (2002a, 2002b) reinforced the necessary steps in administering and interpreting the OASIS-3 to ensure respondents have a clear understanding of the purpose and outcome of each test.

Both instruments use paper and pencil answer sheets with accompanying test booklets. As noted, the AS is timed, while the IS is not timed. Responses can be hand- or machine-scored. The manuals, for both instruments, provide specific information for administering, scoring, and interpreting the results (Parker 2002a; 2002b). Raw data is transformed into stanines and percentile information before the career professional discusses results with the respondent.

For the AS, a transparent Answer Key, for all five subtests, allows administrators to score quickly and directly from the Student Answer Sheet. Practitioners use Appendix A of the manual to convert raw scores to percentiles and stanines (Parker, 2002a).

For the IS, the Student Answer Sheet provides a space for tallying *Likes* and *Dislikes* along rows for each of the twelve interest areas. The manual does not indicate whether students can summarize their scores or whether the test administer needs to tally them; depending on the individuals' maturity and developmental level, the facilitator could delegate this task to the individual test takers. Test administrators calculate raw scores on a Scoring Form and, then, transpose those scores to percentiles (using Appendix A; Parker, 2002b) onto a Student Profile. The accompanying Interpretation Workbook offers respondents a practical way to connect their results with job clusters and career categories on O*NET National Center for O*Net Development (2018) and other career websites.

One clear limitation of the OASIS-3 is the lack of an online version. Computer-run scoring would save time and transposing by the administrator and would likely reduce error in scoring, as well as interpretation of the results. Another limitation is the lack of alternate instructions to accommodate individual needs (e.g. extended time for individuals with ADHD) or different learning styles (e.g. quiet test-taking space). A universal design or alternative forms for the OASIS-3 would increase inclusivity for all test-takers.

Evaluation

The OASIS-3 has several strengths. The OASIS-3 is one of the few assessments that measures both interest and aptitude. Another strength is the ease of the instructions, scoring, and interpretation. Both manuals provide clear and straightforward instructions for administration. Additionally, the assessment has consistent reliability and validity measures (Parker, 2002a; 2000).

Another advantage of the OASIS-3 is that the IS provides an alternative of the universally accepted Holland codes of Realistic, Investigative, Artistic, Social, Enterprising, and Conventional (RIASEC; Niles & Harris-Bowlsbey, 2013). The *Aptitude* factors of the AS align with Gardner's multiple intelligences, which is becoming more accepted in K-12 education (Curry & Milsom, 2017). For example, virtual-spatial intelligence might correlate with Spatial Aptitude. Although Holland's codes are integral to career counseling, twelve interest areas, rather than six, might be more informational and beneficial to students entering the career exploration process.

This instrument could be helpful, particularly in assessing aggregate data to inform in-house or district-wide gaps that need development in comprehensive career programs for students. On the individual level, curriculum developers could conduct pre- and post-test use of the Aptitude Scale to measure progress along specific factors, such as General Ability and Verbal Ability, to indicate whether curriculum is effective.

Cultural Considerations and Implications

Based on the standardization and normative data provided in the manual, Parker (2002a, 2002b) based the norms on a majority of public school students from the 1990s. With the changing demographics in society and the influx of immigrant students (National Center for Education Statistics, 2017; U.S. Department of Education, 2015), revised editions should include a more diverse sampling group. As with this revision of the OASIS, any future revisions would want to use norms based on the most current U.S. Census Bureau data.

In addition, developers could re-categorize norming, reliability, and validity populations for future editions. For example, developers could use urban, suburban, and rural for norming and could view urban and suburban as distinctly different geographic areas. Additionally, Parker (2002a, 2002b) used four categories of race and two categories for gender in validity measures for the initial version; any future revisions should expand these options to include current definitions of gender and race. The categorical demographics, although appropriate at the time the OASIS-3 was developed, are too limiting for the current U.S. population.

Research and Evaluation/Assessment Uses

Despite the longevity and credibility of the OASIS-3, there appears to be limited active use or research of the instrument, based on informal and formal searches. Lenz (2013) provided a comprehensive review of the OASIS-3, and there appears to be limited studies using the OASIS-3 since then. An exhaustive search of several educational and psychological databases yielded few recent studies. However, Kellems, Springer, Wilkins, and Anderson (2016) recognized the OASIS-3 IS in a comprehensive list of appropriate transition assessments in special education, and authors include the OASIS-3 often in career counseling textbooks (e.g. Curry & Milsom, 2017). The OASIS-3 remains a common assessment in career development and professional guidance, and has been referred to in recent books and publications (Curry & Milsom, 2014; Osborn & Zunker, 2015).

One recent study took place in the Philippines, although the study used the OASIS-2. Elnar (2014) conducted a regression analysis with the OASIS-2-IS and age, sex, college course, and personality traits (self-control, tough-mindedness, and independence) of 236 first-year college students in an effort to gain insight into the development of a career guidance program for college students. He found that age had no predictive relationship with interests on the OASIS-2 but that gender and college courses were predictors of several interest areas (e.g. Nature, Protective, Mechanical).

With the continued need for research of vocational evaluation for individuals with diagnosed autism and with other special education needs, an updated OASIS-3 could be useful because of its unique combination of the aptitude and interest instruments. Alternate versions that would accommodate different learning styles, physical abilities, and multiple intelligences (albeit a timely and rigorous endeavor to develop) would contribute tremendously to the fields of special education, rehabilitation counseling, and career development.

227

Recommendations to improve on OASIS-3's strong foundation further would be to include a web-based option and consider changes for increased accessibility or a universal design. A web-based option would increase efficiency and, possibly, comfort level for both the respondent and scorer. With online data available, practitioners and researchers could download results to statistical software for further analysis for grants and other research interests.

Additionally, the IS's Mechanical and Industrial subtests would integrate well into research and program planning in the current trends of Science, Technology, Engineering, and Math (STEM), Science, Technology, Engineering, Art and Math (STEAM), and Career and Technical Education (CTE) movements. The AS instrument could supplement information gained from the IS to match interests in middle school and connect students with aptitudes from relevant AS scales to meet the increased workforce demands in CTE.

Overall, the OASIS-3 contributes to field of career assessment for students in the self-exploration phase. With updated norming data, terminology, and online access, any future revisions of the OASIS-3 could be indispensable in the field of career development as society moves toward a new era of K-12 education, CTE, and a global workforce.

References

Anastasi, A. & Urbina, S. (1997). *Psychological testing* (7th ed.). New York: Prentice Hall.

Curry, J. & Milsom, A. (2017). *Career and college readiness in P-12 Schools* (2nd ed.). New York: Springer.

Elnar, R. D. B. (2014). Personality traits and occupational interest: Basis for career guidance program. *Developing Country Studies, 4*(13), 91-102.

Farr, J. M., Ludden, L., & Shatkin, L. (2001). *Guide for occupational exploration* (3rd ed.). Indianapolis, IN: JIST Works.

Holland, J., Fritzche, B. & Powell, A. (1994). *The Self-Directed Search (SDS): Professional-user's guide-1994 edition.* Odessa, FL: Psychological Assessment Resources.

Kellems, R. O., Springer, B., Wilkins, M. K. & Anderson, C. (2016). Collaboration in transition assessment: School psychologists and special educators working together to improve outcomes for students with disabilities. *Preventing School Failure, 60* (3), 215-221.

Lenz, A. S. (2013). Occupational Aptitude Survey and Interest Inventory Schedule, Third Edition [Review]. In C. Woods and D. Hays, (Eds.). *A counselor's guide to career assessment instruments* (6th Ed.). Broken Arrow, OK: NCDA.

Mayall, D. & Maze, M. (Eds.). (1995). *The enhanced guide for occupational exploration.* Indianapolis, IN: JIST Works.

McGee, M. (1979). Human spatial abilities: Psychometric studies and environmental, genetic, hormonal, and neurological influences. *Psychological Bulletin, 86,* 889-918.

National Career Development Association (NCDA). (2015). NCDA Code of Ethics. Broken Arrow, OK: Author.

National Center for Education Statistics. (2017). *Fast facts.* Retrieved from https://nces.ed.gov/fastfacts/display.asp?id=372

National Center for O*NET Development. (2018). *O*Net Online.* Retrieved from https://www.onetonline.org

Niles, S. G., & Harris-Bowlsbey, J. H. (2013). *Career development interventions in the 21st century.* Upper Saddle River, NJ: Pearson.

Osborn, D. S., & Zunker, V. G. (2015). Using assessment results for career development (9th ed.). Boston: Cengage.

Parker, R. M. (2002a). *Occupational Aptitude Survey and Interest Schedule, Third Edition: Aptitude Survey Examiner's Manual.* Austin, TX: Pro-Ed.

Parker, R. M. (2002b). *Occupational Aptitude Survey and Interest Schedule, Third Edition: Interest Schedule Examiner's Manual.* Austin, TX: Pro-Ed.

U.S. Department of Defense. (1993). *ASVAB 12/19 Technical manual.* North Chicago, IL: U.S. Military Entrance Processing Command.

U.S. Department of Education. (2015). *Educational resources for immigrants, refugees, asylees, and other new Americans.* Retrieved from https://www2.ed.gov/about/overview/focus/immigration-resources.html

QUANTITATIVE

STANDARD SELF-DIRECTED SEARCH

Instrument Acronym or Preferred Short Name: Standard SDS

Instrument Authors: John L. Holland, PhD and Melissa A. Messer, MHS

Publisher: PAR, Inc.

Publisher Address: 16204 N. Florida Ave, Lutz, FL 33549
http://www.self-directed-search.com/

Statement of Purpose: The Standard Self-Directed Search is a career interest and exploration tool that asks questions about a client's aspirations, activities, skills, and interests in different jobs then generates a three-letter Summary Code that can be used to find occupations and fields of study that match well with the client's personality.

Target Population: Ages 11 years and older

Norm Group(s) on which Scores are Based: 1,739 individuals ranging in age from 11 to 70 years of age. The sample was well-matched to the U.S. population parameters for gender, race/ethnicity, and education.

Titles of Subtests, Scales, Scores Provided: Sections include Occupational Daydreams, Activities, Competencies, Occupations, and Self-Estimates. A three-letter Summary Code is generated based on the total scores for each of the six RIASEC types. This code can then be used to help the individual find his or her occupational or educational match.

Forms and Levels Available with Dates of Publication/Revision of Each: Assessment Booklet, Occupations Finder, You and Your Career Workbook, Educational Opportunities Finder. All revisions 2017.

Date of Most Recent Edition of Manual, User's Guide, etc.: 2017

Available in which Languages: In addition to English: Publications: Brazilian Portuguese Finnish Hebrew Italian Korean Norwegian Romanian Russian Spanish Swedish Ukrainian Translations: Arabic Chinese (Simplified & Traditional) Slovak Swahili

Actual Test Time: 25-35 minutes

Total Administration Time: 35-45 minutes (including scoring)

Required Level of Training and/or Credentials for Administrator: No special qualifications are required.

Types of Scores: Total Score for each of the six RIASEC types, plus a three-letter summary code.

Report Format/Content: Depending on the respondent's answers, he or she will receive a StudentSDS report (for middle/high school students), a VeteranSDS report (for active military/veterans), or a StandardSDS report (general use), all of which include: -A personalized Summary Code, which is based on the results of the assessment. -A description of each of the six RIASEC types. -A personalized list of occupations and programs of study associated with the Summary Code, which can be further customized by the user. Each occupation is linked to its Occupational Information Network (O*NET) Web page to allow the user to easily search for additional information. Similarly, each program of study is linked to its Classification of Instructional Programs (CIP) Web page. -An additional personalized list of occupations based on daydream occupations. -An overview of salary data associated with listed occupations as well as links to Monster.com job listings in the user's ZIP code -A list of additional careers organized by career cluster, which can be used for an even deeper self-directed search. -Links to resources to assist with educational and career planning. -For active Military or Veterans additional information on transition planning and occupational recommendations based on military skills is also included.

Report Format/Content for Group Summaries: Not Available

Availability of Machine Scoring Service? No

Availability of Hand Scoring? Yes

If yes, time required for hand scoring? 10 minutes

If yes, who is it scored by? Can be scored by individual test taker or administrator

Availability of Local Machine Scoring Service? Not Available

Availability and Options for Computer Software? Computer Software Available, Standard administration on-line

If available, describe the ways in which computer/online version differs (if any): (information not provided by publisher)

Links to webpage that specifies the costs of materials:
http://www.self-directed-search.com/
http://www4.parinc.com/Products/Product.aspx?ProductID=SDS-R-5#

Additional Comments of Interest to Users (e.g. forthcoming revisions, new material, etc): Replaces the SDS Form R, 5th Edition. All of the exceptional features that make the SDS such a useful tool are still present, but this new edition also includes a bold and modern look, innovative features, and even more user-friendly support materials that continue to build on the legacy of the SDS and on John Holland RIASEC theory. The StandardSDS, along with other career counseling products, is part of the Aspira360 system. Aspira360.com is a Web-based portal that streamlines and enhances the career search experience.

Published Reviews of the Instrument in the Last 15 years:

Bailey, T. R., Blackwell, T. L., & Crtalic, A. K. (2015). Review of Self-Directed Search fifth edition. *Rehabilitation Counseling Bulletin, 59*(1), 55-59. doi:10.1177/0034355214560027

Bullock-Yowell, E., & Tirre, W. C. (2017). The Self-Directed Search, 5th edition [Test review]. In J. F. Carlson, K. F. Geisinger, & J. L. Jonson (Eds.) *The twentieth mental measurements yearbook*. Lincoln, NE: Buros Center for Testing.

STUDENT SELF-DIRECTED SEARCH

Instrument Acronym or Preferred Short Name: Student SDS

Instrument Authors: John L. Holland, PhD and Melissa A. Messer, MHS

Publisher: PAR, Inc.

Publisher Address: 16204 N. Florida Ave, Lutz, FL 33549

http://www.self-directed-search.com/

Statement of Purpose: The Student Self-Directed Search is a career interest and exploration tool that asks questions about a student's aspirations, activities, skills, and interests in different jobs then generates a two-letter Summary Code that can be used to find occupations and fields of study that match well with the student's personality.

Target Population: Students in middle school, junior high and high school, ages 11 years and older.

Norm Group(s) on which Scores are Based: 318 middle and high school students.

Titles of Subtests, Scales, Scores Provided: Sections include Occupational Daydreams, Activities, Competencies, Occupations, and Self-Estimates. A two-letter Summary Code is generated based on the total scores for each of the six RIASEC types. This code can then be used to help the student find his or her occupational or educational match.

Forms and Levels Available with Dates of Publication/Revision of Each: Assessment Booklet, Career Finder, You and Your Future Workbook, Educational Opportunities Finder. All revisions 2017.

Date of Most Recent Edition of Manual, User's Guide, etc.: 2017

Available in which Languages: English Only

Actual Test Time: 25-35 minutes

Total Administration Time: 35-45 minutes (including scoring)

Required Level of Training and/or Credentials for Administrator: No special qualifications are required.

Types of Scores: Total Score for each of the six RIASEC types, plus a two-letter Summary Code.

Report Format/Content: StudentSDS report includes: A personalized Summary Code, which is based on the results of the assessment. A description of each of the six RIASEC types. A personalized list of occupations and programs of study associated with the Summary Code, which can be further customized by the user. Each occupation is linked to its Occupational Information Network (O*NET) Web page to allow the user to easily search for additional information. Similarly, each program of study is linked to its Classification of Instructional Programs (CIP) Web page. An additional personalized list of occupations based on daydream occupations. An overview of salary data associated with occupations. A list of additional careers organized by career cluster, which can be used for an even deeper self-directed search. An individual career/education plan. Links to resources to assist with educational and career planning.

Report Format/Content for Group Summaries: Not Available

Availability of Machine Scoring Service? No

Availability of Hand Scoring? Yes

If yes, time required for hand scoring? 10 minutes

If yes, who is it scored by? Individual Test Taker

Availability of Local Machine Scoring Service? Not Available

Availability and Options for Computer Software? Computer Software Available, Standard administration on-line

If available, describe the ways in which computer/online version differs (if any): (information not provided by publisher)

Link to webpage that specifies the costs of materials: http://www.self-directed-search.com/

and http://www4.parinc.com/Products/Product.aspx?ProductID=SDS_CE

Additional Comments of Interest to Users (e.g. forthcoming revisions, new material, etc): The Student Self-Directed Search (StudentSDS) is based on the Standard SDS and is designed to be used primarily with middle school, junior high and high school students (ages 11 to 18 years). Replaces the SDS Career Explorer. The StudentSDS, along with other career counseling products, is part of the Aspira360 system. Aspira360.com is a Web-based portal that streamlines and enhances the career search experience.

Published Reviews of the Instrument in the Last 15 years:

Bailey, T. R., Blackwell, T. L., & Crtalic, A. K. (2015). Review of Self-Directed Search fifth edition. *Rehabilitation Counseling Bulletin, 59*(1), 55-59. doi:10.1177/0034355214560027

Bullock-Yowell, E., & Tirre, W. C. (2017). The Self-Directed Search, 5th Edition [Test review]. In J. F. Carlson, K. F. Geisinger, & J. L. Jonson (Eds.) *The twentieth mental measurements yearbook*. Lincoln, NE: Buros Center for Testing.

The Self Directed Search

Reviewed by

Chad Luke
Tennessee Technological University

Zach Budesa
The University of Tennessee

Introduction/Description

The Self-Directed Search (SDS; Holland & Messer, 2017a) is a straightforward, self-administered assessment designed to help individuals explore career-related activities, skills, and interests. Participants interpret their results themselves and utilize additional materials to identify career and occupational interests and educational opportunities related to those interest areas. John Holland and Melissa Messer developed the current version of the SDS based on Holland's (Holland, 1959) theory of vocational choice. Holland's theory categorizes individuals and occupations based on six categories of personality; each personality type corresponds with environmental types: Realistic (R), Investigative (I), Artistic (A), Social (S), Enterprising (E), and Conventional (C).

There are two current versions of the SDS: Standard Self-Directed Search (StandardSDS) and Student Self-Directed Search (StudentSDS). Both versions are based on the SDS Form R, 5th Edition, which was last revised in 2013. The update is primarily cosmetic; developers collected no new data and the forms are mostly interchangeable (Holland & Messer, 2017a). The StandardSDS includes an *Assessment Booklet, Occupations Finder (OF), You and Your Career* (YYC) workbook, and *Professional Manual*. The StudentSDS includes an *Assessment Booklet, Career Finder (CF), You and Your Future* (YYF) workbook, and *Professional Manual* with an included teacher's guide. Also included is the *Educational Opportunities Finder (EOF)*, which is the same for both versions. The StandardSDS is for use with individuals 11 to 70 years of age, and the StudentSDS is for use with individuals 6 to 12 years of age, although the developers recommend the Student SDS version for use up to age 17.

The StandardSDS *Assessment Booklet,* based on the SDS Form R, 5th Edition (Holland & Messer, 2013), is divided into five sections: (1) *Occupational Daydreams*; (2) *Activities, Competencies, Occupations, and Self-Estimates*; (3) *How to Organize Your Answers*; (4) *What Your Summary Code Means*; and (5) *Resources*. Instructions in the *Occupational Daydreams* section have participants list occupations they might be considering already and find the three digit occupation code in the StandardSDS *Occupation Finder*. Section two consists of four subsections, including Activities, with six scales of 14 items; Competencies, with six scales of 14 items; Occupations, with six scales of 14 items; and Self-Estimates, with 2 scales of 6 items, with a total of 252 binary choice questions and 12 seven-point Likert scale questions. *How to Organize Your Answers* walks participants through scoring section two. Sections two and three divide questions into each of the six Holland categories (RIASEC) in order to identify a three letter Summary Code for each participant. Section four refers participants back to the StandardSDS *Occupations Finder* to find the occupations listed by Summary Codes, as well as to find as many potential three letter Summary Code combinations and related occupations. Finally, section five lists available resources to explore career and occupational possibilities further.

Most recently revised in 2017, the StandardSDS *Occupations Finder* (Holland & Messer, 2017b) contains over 1,400 occupations listed both alphabetically and by Holland Occupational Codes (HOCs). HOCs are three digit codes that correspond to three digit Summary Codes identified in the *Assessment Booklet*. Each occupation is listed with information about the HOC, O*NET codes, educational requirements (on an ascending scale from 1 to 5), career cluster, and the outlook for the field of work. Career clusters divide the listed occupations into 16 general groupings based on required skills that differentiate between fields such as Information Technology, Manufacturing, Health Science, etc. Occupational outlook identifies whether occupations are emerging or projected to grow much more quickly than average job growth.

The *You and Your Career* (*YYC*; Holland & Messer, 2017c) workbook, also revised in 2017, explains the RIASEC theory and typology characteristics. The use of Summary Codes helps further career exploration and education planning. The *Professional Manual* suggests that practitioners provide all participants with a copy of the *YYC* workbook (Holland & Messer, 2017a).

The StudentSDS *Assessment Booklet* is based on the SDS Form R, 5th Edition also. As such, it consists of the same five sections and includes the same number, layout, and scoring process (Holland & Messer, 2017d). The two different versions are functionally identical, with a few exceptions. First, the StudentSDS refers participants to the *Career Finder* and *You and Your Future* rather than to the *Occupations Finder* and *You and Your Career*. Additionally, rather than identifying a three digit Summary Code, the StudentSDS version identifies only a two digit Summary Code.

Much like the *Occupations Finder* (*OF*), the *Career Finder* (*CF*; Holland & Messer, 2017e) lists occupations alphabetically and by HOCs. Additionally, the authors listed the 400 or so occupations by career clusters in a third index. Career clusters are groups of different occupations based on general skill requirements. In each of the three indices, occupations are listed with the HOC, O*NET code, educational requirements (i.e., less than High School, High School, Some College, College, Graduate School), career cluster, and the outlook for the field of work. In another departure from the *OF*, the *CF* uses two digit HOCs that correspond to the StudentSDS results.

The *You and Your Future* (*YYF*; Holland & Messer, 2017f) workbook operates much like the *YYC* workbook but is aimed at a younger audience. The *YYF* workbook provides a simple explanation of the RIASEC theory, explains careers and occupations, and helps students explore work-related interests, and education planning for middle school, high school, and college bound levels.

Exploration of educational needs continues in the *Educational Opportunities Finder* (*EOF*; Holland & Messer, 2017g), revised in 2017. The *EOF* lists programs of study by their associated HOC, and includes Classification of Instructional Programs (CIP) category and code. Most programs of study listed are programs available through post-secondary institutions, such as community colleges and 4-year colleges and universities. There is only one version of the *EOF* rather than separate StandardSDS and StudentSDS versions.

In addition to the StandardSDS and StudentSDS versions, SDS Form R, 5th Edition, has been translated into more than 30 languages. It is available in Spanish, has been modified specifically for Veterans, and includes a Military Occupations Finder. In addition, earlier versions of the SDS are available in English Canadian (Form R and Form E, 4th Edition), and French Canadian (Form R, 4th Edition). Finally, the SDS is available online at http://www.self-directed-search.com

Technical Considerations

The StandardSDS and StudentSDS utilize the same set of items as the previous SDS Form R, 5th Edition, which was published in 2013 (Holland & Messer, 2017a). As such, the same data gathered during the development process of the 5th Edition is supplied for the StandardSDS and StudentSDS. The authors of the *Professional Manual* detail the development process for both the 2017 and 2013 versions of the SDS. Authors of the fifth edition sought to update the previous edition, from 1994. After seeking feedback from career counseling professionals initially, the authors developed, refined, and removed items. To ensure face validity, they based each item on: "(a) the quality of the item; (b) the degree to which the item represented the associated letter, or type; (c) the face validity/relevance of the item; and (d) potential bias or other problems" (Holland & Messer, 2017a, p. 32). This process resulted in a pilot version of the StandardSDS *Assessment Booklet*, which the authors, then, used to develop the final version.

Listed in the StandardSDS *Professional Manual*, the fifth edition of Form R was administered to a total of 1,739 people to obtain normative data. This sample included individuals ranging in age from 11 to 70, with an average age of 34.5. The population consisted of 879 females and 860 males, with education levels ranging from Grade 5 through 16+ years of education. The sample consisted of 61.6% white, 17.4% Latinx, 13.7% black, 7.0% other groups, and 0.3% unreported ethnicities.

The developers measured internal consistency for the Activities, Competencies, and Occupations scales in section two of the *Assessment Booklet*, the two Self-Estimates ratings scales, and summary scores (Holland & Messer, 2017a). For the Activities, Competencies, and Occupations scales, internal consistency coefficients ranged from .71 to .93, with the lowest coefficients found in the scores of high school students. Coefficients for the two Self-Estimate rating scales are between .20 and .73, which the authors stated indicates "that the ratings contain shared variance, but each contributes some unique variance" (Holland & Messer, 2017a, p. 39). Similar to the Activities, Competencies, and Occupations scales, summary score coefficients ranged from .88 to .94.

The developers examined test-retest reliability of the summary scores over two different time intervals that spanned a range of two weeks to four months. Test-retest reliability over the short period of two to four weeks ranged from .78 to .98. Over the long period of two to four months, test-retest reliability ranged from .84 to .96. Over the entire test-retest sample, reliability ranged from .82 to .96. Pointing toward the summary scores absolute mean change ranging from 1.09 to 2.98, the authors concluded the "results collectively indicate that the summary scores have substantial stability" (Holland & Messer, 2017a, p. 39).

Due to the self-scored nature of the SDS, the authors detailed inter-scorer agreement in the *Professional Manual*, as well. Two researchers scored randomly selected assessments, one with a calculator and one without. Through this process, these researchers found that using a calculator associates with a 3.3% error rate, while not using a calculator associates with a 10% error rate. This led the authors to suggest the use of a calculator when scoring the assessment.

Previous editions of the SDS have supported concurrent validity of the assessment (Holland et al., 1994, as cited in Holland & Messer, 2017a). The fourth edition of the SDS and the current StandardSDS were each administered to a sample of 60 ranging in age from 12 to 70. Correlations between the summary scores from each edition ranged from .74 to .95. Developers established additional concurrent validity by comparing current occupation, current satisfaction level with occupation, and Summary Code from the completion of the SDS. More than 40% of individuals who indicated high satisfaction with their current occupation had summary codes that matched the HOC of their current occupation. In contrast, only 21% of individuals who were unsatisfied with their current occupation had a match between their summary codes and the HOC of their occupation.

To address convergent validity, developers compared the StandardSDS to several other assessments in the areas of career interest, personality, and career thoughts. A sample completed the StandardSDS, the Strong Interest Inventory (SII; Donnay, Morris, Schaubhat, & Thompson, 2005), and the O*NET Interest Profiler (National Center for O*NET Development, 1999). Researchers found significant correlations between the StandardSDS and both the other inventories (Holland & Messer, 2017a). Researchers identified the Zener-Schnuelle Index of Agreement between the StandardSDS and both other inventories. The first letter of the Summary Codes corresponded in more than 37% and 33% of the sample, respectively, while the first and second letters of the Summary Codes matched any two letters of the SSI or O*NET Interest Profiler codes in approximately 19.6% and 17.6% of the sample.

In a comparison between the StandardSDS and the NEO Personality Inventory-3 (NEO-PI-3; Costa & McCrae, 2010), researchers noted strong positive correlations between the *Investigative* and *Artistic* scales of the StandardSDS and the NEO-PI-3's *Openness to Experience* scale (Holland & Messer, 2017a). Additionally, researchers found strong correlations between the *Social* and *Enterprising* scales of the StandardSDS and the NEO-PI-3's *Extraversion* scale. Researchers found weak correlations between the NEO-PI-3 scales and the StandardSDS's *Realistic* and *Conventional* scales.

Finally, researchers have compared the StandardSDS to another self-administered assessment, the Career Thoughts Inventory (Sampson, Peterson, Lenz, Reardon, & Saunders, 1999). In this comparison, researchers found that individuals who scored high in the *Social* and *Enterprising* types were more likely to have dysfunctional career thoughts than individuals who do not score as high in these areas. Wright, Reardon, Peterson, and Osborn (2000) suggested that this might be the result of an individual who is able to pick a general field of career interest but is unable to find a subfield to which they are able to commit.

Use/Interpretation/Evaluation

Since its initial release, Holland and Messer (2017a) have conceived the Self-Directed Search as "a self-administered, self-scored, and self-interpreted career counseling tool" (p. 1). Equipped with the *Assessment Booklet* and the *Occupations Finder* alone, participants are able to complete and score the entire assessment and match their results to the many available occupations. The authors do recommend the use of a calculator, to prevent mistakes, because scoring the assessment does consist primarily of arithmetic across the pages of the *Assessment Booklet*. The authors recommend that a practitioner be involved in the use of the SDS "to monitor its use, correct deficiencies, and help people when they have difficulty" (Holland & Messer, 2017a, p. 15).

Instructions guide users in scoring the *Assessment Booklet* and instruct participants to score as they proceed through the assessment. Developers wrote all test materials, for both versions, at a seventh grade level for ease of understanding. The StandardSDS and StudentSDS direct participants to mark their answer for each scale, then calculate those scales' totals prior to continuing. Each scale is labeled clearly with the letter of the type to which it corresponds (R, I, A, S, E, or C). Following the completion of the assessment, the scoring page lists the HOC letter, the scale (Activities, Competencies, Occupations, or Self-Estimates), the page(s) from which users should transpose the scores, and clear directions for the transposition and totaling of scores. The highest three scores represent the resulting Summary Code. Following identification of a Summary Code, the SDS instructions provide clear and easy to follow instructions about the use of the additional materials provided.

In addition to the testing materials, the StandardSDS *Professional Manual* and the StudentSDS *Professional Manual with Teacher's Guide* provide detailed information about the history and context of Holland's work and theory, the use of the assessment, and guides and practice examples for the administration and scoring of the *Assessment Booklet*. The removal of more detailed technical information and the addition of a teacher's guide to the StudentSDS *Professional Manual* tailors the experience for the setting in which it will be used most. Both versions ensure that practitioners who administer the SDS will be capable of assisting participants in the completion, scoring, and interpretation of the assessment.

In counseling, the SDS can be an incredibly useful tool for individuals who struggle to identify career interests. Career professionals can use the SDS with individuals from middle school to middle- or older adulthood who might have difficulty deciding on a career or education path, who might be considering a second career, or who might be experiencing dissatisfaction in their current career. Because the SDS doubles as an interest assessment, practitioners might use it with individuals seeking avocational activities, such as hobbies or groups, to join. Scores in each of the six personality types could help individuals discuss their skills, abilities, and accomplishments, and reflect on those types. To aid younger participants, developers reduced the Summary Codes from three to two letters for the StudentSDS, which allows more room to explore careers and areas of interest.

Due to the self-administered nature of the SDS, one limitation of the SDS is the possibility of completing the assessment out of the context of career counseling or as an interest inventory devoid of context with the rest of the instrument. Much like employers use the Myers-Briggs Type Inventory as a commonly administered assessment for hiring, Human Resources, or leadership development purposes, this use may divorce the assessment from its valid uses (Michael, 2003).

Overall, the StandardSDS and StudentSDS provide an easy to use, age-appropriate, and comprehensive assessment of career interests. Both versions are based on the fifth edition of the SDS Form R, which has a history of robust evidence and support for its use in many areas (Nauta, 2010). The assessments are based on Holland's RIASEC theory, which spans more than fifty years of research that continues today.

Throughout its history, practitioners have administered the SDS to American audiences primarily. As indicated in the *Professional Manual*, developers selected the normative population for the StandardSDS to match the demographic distribution in the U.S. (Holland & Messer, 2017a). One concern with the current version is that the developers collapsed demographic categories of American Indian or Alaska Native, Asian, and Native Hawaiian or Other Pacific Islander into an Other category that made up 7.0% of the normative population. In previous versions, developers specified some of these groups, including Asian-American and Native American (Ciechalski, 2002).

In studies using the SDS, researchers found that socio-economic factors might influence results more strongly than is considered currently. For developing countries, van Wijk and Fourie (2017) found that factors, such as high unemployment, might aid in the violation of the assumption of Holland's theory that people search for work environments that match their personality types. Similarly, research that included Chinese students as participants found that, although practitioners can apply Holland's model with this population of individuals, adaptation is necessary, possibly due to the difference between collectivist and individualist cultures (Yang, Stokes, & Hui, 2005). Specifically, these authors' results have lead them to theorize that, as local cultures become more like U.S. culture, Holland's theory becomes more transferable to foreign contexts. Zarrin, Baghban, & Abedi, (2011) found significant support for the use of the SDS with Iranian high school and college students, where results reproduced Holland's RIASEC-order hexagon.

To assess for use with neurodivergent individuals, Murray, Hatfield, Falkmer, and Falkmer (2016) completed a meta-analysis of vocational tools and rated the SDS as good in comparison to others. Mattie (2000, as referenced in Murray et al., 2016) found no significant difference between neurodivergent and neurotypical assessment participants. In the same study, researchers were able to demonstrate internal consistency in results between readers and non-readers with learning disabilities, and individuals with developmental disabilities.

Research and Evaluation Uses

Several categories of research and treatment efficacy exist related to the SDS. The first involves studies that used the SDS to ascertain the appropriateness and effectiveness of online, self-administered, and self-scored instruments. Skeptics of these types of measures have made a reasonable case for confining these assessments to the context of counseling and education (Michael, 2003). However, researchers have demonstrated, also, the vitality of instruments, such as the SDS, to promote access to career assessment and resources for those who might not seek support otherwise (Behrens, & Nauta, 2014; Kronholz, 2015; Dozier, Sampson, Lenz, Peterson, & Reardon, 2015; Reardon, 2017).

A second category of research focuses on the outcomes of participants related to the use of the SDS. Large volumes of career assessment and development research exist that demonstrate the efficacy of career interventions over no intervention (Brown & Roche, 2016). Individuals using the SDS experience greater career-related options, partly by virtue of the increased exposure to the variety of occupational titles. This increased awareness can lead, in turn, to increased exploration (Betz, 2007). Identifying meaningful individual personality traits that correspond with occupations can validate both the individual's identity and the sense of place in the world (Luke, 2018).

References

Behrens, E. L., & Nauta, M. M. (2014). The Self-Directed Search as a stand-alone intervention with college students. *Career Development Quarterly, 62,* 224-238. doi:10.1002/j.2161-0045.2014.00081.x

Betz, N. E. (2007). Career self-efficacy: Exemplary recent research and emerging directions. *Journal of Career Assessment, 15,* 403-422. doi:10.1177/1069072707305759

Brown, S. D., & Roche, M. (2016). The outcomes of vocational interventions: Thirty (some) years later. *Journal of Career Assessment, 24,* 26-41. doi:10.1177/1069072715579666

Ciechalski, J. C. (2002). Self-Directed Search. In J. T. Kapes & E.A. Whitfield (Eds.), *A counselor's guide to career assessment instruments (4th ed., pp. 276-287).* Columbus, OH: National Career Development Association.

Costa, P. T., & McCrae, R. R. (2010). *NEO Personality Inventory-3.* Odessa, FL: Psychological Assessment Resources.

Donnay, D. A. C., Morris, M. L., Schaubhut, N. A., & Thompson, R. C. (2005). *Strong Interest Inventory manual: Research, development, and strategies for interpretation.* Mountain View, CA: CPP.

Dozier, V. C., Sampson, J. P., Jr., Lenz, J. G., Peterson, G. W., & Reardon, R. C. (2015). The impact of the Self-Directed Search Form R Internet version on counselor-free career exploration. *Journal of Career Assessment, 23,* 210-224. doi:10.1177/1069072714535020

Holland, J. L. (1959). A theory of vocational choice. *Journal of Counseling Psychology, 6*, 35. doi:10.1037/h0040767

Holland, J. L., Messer, M. (2013). *Self-directed search, 5th Edition.* Lutz, FL: Psychological Assessment Resources.

Holland, J. L., Messer, M. (2017a). *Professional manual, Standard Self-Directed Search.* Lutz, FL: Psychological Assessment Resources.

Holland, J. L., Messer, M. (2017b). *The occupations finder.* Lutz, FL: Psychological Assessment Resources.

Holland, J. L., Messer, M. (2017c). *You and your career.* Lutz, FL: Psychological Assessment Resources.

Holland, J. L., Messer, M. (2017d). *Professional manual and teacher's guide, Student Self-Directed Search.* Lutz, FL: Psychological Assessment Resources.

Holland, J. L., Messer, M. (2017e). *Career finder.* Lutz, FL: Psychological Assessment Resources.

Holland, J. L., Messer, M. (2017f). *You and your future.* Lutz, FL: Psychological Assessment Resources.

Holland, J. L., Messer, M. (2017g). *Educational opportunities finder.* Lutz, FL: Psychological Assessment Resources.

Kronholz, J. F. (2015). Self-help career services: A case report. *Career Development Quarterly, 63*, 282–288. doi:10.1002/cdq.12019

Luke, C. (2018). *Essentials of career-focused counseling: Integrating theory, practice, and neuroscience.* San Diego, CA: Cognella.

Michael, J. (2003). Using the Myers-Briggs Type Indicator as a tool for leadership development? Apply with caution. *Journal of Leadership & Organizational Studies, 10*(1), 68-81. doi:10.1177/107179190301000106

Murray, N., Hatfield, M., Falkmer, M., & Falkmer, T. (2016). Evaluation of career planning tools for use with individuals with autism spectrum disorder: a systematic review. *Research in Autism Spectrum Disorders, 23*, 188-202. doi:10.1016/j.rasd.2015.12.007

National Center for O*NET Development. (1999). *O*NET Interest Profiler.* Raleigh, NC: Author.

Nauta, M. M. (2010). The development, evolution, and status of Holland's theory of vocational personalities: Reflections and future directions for counseling psychology. *Journal of Counseling Psychology, 57*, 11. doi:10.1037/a0018213

Reardon, R. C. (2017). Enhancing self-help career planning using theory-based tools. *Journal of Career Assessment, 25*, 650-669. doi:10.1177/1069072716653376

Sampson, J. P., Jr., Peterson, G. W., Lenz, J. G., Reardon, R. C., & Saunders, D. E. (1999). *The use and development of the Career Thoughts Inventory.* Florida State University, Center for the Study of Technology in Counseling and Career Development.

Van Wijk, C. H., & Fourie, M. (2017). The appropriateness of using the Self-Directed Search questionnaire in developing countries: A pilot study with South African Navy divers. *Open Journal of Social Sciences, 5*, 60-69. doi:10.4236/jss.2017.52007

Wright, L. K., Reardon, R. C., Peterson, G. W., & Osborn, D. S. (2000). The relationship among constructs in the Career Thoughts Inventory and the Self-Directed Search. *Journal of Career Assessment, 8*(2), 105-117.

Yang, W., Stokes, G. S., & Hui, C. H. (2005). Cross-cultural validation of Holland's interest structure in Chinese population. *Journal of Vocational Behavior, 67*, 379-396. doi:10.1016/j.jvb.2004.08.003

Zarrin, S. A., Baghban, I., & Abedi, M. R. (2011). Reliability and correlation of interest inventories: Strong Interest Inventory (SII) and Self-Directed Search (SDS). *International Journal of Psychology and Counselling, 3*, 111-116.

QUANTITATIVE

WORK VALUES INVENTORY

Instrument Acronym or Preferred Short Name: WVI

Instrument Authors: Melissa A. Messer, MHS and Jennifer A. Greene, MSPH

Publisher: PAR, Inc.

Publisher Address: 16204 N. Florida Ave, Lutz, FL 33549

http://www4.parinc.com/Products/Product.aspx?ProductID=WVI

Statement of Purpose: The Work Values Inventory (WVI) is a career exploration and job selection tool developed to assess an individual's work values. Work values, also referred to as vocational needs, can be described as a set of standards that determines an individual's attitude, choices, and actions related to the workplace.

Target Population: Ages 18 to 70 years

Norm Group(s) on which Scores are Based: Standardization sample (N = 526) included employees across eight common O*NET job families who had been in their current positions for at least a year.

Titles of Subtests, Scales, Scores Provided: Achievement, Independence, Support, Relationships, Working Conditions, and Recognition. Scores are also generated for Profile elevation, Differentiation, and Commonness.

Forms and Levels Available with Dates of Publication/Revision of Each: Assessment Booklet, Score Summary Sheet, and Occupations Index. All versions published in 2016.

Date of Most Recent Edition of Manual, User's Guide, etc.: 2016

Available in which Languages: English Only

Actual Test Time: 10 minutes

Total Administration Time: 15 minutes (including scoring)

Required Level of Training and/or Credentials for Administrator: No special qualifications are required.

Types of Scores: Percentiles. For Diagnostic indicators, descriptive classifications are also available.

Report Format/Content: (information not provided by the publisher)

Report Format/Content for Group Summaries: Not Available

Availability of Machine Scoring Service? No

Availability of Hand Scoring? Yes

If yes, time required for hand scoring? 5 minutes

If yes, who is it scored by? Test Administrator

Availability of Local Machine Scoring Service? Not Available

Availability and Options for Computer Software? None Available

Link to webpage that specifies the costs of materials: http://www4.parinc.com/
Products/Product.aspx?ProductID=WVI

Additional Comments of Interest to Users (e.g. forthcoming revisions, new
material, etc): (information not provided by publisher)

Published Reviews of the Instrument in the Last 15 years: (information not
provided by publisher)

WORK VALUES INVENTORY

Reviewed by
S. Autumn Collins
The University of New Mexico

Authors Melissa A. Messer and Jennifer A. Greene developed the Work Values Inventory (WVI; Messer & Ureksoy, 2014) to provide a multidimensional assessment that characterizes a person's work values. Messer and Greene (2016a) defined work values as a set of workplace principles that are important for an individual's mindset, preferences, and desired behaviors related to work. Individuals and career counselors can use the WVI for career exploration, and human resources (HR) professionals can use the WVI when selecting and hiring employees.

The WVI grew from the foundations of *Theory of Work Adjustment* (Dawis, England & Lofquist, 1964), alongside the evolution of the U.S. Department of Labor's Occupational Information Network (O*NET), to become what it is today. WVI utilizes O*NET, which is a government database with a robust classification system of almost 1,000 occupations (O*NET, 2018). O*NET includes a category, *Work Values Model* (O*NET, 2018), and the WVI captured the model's six constructs: Achievement, Independence, Support, Relationship, Working Conditions, and Recognition (Messer & Greene, 2016a). Career practitioners should not confuse the WVI with Super's Work Values Inventory (1973), which Super based on 12 scales, even though the WVI bears the same name. Published in 2016, the WVI is the most up-to-date tool that utilizes the Work Values' taxonomy from O*NET for assessing an individuals' work values. The WVI is user-friendly and includes straightforward scoring and interpreting features.

The 61-item WVI is appropriate for ages 18 and older, is written at a seventh grade reading level, and takes approximately 10 minutes to complete. Users respond to prompts on a four-point Likert scale (*not valued; somewhat valued, highly valued; and very highly valued*). Practitioners can administer the WVI individually or in a group setting. The WVI includes a Score Summary Sheet, and scoring takes only five minutes. Messer and Greene (2016b) indicated individuals can self-score the assessment, as well; however, they recommended a professional perform the interpretation.

There are 10 items per the six scales and each scale has two facets: Achievement (ability utilization, accomplishment), Independence (autonomy, responsibility), Support (organization policies and practices, supervision), Relationship (interpersonal relationships, collaborative environment), Working Conditions (activity/variety, security), and Recognition (acknowledgement, leadership/ influence). Guidelines instruct respondents to answer the items regarding any job, not solely based on where they are working or considering currently.

Items 1-60 begin with: "In a job, I value the opportunity to..." followed by statements that fall under each scale: Achievement: "...use my skills and abilities to their fullest"; Independence: "demonstrate my ability to work self-sufficiently"; Support: "work with a supervisor who provides clear and understandable instructions"; Relationships: "work in a warm and friendly environment"; Working Conditions: "earn a consistent and predictable salary; Recognition: "have an influence on the future of the organization" (Messer & Greene, 2016b). Item 61 is a binary response item (*yes* or *no*) as to whether individuals have responded honestly to the items on the survey.

Technical Considerations

The authors used a standardization sample (N = 526), which matched that of the U.S. population, ranging in ages from 18 to 70 years old. The sample comprised employees who had been in their current job for a minimum of a year and whose job fell into one of O*NET's eight job families (i. e., Management; Business and Financial Operations; Computer and Mathematical; Education, Training, and Library; Healthcare Support; Office and Administrative Support; Sales and Related Occupations).

Messer and Greene (2016b) reported Cronbach's alpha reliability coefficients as ranging from .81 to .94. Test-retest reliability ranged between .82 and .95 for the scales, indicating satisfactory consistency. In addition, Messer and Greene found high inter-scorer reliability. An expert panel assessed the WVI as having reasonable face validity and suggested the use of a 4-point Likert scale, instead of the typical 5-point format, for the response criterion on the first 60 items. The developers found intercorrelations ranging from .46 to .72, with the strongest relationships between Achievement and Independence ($r = .64$ for males; $r = .60$ for females) and Relationships and Support ($r = .72$ for males and $r = .72$ for females).

Messer and Greene (2016b) tested convergent validity by administering the WVI concurrently with three assessments containing similar constructs as the WVI. They found a moderately strong relationship between the Enterprising scale of the Self-Directed Search (SDS) and Independence ($r = .44$), Recognition ($r = .38$), and Support ($r = .38$) scales of the WVI for males; however, there were no significant correlations for females. A comparison between the NEO Personality Inventory-3 (NEO-3) and the WVI yielded strong positive correlations between Agreeableness and Relationships ($r = .62$) for women. There was a strong positive correlation between Openness to Experience and Relationships ($r = .53$) for men. The Working Styles Assessment (WSA) working styles correlated strongly with the appropriate working styles of the WVI and across gender with associated work values, thus, demonstrating a distinct relationship between the WVI work values and similar WSA work styles. The Test of General Reasoning Ability (TOGRA) did not have significant findings with any of the scales of the WVI.

Developers of the WVI addressed construct validity using incumbent raters to assess to what extent the O*NET occupation met each of the work values of WVI. A large majority (96.2%) of the occupations matched one work value of each of the occupation families. The raters matched two work values on approximately 55.6% to 87.5%. Very few matched all three work values. This process provided support for construct validity in the WVI.

When testing for concurrent validity, the authors divided the sample into two groups: participants who were extremely/very satisfied with their jobs (n = 196) and those workers who were somewhat/not at all satisfied in their work (n = 101). Of the unsatisfied workers, 59% had their highest ranked work value match one of the occupational values. Two work values matched at a rate of 50% of their occupational work values. The satisfied workers matched one value at 63% and two at a rate of 54%. This consistency reflected concurrent validity for the WVI assessment in that a large portion of individuals who are satisfied workers can find a top work value that will help illuminate a satisfying occupation for that worker.

Use/Interpretation/Evaluation

The WVI Professional Manual (2016) is fully comprehensive and includes information on the functionality, development, administration, scoring, summarization, and interpretation of the assessment. The WVI Fast Guide (2016) is a condensed format (i.e., 11 pages) and is user-friendly. The WVI appears to have strong psychometrics. The WVI Assessment Booklet articulates instructions for taking the assessment, as well for as scoring and interpretation, and provides other support resources, particularly O*NET. There is a WVI Occupations Index that guides users in discovering potential occupations linked to the "highest-rated work values" resulting from the WVI Assessment Booklet (Greene & Messer, 2017).

The WVI could be used in individual or group settings in workforce centers, college settings, adult learning centers, and in places of employment by HR professionals or managers. A career practitioner would use this in assisting a client in career exploration, career restructuring or changing, or career decision-making. The career practitioner can help the individual identify workplaces that might be appealing based on the person's work values. One critique is that the WVI might not be useful for individuals with no prior work experience because they would have little or no fund of knowledge or experience from which to indicate preferences. The WVI is available in English only, so providing versions of the assessment in other relevant languages might be useful in assisting a wider diversity of clients. Many organizations have employees who are not native English speakers. This option might be helpful for those workers and expand the scope of the use of this tool.

Employers might use this assessment to identify workers who might or might not be a good fit for specific types of jobs within their corporation or organization. Employers could use the WVI with both potential and current employees. With a 2016 publication date, this is a contemporary instrument with little evidence of usage in research or other applications. The developers administered the WVI with a standardized sample that was directly reflective of the U.S. population from 2016, and no cultural implications emerged. Overall, the WVI instrument is easy to administer and score, and provides a helpful lens into an individual's values in a workplace setting.

Research and Evaluation/Assessment Uses

Jin and Rounds (2012) conducted a meta-analysis examining work values over the career span, with the goals of learning how stable work values are or how much they change. Results indicated individuals' values had the least stability between ages 18 and 22 and were most stable after entering the world of work (e. g., age 22 and older). In addition, Jin and Rounds found that personality traits were less stable than work values and that Baby Boomers have more stable work values than Generation X. Using WVI to assess possible differences in work values between Generation Y and Z might be a valuable use for this assessment. Conducting future research, using the WVI in conjunction with O*NET, could also generate very important data that might prove useful in contexts such as private and public organizations and university career counseling centers.

References

Dawis, R. V., England, G., & Lofquist, L. H. (1964). *A theory of work adjustment (Minnesota studies in vocational rehabilitation: XV, under support of the US Department of Health, Education, and Welfare)*. Minneapolis, MN: University of Minnesota. Industrial Relations Center.

Greene, J. A., & Messer, M. A. (2017). Best practices for selecting, administering, and interpreting career assessments: A case study with the Work Values Inventory. *Career Planning & Adult Development Journal, 33*(4), 33-44.

Jin, J., & Rounds, J. (2012). Stability and change in values: A meta-analysis of longitudinal studies. *Journal of Vocational Behavior, 80*, 326-339.

Messer, M. A., & Greene, J. A. (2016a). *Work Values Inventory fast guide*. Lutz, FL: PAR.

Messer, M. A., & Greene, J. A. (2016b). *Work Values Inventory professional manual*. Lutz, FL: PAR.

Messer, M. A., & Ureksoy, H. (2014). *Working Styles Assessment*. Lutz, FL: PAR.

Occupational Information Network [O*NET]. (2018). *O*NET resource center*. Retrieved from https://www.onetcenter.org/content.html

Super, D. E. (1973). The Work Values Inventory. In D. G. Zytowski (Ed.), *Contemporary approaches to interest measurement* (pp. 189–205). Minneapolis, MN: University of Minnesota Press.

Career Construction Interview

Reviewed by
Louis A. Busacca
Old Dominion University

The Career Construction Interview (CCI; Savickas, 2013; 2015) is a qualitative assessment method for helping individuals author career stories that connect their self-concepts to work roles and construct meaning through narratives about self and work. As a central component in career construction counseling (Savickas, 2005), the CCI rests on the narrative paradigm to help uncover life themes and inform decision making about a client's current transition. Because an individual's identity is formed by and expressed in narratives, practitioners can enhance client reflexivity, self-awareness, and clarify identity through use of the CCI (Busacca, 2017). As such, Savickas (2013; 2015) designed the CCI to meet the needs of individuals faced with change and uncertainty in a precarious 21st century work environment.

Background

The Career Construction Interview evolved over 30 years of work by Mark Savickas to apply career counseling practice to career construction theory. The semi-structured interview has undergone several revisions over the years, beginning first as the Career Style Interview (Savickas, 1998; 2005; 2009a) which used eight questions, then later amended to the Career Story Interview (Savickas, 2011), and currently renamed to the Career Construction Interview (CCI; Savickas, 2013; 2015); both use five questions. The CCI parallels the name of the theory and retains the same questions found in the Career Story Interview. The CCI applies constructionist and narrative practices to career counseling to motivate individuals to tell their life-career stories subjectively rather than view themselves objectively through scores and norms. Although practitioners used the earlier versions of the CCI, initially, with individuals' undecided about their career choice, the ability of the CCI to address a broad spectrum of career concerns has encouraged its use in diverse settings and with clients ranging from adolescents to adults.

The CCI contains a sequence of questions designed to prompt the telling of an individual's life story in a series of small, micro stories. Having its roots in

Adler's Individual Psychology (Savickas, 1989), the CCI questions elicit the experiences and stories of clients relevant to their career problem. From the telling of the life story, client and counselor co-construct a life portrait that entails an autobiographical narrative about the client's central life theme. Life themes contain an individual's beliefs and values, which in turn guide behavior and have an impact on the person's future (Savickas, 2005). In co-constructing a life portrait, the counselor assists the client with relating the life theme to a career problem or transition currently faced.

Content

The Career Construction Interview is a semi-structured qualitative interview based on five questions that have worked best, in Savickas's experience, using a protracted trial-and-error method (Savickas, 2011). Reflecting the narrative paradigm, the CCI comprises an initial question that sets the scene and five questions to understand different aspects of a life story: role models; magazines, television, websites; favorite story; favorite saying, and early recollections (Savickas, 2015).

The Career Construction Interview sets and empowers the client to tell her or his story. The counselor begins by eliciting counseling goals by asking, "How can I be useful to you as you construct your career?" This opening question places the counselor in a supporting role to that of the client who is the expert on herself or himself (Hartung, 2015). The counselor informs the client that several questions will be asked and explored to get to know her or him better.

For the first question in the interview, the interviewer elicits role models by asking, "Whom did you admire when you were growing up?" The role model can be a real person, fictional character, historical figure, or even an animal. Clients use role models to describe the self and as a way to overcome difficulties and move toward a goal. Unlike parents, clients choose role models deliberately because they share a dilemma similar to the client's own. Also, the counselor might elicit a description of the role model and ask the client how she or he is similar or different from the model.

The second question is, "What are your favorite magazines, TV shows, websites, podcasts, video sharing, or social-media websites? What do you like about them?" This helps inform the counselor about the preferred educational and occupational environments that fit the client's career style. These environments reflect the manifest interests of the client. Also important is gathering details about the section of the magazine or most interesting parts of the TV shows, films, or what the client reviews or reads first when logging onto Facebook, YouTube, or Vimeo, for example.

The third question is, "What is your current favorite book or movie? Tell me the story." Implicit in the story might be an emerging script or plan for the next episode in the life story (Savickas, 2015). Practitioners explore favorite stories by asking clients to describe nonfiction or fiction books, or even a story in a play, musical, or comic book, for example. Clients choose a story often because the story contains cultural scripts and provides perspective on the current problem, preoccupation, or discomfort. According to Savickas (2009a), "People are attracted to books in which a major character experiences problems similar to their own problem" (p. 193). Often, the character provides the client the means for working through the challenge.

The fourth question is, "Tell me your favorite saying or motto." Exploration of mottos comes next because they offer a solution to the problem. Mottos or favorite sayings require listening closely to how clients title their life story because the motto offers self-advice, support, and strategies for constructing the next episode in the story.

Revealing the client's perspective on the current problem, the final question is, "What are your earliest recollections (ER)?" Although ERs are fragments of a larger story, the projective information elicited can be helpful to the counselor by offering a prototype for a plot of life and career and can uncover how an individual is striving toward a goal of superiority or the actualization of an ideal (Cochran, 1997). During the interview process, the counselor elicits, preferably, three early recollections between the ages of three to six years old, or as early as the client can remember. The ERs might portray a preoccupation or express pain (Savickas, 2005). For general interpretation, the counselor identifies recurring themes and feelings in each ER and relates them to information gathered from the other CCI questions to create a profile. Early recollections can serve as a validating process for uncovering a client's recurring life theme and feelings (Busacca, 2007). Using early recollections in career counseling requires basic knowledge of Adlerian psychology along with advanced training.

After administering the questions of the CCI, the counselor builds a life portrait that ties together the small stories to form a larger macro-narrative that unfolds meaning and fosters decision making (Savickas, 2015). Presenting the portrait to the client, the counselor and client work collaboratively and engage in narrative counseling to co-construct plans. Assessment and intervention are intertwined and become a personal process for the client based in emotion and action.

General Utility

Savickas designed the Career Construction Interview, primarily, for use by a counselor within a professional relationship with a client. To expand its use, professionals and practitioners have developed CCI workbooks and guides for a variety of settings. Savickas and Hartung (2012) developed the *My Career Story* workbook (MCS) for use by individuals, with groups, or in educational settings. Clients can complete the MCS on their own or with a counselor. The MCS is helpful in that it provides specific directions and self-reflective questions that guide the individual through the process of completing and processing their story. The MCS aims to increase narrative identity and intentionality (Hartung, 2012). To assist counselors in the use of the MCS, Rehfuss (2017) provided a case study demonstration. The CCI, along with the MCS and worksheets, are available for free at http://www.vocopher.com, and provide structured space for recording responses to each question, as well as several structured pages to help the counselor organize and process the responses. To facilitate the CCI in a group setting with adolescents and adults, Barclay and Stoltz (2016) prepared a guide that contains procedures for leading groups of individuals in deconstructing and constructing themes uncovered in the narrative of group participants. In addition, video demonstrations of career construction counseling are available to help counselors evaluate the usefulness of the CCI (Savickas, 2006; 2009b).

Empirical Support

Several authors have discussed the efficacy and use of the Career Construction Interview in practice. Published articles have been pedagogical in nature—instructing counselors on the use of the CCI—and others have provided case study demonstrations. Busacca (2007) provided a practitioner friendly primer on career construction theory and application of the CCI. Rehfuss (2009) advocated teaching the CCI to counselors and presented various techniques for increasing counselors' career counseling competencies. In addition, techniques for using the CCI in group settings were discussed by Barclay (2017), Barclay and Stoltz (2016), and Barclay, Stoltz, and Wolff (2011). To assist counselors in the use of the CCI, Taber, Hartung, Briddick, Briddick, and Rehfuss (2011) organized an overview of the CCI, along with a case study, as a guide. In another case study, Taber and Briddick (2011) discussed counseling an adult seeking career direction in the face of uncertainty as a contract worker.

Qualitative researchers have examined the usefulness of the CCI from client and counselor perspectives. Because the questions on the Career Story Interview (CSI) are the same in the CCI, noting counselor impressions and outcomes in several studies using the CSI is important. In a qualitative study, Rehfuss, Del Corso, Glavin, and Wykes (2011) studied participants (n = 18) with whom they assessed for the overall impact of the CSI on participants' career concerns and career narrative, as well as their recall of career style components and engagement in career exploration behaviors two weeks after participating in the CSI. The results indicated that, after completing the CSI, participants generally felt helped and, typically, reported more awareness, self-confidence, direction, confirmation, and a sense of encouragement related to their career concern. In another qualitative study, Rehfuss, Cosio, and Del Corso (2011) presented findings which explored the impressions of practicing counselors (n = 34) who had implemented use of the CSI in counseling sessions with clients who expressed concern regarding their career. The results showed that counselors described the CSI as enlightening and acknowledged its value in identifying life themes.

Two international studies have also been conducted using earlier versions of the CCI. The first employed a qualitative study using the Career Story Interview, and the second was the only experimental design to date incorporating the CSI. In a qualitative study in the United Kingdom, Reid and West (2011) had eight career guidance practitioners use the CSI with a sample (n = 10) of adolescent students in transition. First, practitioners self-trained through watching a Savickas DVD (2006), readings, role-play, and recorded discussion. Results included qualitative increases in self-control and self-understanding of the participants, yet some practitioners found it difficult to find the time, space, and confidence to apply a new approach. In an experimental study, in Italy, of a group-based Life Design Counseling intervention, Di Fabio and Maree (2012) examined the CSI for its effectiveness. Di Fabio and Maree used written exercises to implement the topics in the CSI (i.e., role models, magazines/entertainment, favorite books, free time, favorite mottos, school subjects, and earliest memories). The study employed an experimental design that involved two groups of Italian entrepreneurs from the agricultural and trade sectors: an experimental group (n= 38), who received Life Design Counseling (Savickas, 2010) and a control group (n = 34). The results showed a decrease in career decision-making difficulties and an increase in career decision-making self-efficacy in the experimental group, thus suggesting the value of group-based Life Design Counseling using the CSI.

Recently, several researchers have used new qualitative designs to investigate how career construction counseling, using the CCI as an intervention, promotes reflection and develops reflexivity (Hartung & Vess, 2016; Maree, 2016; Reid, Bimrose & Brown, 2016). For example, Hartung and Vess used the Interpersonal Process Recall (IPR) procedure to determine what parts of the intervention, if any, prompted reflection and reflexivity. In a single case analysis method using the CCI, they examined a single episode of career construction counseling, conducted in two sessions, to determine a 24-year old Caucasian woman's perspective on what prompts client change and reflexivity in the counseling process. Post-counseling IPR with the client of her videotaped career construction counseling session indicated five major themes: (a) role models prompt identity reflection, (b) early recollections foster cohesion, (c) follow-up questions add depth to the story, (d) counselor as audience provides clarity and validation, and (e) career construction interview questions illuminate perspective and need for action. Results support prior research indicating the usefulness of career construction counseling for promoting reflexive action in life design.

The CCI has also been examined for its efficacy and use in group career counseling. In examining the efficacy of the Life-Design Group career counseling intervention to help members explore their personal identities, envision possible selves, and plan purposeful action, Barclay and Stoltz (2016) presented case study results for Caucasian undergraduate students (n = 3) who were struggling with gaining movement in their career trajectories. Participants engaged in the CCI as part of the group intervention, and data collection included pre- and post-test quantitative career measures. Results indicated decreases in career uncertainty and indecision, and increases in readiness for making academic major and career decisions. Also, thematic content from the CCI aligned well with all the participants' Holland code.

Researchers have also investigated the validity of the CCI. Although further exploration and validity assessment of the CCI is necessary, one such study demonstrates promising results. Using the Career Construction Interview (CCI), Barclay and Wolff (2012) investigated the concurrent validity and usefulness of the CCI of college juniors and seniors (n = 83) for identifying students' RIASEC codes. They derived a correlation (r = 0.466) between the participants' written narrative responses to the CCI and their Strong Interest Inventory (SII; Donnay, Thompson, Morris, & Schaubhut, 2004) RIASEC theme codes. Results indicated moderate correlations between the CCI and SII and suggested that the CCI was effective at identifying participants' career interests.

Conclusion

The Career Construction Interview (CCI) aims to help clients tell, hear, and enact their life-career stories. By turning to qualitative career assessment in the form of narrative models and methods such as the CCI, counselors have a culturally embedded and contextualized approach to help clients author their life stories.

References

Barclay, S. R. (2017). Constructing a course: Constructivist group career counseling with low-income, first-generation college students. In L. A. Busacca & M. C. Rehfuss (Eds.), *Postmodern career counseling: A handbook of culture, context, and cases* (pp. 23-36). Alexandria, VA: American Counseling Association.

Barclay, S. R., Stoltz, K. B. (2016). The life design group: A case study vignette in group career construction counseling. *Journal of Student Affairs, Research and Practice, 53*, 78-89.

Barclay, S. R., Stoltz, K. B., & Wolff, L. A. (2011). Career development through career construction counseling: A group method. In T. Fitch, & J. L. Marshall (Eds.), *Group work and outreach plans for college counselors* (pp. 49–54). Alexandria, VA: American Counseling Association.

Barclay, S. R., & Wolff, L. A. (2012). Exploring the career construction interview for vocational personality assessment. *Journal of Vocational Behavior, 81*(3), 370–377.

Busacca, L. A. (2007). Career construction theory: A practitioner's primer. *Career Planning and Adult Development Journal, 23*, 57-67.

Busacca, L. A. (2017). Career counseling in postmodern times: Emergence and narrative conceptions. In L. A. Busacca & M. C. Rehfuss (Eds.), *Postmodern career counseling: A handbook of culture, context, and cases* (pp. 23-36). Alexandria, VA: American Counseling Association.

Cochran, L. (1997). *Career Counseling: A Narrative Approach.* Thousand Oaks, CA: Sage.

Di Fabio, A., & Maree, J. G. (2012). Group-based life design counseling in an Italian context. *Journal of Vocational Behavior, 80,* 100–107.

Donnay, D. A. C., Thompson, R. C., Morris, M. L., & Schaubhut, N. A. (2004). *Technical brief for the newly revised Strong Interest Inventory assessment: Content, reliability, and validity.* Mountain View, CA: Consulting Psychology. Retrieved from https://www.cpp.com/Pdfs/StrongTechnicalBrief.pdf

Hartung, P. J. (2012, June). *My career story: An autobiographical workbook for life-career success.* Paper prepared for presentation at the annual meeting of the National Career Development Association, Atlanta, GA.

Hartung, P. J. (2015). The career construction interview. In M. McMahon & M. Watson (Eds.), *Career assessment: Qualitative approaches,* (pp. 115-121). The Netherlands: Sense Publishers.

Hartung, P. J., & Vess, L. (2016). Critical moments in career construction counseling. *Journal of Vocational Behavior, 97,* 31-39.

Maree, J. G. (2016). How career construction counseling promotes reflection and reflexivity: Two case studies. *Journal of Vocational Behavior, 97,* 22-30.

Rehfuss, M. C. (2009). Teaching career construction and the career style interview. *Career Planning and Adult Development Journal, 25,* 58–71.

Rehfuss, M. C. (2017). Using the My Career Story workbook with an African-American high school student. In L. A. Busacca & M. C. Rehfuss (Eds.), *Postmodern career counseling: A handbook of culture, context, and cases* (pp. 91-103). Alexandria, VA: American Counseling Association.

Rehfuss, M. C., Cosio, S., & Del Corso, J. (2011). Counselors' perspectives on using the career style interview with clients. *Career Development Quarterly, 59,* 208–218.

Rehfuss, M. C., Del Corso, J., Glavin, K., & Wykes, S. (2011). Impact of the Career Style Interview on individuals with career concerns. *Journal of Career Assessment, 9,* 405–419.

Reid, H., Bimrose, J., & Brown, A. (2016). Prompting reflection and learning in career construction counseling. *Journal of Vocational Behavior, 97,* 51-59.

Reid, H., & West, L. (2011). "Telling tales": Using narrative in career guidance. *Journal of Vocational Behavior, 78*(2), 174–183.

Savickas, M. L. (1989). Career style assessment and counseling. In T. Sweeney (Ed.), *Adlerian counseling: A practical approach for a new decade* (3rd ed., pp. 289-320). Muncie, IN: Accelerated Development.

Savickas, M. L. (1998). Career style assessment and counseling. In T. Sweeney (Ed.), *Adlerian counseling: A practitioner's approach* (4th ed., pp. 149-205). Philadelphia: Accelerated Development.

Savickas, M. L. (2005). The theory and practice of career construction. In S. D. Brown & R. W. Lent (Eds.), *Career development and counseling: Putting theory and research to work* (pp. 42-70). Hoboken, NJ: John Wiley & Sons.

Savickas, M. L. (2006). *Career counseling* [DVD]. Washington D.C.: American Psychological Association.

Savickas M. L. (2009a). Career-style counseling. In T. J. Sweeney (Ed.), *Adlerian counseling and psychotherapy: A practitioner's approach* (5th ed., pp. 183–207). New York, NY: Routledge.

Savickas, M. L. (2009b). *Career counseling over time: Psychotherapy training video* [DVD]. Washington, D.C.: American Psychological Association.

Savickas, M. L. (2010). *Life Designing: Framework and introduction.* Paper presented at the 27th International Congress of Applied Psychology, Melbourne, Australia.

Savickas, M. L. (2011). *Career counseling.* Washington, DC: American Psychological Association.

Savickas, M. L. (2013). The theory and practice of career construction. In S. Brown, & R. Lent (Eds.), *Career development and counseling: Putting theory and research to work (2nd ed. pp. 147-183).* New York: John Wiley.

Savickas, M. L. (2015). *Life-design counseling manual.* Rootstown, OH: Retrieved from http://www.vocopher.com/LifeDesign/LifeDesign.pdf

Savickas, M. L., & Hartung, P. J. (2012). *My career story: An autobiographical workbook for life-career success.* Retrieved from http://www.vocopher.com/CSI/CCI_workbook.pdf

Taber, B. J., & Briddick, W. C. (2011). Adlerian-based career counseling in the age of protean careers. *Journal of Individual Psychology, 67,* 107-121.

Taber, B. J., Hartung, P. J., Briddick, W. C., Briddick, H., & Rehfuss, M. (2011). Career Style Interview: A contextualized approach to career counseling. *Career Development Quarterly, 59,* 274–287.

CAREER GENOGRAM

Reviewed by

Tina M. Anctil

Portland State University

Introduction

As career counseling theories have evolved into postmodern approaches, which allow for more individualized and culturally sensitive assessments, the career genogram has increased in relevance and is widely believed to be the most common qualitative career assessment in use (Chope, 2005). The assessment is described as a post-modern tool used to empower individuals to make meaning from their past to transform their future. Bowen (1980) created the genogram for use in family therapy as a mechanism to record information about the family of origin quickly, especially during the initial interview. The career genogram (Dagley, 1984; Gysbers & Moore, 1987; Okiishi, 1987) was created as an adaption of the genogram and is a qualitative assessment designed to gather information about the influence of the family in career decision making through a three-generational graphic model of the family origin and corresponding careers. The career genogram meets a critical career exploration and counseling need by allowing practitioners to understand the historical and multigenerational career development patterns, including roles, behaviors, and attitudes of family members, toward work and career (Chope, 2005). The utility of the assessment includes use with children and adolescents in classroom guidance activities (Gibson, 2005; Malott & Magnuson, 2004), with undergraduates in career centers (Grier-Reed & Ganuza, 2011; Grier-Reed & Ganuza, 2012; McMahon, Patton, & Watson, 2003), and with adults in private practice settings (Chope, 2005; Malach-Pines & Yafe-Yanai, 2001; Swanson & Fouad, 2014).

Description

The career genogram is a non-standardized qualitative tool that practitioners can use individually and in groups or classrooms. Okiisha (1987) suggested a simple three-step approach for administration of the career genogram with adults: construction of the genogram, identification of occupations, and exploration with the client. Allowing the client to choose non-biologically significant others who have acted as family members to the client throughout the use of the genogram is important. Notably, genogram activities might trigger clients with trauma histories that originated in the family: thus, instructions to the client must include the option of allowing the client to select which individuals to include and discuss. Career practitioners who are not trained mental health counselors should use this tool with caution and awareness of the potentially triggering effect of the genogram. Finally, the depth of the discussion indicates the amount of time required to use the career genogram.

Step One:
Construction of the Career Genogram

This step includes giving the client basic instructions regarding the purpose of the genogram and suggestions on how to gather historical family information. Completion of the genogram can occur at home or in person with the practitioner, which allows for help from the counselor or facilitator. Generally, the directions include having clients identify three-generations of family members on each side of the family tree, inclusive of grandparents, aunts, uncles, cousins, parents and/or stepparents; brothers, sisters, and the client. Again, clients should be allowed to include significant individuals who have been in family roles and adapt the genogram accordingly. Once the client has gathered information about family members, the practitioner and the client can work collaboratively to construct the career genogram either manually or with the use of an online tool (there are thousands of free options available through a Google search). Practitioners and clients use standard symbols for a person's sex or gender in the genogram. A square represents a man or boy, and a circle represents a woman or girl. The genogram symbol for a person whose gender is non-binary is a rhombus or triangle. Some non-binary people might prefer to have themselves represented by a genderless symbol.

Step Two:
Identification of Occupational History

Client frustration is common when there is a lack of available historical family knowledge. Some might be unwilling or unable to connect with family members who have this information. In such cases, the career practitioner can encourage clients to complete as much of the information as they know because the process is still valuable. After clients learn more history, they can add family members and primary occupations to the constructed genogram.

Step Three:
Genogram Analysis

The analysis of the career genogram involves using guiding questions with the individual to facilitate gaps in the information and develop meaning from the data. Because this is a non-standardized assessment, career practitioners should feel open to adapt questions to the context and needs of the person. When working with vulnerable populations, such as youth in foster care, clients from systemic poverty environments, or those with family trauma histories, practitioners must use care and skill during this exploration stage. Whenever practitioners conduct this analysis outside a one-on-one career counseling session, they should honor the person's right to privacy.

Gysbers, Heppner, and Johnston (2014) suggested these as general questions practitioners might ask:

- How would you describe the family in which you grew up?
- What is/was your role in the family (now and when growing up)?
- Who are you most like in your family?
- What is your spouse's relationship with your family? (p.201)

Chope (2005) compiled some suggested questions from the literature to guide the discussion, including:

- What family patterns exist?
- Which family members had a clearly formed work identity?
- Which family members did you most admire?
- Whose career aspirations are similar to your own?
- Which person was most influential in the creation of your own career identity?
- What pressures do you feel when you compare yourself to your family?
- What were the dominant values in the family?
- What pressures does each family member observe with regard to decision making and economic status and position?
- What is the meaning of success? (p. 407-408).

Questions such as these elicit a considerable amount of information and will include such issues as family role expectations, beliefs about higher education, work values, patterns in vocational choices, the impact of disability, addiction or poverty on the family, and overall family values related to work and family roles. Practitioners who are trained counselors might use this information to process vocational patterns, and discuss similarities and differences in values, interests, and opportunity structures among family members. If a client is experiencing career stress or conflict, these discussions can be insightful and could lead to clarity in the career decision making process. In addition, this process might unveil larger unfinished family business that practitioners can address with a referral for individual or family counseling, as appropriate.

Qualitative Considerations: Application to Theory

Murray Bowen (1980) created the genogram as a tool to gather pertinent structural family information in the initial interview of family therapy. The career genogram (Dagley, 1984; Gysbers & Moore, 1987; Okiishi, 1987) is viewed widely as the most popular qualitative career assessment measure to date. Non-standardized qualitative assessments are grounded in constructivism, which "provides a means for individuals to reflect on their real-life experiences through the use of narratives, enabling them to construct understandings of their situations and circumstances" (Gysbers, 2006, p. 97). As such, the career genogram is useful to practitioners as a holistic and integrative assessment approach. Its theoretical application is interdisciplinary and broad, and is useful with career counseling theories that acknowledge and assess the family's influence on career decision making. Examples of this come from Super's Life Span Life Space approach, Life Design Theory, and Existential Career theory.

Super (1963) explored how one's family influences career decision and identified self-concept as a critical influence in career decision making. Super's contributions to understanding the developmental tasks associated with planning, exploring, and making decisions, through the emergence of self-concept, are foundational to career planning (Super, 1963; Phillips & Blustein, 1994). In a seminal review of research, Osipow (1983) explored Super's self concept theory in career development and concluded that there is ample evidence that people seek to implement their self-concept through their occupational choices. Academic self-concept, or how people perceive their abilities in a certain area of study, is an important predictor of future study and career choice (Valentine, Dubois, & Cooper, 2004). Self-concept was important to the retention of nursing students (Cowin & Hengstberger-Sims, 2006) and predicted academic self-concept and career aspirations (Nagengast & Marsh, 2012) in science students. In their qualitative study of first-generation college students, Byrd and Macdonald (2005) found that a negative self-concept was a significant factor in delaying college. Additionally, self-concept in the workplace operates at implicit levels and influences the attitudes and behaviors of workers (Johnson & Saboe, 2011). Use of the career genogram allows for the facilitation of a discussion to explore how the family influenced the individual's understanding of his or her occupational or academic self-concept. This information is foundational to career decision making.

The family career story is fundamental to life design theory, and the career genogram is in direct alignment with this career development theory. Practitioners and facilitators can align the questions they use in the discussion and analysis of the career genogram directly to life design theory (Di Fabio, 2010), which relies on the construction of identity and meaning from early life experiences or stories. Savickas (2013) described how the past relates to a person's understanding of the present and, then, guides the individual into the future. Di Fabio described the career construction genogram as facilitating "the concepts of "historical, familial and cultural forces in sharing career decision making" (p. 382). The process of helping the client identify the career motto of parental lines leads to understanding of lifelong career meanings and expectations of work. (Di Fabio, 2010, 2017.) Use of the career genogram aids clients in identifying congruence and incongruence in family career stories, which facilitates the client's new career story (Di Fabio, 2017).

Finally, Malach-Pine and Yafe-Yanai (2001) provided applications of the career genogram from a psychodynamic-existential perspective. The psychodynamic career perspective focuses on significant childhood experiences, family dynamics, and familial vocational choices as the basis for understanding unconscious career choices. Practitioners use the career genogram to help clients bring the unconscious career narratives to the surface so they can be aware of the influence and power of career narratives, particularly as those relate to "linking people's behavior and feeling about themselves to the existential need to find and assure a place of belonging" (p. 172). Malach-Pine and Yafe-Yanai explored this theory with a case study methodology using the career genogram to help clients who were experiencing career burnout to identify the unconscious layers that might have forbidden or hindered career decision making. Use of the career genogram helps to answer specific questions about dominant values and family legends that still have influence on the family. This is an effective tool to facilitate career decision making with adults who are experiencing career burnout.

Research on the consistency and credibility of the career genogram is quite limited. To date, Di Fabio (2012, 2015, 2017) has published, perhaps, the only experimental study using the career construction genogram as the intervention variable. Her study found that the group who received the intervention had more specific life and occupational goals than those who did not receive the intervention. Grier-Reed and Ganuza (2011) completed a quasi-experimental study, using the career genogram as part of a classroom-based intervention with Asian American and African American college students, and Grier-Reed and Ganuza (2012) evaluated the career construction approach with first generation college students in the United States. Results indicated a significant increase career decision self-efficacy after completion of the course. As life design theory grows in popularity across the globe, more research on the efficacy and use of the career genogram across cultures and populations will likely expand.

Career Genogram Applications

Beyond the individual application, school counselors and college career counselors have adapted the career genogram successfully for classroom and small group use. Gibson (2005) described how counselors can utilize the career genogram as part of the comprehensive guidance program with elementary, middle, and high school students. Career counselors and educators must be sensitive to students who are not able to gather this information for any number of reasons (e.g., the student lives in foster care, the student does not know one of side of their family, unemployment trends/multiple jobs, etc.). Further, during the interpretation or discussion of the genogram, some students might be embarrassed or might want to keep their responses private from their peers, which facilitators must honor.

Elementary School

At the elementary school level, the general purpose of the career genogram is to increase career awareness. The procedure involves gathering family occupational information through family discussions at home. There are readily available family tree pictures that practitioners can use as a paper handout to accompany the assignment, thus allowing students to be creative with the visual representation of their career genogram. Once students return with their completed occupational family tree, the analysis stage includes sharing the career genograms with classmates. Genogram practitioners can structure classroom activities to facilitate learning about the world of work, increase awareness of gender roles, and help students understand the relationship between educational levels and careers (Gibson, 2005).

Middle School

With middle school students, practitioners can instruct students in the same approach to complete the career genogram, but they can adapt the process to help students deepen their understanding of career and the relationship to education and training. Likewise, practitioners can use the information students gather about family members' occupations as a springboard to using career information systems and related information gathering (e.g., online gamification of career information systems or O*NET).

High School

In a high school, career and technical education specialists and school counselors must support students as they explore postsecondary education and training. These professionals can use the career genogram to help students with identifying and describing family and motivational values associated with work, higher education, and training. To facilitate greater depth of the genogram analysis, practitioners might have students interview three family members about specific areas or themes, such as how/whether their interests relate to their career, what career opportunities they did or did not have, or their career decision making process. Practitioners can have students complete journal or writing assignments, or have students record video blogs about themes and their self-discovery process they identified through the constructions of their career genogram (Gibson, 2005).

Higher Education

In higher education settings, many report the use of career genograms in classroom and career centers, yet there is sparse discussion of this in the literature. Malott and Magnuson (2004) provided an example of a 5-session group experience they developed in which they used a highly structured sequence of activities to explore the career genogram within a one-credit career exploration college course. The basic procedures were a three-step process that included creation of the career genogram, responding to a series of guiding questions through a writing assignment, and, then, individual process meetings. The instructors invited students to include persons outside of the family who had a significant influence on them and their career development. The individual meetings were 50 minutes long and allowed students to discuss more personal issues, concerns, and insights that emerged from the activity. This is a suggested best practice for use of the career genogram in higher education (Malott & Magnuson, 2004).

Beyond the use of career genograms in individual, dyadic, small group, or classroom settings, the genogram has a broad appeal and use with diverse populations, including people of color, people with disabilities, and those who experience economically disadvantages. DeMaria, Weeks, and Hof (1999) identified the construction of a multicultural genogram as a counseling intervention designed to help individuals understand their racial/ethnic backgrounds, as well as the sociopolitical influences such as immigration, religion, and class on their development. By extension, practitioners might use the career genogram to help clients understand how cultural factors have influenced the careers of family members and how this could be influencing the current career decision making process of the client. Use of the career genogram allows clients to externalize problems (e.g., I am the first person in my family to go to college) and become aware of issues they have internalized (e.g., I don't fit in with many of my college friends), which allows for new understanding of the context of the problem (Sexton & Cheney, 2001).

Gibson and Taylor (2017) described how the career genogram can be helpful, particularly when working with clients who are disadvantaged economically because use of the genogram helps individuals to illuminate and externalize issues related to social capital that can be disempowering. The working poor have less access and fewer opportunities to explore career interests, values, and abilities; yet, this might be hidden from the client's awareness. Using the career genogram to discuss these issues can lower the client's defensiveness, which facilitates understanding of how the client has internalized these social influences without awareness of their influence on career decision making. For example, a female client becomes aware she is the first woman in her family to work outside the home, or a male client realizes the past two generations of lumber mill workers did not have any opportunity to explore a trade or career.

Conclusion

The career genogram is a tool that guides an understanding of the client's historical and multigenerational career development patterns, including roles, behaviors, and attitudes, of family members toward work and career. This review provides examples as to how practitioners might use the career genogram in individual, dyadic, small group, and classroom settings with children, adolescents, and adults across cultures. Utilizing the career genogram as a qualitative career assessment allows career practitioners to empower clients to understand how their family has influenced their work and career journeys, which, in turn, facilitates the career exploration process and the development of a career goal.

References

Bowen M. (1980). *Key to the Genogram*. Washington, DC: Georgetown University Hospital.

Byrd, K., & Macdonald, G. (2005). Defining college readiness from the inside out: First-generation college student perspectives. *Community College Review, 33*, 22-37. doi: 10.1177/009155210503300102

Chope, R. (2005). Qualitatively assessing family influence in career decision making. *Journal of Career Assessment, 13*, 395-414.

Cowin, L., & Hengstberger-Sims, C. (2006). New graduate nurse self-concept and retention: A longitudinal survey. *International Journal of Nursing Studies, 43*, 59-70. doi: 10.1016/j.ijnurstu.2005.03.004

Dagley, J. (1984). *A vocational genogram*. Unpublished document, University of Georgia, Athens, GA.

DeMaria, R., Weeks, G, & Hof, L. (1999). *Focused genograms: Intergenerational assessment of individuals, couples, and families.* Philadelphia, PA: Taylor & Francis.

Di Fabio, A. (2010). Life designing in 21st century: Using a new, strengthened career genogram. *Journal of Psychology in Africa, 20,* 381-384.

Di Fabio, A. (2012). Evaluation of the effectiveness of the career construction genogram. *Cypriot Journal of Educational Sciences, 7,* 287-297. Retrieved from http://archives. sproc.org/index.php/cjes/article/view/913/pdf_96

Di Fabio, A. (2015). The life design genogram. In M. McMahon & M. Watson (Eds.), *Career assessment: Qualitative approaches* (pp. 97-103). Rotterdam: Sense Publishers. doi: 10.1007/978-94-6300-034-5_11

Di Fabio, A. (2017). The life design genogram: Self-construction with an Italian female transitioning to the world of work. In L. A. Busacca & M. C. Rehfuss (Eds.), *Postmodern career counseling: A handbook of culture, context, and cases* (pp. 229-244). Alexandria, VA: American Counseling Association.

Gibson, D. (2005). The use of genograms in career counseling with elementary, middle, and high school students. *The Career Development Quarterly, 53,* 353-362.

Gibson, D. M., & Taylor, J. V. (2017). Using the genogram for career assessment and intervention with an economically disadvantaged client. In L. A. Busacca, & M. C. Rehfuss (Eds.), *Postmodern career counseling: A handbook of culture, context, and cases* (pp. 163-176). Alexandria, VA: American Counseling Association.

Grier-Reed, T., & Ganuza, Z. (2011). Constructivism and career decision self-efficacy for Asian Americans and African Americans. *Journal of Counseling and Development, 89,* 200-205.

Grier-Reed, T., & Ganuza, Z. (2012). Using constructivist career development to improve career decision self-efficacy in trio students. *Journal of College Student Development, 53,* 464-471.

Gysbers, N. (2006). Using qualitative career assessments in career counselling with adults. *International Journal for Educational and Vocational Guidance, 6,* 95-108.

Gysbers, N. C., Heppner, M. J., & Johnston, J. A. (2014). *Career counseling: Holism, diversity, and strengths.* John Wiley & Sons.

Gysbers, N. C. & Moore, E. J. (1987). *Career counseling: Skills and techniques for practitioners.* Englewood Cliffs, NJ: Prentice Hall.

Johnson, R., & Saboe, K. (2011). Measuring implicit iraits in organizational research: Development of an indirect measure of employee implicit self-concept. *Organizational Research Methods, 14,* 530-547. doi: 10.1177/1094428110363617

Malach-Pines, A., & Yafe-Yanai, O. (2001). Unconscious determinants of career choice and burnout: Theoretical model and counseling strategy. *Journal of Employment Counseling, 38*(4), 170-184.

Malott, K., & Magnuson, S. (2004). Using genograms to facilitate undergraduate students' career development: A group model. *The Career Development Quarterly, 53*, 178-186.

McMahon, M., Patton, W., & Watson, M. (2003). Developing qualitative career assessment processes. *The Career Development Quarterly, 51*, 194-202.

Okiishi, R. (1987). The genogram as a tool in career counseling. *Journal of Counseling and Development, 66*, 139-143.

Osipow, S. H. (1983). Theories of career development (3rd ed). Englewood Cliffs, NJ: Prentice Hall.

Nagengast, B., & Marsh, H. (2012). Big fish in little ponds aspire more: Mediation and cross-cultural generalizability of school-average ability effects on self-concept and career aspirations in science. *Journal of Educational Psychology, 104*, 1033-1053. doi: 10.1037/a0027697

Phillips, S. D., & Blustein, D. L. (1994). Readiness for career choices: Planning, exploring, and deciding. *The Career Development Quarterly, 43*(1), 63-73.. doi: 10.1002/j.2161-0045.1994.tb00847.x

Savickas, M. L. (2013). *Career development and counseling putting theory and research to Work* (2nd ed). Hoboken, NJ: Wiley.

Sexton, E. & Cheney, C. O. (2001, Fall). The use of genogram with students with emotional and behavioral disorders. *Beyond Behavior,* 27-29.

Super, D. E. (1963). Self-concepts in vocational development. In D. E. Super (Ed.), *Career development: Self-concept theory* (pp.1-16). New York: College Entrance Examination Board.

Swanson, J. L, & Fouad, N. A. (2014). *Career theory and practice: Learning through case studies.* Thousand Oaks, CA: Sage Publications, Inc.

Valentine, J., DuBois, D., & Cooper, H. (2004). The relation between self-beliefs and academic achievement: A meta-analytic review. *Educational Psychologist, 39*, 111-133. doi: 10.1207/s15326985ep3902_3

QUALITATIVE

KNOWDELL CARD SORTS

Instrument Author: Richard L. Knowdell

Publisher: Career Research & Testing, Inc.

Publisher Address: P.O. Box 611930   San Jose, CA 95161-1930 USA
https://www.knowdellcardsorts.com/

Statement of Purpose: Identify and rank order Career Values, Motivated Skills, Occupational Interests and Leisure/Retirement Activities

Target Population: High School, College Students and Adults

Norm Group(s) on which Scores are based: Not normed instruments

Titles of Subtests, Scales, Scores Provided: Career Values Card Sort, Motivated Skills Card Sort, Occupational Interest Card Sort, Leisure/Retirement Card Sort

Forms and Levels Available with Dates of Publication/Revision of Each: 1977, 1997, 2002, 2016

Date of Most Recent Edition of Manual, User's Guide, etc.: 2002

Available in which Languages: In addition to English, Career Values and Motivated Skills available in Arabic, Chinese and Korean

Actual Test Time: Not Timed Instruments

Total Administration Time: Each Instrument can be completed in 45 to 60 minutes

Required Level of Training and/or Credentials for Administrator: None Required

Types of Scores: Rank Ordered

Report Format/Content: Rank Ordered and on Bell Curve Form

Report Format/Content for Group Summaries: Individual Rank Order. No Group Results

Availability of Machine Scoring Service? No

Availability of Hand Scoring? Yes

If yes, time required for hand scoring? 30 to 45 minutes

If yes, who is it scored by? Individual Test Taker

Availability of Local Machine Scoring Service? Not Available

Availability and Options for Computer Software? Computer Software Available; Standard administration online

If available, describe the ways in which computer/online version differs: see https://www.knowdellcardsorts.com/

> **Link to webpage that specifies the costs of materials**: www.knowdellcardsorts. com
>
> **Additional Comments of Interest to Users (e.g. forthcoming revisions, new material, etc)**: see https://www.knowdellcardsorts.com/
>
> **Published Reviews of the Instrument in the Last 15 years**: *Counselors Guide to Career Assessment Instruments*, 5th Edition

KNOWDELL CARD SORTS

Reviewed by

Tanya M. Campos

University of New Mexico

INTRODUCTION

The four sets of Knowdell Card Sorts consist of the Career Values Card Sort (CVCS; Knowdell, 2005a, 2006, 2011a), the Motivational Skills Card Sort (MSCS; Knowdell, 2005b; 2011b, 2017a), the Occupational Interests Card Sort (OICS; Knowdell, 2010, 2015a, 2017b), and the Leisure and Retirement Activities Card Sort (LRCS; Knowdell, 2009, 2015b, 2017c). Describing how the CVCS originated, Knowdell (2006) wrote that in the mid-1970s, as the Chief Counselor and Employee Assistance Division Manager at Lawrence Livermore National Laboratoi y, his employer asked him to lead an effort to create a career planning and development program for the lab's 5,000 plus employees. In searching through career assessments and tools available in that period, he grew frustrated not being able to find assessments he believed were user friendly and normed to the general public. Using a q-sort technique he learned in graduate school, along with occupation card exercises observed at counseling conferences, Knowdell combined a list of 41 values that, ultimately, formed the CVCS Card Sort in 1977. Since then, Knowdell added the MSCS, the OICS, and the LRCS. Knowdell revised or updated the card sorts in 2002 and 2004, as well as implemented online activities in 2012. In addition, users will locate card sorts in other languages, such as Russian, Spanish, German, Japanese, Vietnamese, Dutch, Swedish, and Islandic (Knowdell, 2006). All of Knowdell's card sorts, worksheets, and planning manuals are available on Knowdell's Career Trainer webpage (Career Trainer, 2018) along with additional instructional books, CDs, and DVDs.

Although each of the Knowdell card sorts is unique, the same theoretical foundation, structure, and general format serve as foundations for each. Each card sort comes in a visually appealing and user-friendly package that consists of a deck of cards, a worksheet, and a planning manual. Knowdell (2006; 2017a; 2017c) described the card sort process as an activity similar to the card game called Solitaire – a deck of cards that clients deal by grouping and sorting the cards into several categories depending on the assessment (values, skills, interests, activities, occupations). Clients rank these categories by level of motivation and interest. Knowdell (2006; 2011b; 2017a; 2017c) recommended clients complete this solitaire process rather quickly by deferring to their first, or gut, instinct rather er doing a deep reflection process. Once clients complete the card sort process, they can proceed to use any of the wide-range of worksheets and activities in all the four planning manuals to establish next-step career development goals and outcomes.

Career Values Card Sort (CVCS)

Knowdell designed the CVCS to assist clients in understanding personal value systems for the purpose of aligning values with certain job settings and the world of work. Knowdell (2006) believed this clarification and alignment would lead to stronger job and career satisfaction. Practitioners use the CVCS to help clients identify their values. Next, practitioners have clients rate their values in an ordered type of rating system (i.e., always valued, often valued, sometimes valued, seldom valued, never valued), which helps determine the clients' intensity, or strength, associated with each of the values, as well as provide space to explore areas of value conflict or congruence. Once clients complete both steps, they apply what they learned to making career decisions.

Motivated Skills Card Sort (MSCS)

The MSCS helps clients identify their level of competence and motivation in a wide variety of employability skills. Career specialists can use the MSCS for diverse groups of people; however, as Knowdell (2017) wrote, these clients, "share at least one factor in common: not being unmarketable, but a perception they are unmarketable" (p. 2). Examples might include recent graduates who believe they lack the skill level to be competitive candidates, or clients who have been out of the job market for some time and believe their job skills are out-of-date. Practitioners can use the MSCS as a tool to assist clients in identifying skills used in other parts of their lives and clarifying how these skills can be transferrable to the world of work. In addition, the MSCS can help clients identify the level of interest, or motivation, to use certain skills in career-related activities. For clients who are recently unemployed and need to find new work, sometimes in different job sectors, the MSCS can help identify the important transferrable skills possessed by the client.

Occupational Interests Card Sort (OICS)

Knowdell designed the OICS to assist clients in both defining occupations of interests and identifying common characteristics within occupational themes. The OICS is helpful to clients who might need to broaden their view of occupations for career decision-making. For example, those students or recent graduates lacking significant exposure to the world of work and diverse types of occupations benefit from developing lists of specific occupational interests. Similarly, clients who have been in a specified occupation or position for some time and are having difficulty envisioning themselves in different occupational roles, or not even knowing what is available to them in other professional fields, learn about other occupational possibilities. Once clients identify occupations and common themes, practitioners can work with clients to assess their level of readiness to purse those occupations, as well as help them assess the skills and knowledge needed to build, or gain, competency to enter other occupations.

Leisure and Retirement Activities Card Sort (LRCS)

The LRCS addresses developmental factors and personal planning related to transitioning from the formal world of work to leisure activities and retirement. Practitioners can use the LRCS to work with clients in identifying factors related to leisure and retirement satisfaction through grouping a series of activities and specifying their desired level of engagement in these activities. Also, the LRCS assists clients in acknowledging retirement as a major life transition and identifying the importance of planning and preparing for this transition. Practitioners can use the LRCS to challenge clients' views about retirement, particularly those beliefs clients use to view retirement as an end-of-life stage.

Technical Considerations

Several authors (Fields, 2013; Kinner & Kernes, 2001) have acknowledged a lack of empirical testing regarding the validity and reliability of the card sorts. In a review of literature, Fields (2013) indicated he found no references to empirical testing or evidence of methodological rigor, and a literature review since then for this current review also found none.

Knowdell (2006) cited the high face validity as one of the strengths to the card sorts. Clients are making the determination of how to categorize each of the cards in terms of their preferences, so, certainly, clients will agree that the final summaries reflect their values, skills, occupational interests, and interests related to leisure/retirement. Fields (2013) referenced the work of Slaney, Moran, and Wade (1994) and discussed how the card sort processes will elicit this direct feedback and outcome simply because of the nature of the card sort experience. Kinnier and Kernes (2001) acknowledged the high face validity of the card sorts but, also, recommended more psychometric work, specifically arguing that the list of values be more formally validated. Kinnier and Kernes (2001) stated that a test-retest study could provide additional support for the validity of the list of values. .

Slaney et al. (1994) referenced Goldman's (1982) view that card sorts are more examples of qualitative than quantitative assessment approaches. If so, users can view the Knowdell Card Sorts as a qualitative or, more likely, a mixed-methods assessment, which would lead to a different, and more appropriate, set of methods and technical considerations, such as credibility and replicability in an evaluation.

Use/Interpretation/Evaluation

With the CVCS, MSCS, OICS, and LRCS each having its own focus area (values, skills, occupational interest, and interests related to leisure/retirement), a practitioner has a diverse set of resources with the four separate Knowdell Card Sorts. Knowdell did not develop the card sorts for practitioners to use specifically as a whole unit; however, as noted earlier, their intertwining themes and shared common modalities allow practitioners to use multiple card sorts together to develop detailed client profiles that ultimately can assist clients in reaching career goals and outcomes.

Although Knowdell (2006) described the card sorts as being used with "equal effectiveness" (p. 21) with both individuals and groups, the worksheets for all four card sorts and three of the planning manuals (with the exception of the LRCS) emphasize the individual. However, with minimal editing, practitioners can utilize these materials for group activities. One caution for practitioners is to be cognizant of the dynamics of the group in relation to time.

Practitioners can also use all four card sorts interchangeably and multiple times with clients, depending on client career needs and life stages. This includes the LRCS; the concept of identifying pleasurable leisure activities for a healthy work-life balance is beneficial for everyone and in all stages of work and life. However, having the word *retirement* in the title might prompt both practitioners and clients to associate using this card sort for those at the retirement stage; therefore, a recommendation would be to look into reformatting the title.

Knowdell (2006) identified six strengths shared among the four career assessments: the card sorts are (1) nonthreatening; (2) flexible; (3) energizing; (4)

almost effortless; (5) a catalyst; and (6) high in face validity. Fields' (2013) review cited the game like qualities that makes these assessments familiar, user-friendly, and, in a way, nostalgic and even comforting to clients. Because of their gamelike structure, clients can complete these assessments in flexible environments (e.g., strewn across a table or put together on the floor. This game like quality makes them appealing not just to adults, but also to younger clients, such as high school students, or even younger students. Overall, the ease, informal structure, and engaging qualities of the Knowdell Card Sorts make them very appealing to a wide-range of clients. However, the card sorts, including the worksheets and activities, reference almost entirely adult working clients. Fields (2013) cited the benefits of using these card sorts with clients who have been victims of the economic collapse in the last decades and clients with limited work experience. However, Fields (2013) also wrote how the age level and limited work experience of clients could hinder their understanding of some of the terms used and that clients would need additional assistance from practitioners to clarify language and/or meaning. However, like the group activities described above, a practitioner, including school career counselors and other practitioners who work with younger clients or even with students, can edit the card sort and activities successfully to align them better with the age appropriateness, level of experience, and knowledge of their clients' world of work. In fact, Slaney et al.'s (1994) review noted that, with modification, career specialists could use the card sorts in university and college settings to assist students deciding on college majors. Knowdell (2006) discussed the 'right-brained' nature of these assessments "that reenergizes the client who may be overloaded with cognitive, left-brained content" (p. 21). These assessments are hands-on in that the client is manipulating the deck of cards physically and writing the information on the worksheets provided, all while engaging in discussion with the practitioner. Even though clients are making lists, something that is usually considered tedious and boring, the organizing and ranking of information in these card sorts is engaging and has an effortless quality. Overall, Knowdell's assessments strike a good balance between the more artistic career activities that might not be appropriate for every client and the more formal, structured assessments.

Clients utilize career practitioners for many reasons, and sometimes those reasons (e.g., recently terminated, long-term unemployed, seeking career assistance because of a separation or divorce) align with very personal issues. In addition, clients who have never been part of a client-practitioner relationship can be uncomfortable and cautious with the process. Knowdell (2006) described how focusing on the concept printed on the cards can act as a non-threatening catalyst for clients to share private information, concerns, and issues.

Research and Evaluation/Assessment Use

Overall, the CVCS, MSCS, OICS, and LRCS are useful career assessments to assist clients in identifying their values, skills, interests, occupations, and to determine their level of motivation and interest for employment or retirement purposes. The supplemental activities and worksheets can help jumpstart the third process, which is to move clients from the identification stage to making actual changes and producing desired outcomes in their career development processes. These activities range from artistic and creative forms to very focused, list driven exercises, so chances are most clients will find an activity conducive to their learning style. For example, one activity from the MSCS manual (2017a) is the *Skill Wheel*, where clients list their two strongest motivated skills and, then, brainstorm ways they can implement them in the world of work (e.g., projects, work settings). The CVCS workbook (2006) includes a Career Values Diary that clients can use to track their highest values parallel to their present work activities for up to a month. Instructions have clients write a narrative account of this progression so they can become more conscious of how their values align with their present work. This can lead to either reinforcing their current profession or making career changes. The OICS manual (2017b) contains an occupation interest worksheet that lists a series of questions clients answer to rate their knowledge level of occupations and expertise. One prompt has clients write the occupation that interests them the most, and, then, write possible variations of that occupation in terms of work settings, clientele, and organizations. In the LRCS manual (2017c), clients have a range of activities from which to choose, including the Retirement Research activity, where they identify five people who have retired and interview those five using a series of questions from the worksheet. Such questions include, "What do you like best and least about being retired?" "What has been the biggest surprise?" and "What sources of meaning have you discovered once retired?"

Outside of the supplemental activities and worksheets provided by all four card sorts, clients and counselors can use other activities and methods to evaluate client change and progression. For example, career practitioners have used the CVCS and MSCS for assisting clients to either update or create a resume and for interview preparation. Practitioners who work with college students have used the CVCS, MSCS, and OICS to help student decide on, or change, a college major and have used these card sorts with graduate students to help them narrow their scope of practice within a specific industry.

Although Knowdell (2006; 2011a; 2011b; 2015a; 2015b; 2017a; 2017b; 2017c) and other evaluators (Fields, 2013; Kinnier & Kernes, 2001) have cited the ease and user-friendliness of the Knowdell Card Sorts, the simplicity of these assessments should not be construed as promoting clients to complete them, including the activities, without the assistance of a trained and skilled practitioner. As noted earlier, Knowdell (2006) articulated how the card sorts can be catalysts for clients to express deep reflection and thoughts. Although all next-step examples mentioned in this section allow clients to move toward more measured outcomes and career development goals, these examples demonstrate, clearly, the need for clients to use the card sorts in the context of a client-practitioner relationship.

References

Career Trainer. (2018). *Knowdell assessment supplies.* Retrieved from http://www.career-trainer.com/trainingsys/knowdell-assessment-supplies-ff80818123928a090124178 5cf9d5150-c.html#

Fields, J. R. (2013). Knowdell card sorts: Career values card sort, motivated skills card sort, and occupational interests card sort. In C. Wood & D. G. Hayes (Eds.), *A counselor's guide to career assessment instruments* (6th ed., 482-485). Broken Arrow, OK: National Career Development Association.

Kinnier, R. T., & Kernes, J. L., (2001). Career values card sort kit (CVCS). In J. T. Kapes & E. A. Whitfield (Eds.), *A counselor's guide to career assessment instruments* (4th ed., pp. 218-221). Columbus, OH: National Career Development Association.

Knowdell, R. (2005a). *Career values: Card sort card deck.* San Jose, CA: Career Research & Testing.

Knowdell, R. (2005b). *Motivated skills: Card sort card deck.* San Jose, CA: Career Research & Testing.

Knowdell, R. (2006). *Exploring your career values workbook.* San Jose, CA: Career Research & Testing.

Knowdell, R. (2009). *Leisure/Retirement: Card sort card deck.* San Jose, CA: Career Research & Testing.

Knowdell, R. (2010). *Occupational interests: Card sort card deck.* San Jose, CA: Career Research & Testing.

Knowdell, R. (2011a). *Knowdell career values worksheet.* San Jose, CA: Career Research & Testing.

Knowdell, R. (2011b). *Knowdell motivated skills worksheet.* San Jose, CA: Career Research & Testing.

Knowdell, R. (2015a). *Knowdell occupational interests worksheet.* San Jose, CA: Career Research & Testing.

Knowdell, R. (2015b). *Knowdell leisure/retirement activities worksheet: Card sort card deck.* San Jose, CA: Career Research & Testing.

Knowdell, R. (2017a). *Motivated skills: Card sort career planning manual.* San Jose, CA: Career Research & Testing.

Knowdell, R. (2017b). *Occupational interests card sort planning manual.* San Jose, CA: Career Research & Testing.

Knowdell, R. (2017c). *Leisure & Retirement: Card sort planning manual.* San Jose, CA: Career Research & Testing.

Slaney, R. B., Moran, W. J., & Wade, J. C. (1994). Vocational card sorts. In J. T. Kapes, M. M. Mastie, & E. A. Whitfield (Eds.), *A counselor's guide to career instruments* (3rd ed., pp. 347-360). Alexandria, VA: National Career Development Association.

Bendill – Icelandic Interest Inventory

Reviewed by

Sif Einarsdóttir
University of Iceland

James Rounds
University of Illinois

Bendill, an indigenous interest inventory, was developed in Iceland to reflect the local labor market and for use with young people making career choices and adults facing career transitions. We constructed four interest inventories: *Bendill I* for 10th graders, age 15 - 16 (completing compulsory education), *Bendill II* for upper secondary students (age 16 - 20+), *Bendill III* for higher education students, and, finally, *Bendill IV* for adults in the labor market. We designed the Icelandic interest inventories to capture Holland's (1959; 1997) RIASEC interest types and up to 35 ecologically valid basic interests (I-BIS; Einarsdóttir, Eyjólfsdóttir & Rounds, 2013). Finally, we designed the Icelandic interest assessment system with the goal of providing low cost, accessible and effective on-line interest inventories for career counselling and research.

The Structure of the Instruments

Bendill I through IV include six RIASEC scales to measure broad interests. Bendill II through IV contain also 27 - 35 narrow-band basic interest scales that reflect the local labor market (BIS; Day & Rounds, 1997; Einarsdóttir et al, 2013). Table 1 gives an overview of the number of scales and items in each of the four Icelandic interest inventories. Three types of items were used: *work activities* (e.g. cut fish in a machine, design a computer program, assist disabled children in school) based on job descriptions; *school subjects* offered in the upper secondary education system (e.g. history, use of tools, bookkeeping); and *occupational titles* (e.g. nurse, bus driver, actor) selected from the Icelandic occupational classification (Statistics, Iceland 1994; 2009). The clients respond to items on a 5-point Likert-type scale (1 = dislike very much, 3 = neutral, 5 = like very much).

Table 1. *Scales, Number of Items and Types in the Four Icelandic Interest Inventories*

		Scale type and # of items each scale	
Inventory	Item type	RIASEC	I-BIS
Bendill I	School subjects, activities	15 - 20	not included
Bendill II	Work activities, occupational titles	15 - 23	28 scales, 4 - 13
Bendill III	Work activities, occupational titles	15 - 23	27 scales, 5 - 13
Bendill IV	Work activities, occupational titles	15 - 23	35 scales, 5 - 13

Administration

Bendill I through IV are available for online assessment through computers and smart phones. Practitioners can use these with individuals, but they are designed, especially, to facilitate group counselling. Administration of Bendill I takes only 10-12 minutes and 15-25 minutes for Bendill II –IV. The manual was published when the website and the Bendill I and II were first launched (Einarsdóttir & Rounds, 2007), and we added an updated version with the introduction of the Bendill III in 2013. Psychometric information and user friendly explanation of vocational interests are available on the website (www.bendill.is).

Scoring is computerized, and results appear graphically after all items have been completed (see Figure 1). The circumplex structure with the six RIASEC scales at the center and the Icelandic basic interest scales (I-BIS) in the outer circle is called the *Icelandic interest model* (for Bendill II – IV). T-scores (mean of 50 and standard deviation [sd] of 10) are used to present individual scores on all scales, along with color coding for ease of interpretation for test takers (see more below). Career and guidance counsellors (who need a master's degree for licensing) need to attend a half day qualification course and have access to the manual for permission to use the Icelandic interest inventories in practice. The Bendill I costs 1,400 iskr ($11 U.S.) per administration, and the Bendill II through III costs 3,700 iskr ($30 U.S.). Qualified professionals can contact bendill@bendill.is for access to the inventory.

Technical Considerations

The development of Bendill is grounded firmly in current conceptions of vocational interests and theoretical approaches to test construction (Einarsdóttir &

Figure 1. Icelandic interest model, Bendill IV graphic representation of results

Rounds, 2007; 2013, Einarsdóttir, Rounds, & Su, 2010; Einarsdóttir et al., 2013). We created both general interest scales, to capture known structural models, and homogenous narrow-band basic interest scales. We used occupational classifications (Statistics Iceland, 1994) to select occupational titles and work activities with the aim of representing approximately 80-85% of the jobs in the labor market. This sampling resulted in 125 occupations (e.g., seaman/fisherman, preschool director) and 133 work activities (e.g., shell and clean shrimps, show and sell houses to buyers) for a total of 258 items selected from 350 occupational groups. In addition, we selected items to represent the six RIASEC types as defined by Holland (1997). Finally, we included school subjects for the youngest age group facing educational transitions at the age of 15-16. Therefore, we sampled 136 school subjects based on courses offered in all the upper secondary schools in Iceland. The aim was to select both common subjects offered (e.g., Icelandic, math, history) and subjects that reflect the full range of vocational education offered in the comprehensive upper secondary school system (e.g., welding, carpentry, cutting hair and coloring).

The 258 work activities and occupational titles were administered to a developmental sample of 1,043 upper secondary education students across Iceland. Participating schools represented all educational opportunities (academic and vocational) offered at this level in the school system. In addition, we collected data from a sample of 864 10th grade students based on a random sample of 26 compulsory education schools. The 10th graders responded to 133 work activities and 136 school subjects.

Scale Construction

First, we constructed RIASEC scales based on series of analysis of the responses of 597 upper secondary students from the developmental sample. Only students who had reached the age of 18 years were included to rule out maturation issues. The majority of the job-related items were based on occupational descriptions that had been RIASEC-coded by three career counselors (Einarsdóttir, 2005a).

General RIASEC scales. We constructed the scales in a five-step procedure. First, we assigned items to one of the six scales based on the respective RIASEC expert codes. Second, we applied multidimensional scaling to the 258 items. The location of each item in the two-dimensional spaces were conjointly used with their Holland code to determine whether we should retain an item. Third, we calculated the item scale correlations and inspected the full matrix to check whether the correlations conformed to expectations of the structural model. We retained items with the highest correlation to its own scale and lowest to the opposite scale, as specified by the relations of RIASEC types in the model. Finally, we reviewed the items making up each of the six scales for conceptual breadth against the definitions and descriptions provided by Holland (1997) for the respective interest type.

The compulsory education sample responded to work activities and school subjects. The same work activities that had been selected for the RIASEC scales in the upper secondary school sample were assigned to their respective scale and then we added school subjects and reduced the scales based on the steps and criteria described above. Finally, we applied a randomization test (Rounds, Tracey, & Hubert, 1992) to the inter-correlations of the final version of the scales to test Holland's circular RIASEC model. The Correspondence (CI) indices were .61, .63, and .76 for the 15-16 years old (10th grade), 16-17 years, and 18 years and older samples, respectively. The results indicated that the fit of the RIASEC scales to Holland´s model increased with age.

Narrow band basic interest scales. We constructed the 28 basic interest scales, for use in career counselling with young people heading into the labor market, vocational training, or academic education using 1,368 upper secondary students. We added 30 new items to the relevant basic interest scales. This resulted in 28 basic interest scales, including indigenous-Icelandic scales (e.g., fishing, public administration, humanities; see Einarsdóttir et al. 2013).

We published Bendill I for 10th graders and Bendill II for upper secondary school students in 2007. Both were well received among career counsellors and young people facing career transitions in Iceland. The aim was to create a comprehensive system of interest assessment for all age groups, especially adults in career transition specifically targeted by policy makers (Ministry of Education and Culture, 2010). We designed two additional interest inventories, one for higher education students (Bendill III) and another for working adults (Bendill IV). Bendill III, designed for university students, contains 27 basic interest scales, and Bendill IV, constructed for adults in the labor market, contains all 35 basic interest scales. Bendill II through IV use the same items in the RIASEC scales. The Bendill score profile is presented graphically in a concentric circle (Tracey & Rounds, 1995) with the RIASEC scales in the middle and the basic scales in the outer circle (see Figure 1). We determined the placement of the BIS, in relation to the RIASEC types, based on their intercorrelation and by applying Circular Unidimensional Scaling (CUS; Hubert, Armstrong, & Rounds, 2003).

Norms

The norms used to calculate T-scores are based on four standardization samples selected from the Icelandic population (see Table 2 for overview). We administered the Bendill I to all the students in the graduating class in 21 schools. For Bendill-II, 22 upper secondary schools participated. The norms were based on weighted means according to population statistics. Five out of seven universities in Iceland sent e-mails to their students asking them to participate in the data collection for the standardization and finalization of Bendill III. The sample did reflect the distribution of the higher education student population over eight major fields of study provided by Iceland statistics. Finally, for the standardization of Bendill-IV, we selected a random sample of 2,000 adults from the national registry, which yielded 820 adults belonging to the defined population of adults in the labor market (employment seekers, parental leave, and people on disability included) used for standardization (see Einarsdóttir & Rounds, 2013 and www.bendill.is for more detail).

Table 2. *Standardization Samples Used in Norming the Icelandic Interest Inventories*

Inventory	Users	Age	N
Bendill I	10th. graders	15 - 16	485
Bendill II	Upper secondary students	16 - 20+	1368
Bendill III	Higher education students	20 - 30+	2218
Bendill IV	Working adults	18 - 60	820

Reliability

To estimate reliability, we calculated Cronbach Alpha based on the standardization sample (see Table 3). Cronbach alpha is mainly in the .90 range for the RIASEC scales but is lower for the shorter BIS scales.

Table 3. *Reliability and Validity Indices for Scales*

	Alpha		CI index
Inventory	RIASEC	BIS	RIASEC
Bendill I	.91 - .93	-	.69
Bendill II	.91 - .95	.82 - .93	.58
Bendill III	.89 - .94	.80 - .94	.76
Bendill IV	.92 - .96	.82 - .93	.65

Eight-month test-retest reliability in a sample of 22 upper secondary students ranged from .75-.95 for all six RIASEC and 28 BIS scales in Bendill-II. A recent study on the standardization sample shows that the long term rank order stability of the RIASEC scales in Bendill - I increases with age; .49 for ages 16-18, .66 for ages 18-22, and .74 for ages 22-24 (Hoff, Song, Einarsdóttir, Briley & Rounds, 2019). The results are comparable to U. S. studies (Hoff, Briley, Wee, & Rounds 2018; Low, Yoon, Roberts, & Rounds, 2005).

Validity

The goal of our Bendill developmental procedures was to construct an eco-logically valid interest inventory for use among Icelanders. The creation of an indigenous and extensive item pool that reflects the Icelandic labor market and the expert assignment of RIASEC codes to all items played a key role in ensuring content validity and conceptual breadth of scales. We paid close attention to con-textual issues, especially in constructing the indigenous basic interest scales that reflect the Icelandic labor market. The final version of the RIASEC scales in the four standardization samples conform largely to Hollands structural hypothesis, thus, supporting its construct validity as a measure of the six interest types (see Table 3).

To test the concurrent validity of the scales, we used multivariate discrim-inant function analysis to predict 17 major fields in the sample of 2,218 higher education students. The RIASEC scales assigned 23.4% of participants correctly to majors, compared to 42.4% for the basic interest and 5.9% chance hit rate for the 17 majors (Ágústsdóttir, 2011). This supports the concurrent validity of both types of scales and the incremental validity of basic interest scales above RIASEC scales. The results largely mirror previous studies (Ralston, Borgen, Rottinghaus, & Donnay, 2004).

Use/Interpretation/Evaluation

We constructed Bendill (which means *cursor* in English) to use in counselling with individuals who face career transitions in the context of Icelandic education-al system and world of work. We designed the four inventories for specific age groups that go through normative transitions and have to make choices based on educational and work-related opportunities. We applied Holland's theory and the circumplex model because they enhance exploration and are flexible enough to provide interests at both general and specific levels to meet diverse decision-mak-ing needs. For example, general interest assessment is useful for broad explora-tion of the labor market when choosing an academic versus a vocational degree in upper secondary school. The more specific BIS scale might be useful in selecting a specific major at universities. Users investigating the extensive continuing edu-cation options, available when making voluntary or unexpected transitions after years in the labor market, might benefit from exploration of both breadth and depth of interests.

As the name implies, users control the cursor in the modern-day electronic world. Likewise, self-determination is a core ideology guiding the use of Bendill in practice. We designed the scales to help clients be more purposeful and in-strumental in their career exploration, and recognize they control the cursor in responding and surfing for information. We developed an information system, and we coded and organized all educational opportunities in upper secondary and higher education according to the RIASEC model so clients can base their search on their interest codes. This is the case for almost 300 available occupational descriptions (www.bendill.is), which is available, also, through a portal for adult learners (www.naestaskref.is). The ease of access, the short time to yield results, and the graphic representation makes Bendill easy to use with groups and in career education courses.

Presentation and Interpretation

The results appear graphically as can be seen in Figure 1 (for Bendill IV). The general scales present as a pie, in the middle, with six sides each representing a RIASEC interest type. In the outer circle, cones represent the specific basic interest scales. The T-scores, based on the standardization sample, appear and are colored green if the person scores one sd above the mean (60 or higher) and yellow if between sd of -1 to 1 (40-59), but gray if 1 sd below the mean (below 40). We used color codes to ease understanding for clients, but the T-scores are also informative when explained by the counsellor to the client. We recommend the six-step procedure of administration and interpretation as described in the handbooks.

The graphical representations and color-coding make it easier for counsellors to explain the theoretical foundation and meaning of the results. The main advantages of the Bendill system are cultural relevance, low cost, accessibility, and immediate inventory results. Large gender differences appear on the RIASEC scales, which reflects the largely gendered labor market common in Nordic countries (Einarsdóttir, 2005b). Gender difference awareness is important in the use of interest inventories under the gender equality law in Iceland (nr.10/2008). We discussed methods to make test takers aware of gender stereotyping and its influence on career choices in the handbooks.

The generalizability of the instrument to other cultures is unknown. The items are either one word occupational titles (actor) or school subjects (math) and activities in short sentences (paint a house inside and outside). The reading level is aimed at 10th grade, and was pretested. Bendill is still only available online in Icelandic and, therefore, poses challenges for use with immigrants who work and live in Iceland but do not speak the language. An English version can be obtained from the authors. Bendill has been used as part of empirically evaluated career interventions in upper secondary schools (Björnsdóttir, 2018), for research on the structure of interest in Iceland (e.g. Einarsdóttir et al., 2010; 2013), and for evaluating developmental changes in recent longitudinal studies (Hoff, Song et al. 2019).

Summary

Bendill is a comprehensive interest assessment system accompanied by corresponding educational and occupational information portals. Bendill is culturally sensitive, accessible, and provides affordable and effective assessment that results in easily interpretable results. Bendill accommodates the needs of the Icelandic population from age 15 and upward, except for foreign language speakers. Researchers have provided reliability and validity evidence, although there are indications that Holland´s aging RIASEC model does not fully capture the Icelandic interest space of today´s labor market (Einarsdóttir et al., 2010; 2013). An indigenous structural model, based on the culturally sensitive basic interest scales, needs to be tested in future developments of Bendill.

References

Ágústsdóttir, I. M (2011). Áhugakönnunin Bendill II. Hugsmíða og samtímaréttmæti meðal háskólanema hérlendis [Construct and concurrent validity of Bendill II in a sample of university students]. Unpublished MA thesis. University of Iceland.

Björnsdóttir, M. D. (2018). *Evaluation of career interventions: Short and long term outcomes for students finishing upper secondary school in Iceland.* Unpublished PhD thesis. University of Iceland.

Day, S. X., & Rounds, J. (1997). "A little more than kin, and less than kind": Basic interests in vocational research and career counseling. *The Career Development Quarterly, 45,* 207-220. doi 10.1002/j.2161-0045.1997.tb00465.x

Einarsdóttir, S. (2005a). „Læknir lögfræðingur eða prestur" Flokkun íslenskra starfslýsinga samkvæmt kenningu Hollands um starfsáhuga [RIASEC expert ratings of Icelandic occupational descriptions]. *Netla, 3. júní.*

Einarsdóttir, S. (2005b). Kynjamunur í starfsáhuga-raunerulegur eða skekkja í áhugakönnunum? Áhrif kynbundinna staðalmynda á starfsáhuga karla og kvenna [Are gender-differences in interest inventories real or measurement bias? The influence of gender stereotypes on the interests of men and women]. In A. JónsdóttirS. H. Lárusdóttir, & Þ. Þórðardóttir (ed.). *Kynjamyndir í skólastarfi [Gender stereotyping in schools].* Reykjavík: Rannsóknastofnun Kennaraháskóla Íslands.

Einarsdóttir, S., Eyjólfsdóttir, K. Ó., &, Rounds, J. (2013). Development of Indigenous basic interest scales: Re-structuring the Icelandic interest space. *Journal of Vocational Behavior, 82,* 105-115. doi 10.1016/j.jvb.2013.01.001

Einarsdóttir, S., & Rounds, J. (2007). *Bendill: Þróun og notkun netvæddrar áhugakönnunar* [Bendill: Development and use of a web-based Icelandic Interest inventory]. Reykjavík: Iceland University Press.

Einarsdóttir, S., & Rounds, J. (2013). *Bendill: Þróun og notkun netvæddrar áhugakönnunar,* 2. útg [Bendill: Development and use of a web-based Icelandic Interest inventory, 2nd ed.]. Reykjavík: Icelandic Educational Evaluation Institute.

Einarsdóttir, S . Rounds, J., & Su, R. (2010). Holland in Iceland revisited: An emic approach to testing U.S. interest models. *Journal of Counseling Psychology, 57,* 361-367. doi:10.1037/a0019685

Hoff, K. A., Briley, D. A., Wee, C. J. M., & Rounds J. (2018). Normative changes in interests from adolescence to adulthood: A meta-analysis of longitudinal studies. *Psychological Bulletin, 144.* 426 – 451. doi:10.1037/bul0000140

Hoff, K. A., Song, Q. C., Einarsdóttir, S., Briley, D. A., & Rounds, J. (2019). Developmental structure of personality and interests: A 4-wave, 8-year longitudinal study. *Journal of Personality and Social Psychology.* Advance online publication. doi:10.1037/pspp0000228

Holland, J. L. (1959). A theory of vocational choice. *Journal of Counseling Psychology, 6,* 35–45. doi:10.1037/h0040767

Holland, J. L. (1997). *Making vocational choices: A theory of vocational personalities and work environments* (3rd ed.). Odessa, FL: Psychological Assessment Resources.

Armstrong, P. I., Hubert, L., & Rounds, J. (2003). Circular unidimensional scaling: A new look at group differences in interest structure. *Journal of Counseling Psychology, 50,* 297–308. https://doi.org/10.1037/0022-0167.50.3.297

Lög um jafna stöðu og jafnan rétt kvenna og karla nr. 10/2008 [Statue on gender equality]. Velferðarráðuneytið [Ministry of Welfare].

Low, K. S. D., Yoon, M., Roberts, B. W., & Rounds, J. (2005). The stability of interests from early adolescence to middle adulthood: A quantitative review of longitudinal studies. *Psychological Bulletin, 131,* 713-737. doi 10.1037/0033-2909.131.5.713

Ministry of Education and Culture. (2010). *Mótun stefnu um nám alla ævi: Þróun menntastefnu á Íslandi í evrópsku samhengi* [Life long educuation policy. Educational policy making in European context]. Reykjavík: Mennta- og menningarmálaráðuneytið.

Ralston, C. A., Borgen, F. H., Rottinghaus, P. J., & Donnay, D. A. C. (2004). Specificity in interest measurement: Basic interest scales and major field of study. *Journal of vocational behavior, 65,* 203-216 DOI: 10.1177/1069072706294516

Rounds, J., Tracey, T. J., & Hubert, L. (1992). Methods for evaluating vocational interest structure hypothesis. *Journal of Vocational Behavior, 40,* 239-259. doi: 10.1016/0001-8791(92)90073-9

Statistics, Iceland (1994). Ístarf95: Íslensk starfaflokkun [Icelandic occupational classification system]. Reykjavík, Iceland: Author.

Statistics, Iceland (2009). Skráðir nemendur í framhalds- og háskólum haustið 2008. [Registered students in upper secondary and tertiary education, fall 2008]. Retrieved September 25th, 2010 from https://hagstofa.is/?PageID=421&itemid=81190473-7ae4-4948-932f-73b99fc46bb0

Tracey, T. J. G., & Rounds, J. (1995). The arbitrary nature of Holland's RIASEC types: A concentric-circles structure. *Journal of Counseling Psychology, 42,* 431–439. doi 10.1037/0022-0167.42.4.431

Career Decision-making Difficulties Questionnaire

Reviewed by

Itamar Gati

Viktoria Kulcsar

YISSUM, Hebrew University of Jerusalem

The Purpose

The goal of the Career Decision-making Difficulties Questionnaire (CDDQ) is to locate causes of those difficulties that might (a) delay beginning the career decision-making process, (b) halt the process before a decision is made, or (c) lead to a less than optimal decision. Career indecision can result from a single difficulty or a combination of them. The CDDQ is based on a taxonomy of difficulties derived from decision-making theory (Gati, Krausz, & Osipow, 1996).

The CDDQ is for adolescents (from age 16; ten-grade reading level), young adults (18-30), and adults. The CDDQ is targeted, primarily, at young adults who are making their first career decisions (e.g., what college to attend, what professional training to pursue, what major to choose, what job to select after graduation), but practitioners can use the CDDQ for adults who are facing a voluntary or imposed career transition.

The total score of the CDDQ provides information about the individual's overall level of career indecision. The scores for the three major clusters provide information about the individual's difficulties involving *Lack of readiness, Lack of information,* and *Inconsistent information.* The ten specific scales refer to the following constructs: for Lack of readiness – *lack of motivation, general indecisiveness,* and *dysfunctional beliefs;* for Lack of information – *lack of knowledge about the process, lack of information about the self, about career alternatives,* and *about sources of help and information;* and for Inconsistent information – *unreliable information, internal conflicts,* and *external conflicts.*

Practitioners can use the questionnaire to (a) assess individuals' career indecision in counseling, (b) diagnose an individual's specific pattern of difficulties, (c) map the pattern of difficulties prior to a group intervention so as to tailor it to the participants' needs, and (d) assess the effectiveness of a career intervention by administering it before and after the intervention.

Structure of the Instrument

The CDDQ provides for a multidimensional, multilevel assessment of career decision-making difficulties. The original assessment (Gati et al., 1996) comprised 44 items; the revised shortened version comprises 34 items (Gati & Saka, 2001). Each item represents one of the 10 difficulty categories and the three major clusters (*Lack of Readiness, Lack of Information,* and *Inconsistent Information*). The revised and shortened version of the CDDQ has 34 items (Gati & Saka, 2001), with a 9-point response scale (1=does not describe me to 9=describes me well), including two validity items.

The individual's difficulties are captured by a 10-scale score profile corresponding to the 10 difficulty categories, each defined as the mean of the responses to the items included in the category. The three clusters and the 10 scales are:

Lack of Readiness. This cluster consists of three difficulty categories.

Lack of motivation. A high score on this scale reflects a lack of willingness to make a decision at this point (e.g., "Work is not the most important thing in my life and therefore the issue of choosing a career doesn't worry me much.").

General indecisiveness. A high score on this scale reflects a general difficulty in making decisions (e.g., "It is usually difficult for me to make decisions.").

Dysfunctional beliefs. A high score on this scale reflects a maladaptive perception of the career decision-making process, unreasonable expectations of it, and dysfunctional thoughts about it (e.g., "I believe there is only one career that is good for me.").

Lack of Information. This cluster consists of four difficulty categories.

Lack of knowledge about the decision-making process. A high score on this scale reflects a lack of knowledge about how to make a decision wisely, especially a lack of knowledge of the specific steps involved in career decision-making (e.g., "I find it difficult to make a career decision because I don't know what steps to take.").

Lack of information about the self. A high score on this scale reflects a situation where a person feels he or she does not have enough information about his- or herself (e.g., about career preferences, vocational interests, work values, or abilities and skills). An example is "I find it difficult to make a career decision because I still don't know which occupations I am interested in".

Lack of information about career alternatives (e.g., occupations, majors). A high score on this scale reflects a lack of information about existing career options, such as what alternatives there are and/or what each alternative is like (e.g., "I find it difficult to make a career decision because I don't know what careers will look like in the future.").

Lack of Information about ways of obtaining information. A high score on this scale reflects a lack of information about ways of obtaining additional information or help that might facilitate decision making (e.g., "I find it difficult to make a career decision because I don't know how to obtain additional information about myself [for example, my abilities or my personality traits]").

Inconsistent Information. This cluster consists of three specific difficulty categories.

Unreliable Information. A high score on this scale indicates that an individual feels that he or she has contradictory information about his- or herself or about the considered occupations (e.g., "I find it difficult to make a career decision because I have contradictory data about the existence or the properties of a particular occupation or training program.").

Internal Conflicts. A high score on this scale reflects a state of internal confusion which might stem from difficulty in compromising on the many factors the individual views as important, when some of these factors are incompatible with one another (e.g., "I find it difficult to make a career decision because I don't like any of the occupation or training programs available to me.").

External Conflicts. A high score on this scale might indicate a gap between an individual's preferences and the preferences voiced by significant others or a contradiction between the opinions of two significant others (e.g., I find it difficult to make a career decision because there are contradictions between the recommendations made by different people who are important to me about the career that is good for me or what career characteristics should guide my decisions.").

Administration

The CDDQ is available in two versions: Paper and Pencil (with hand scoring by the career counselor) and on the Internet www.cddq.org (with automatic scoring and immediate interpretive feedback); both are free. Research has supported the equivalence of the two versions (Gati, & Saka, 2001; see also Kleiman & Gati, 2004). The typical time for completing the CDDQ is 5-8 minutes. Practitioners can administer the CDDQ individually or in groups.

The instrument was developed cross-culturally (with both Israeli and American samples). It has been translated and adapted world-wide into 46 languages and used in 58 countries. Currently, the CDDQ is available in Albanian, Arabic, Bulgarian, Chinese, Croatian, Dutch, English, Flemish, French, German, Greek, Hebrew, Hungarian, Italian, Korean, Nepali, Norwegian, Polish, Persian,

Portuguese, Romanian, Spanish, Taiwanese, Turkish, Ugandan, and Vietnamese.

Each scale score is defined as the mean of the items that comprise the scale; the three major cluster scores are defined as the mean of the scales that comprise the cluster. The simple rule of thumb is that a scale (or a cluster) score with a mean of 6.34 and above indicates a "salient" difficulty, below 3.33 is "negligible", and in-between is "moderate." A more sophisticated interpretation procedure, based on the relative salience of the individual's difficulties, was developed and validated using career-counseling experts' judgments (see Amir, Gati, & Kleiman, 2008). This interpretative algorithm is incorporated into the Internet version of the CDDQ in addition to the automatic scoring. The interpretive report highlights the salient and moderate foci of the clients' career-decision making difficulties, with recommendations on how to deal with them.

As mentioned earlier, the CDDQ is available free for individuals, counselors, and researchers. The online version, which includes an automatic immediate scoring and interpretation, is available at www.cddq.org . Requests for the paper-and-pencil version should be addressed to itamar.gati@huji.ac.il.

Technical Considerations

Reliability

The Cronbach α internal-consistency reliability estimate of the total scale is very high (Cα=.95; Gati et al., 1996), with similar results found in subsequent studies (Osipow & Gati, 1998; Gati, Osipow, Krausz, & Saka, 2000; Gati & Saka, 2001; Mau, 2001). The lower bound estimate of the test-retest reliability of the CDDQ is .80 (Gati et al., 1996).

The low reliability of the dysfunctional beliefs scale is inherent in the nature of such beliefs; the recently developed *Dysfunctional Beliefs about Career Decision Making* questionnaire (Hechtlinger, Levin, & Gati, in press) helps reveal the individual's particular dysfunctional beliefs.

Validity

Content validity. The items of the CDDQ represent causes of difficulty in making career decision reported by career counselors, as well as by individuals facing difficulty in making career decisions.

Construct validity. The empirical structure of the ten scales was very similar or identical to the one proposed in the theoretical model (Gati et al., 1996; Gati & Saka, 2001; Kleiman & Gati, 2004). High positive correlations ($r=.77$) were found with the sum of the 16 indecision items of the Career Decision Scale (CDS, Osipow, Carney, & Barak, 1976) and a moderate negative correlation ($r = -.50$; Osipow & Gati, 1998) with the Career Decision Self-Efficacy scale (CDSE, Taylor

& Betz, 1983), which supports the construct validity of the CDDQ. The validity of the conclusions from the CDDQ were validated using expert career counselors' judgments as the criteria (Gati et al., 2000).

Concurrent/predictive validity. Concurrent validity was tested with the *Range of Considered Alternatives* question (Perez & Gati, 2017), which assesses the individual's career decision status. Individuals with more advanced career decision status had fewer career decision-making difficulties (Perez & Gati, 2017; Vertsberger & Gati, 2015). Concurrent validity was also tested in a study with high-school students, and the results showed that those who labeled themselves "undecided" had greater difficulties than those who labeled themselves "decided" (Gati & Saka, 2001).

Predictive validity was tested in a study with young adult college students. Those who reported more difficulties at the beginning of the school year also reported a less advanced career decision status towards the end of the year (Anghel & Gati, 2019; Lipshits-Braziler, Gati, & Tatar, 2015).

Convergent/divergent validity. The convergent validity results indicate that the CDDQ and the CDS measure similar constructs (Lancaster, Rudolph, Perkins, & Patten, 1999). The discriminant validity study (Lancaster et al., 1999) results revealed that most of the CDDQ subscales have a negative correlation with social desirability as measured by the Marlowe-Crowne Social Desirability Scale (M-C SDS; Crowne & Marlowe, 1960) and a positive correlation with anxiety as measured by the Beck Anxiety Inventory (BAI; Beck, Epstein, Brown, & Steer, 1988).

There are no norms for interpreting the CDDQ, as the interpretation of the scores is within each individual (i.e., comparing the individual's scale scores and locating his or her salient, moderate, and negligible difficulties).

Use/Interpretation/Evaluation

Career professionals can use the instrument for initial screening of clients according to the three major difficulty clusters or the 10 specific difficulty categories and by directing clients to the most relevant intervention options (e.g., face-to-face counseling, relevant Internet sites). Practitioners can use the CDDQ to assess the client's difficulties, which will provide the practitioner with initial relevant data regarding the foci of the client's difficulties (see an example of printed feedback in www.cddq.org, section for experts).

Also, practitioners can use the CDDQ as a needs assessment for collecting information about the types of difficulties that occur frequently in a particular group (e.g., high school students, men vs. women, particular minority groups [Gati & Saka, 2001]).

In addition, the CDDQ serves as a tool for evaluating not only the overall effectiveness of career interventions, but also the differential effectiveness of an intervention to reduce difficulties (e.g., comparing before and after difficulties [Gati, Saka, & Krausz, 2001; Fouad, Cotter, & Kantamneni, 2009]).

User Manual and Scoring Reports

The User Manual is aimed at providing information about the theoretical rationale and the assumptions underlying the CDDQ, its scoring and interpretation, its psychometric characteristics (reliability and validity), suggestions for possible uses of the questionnaire, and additional sources of relevant information. The manual describes the three major categories and subscales and the scoring of the instrument. One advantage of the online CDDQ is that it computes the scores and generates the interpretation and recommendations automatically.

Strengths and Weaknesses of the CDDQ

The CDDQ provides information not only about the individual's overall level of career indecision (total score), but also about its three clusters and ten difficulty categories. This makes the CDDQ one of the most comprehensive multidimensional assessments of career indecision. The number of items is sufficient for a multidimensional measure, but the CDDQ is short enough to be applied easily; completing it does not consume much time. Another advantage of the instrument is that it can be used in both printed and online formats, and the online version makes the score calculation and interpretation easier. However, for the counselor to interpret the results might require practice in using the instrument.

The CDDQ provides information about the foci and the causes of the client's career decision-making difficulties and highlights those that need the counselor's attention. This helps the counselor tailor the intervention to the client's particular needs (Gati, 2010; Rochat, in press). Practitioners can use the CDDQ for evaluating the effectiveness of counseling (i.e., in reducing difficulties) if used pre- and post-intervention.

Presentation and Interpretation

The online format of the CDDQ makes it a generally easily administrable tool and one in which the individual can complete the questionnaire quickly; the scores calculate automatically, and the interpretation and the recommendation are straightforward and provided immediately. Completing the printed form is simple, and practitioners can complete the scoring manually. The interpretation of the scores is quite straightforward, as it is within each individual (i.e., comparing the scale scores and locating the individual's salient, moderate, and negligible difficulties).

The CDDQ is a theoretically derived multidimensional measure of career indecision. The 10 difficulty categories and the three clusters allow a multilevel assessment. In contrast to unidimensional measures, which provide only an overall score of career indecision (e.g., the Career Decision Scale), the CDDQ provides information about the salient difficulties of the client. Therefore, the CDDQ is useful for pinpointing the client's salient difficulty areas that need the counselor's attention. Practitioners can use the CDDQ for evaluating the effectiveness of career interventions (individual counseling, group interventions and courses, and self-help career guidance sites). If a researcher or a counselor is interested in not just an overall assessment of career indecision, but more information about the specific causes of the client's career decision-making difficulties, then the CDDQ is a good choice.

The measurement invariance of the English version of the CDDQ has been tested and supported across seven countries, both male and female populations, and various age groups (Levin, Braunstein-Bercovitz, Lipshits-Braziler, Gati, & Rossier, 2019). Another ongoing study is testing the measurement invariance across different linguistic versions of the CDDQ in more than 20 countries (Levin et al., 2019).

Career Counseling Practice Considerations

Researchers can use the instrument to generally assess career indecision or the various categories of career decision-making difficulties. Counselors can use it for initial screening of a client, diagnosing difficulties, needs assessment (Gati & Saka, 2001), and evaluating interventions (e.g., Fouad et al., 2009; Gati, Saka, & Krausz, 2001; Milot-Lapointe, Savard, & Le Corff, 2018).

Summary

On the basis of Gati et al.'s (1996) taxonomy of career decision-making difficulties, the CDDQ provides multidimensional information about a client's career decision-making difficulties on three levels: (1) the ten difficulty categories, based on the mean responses to the items in each scale, (2) the three major difficulty clusters, based on the mean of the scales included in each cluster, and (3) globally, based on the mean of the ten difficulty scales. The CDDQ assesses the foci and causes of individuals' career decision-making difficulties.

The CDDQ is recommended for initial screening and diagnosing the client's career decision-making difficulties, which helps counselors tailor their intervention to the client's specific needs and allows counselors to have a better understanding as to why their client sought counseling (e.g., due to lack of readiness, lack of information, inability to use the information at hand, or a combination of several difficulties). This information can facilitate counseling by allowing counselors to focus on issues that prevent their clients from reaching an informed decision– those that brought them to seek professional help in the first place. Practitioners can use the CDDQ, also, as a needs assessment and for evaluating the effectiveness of an intervention. Finally, practitioners can use the CDDQ in research to measure career indecision, generally, or to assess the various difficulty categories of career decision-making. In sum, the ten scales and the three major difficulty clusters make the CDDQ a multidimensional assessment with good psychometric properties that can help deliberating individuals and facilitate career counseling.

References

Amir, T., Gati, I. & Kleiman, T. (2008). Understanding and interpreting career decision-making difficulties. *Journal of Career Assessment, 16*, 281-309. doi:10.1177/1069072708317367.

Anghel, E. & Gati, I. (2019). *The associations between career decision-making difficulties and negative emotional states: A longitudinal study.* Manuscript submitted for publication.

Beck, A. T., Epstein, N., Brown, G., & Steer, R. A. (1988). An inventory for measuring clinical anxiety: Psychometric properties. *Journal of Consulting and Clinical Psychology, 56*, 893-897.

Fouad, N., Cotter, E. W., & Kantamneni, N. (2009). The effectiveness of a career decision-making course. *Journal of Career Assessment, 17*, 338-347.

Gati, I. (2010, April). *Career decision making difficulties: Assessment and treatment.* Invited presentation for the VI Conference on Career Development: Assessment and intervention, Braga, Portugal. https://www.youtube.com/watch?v=Jn3MEtJFcEI&feature=related

Gati, I., & Saka, N. (2001). Internet-based versus paper-and-pencil assessment: Measuring career decision-making difficulties. *Journal of Career Assessment, 9*, 397-416. doi:10.1177/106907270100900406

Gati, I., Krausz, M., & Osipow, S. H. (1996). A taxonomy of difficulties in career decision making. *Journal of Counseling Psychology, 43*, 510-526. doi:10.1037/0022-0167.43.4.510

Gati, I., Osipow, S. H., Krausz, M., & Saka, N. (2000). Validity of the Career Decision-making Difficulties Questionnaire: Counselee versus career counselor perceptions. *Journal of Vocational Behavior, 56*, 99-113. doi:10.1006/jvbe.1999.1710

Gati, I., Saka, N., & Krausz, M. (2001). "Should I use a computer-assisted career guidance system?" It depends on where your career decision-making difficulties lie. *British Journal of Guidance and Counselling, 29,* 301-321. doi:10.1080/03069880124945

Hechtlinger, S., Levin, N., & Gati, I. (in press).dysfunctional career decision-making beliefs: A multidimensional model and measure. *Journal of Career Assessment.* 10.1177/1069072717748677

Kleiman, T., & Gati, I. (2004). Challenges of Internet-based assessment: Measuring career decision-making difficulties. *Measurement and Evaluation in Counseling and Development, 37,* 41-55. doi:10.1080/07481756.2004.11909749

Lancaster, B. P., Rudolph, C. E., Perkins, T. S., & Patten, T. G. (1999). The reliability and validity of the Career Decision Difficulties Questionnaire. *Journal of Career Assessment, 7,* 393-413.

Levin, N., Braunstein-Bercovitz, H., Lipshits-Braziler, Y., Gati, I., & Rossier, J. (2019). *The internal structure of the Career Decision-making Difficulties Questionnaire in seven countries.* Unpublished manuscript.

Levin, N. et al. (2019). *The measurement invariance of the Career Decision-making Difficulties Questionnaire across 25 countries.* Manuscript in preparation.

Lipshits-Braziler, Y., Gati, I., & Tatar, M. (2015). Strategies for coping with career indecision: Concurrent and predictive validity. *Journal of Vocational Behavior, 91,* 170-179. doi:10.1016/j.jvb.2015.10.004

Mau, W. C. (2001). Assessing career decision-making difficulties: A cross-cultural study. *Journal of Career Assessment, 9,* 353–364. doi: 10.1177/106907270100900403

Milot-Lapointe, F., Savard, R., & Le Corff, Y. (2018). Intervention components and working alliance as predictors of individual career counseling effect on career decision-making difficulties. *Journal of Vocational Behavior, 107,* 15-24.

Osipow, S. H., Carney, C. G., & Barak, A. (1976). A scale of educational-vocational undecidedness: A typological approach. *Journal of Vocational Behavior, 9,* 233-243.

Osipow, S. H., & Gati, I. (1998). Construct and concurrent validity of the career decision-making difficulties questionnaire. *Journal of Career Assessment, 6,* 345-363. doi:10.1177/106907279800600305

Perez, M., & Gati, I. (2017). Advancing in the career decision-making process: The role of coping strategies and career decision-making profiles. *International Journal for Educational and Vocational Guidance, 17,* 285–309. doi:10.1007/s10775-016-9334-x

Rochat, S. (in press).The career decision-making difficulties questionnaire: A case for item-level interpretation. *Career Development Quarterly.*

Taylor, K. M., & Betz, N. E. (1983). Applications of self-efficacy theory to the understanding and treatment of career indecision. *Journal of vocational behavior, 22,* 63-81.

Vertsberger, D., & Gati, I. (2015). The effectiveness of sources of support in career decision-making: A two-year follow-up. *Journal of Vocational Behavior, 89,* 151-161. doi:10.1016/j.jvb.2015.06.004

RESEARCH

THE CAREER DISTRESS SCALE

Reviewed by
Peter A. Creed
Michelle Hood
Griffith University, Australia

The *Career Distress Scale* (CDS; Creed, Hood, Praskova, & Makransky, 2016) is a short, unifactorial, 9-item measure that provides a rapid assessment of distress in the career domain. Creed et al. (2016) developed the CDS as a research tool, primarily, although practitioners could use the CDS as a screening devise for clients or as a measure of client change (Creed & Hood, 2015a). The scale assesses negative feelings in young adults that might result from adverse experiences in their career development process. Adverse career-related experiences are many, varied, and include an inability to decide upon a career path (i.e., decision-making problems), difficulty with progressing a career direction (i.e., being confronted with barriers to career progress), or being told by others that you do not have the requisite characteristics to be successful in a particular occupation (i.e., receiving negative feedback).

Career distress is considered specific to the career domain, although negative feelings in one domain (e.g., career) can spill over to other domains (e.g., relationships, work, study), and vice versa. Career distress might be reflected in feelings of frustration, doubt, envy, helplessness, sadness, anxiety, shame, and despair, and can range from mildly upsetting to very incapacitating (Larson, Toulouse, Ngumba, Fitzpatrick, & Heppner, 1994). Most important, career distress can negatively affect other career-related behaviors, such as career exploration, which is necessary for the development of vocational identity and making career and education decisions, which are important for progressing career goals (Skorikov, 2007). These are common reasons students present at campus and school counselling services (Benton, Robertson, Tseng, Newton, & Benton, 2003).

Career distress occurs when young people are unable to manage age-appropriate, career-related tasks (Erikson, 1968; Havighurst, 1972). From a goal-setting, self-regulatory perspective (e.g., Bandura, 1991; Carver & Scheier, 1990), individuals set goals or have them set by others (e.g., parent or work supervisor). These can be simple, short-term, and narrow (e.g., studying for an exam), or complex, long-term, and pervasive (e.g., aspiring to live a morally-informed life). Informed by the environment (e.g., failing an exam or being told that more effort is needed) and self-reflection, individuals appraise how well they are progressing toward their goals (e.g., are they on track?) and become uncomfortable or distressed when there is a negative discrepancy between performance and the set standard. These uncomfortable feelings drive self-regulatory behaviors, which aim to reduce the discrepancy and alleviate the negative feelings (e.g., by lowering the goal, increasing effort, or both). If goal progress is on track or ahead of what is required, positive emotions are likely to result, and self-regulatory responses will be different (e.g., raising the goal, reducing effort).

Few scales are available to assess career distress. Apart from the CDS, researchers and practitioners can consider two other career-specific scales: (a) the 20-item *Korean Career Stress Inventory* (KCSI; Choi et al., 2011), which has four, 4-item subscales measuring career ambiguity, lack of information, employment pressure, and external conflict (see Creed et al., 2016, for review), and (b) the 21-item *Subjective Career Distress and Obstacles Subscale* from the 35-item *Coping with Career Indecision Scale* (Larson et al., 1994), which assesses career-related distress (13 items) and obstacles (8 items; see Creed et al., 2016). In addition, many general distress measures, such as the *General Health Questionnaire* (GHQ; Goldberg & Williams, 1988; see McDowell, 2006, for review), are available. General measures of distress, however, are likely to miss specific career concerns and thus are likely to have weaker associations with other important career variables (Blair & Hunt, 1986).

Structure of the Instrument

Test-takers respond to the nine items in the CDS using a 6-point Likert-like response format (from *strongly disagree* to *strongly agree*). There are no reverse items to code and no subscales; practitioners simply sum the scores to derive a single, total distress score, where higher scores represent greater career distress. Sample items for the scale are "I often feel down or depressed about selecting a career" and "I feel stress or pressure to select a satisfying career." Refer to Creed et al. (2016) for a report of the full nine items.

Administration

Practitioners can administer the CDS as part of a longer questionnaire or as a stand-alone scale, either individually or in a group, and in either a paper-and-pencil format, online, or read aloud to participants. At only nine items, users can complete the CDS in just a few minutes. There is no manual or electronic reporting software; practitioners simply sum the scores to derive a total score representing distress. The CDS is available in the original English-language version and in Indonesian Bahasa (Sawitri, Creed, & Perdhana, 2018). There is no cost associated with using the scale, and permission is not required.

Instrument Development Processes and Procedures

The CDS developers drew from the 21-item *Subjective Career Distress and Obstacles Subscale* of the 42-item *Coping with Career Indecision Scale* (CCIS; Larson et al., 1994), which Larson et al. (1994) devised to assess the domains of perceived obstacles, distress, problem-solving, self-efficacy, lack of support, lack of information, pressure from others, and misconceptions in university students. Using exploratory factor analysis (EFA), Larson et al. reported factor loadings from .35 to .85 for the 13 career distress and eight career obstacle items. Several researchers have used the full 21-item subscale with U. S. undergraduates (Kim & Karan, 2004), U. S. gifted and talented junior high school students (Larson & Majors, 1998), and South Korean university students (Lee, 2005). However, little psychometric data have been provided on the measure (e.g., no independent EFAs or Confirmatory Factor Analyses, CFA), although Lee (2005) reported an internal reliability coefficient (alpha) of .88.

In addition to use of the full scale, researchers have used the 13 distress items alone (i.e., without the obstacle items) from the 21-item *Subjective Career Distress and Obstacles Subscale* (e.g., Creed & Blume, 2013; Creed & Gagliardi, 2015; Creed & Hood, 2015b; Creed & Hughes, 2012; Creed, Wamelink, & Hu, 2015; Praskova, Creed, & Hood, 2015). The use of the distress items without the obstacle items seemed justified by the need to provide a "purer" measure of distress. CFAs lent support to these distress items in forming one unidimensional measure (Creed & Blume, 2013; Creed & Hood, 2015; Praskova et al., 2015) that had high internal reliability (alpha range .89 to .94 with university students). In support of validity, the 13-item measure had expected associations with other career variables (e.g., positively related to career compromise, career goal-performance discrepancy, and negative career feedback from others; negatively related to career satisfaction, career strategies, and career confidence).

In 2016, Creed et al. used CFA and item response procedures with a sample of undergraduate students (mean age 20.5 years) to evaluate the 12 highest loading items from the *Subjective Career Distress and Obstacles Subscale* reported by Larson et al. (1994). These 12 items met a "practical significance" criterion of having factor loadings $\geq$ .50 (actual range .49 to .85). Creed et al. identified nine items (three misfitting items were deleted) that demonstrated "excellent psychometric properties" (p. 732). The 9-item scale was unifactorial, had good internal reliability (Person Separation Index = .86, alpha = .87), did not evidence bias (based on age, sex, employment status, academic achievement, and socio-economic status), and, supported validity in that the scale was related as expected to general measures of negative (*r* = .45) and positive affect (*r* = -.34; *PANAS Scale*; Watson, Clark, & Tellegan, 1988).

Reliability

When formulating the CDS, Creed et al. (2016) reported a sound alpha coefficient of .87 with undergraduate students but reported no test/retest coefficient. Alpha coefficients reported by other authors have been good (i.e., > .90; Gunawan, Creed & Glendon 2018; Creed, Hood, & Hu, 2017). Test/retest statistics have yet to be assessed.

Validity

Content validity of the items is based on information found in the career literature, discussions with career practitioners, evaluating and revising items, and piloting the items with tertiary students (Larson et al., 1994; Larson, Heppner, Ham, & Dugan, 1988). Creed et al. (2016) supported construct validity by demonstrating unidimensionality of the CDS, which Creed et al. (2017) confirmed. For concurrent validity, the *Career Distress Scale* has been shown to be related positively to negative affect (Creed et al., 2016), career goal-performance discrepancies (Creed et al., 2017), and career discrepancies between adolescent and parents (Sawitri et al., 2018), and related negatively to positive affect (Creed et al., 2016), optimism about future employability (Gunawan et al., 2018), employability confidence, proactivity, career goal importance (Creed et al., 2017), and perceptions of career congruence with parents (Sawitri et al., 2018). Predictive validity has not been assessed.

Norms

Normative data are not available for the CDS. Users of the scale can compare their obtained scores against several sets of research data, which typically provide descriptions of sample used, and data means and standard deviations (Creed et al., 2016; Creed et al., 2017; Gunawan et al., 2018; Sawitri et al., 2018).

Use/Interpretation/Evaluation

The CDS (with nine straightforward items and simple format) is easy to use (either in paper, online, or other format), easy to score (by summing item scores), and simple to interpret (as one total score to analyze).

General Utility

The CDS developers devised the inventory for use as a research tool. However, practitioners could use the scale as an aid to counselling, as a screening device for presenting clients, or as a measure of client change. Although the scale has good internal reliability and support for validity, based on its relationship with other constructs, there are no norms. Practitioners can refer to the data reported in research papers (i.e., sample descriptions, means, and standard deviations) and develop sets of local norms over time, if practical.

Presentation and Interpretation

Researchers who employ the CDS can use the total score (or mean item response, depending on preference) when testing their hypotheses. There is evidence that the scale is unifactorial; thus, the scale cannot be analyzed using subscales. Practitioners need to be cautious when reporting the results (e.g., to client or outside body), because there are no suitable normative data for the scale.

Overall Evaluation

Creed et al. (2016) published the 9-item, unifactorial CDS in 2016. The CDS is one of a small number of scales suitable for assessing career-related distress. Given that career concerns are widespread in adolescents and young adults, having tools that can measure this construct is important, and the CDS is such a tool.

Strengths of the CDS include its brevity, and its ease of use, scoring, and interpretation; there is initial evidence of sound psychometric properties. The evidence for content validity of the items is dated (Larson et al., 1994) and additional research needs to determine how well the scale assesses the underlying domains of career distress. Internal reliability is good, but there are no published reports regarding test-retest reliability. Validity support for the scale is based on statistical analyses of research data (e.g., CFA and Rasch analysis) and testing of concurrent validity, but future research needs to assess predictive validity, which is important to both researchers and practitioners.

Cultural Considerations and Implications

The CDS is available in English (original version) and Indonesian, and there is potential for translating the scale into other languages. Translating the items by using translation/back-translation procedures or some similar method should be quite straightforward; however, demonstrating cross-cultural equivalence of the scale is more demanding, as is demonstrating that career distress from a Western perspective translates directly to other cultures (Cha, Kim, & Erlen, 2007).

Career Counseling Practice Considerations

Career distress is widespread, and much of career counseling seeks to alleviate this distress. The CDS can be a useful addition to the practitioner's arsenal when he or she uses it as an aid to counseling (Meier, 2013). The CDS is brief and easy to administer and score, is reliable, has evidence for validity, and, when used as an aid, does not require normative data.

Summary

The CDS is a short, 9-item, unifactorial measure of distress in the career domain. Although devised primarily for use by researchers, the CDS has potential for use by practitioners as a screening tool or for assessing client change. Researchers will find the CDS useful because it fits easily into a questionnaire with other measures, and, currently, practitioners have few scales to assess career distress, which is common in adolescents and young adults. The scale has good internal reliability, and there is validity evidence based on evaluation of the scale's items and structure, and concurrent assessment of its relationships with other career-related constructs. Future research needs to examine test-retest reliability, test for predictive validity, and normative data is required if the scale is to be utilized fully by practitioners.

References

Bandura, A. (1991). Social cognitive theory of self-regulation. *Organizational Behavior and Human Decision Processes, 50,* 248-287. doi:10.1016/0749-5978(91)90022-L

Benton, S. A., Robertson, J. M., Tseng, W. C., Newton, F. B., & Benton, S. L. (2003). Changes in counseling center client problems across 13 years. *Professional Psychology: Research and Practice, 34,* 66-72. doi:10.1037/0735-7028.34.1.66

Blair, J. D., & Hunt, J. G. (1986). Getting inside the head of the management researcher one more time. *Journal of Management, 12,* 147-166. doi:10.1177/014920638601200202

Carver, C. S., & Scheier, M. F. (1990). Origins and functions of positive and negative affect. *Psychological Review, 97,* 19-35. doi:10.1037/0033-295X.97.1.19

Cha, E. S., Kim, K. H., & Erlen, J. A. (2007). Translation of scales in cross-cultural research. *Journal Advanced Nursing, 58,* 386-395. doi:10.1111/j.1365-2648.2007.04242.x

Choi, B. Y., Park, H., Nam, S., Lee, J., Cho, D., & Lee, S. M. (2011). The development and initial psychometric evaluation of the Korean Career Stress Inventory for college students. *Career Development Quarterly, 59,* 559-572. doi:10.1002/j.2161-0045.2011.tb00976.x

Creed, P. A., & Blume, K. (2013). Compromise, well-being, and action behaviours in young adults. *Journal of Career Assessment, 21,* 3-19. doi:10.1177/1069072712453830

Creed, P. A., & Gagliardi, R. (2015). Career compromise, career distress, and perceptions of employability. *Journal of Career Assessment, 23*, 20-34. doi:10.1177/1069072714523082

Creed, P. A., & Hood, M. (2015a). Process variables: Maturity, identity, decision making, and adjustment. In P. Hartung, M. Savickas, & B. Walsh (Eds.). *APA handbook of career intervention* (pp. 351-372). Washington, DC: American Psychological Association.

Creed, P. A., & Hood, M. (2015b). The development and initial validation of a scale to assess career goal discrepancies. *Journal of Career Assessment, 23*, 308-317. doi:10.1177/1069072714535175

Creed, P. A., Hood, M., & Hu, S. (2017). Personal orientation as an antecedent to career stress and employability confidence. *Journal of Vocational Behavior, 99*, 79-92. doi:10.1016/j.jvb.2016.12.007

Creed, P. A., Hood, M., Praskova, A., & Makransky, G. (2016). The Career Distress Scale: Using Rasch measurement theory to evaluate a brief measure of career distress. *Journal of Career Assessment, 24*, 732-746. doi:10.1177/1069072715616126

Creed, P. A., & Hughes, T. (2013). Career development strategies as moderators between career compromise and career outcomes in emerging adults. *Journal of Career Development, 40*, 146-163. doi:10.1177/0894845312437207

Creed, P. A., Wamelink, T., & Hu, S. (2015). Antecedents and consequences to perceived career goal-progress discrepancies. *Journal of Vocational Behavior, 87*, 43-53. doi:10.1016/j.jvb.2014.12.001

Erikson, E. (1968). *Identity: Youth and crisis.* New York, NY: Norton.

Goldberg, D. P., & Williams, P. (1988). *A user's guide to the GHQ.* Windsor, UK: NFER.

Gunawan, W., Creed, P. A., & Glendon, A. I. (2018). Development and initial validation of a Perceived Future Employability Scale for young adults. *Journal of Career Assessment.* Advance online publication. doi:10.1177/1069072718788645

Havighurst, R. J. (1972). *Developmental tasks and education.* New York, NY: McKay.

Kim, J. H., & Karan, O. (2004). The relationships among sex, gender identity factors, and career-decision-situation-specified personality traits. *Asia Pacific Education Review, 5*, 39-49. doi:10.1007/BF03026278

Larson, L. M., Heppner, P., Ham, T., & Dugan, K. (1988). Investigating multiple subtypes of career indecision through cluster analysis. *Journal of Counseling Psychology, 35*, 439-446. doi:10.1037/0022-0167.35.4.447

Larson, L. M., & Majors, M. S. (1998). Applications of the Coping with Career Indecision instrument with adolescents. *Journal of Career Assessment, 6*, 163-179. doi:10.1177/106907279800600204

Larson, L. M., Toulouse, A. L., Ngumba, W. E., Fitzpatrick, L. A., & Heppner, P. P. (1994). The development and validation of Coping with Career Indecision. *Journal of Career Assessment, 2*, 91-110. doi:10.1177/106907279400200201

Lee, K. H. (2005). Coping with career indecision. *Journal of Career Development, 31*, 279-289. doi:10.1007/s1087-005-4741-0

Meier, S. (2013). *Measuring change in counseling and psychotherapy.* New York: Guilford.

McDowell, I. (2006). *Measuring health: A guide to rating scales and questionnaires.* New York, NY: Oxford University Press.

Praskova, A., Creed, P. A., & Hood, M. (2015). Career identity and the complex mediating relationships between career preparatory actions and career progress markers. *Journal of Vocational Behavior, 87*, 145-153. doi:10.1016/j.jvb.2015.01.001

Sawitri, D. R., Creed, P. A., & Perdhana, M. S. (2018). Development and initial validation of a scale to measure discrepancies between individual-set and parent-set career goals. *Journal of Career Assessment, 23*, 308-317. doi: 10.1177/1069072714535175

Skorikov, V. B. (2007). Adolescent career development and adjustment. In V. Skorikov & W. Patton (Eds.), *Career development in childhood and adolescence* (pp. 237-254). Rotterdam, ND: Sense.

Watson, D., Clark, L. A., & Tellegen, A. (1988). Development and validation of brief measures of positive and negative affect: The PANAS scales. *Journal of Personality and Social Psychology, 47*, 1063-1070. doi:10.1037/0022-3514.54.6.1063

Career Resources Questionnaire

Reviewed by
Simona Ingold
Madeleine Haenggli
Andreas Hirschi
University of Bern, Switzerland

Purpose

Vocational and organizational career research has a long-standing interest in identifying factors that allow people to achieve career success (e.g., Schein, 1978). The great interest in this topic has resulted in a wealth of theoretical models, measures, and empirical studies that aim to identify factors that allow people to have successful careers (for an overview see Ng, Eby, Sorensen, & Feldman, 2005; Ng & Feldman, 2014a; 2014b; Spurk, Hirschi, & Dries, 2018). Given this state of affairs, Hirschi, Nagy, Baumeler, Johnston, and Spurk (2018) concluded that there is value in developing an instrument that provides a concise and integrative measurement of key predictors of career success.

Hirschi, Haenggli et al. (2018) and Hirschi, Nagy et al. (2018) developed the Career Resources Questionnaire (CRQ) as a scientifically based self-assessment tool to evaluate critical resources that promote career success. The resources can be divided into four broad domains: (1) Knowledge and Skills; (2) Motivation; (3) Environment; and (4) Activities. These four broad domains consist of 13 different components that practitioners and researchers from various countries consider as important facilitators of subjective (i.e., job satisfaction, career satisfaction) and objective (i.e., salary, promotions) career success. What is important to note is that individuals can modify and develop these resources actively. The developers created the CRQ to assess critical resources of employability and to promote personal career success of employees and students of all age groups and work fields. The results of the CRQ provide a personal career resources profile.

Career specialists can use the questionnaire in career counseling, HR development, and in consulting and coaching services to assess key resources for career success among clients and employees. This allows for a nuanced and informative assessment of the career-related strengths and weaknesses of client and employees. Furthermore, based on the CRQ profile, evaluating the effectiveness of career counselling, coaching, and HR development processes is possible by comparing the client's or employee's career resources before and after an intervention.

In addition to use by practitioners, researchers can use the CRQ as a brief, reliable, and validated assessment of career resources for examining the predictors, outcomes, or development of career resources over time. Researchers can use the questionnaire in its entirety to assess a comprehensive array of career resources. Alternatively, researchers might assess for single resources separately for more specific research questions.

Structure of the Instrument

The CRQ consists of 41 items for employees and 38 items for students, with three to four items per scale (the student version does not contain three organizational career opportunities items because they are not relevant for this population). All items have a response format of a 5-point Likert scale ranging from 1 (*not true at all*) to 5 (*completely true*).

The questionnaire assesses four overarching dimensions: (1) Knowledge and Skills Resources; (2) Motivational Resources; (3) Environmental Resources; and (4) Activities of Career Self-management. These four dimensions encompass 13 specific subscales that each measure a specific resource or activity (for a definition of each scale and sample items see Table 1).

Administration

The CRQ is available in English and German for both students and employees. All versions are validated in different samples. The questionnaire is free and available on www.cresogo.com and takes about 10 minutes to complete. After completing the questionnaire, the results display in a basic report that shows the test taker's individual career resources profile. Also, there is an option to purchase a comprehensive personal report, which gives an additional, more detailed profile of career resources based on norm values and compared to other people who took the CRQ. Moreover, this comprehensive report provides additional background information on each resource and presents recommendations about how to use and develop every resource optimally.

Table 1. *Overview of the four key career resource dimensions and the 13 specific career resources assessed in the Career Resource Questionnaire*

Career Resource	Definition	Example Item
Knowledge and Skills		
Occupational expertise	The degree of possessed occupation specific knowledge and competencies.	*Others see me as an expert in my occupation.*
Job market knowledge	The degree of possessed general knowledge about the job market and employment trends.	*I have a good knowledge of the job market.*
Soft skills	The degree of possessed skills and competencies that are relevant for a broad range of occupations.	*I have many skills that I could use in a range of different occupations.*
Motivation		
Involvement	The degree of affective attachment to the working role.	*My work is a central part of my identity.*
Confidence	The belief that one is capable of successfully developing one's career.	*I am capable of successfully managing my career.*
Clarity	The clarity and self-determination of career goals.	*I have clear career goals.*
Environment		
Career opportunities	The extent to which personally interesting career advancement opportunities exist within one's current organization.	*My organization offers interesting career opportunities for me.*
Organizational career support	The extent to which one's current organization provides support for one's career development.	*My current employer supports my intended career.*
Job challenge	The extent to which one's current job allows one to utilize and develop personally valued skills.	*My work helps me to increase my skills.*

Activities		
Networking	The extent to which social contacts are built, maintained, and utilized to promote one's career development.	*I always try to be well connected in my professional field.*
Career information gathering	The extent to which information about career options is collected.	*I regularly collect information about career opportunities.*
Continuous learning	The extent to which work relevant knowledge and skills are enlarged and updated.	*I continuously develop my work-related abilities.*

Notes: The items will be answered on a 5-point scale: not true at all (1), slightly not true (2), moderately true (3), mostly true (4), completely true (5). All items are poled in the same direction. The individual test value results from the mean value of the items assigned to each scale.

Technical Considerations

Instrument development processes and procedures

In broad terms, the development of the CRQ involved five steps: (1) literature review, (2) item development, (3) item selection, (4) confirmation of the hypothesized factor structure, and (5) establishment of convergent/criterion validity. First, by integrating insights from diverse existing models and adapting the career resources model by Hirschi (2012), the developers identified four key areas of predictors of career success they wanted to assess in the measure. These include: (1) human capital resources, (2) environmental resources, (3) motivational resources, and (4) career management behaviors. Based on existing meta-analyses (Ng et. al, 2005; Ng & Feldman, 2014a, 2014b) and theoretical models on objective and subjective career success, the developers derived a list of 13 critical constructs within four broad dimensions (see Table 1).

Second, for item development, the developers used a recommended multi-step procedure to ensure high item content validity (Hinkin, 1998). For this purpose, they identified existing scales that assessed the same or very closely related constructs as the 13 identified factors in the previous step. Then, they used a deductive item generation strategy (Hinkin, 1998) by either creating new items or adapting items from existing scales. This process resulted in an initial set of 208 items. In addition to a questionnaire for use with working adults, the aim was to create a version for university students. Hence, the developers created a student version of each item in parallel, by adapting the items, if necessary (e.g. "my organization" was changed to "my university/college").

Third, the developers tested the items for content validity. The involved authors evaluated all preliminary items and deleted items that resulted in low agreement for representing the construct. In addition, five post-graduate students received a random set of items with the task of categorizing them into the theoretically presumed higher-order dimensions. Developers deleted or rephrased those items they or the students did not assign correctly, which resulted in a set of 133 items (between 7 and 12 per factor).

Fourth, to provide an empirical evaluation of which items described each factor best and to select a parsimonious and efficient number of final items for each factor, developers conducted a single-factor confirmatory factor analyses (CFA) with the employee and the student sample for each of the 13 factors. Developers identified six items per scale that showed the highest average factor loadings across the two samples. Three of the developers reviewed these items independently for content overlap and, together with a fourth author, the team decided which items to keep for the final version. This resulted in 41 items for the employee group and 38 items for the student group, with 3 to 4 items per scale, which corresponds with best practice recommendations in scale development.

Finally, to confirm dimensionality and structure of the selected items, the developers conducted a confirmatory factor analyses (CFA) in a new employee and student sample with maximum likelihood estimation with robust standard errors. These results supported the hypothesized structure and favored the 13-factor model (respectively, 12-factor model for students) over other models. In addition, the hierarchical 4-factor model showed acceptable fit. This suggested that, in addition to 13 or 12, respectively, individual factors, practitioners and researchers can use the CRQ to represent four broader higher-order dimensions of different career resources (see Table 1).

Reliability

Hirschi, Haenggli et al. (2018) and Hirschi, Nagy et al. (2018) tested the reliability of the CRQ (separately for the student and the employee versions) with the coefficient of internal consistency (Cronbach's alpha). Four studies, among different samples, showed consistently high values of reliability, ranging from $\alpha = .82$ to $.92$ for the employee version and from $\alpha = .73$ to $.91$ for the student version.

Validity

Content validity. All generated items underwent an internal content validity review by the authors of the scale. In addition, several post-graduate students evaluated item content independently.

Construct validity. Several researchers have been able to confirm the dimensionality and structure of the selected items of the CRQ through a series of CFAs in employee and student samples (Hirschi, Haenggli et al., 2018; Hirschi, Nagy et al., 2018). Confirming the construct validity, standardized factor loadings ranged between .67 and .93 in employee samples and between .59 and .91 in student samples.

Concurrent/predictive validity. To test criterion validity, all CRQ factors were correlated with different career success variables. All CRQ factors correlated significantly and positively with *career satisfaction, job satisfaction, salary,* and *promotions.* Generally, *salary* showed lower correlations with the CRQ factors compared to the other success indicators.

Convergent/divergent validity. To assess convergent validity, the CRQ factors were correlated with existing scales measuring closely related constructs. All correlations were highly significant and moderate to high in size ranging from $r = .27$ to $r = .83$. As expected, some correlations (e.g., *job market knowledge, career opportunities, networking*) were high, indicating that some CRQ factors assess constructs that are close to those assessed in existing scales. Other correlations (e.g., *skill variety, job crafting*) were moderate to high, confirming that some CRQ factors assess related constructs to existing scales. Overall, developers were able to confirm the convergent validity of the newly developed scales.

Norms

The reference groups for employees are displayed in Table 2 and for students in Table 3, and separately for the English and the German group. Statistical analyses revealed that manifestations of the different career resources differ significantly between employees in different age groups. For this purpose, the values in the reports are compared to a reference group in the same age group. Statistical analyses among students showed that manifestations of the different career resources differ significantly between women and men. Therefore, the values are compared to a reference group with the same gender. We used the values stanine scores and percentiles ranks to provide comparisons in the provided report.

Use / Interpretation / Evaluation

General utility

The CRQ is suitable as a basis to assess the following questions:

– What support does a client or an employee need to manage professional challenges?

Table 2. *Reference group for employees*

	Number	Age	Level of education						
			Middle school	High school	Vocational technical institution	Junior or community college	Undergraduate program	Master degree	Doctoral degree
English	873 64% female	19-65 years (M = 41; SD = 11)	-	13%	7%	14%	38%	24%	4%
German	748 40% female	19-65 years (M = 42 ; SD = 11)	14%	15%	29%	-	5%	40%	1%

Table 3. *Reference group for students*

	Number	Age	Type of institution				Level of education		
			Four-year college	University of applied science	University	No information	Bachelor degree	Master degree	No information
English	691 77% female	16-30 years (M = 23; SD = 4)	49%	-	49%	2%	75%	25%	-
German	724 69% female	17-30 years (M = 23; SD = 3)	-	31%	69%	-	68%	30%	2%

– On what strengths can clients or employees rely to make progress in their own career?

– In which areas does the client or employee have weaknesses that could hinder occupational development?

Besides using the CRQ in research, practitioners might use the questionnaire for different purposes. The CRQ allows practitioners to obtain a better understanding of the specific counselling and development needs of clients or employees, as well as plan career counselling, coaching sessions, and HR development processes by focusing on the career resources most useful for clients/employees. In addition, practitioners might use the CRQ to evaluate the effectiveness of career development interventions (e.g., counselling sessions, workshops, development programs) by comparing the career resources of clients or employees before and after an intervention. Hence, the CRQ will be a useful tool for practitioners interested in career development, in general, and predictors of career success, more specifically.

Presentation and Interpretation

The CRQ results provide the personal career resources profile of the test taker in four broad domains (knowledge and skills, motivation, environment, and activities) as well as for each of the 13 or 12, respectively, different subfactors, specifically. The report presents the values both numerically and graphically. A higher score on a factor means the person has well developed resources in this area. In the basic report, practitioners can interpret the results regarding where a person has more or fewer resources in comparison across the different resources.

The comprehensive personal report contains norms practitioners can use to compare the level of the different career resources to other people across raw values, standard values (stanine scores), and percentile ranks. Practitioners can interpret the results of this comprehensive report as to where a person has more or fewer resources in comparison to other people. Moreover, the report includes recommendations on how to use each resource optimally and how to increase a resource.

Researchers and practitioners can download further information and additional materials (career resources workbook, interview guide for professionals, career professional's guide, scientific report) from the website (www.cresogo.com).

Evaluation

The CRQ provides a brief, comprehensive, reliable, and validated assessment of the critical factors that help people develop their careers successfully. The CRQ integrates existing international empirical and theoretical work on objective and subjective career success. The CRQ is available for use with both employees and students in two languages (English and German). The automatic generated report, with recommendations for interpretation, provides a comprehensible way to interpret the scoring.

Cultural Considerations and Implications

For cultural considerations, developers confirmed the measurement invariance between the English and the German samples of the CRQ using the step-up approach suggested by Chen (2007). The results for both the English the German samples (employees and students) showed measurement equivalence for all measured factors. Hence, the measurements are comparable between English and German samples.

Career Counselling Practice Considerations

Career professionals can use the CRQ to enrich their practice and career interventions in several ways. First, a brief screening of the available resources of a client with the CRQ could serve as a basis for a preliminary decision about what type and intensity of career intervention is most appropriate for a client. Second, the CRQ results give specific insight to career processionals by providing results about which personal and environmental resources, as well as which career activities, need to be strengthened in a career intervention. Third, if career practitioners administer the CRQ before and after a career intervention, they can determine whether meaningful change has occurred in personal and environmental career resources, as well as in career behaviors. A summary of this process career professionals can follow to integrate the CRQ into their work is: (1) establish the needs and career concerns of the client in a brief interview; (2) screen the available career resources of the client with the CRQ; (3) determine the type of intervention that is most useful and efficient for the client based on the CRQ profile; (4) determine the key areas of intervention that are most useful for the client based on the CRQ profile; (5) help the client activate and utilize existing resources and to improve resources that are currently underdeveloped; and (6) evaluate the changes in career resources with a new CRQ assessment.

Summary

The Career Resources Questionnaire (CRQ) is a brief, reliable, and empirically validated measure practitioners can use to aid their clients in identifying critical resources of employability and in promoting personal career success. The CRQ is suitable for both students and employees of all ages and work fields and provides a personal career resources profile. Those engaged in career counseling, human resources development, consulting or coaching, or research will find the CRQ useful to their work.

References

Chen, F. F. (2007). Sensitivity of goodness of fit indexes to lack of measurement invariance. *Structural Equation Modeling, 14,* 464-504. doi:10.1080/10705510701301834

Hinkin, T. R. (1998). A brief tutorial on the development of measures for use in survey questionnaires. *Organizational Research Methods, 1*(1), 104-121. doi: 10.1177/109442819800100106

Hirschi, A. (2012). The career resources model: an integrative framework for career counsellors. *British Journal of Guidance & Counselling, 40,* 369-383. doi: 10.1080/03069885.2012.700506

Hirschi, A., Haenggli, M., Nagy, N., Baumeler, F., Johnston, C., & Spurk, D. (2018). Karriere-Ressourcen messen: Validierung der deutschsprachigen Version des Karriere-Ressourcen Fragebogens [Assessing career resources: Validation of the German version of the Career Resources Questionnaire]. *Diagnostica.*

Hirschi, A., Nagy, N., Baumeler, F., Johnston, C. S., & Spurk, D. (2018). Assessing key predictors of career success: Development and validation of the Career Resources Questionnaire. *Journal of Career Assessment, 26*(2), 338–358. doi: 10.1177/1069072717695584

Ng, T. W. H., Eby, L. T., Sorensen, K. L., & Feldman, D. C. (2005). Predictors of objective and subjective career success. A meta-analysis. *Personnel Psychology, 58,* 367-408. doi: 10.1111/j.1744-6570.2005.00515.x

Ng, T. W. H., & Feldman, D. C. (2014a). A conservation of resources perspective on career hurdles and salary attainment. *Journal of Vocational Behavior, 85*(1), 156-168. doi: 10.1016/j.jvb.2014.05.008

Ng, T. W. H., & Feldman, D. C. (2014b). Subjective career success: A meta-analytic review. *Journal of Vocational Behavior, 85*(2), 169-179. doi: 10.1016/j.jvb.2014.06.001

Schein, E. H. (1978). *Career dynamics : Matching individual and organizational needs.* Reading, Mass.: Addison-Wesley Pub. Co.

Spurk, D., Hirschi, A., & Dries, N. (2018). Antecedents and outcomes of objective versus subjective career success: Competing perspectives and future directions. *Journal of Management.* doi:10.1177/0149206318786563

DECISIONAL PROCESS INVENTORY

Reviewed by

Paul J. Hartung
Northeast Ohio Medical University

Purpose

The Decisional Process Inventory (DPI; Hartung, 1994) offers counselors and researchers a brief measure of career indecision. A complex construct, career indecision relates closely to broader constructs of career choice and decision making and serves as the focus of a sizeable literature (e.g., Gati, 2013; Osipow, 1999; Phillips & Jome, 2005; Savickas, 2000; Tinsley, 1992; Whiston & Rose, 2013). Career indecision has long denoted an inability to express an educational or occupational choice, when asked to do so, and a delay in bringing closure to the career-choice process (Slaney, 1988). Alternatively, indecision signals a wavering, pause, or hesitation in career development (Savickas, 2011), an openness to alternative career pathways (Krumboltz, 2009), and a state of adaptive uncertainty (Krieshok, Black, & McKay, 2009; Phillips, 1997).

Gestalt counseling homeostasis theory (Perls, Hefferline, & Goodman, 1951/1969; Polster & Polster, 1973) informed construction of the DPI via a model – namely, the Gestalt Career Decision Making Cycle (CDMC; Hartung, 1995; Hartung & Marco, 1998) – adapted for use in a career decision-making context. Like other adaptations of counseling theory to career development, the adapted model and measure seemed appropriate for use in career counseling. That is because the Gestalt CDMC and the DPI emphasize process elements that affect career decision making. Process elements include thoughts and feelings about career decision making, the meaning and importance of work and career, and levels of investment and involvement in career exploration and choice processes. Most career decision-making measures focus on assessing content-based or structural aspects of career indecision emphasized in Parsons' (1909) venerable tripartite model. Such factors include insufficient occupational information and lack of knowledge of one's interests, aptitudes, or abilities to make a decision. The

DPI emphasizes individual perceptions about and, experiences of, career decision making.

The DPI aims to operationalize contact and resistance constructs articulated in the Gestalt CDMC and apply those constructs to comprehending and assessing career decision making and indecision. Gestalt homeostasis theory offers a well-articulated model of process factors involved in human need fulfillment (Clarkson, 1989; Perls et al., 1951/1969; Polster & Polster, 1973; Wheeler, 1991). Personal homeostasis, or organismic self-regulation, involves processes whereby humans balance personal needs with environmental demands and circumstances. In theory, contact processes, such as awareness and action, promote career decision making and need fulfillment. Resistance processes, such as introjection and deflection, inhibit successful resolution of the career decision-making process. The Gestalt CDMC conceptualizes career decision making as a cyclical process of contact and need fulfillment, or resistance to contact and need inhibition. In successful, or contactful, resolution of this process, individuals use internal and external resources effectively to satisfy personal needs and cope with environmental demands, reach a satisfying career-decided state, and, thereby, maintain psychological homeostasis or balance. When individuals lack awareness of personal and environmental resources or cannot access or use those resources effectively, they fail to satisfy their needs, prove ineffective in coping with the demands of the environment, remain undecided, and experience dishomeostasis. Movement through the decisional process will lead, ultimately, to some degree of homeostatic closure and a decided state or to dishomeostasis and continued indecision.

Structure

The DPI contains 25 items designed to measure level of career decidedness defined in terms of progress and problems in moving through the Gestalt CDMC. Respondents rate all DPI items on a 5-point scale with two anchors (e.g., "As far as being able to make a career decision, I am: unprepared/prepared"). An exploratory factor analysis (Hartung & Marco, 1998) indicated the DPI assesses three latent dimensions of the Gestalt CDMC: career decision-making orientation (CDO; 11 items dealing with readiness to make a career choice; e.g., "The subject of career planning makes me feel: uncomfortable/comfortable"), career decision-making closure (CDC; 7 items dealing with action to make a career decision; e.g., "The thought of putting effort into making a career decision makes me feel: empty/fulfilled"), and career decision-making resistance (CDR; 7 items dealing with interruption of the decision-making process; e.g., "The thought of me actually deciding on a career is: realistic/unrealistic"). Administrators scores items 1-18 (CDO and CDC) and add that total to the reverse-scored sum of items 19-25 (CDR) for a DPI total Indecision score, which could range from 25 to 125. Summing the items for each scale yields score ranges of 11-55 on CDO, 7-35 on CDC, and 7-35 on CDR. Higher scores on CDO purport to indicate more readiness for making a career choice. Higher scores on CDC purport to indicate more involvement in the career-choice process. Higher scores on CDR purport to indicate more difficulty in making a career decision.

Administration

The DPI is currently available in a paper-and-pencil, hand-scored English language version only. Administration is easy, either individually or in groups, and response time averages approximately 15 minutes. No scoring report is available at present. Counselors and researchers wanting to use the instrument may do so at no cost by obtaining permission from the test author: Paul J. Hartung, Ph.D., Department of Family and Community Medicine, Northeast Ohio Medical University, Rootstown, OH, USA, phartung@neomed.edu.

Technical Considerations

Development

To construct the DPI, I generated an initial pool of 70 items from a review and synthesis of the Gestalt counseling theory literature and content analyzed by ten expert judges. Alpha factor analysis of these 70 items, based on a sample of 248 community college students in an initial study of the DPI, produced seven identifiable factors and 42 items (Hartung, 1995). These factors were Career Orientation, Decisional Involvement, Expressiveness, Perceived Opportunity, Decisional Salience, Directedness, and Clarity. Alpha factor analysis of the 42-item DPI, in a second study involving 183 undergraduate college students, produced a three-factor solution and reduced the DPI to 25 items (Hartung & Marco, 1998). These factors were: Career Decision-Making Orientation (CDO), Career Decision-Making Closure (CDC), and Career Decision-Making Resistance (CDR).

Reliability

Three studies have examined the internal consistency reliability of the DPI items and subscales. In the first study (Hartung, 1995), analysis of the initial 70-item version produced Cronbach's alpha coefficients for the subscales ranging from .09 to .85 ($M = .60$). The second study of the 42-item version (Hartung & Marco, 1998) reported Cronbach's alpha coefficients for the subscales ranging from -.25 to .92 ($M = .63$). In the third study (Marco, Hartung, Newman, & Parr, 2003), analysis of the 25-item version yielded Cronbach's alpha coefficients of .89

for CDO, .79 for CDC, .81 for CDR, .91 for the composite Contact scale (CDO + CDC), and .93 for the DPI total. These values indicated that the items, sub-scales, and composite Contact scale of the DPI show high internal consistency. Consistent with the Marco et al. (2003) study, subsequent analysis (Uthayakumar, Schimmack, Hartung, & Rogers, 2010) yielded an alpha of .93 for the DPI total. Test-retest reliability data is lacking for the measure.

Validity

Evidence has been provided for the concurrent validity of DPI scores on the 70-item (Hartung, 1995), 42-item (Hartung & Marco, 1998), and 25-item (Marco et al., 2003) versions. Contact subscale scores have been shown to correlate significantly and inversely with scores on two different measures of career inde-cision, with values ranging from $r = -.44$ to $r = -.70$. Contact subscale scores have been related positively to scores on a measure of vocational identity ($r = .74$). Re-sistance subscale scores have been shown to correlate significantly and positively with career indecision scores, having values ranging from $r = .35$ to $r = .65$. In addition, resistance scores have been shown to correlate inversely with vocational identity scores ($r = -.67$). A direct relationship has been found between DPI total scores and subjective well-being and an inverse relationship was supported be-tween DPI total scores and depression (Uthayakumar et al., 2010).

The study by Marco et al. (2003) supported DPI discriminant validity. Ex-pressed career-decided students in the study scored significantly higher on CDO ($M = 39.4$) and CDC ($M = 27.4$) than did expressed career-undecided individ-uals on these subscales ($M = 33.2$, $M = 24.9$, respectively). Likewise, expressed career-decided students scored significantly lower on CDR ($M = 13.3$) than did expressed career-undecided individuals ($M = 16.5$).

In terms of construct validity, the two initial studies of the DPI yielded item reductions and factor structures that included empirical support and support through the need to produce a brief measure that would accommodate well for use in both career counseling practice and research contexts. A third study in-dicated that additional work was needed to improve the measure and clarify its factor structure (Marco et al. 2003). Toward this end, Uthayakumar et al. (2010) performed a subsequent study using maximum likelihood Confirmatory Factor Analyses (CFA) on three alternative models proposed by Marco et al. (2003). Results of the CFAs could not confirm the three-factor structure proposed by Hartung and Marco (1998) nor the alternative models suggested by Marco et al. (2003). Therefore, Uthayakumar et al. (2010) conducted a principal axis factor analysis of the DPI items. Results suggested a one-factor model for the data ac-counting for 70% of the common variance. Coefficient alpha for this one-factor model was .93. Combined, their results supported using the total DPI score as a measure of overall career decidedness. Uthayakumar et al. (2010) concluded, that of the four models they tested, the original three-factor structure appears most promising for further study. Given the strength of the theory that underlies the development of the DPI coupled with the CFA results, they encouraged further research to revisit the three sub-scale structure at the item level in an effort to strengthen construct validity.

Use/Interpretation/Evaluation

Counselors might use data from DPI scores to assess and intervene with clients according to their levels of career decision-making contact and resistance (Hartung & Marco, 1998). For example, clients with low CDO scores might benefit from interventions aimed at increasing orientation to the role of work in their lives. Clients with low CDC scores might benefit from focused career exploration, interest assessment, and values clarification. Clients with high CDR scores might need interventions to increase decisional salience, problem ownership, and realism in career decision making. As a caveat, however, future investigations aimed at clarifying the DPI's factor structure are needed to guide and ensure appropriate use and interpretation of the three DPI subscale scores in career assessment and counseling contexts. Meanwhile, and minimally, practitioners can feel confident in using total DPI scores to index overall level of career indecision.

Ultimately, to refine and strengthen the DPI, future research should involve administering the instrument to larger and more systematically selected samples. Such research could include random stratified samples representing different age groups, different ethnic groups, and a variety of educational backgrounds. A more rigorous sampling methodology could both aid a more definitive understanding of the DPI and bolster the external validity of the measure. With further establishment of the DPI's reliability and validity and clarification of its factor structure, future research might examine the discriminant validity of the DPI further when compared to other measures of career indecision, such as the Career Decision Scale (Osipow, Carney, Winer, Yanico, & Koschier, 1976), the Career Factors Inventory (Chartrand, Robbins, Morrill, & Boggs, 1990), and the Career Decision-Making Difficulties Questionnaire (Gati, Krausz, & Osipow, 1996). Such studies could address the question of what each of these career decision-making measures assesses best. Examining the efficacy of the DPI as a treatment outcome measure as part of an intervention study could be the focus of future research. Finally, future research might include the use of cluster analytic techniques to determine whether DPI scores differentiate subtypes of people that practitioners could use to guide selection of specific types of interventions.

Summary

Career indecision has long been a focus of theory, research, and practice in career development. For decades, practitioners and researchers have made attempts to understand career indecision, both theoretically and psychometrically. The DPI has shown promise for appraising aspects of a career decision-making model grounded in Gestalt counseling theory. Research evidence indicates that practitioners and researchers can use DPI total scores with confidence to measure overall level of career indecision. However, work remains on clarifying the dimensional structure of the measure with regard to using the three proposed subscales identified in a refinement of the measure (Hartung & Marco, 1998). With additional development and investigation, the DPI might, ultimately, offer researchers and practitioners a rationally and empirically-derived tool useful for understanding dimensions of the career decision-making process and for dealing with career indecision as a problem that can interrupt that process.

References

Chartrand, J. M., Robbins, S. B., & Morrill, W. H., & Boggs, K. (1990). Development and validation of the Career Factors Inventory. *Journal of Counseling Psychology, 37*, 491-501.

Clarkson, P. (1989). *Gestalt counselling in action.* London: SAGE.

Gati, I. (2013). Advances in career decision making. In W. B. Walsh, M. L. Savickas, & P. J. Hartung (Eds.), *Handbook of Vocational Psychology* (4th ed., pp. 183-215). New York, NY: Routledge.

Gati, I., Krausz, M., & Osipow, S. H. (1996). A taxonomy of difficulties in career decision making. *Journal of Counseling Psychology, 43*, 510-526.

Hartung, P. J. (1994). The Decisional Process Inventory. [Copyrighted psychological test.] Rootstown, OH. Author.

Hartung, P. J. (1995). Developing a theory-based measure of career decision making: The Decisional Process Inventory. *Journal of Career Assessment, 3*, 299-313.

Hartung, P. J., & Marco, C. (1998). Refinement and further validation of the Decisional Process Inventory. *Journal of Career Assessment, 6*, 147-162.

Krieshok, T. S., Black, M. D., & McKay, R. A. (2009). Career decision making: The limits of rationality and the abundance of non-conscious processes. *Journal of Vocational Behavior, 75*, 275–290. doi:10.1016/j.jvb.2009.04.006

Krumboltz, J. D. (2009). The happenstance learning theory. *Journal of Career Assessment, 17*, 135-154.

Marco, C. D., Hartung, P. J., Newman, I., & Parr, P. (2003). Validity of the Decisional Process Inventory. *Journal of Vocational Behavior, 63*, 1-19.

Osipow, S. H. (1999). Assessing career indecision. *Journal of Vocational Behavior, 55,* 147-154. doi: 10.1006/jvbe.1999.1704

Osipow, S. H., Carney, C. G., Winer, J. L., Yanico, B., & Koschier, M. (1976). *The Career Decision Scale* (3rd revision). Odessa, FL: Psychological Assessment Resources.

Parsons, F. (1909). *Choosing a vocation.* Boston, MA: Houghton-Mifflin.

Perls, F. S., Hefferline, R., & Goodman, P. (1951/1969). *Gestalt therapy: Excitement and growth in the human personality.* New York: Bantam.

Phillips, S. D. (1997). Toward an expanded definition of adaptive decision making. *Career Development Quarterly, 45,* 275-287.

Phillips, S. D., & Jome, L. M. (2005). Vocational choices: What do we know? What do we need to know? In W. B. Walsh, & M. L. Savickas (Eds.), *Handbook of vocational psychology* (3rd ed., pp. 127-153). Mahwah, NJ: Erlbaum.

Polster, E., & Polster, M. (1973). *Gestalt therapy integrated.* New York: Random House.

Savickas, M. L. (2000). Assessing career decision making. In C. E. Watkins, & V. Campbell (Eds.), *Testing and assessment in counseling practice* (2nd ed., pp. 429-477). Hillsdale, NJ: Erlbaum.

Savickas, M. L. (2011). *Career counseling.* Washington, DC: American Psychological Association.

Slaney, R. B. (1988). The assessment of career decision making. In W. B. Walsh, & S. H. Osipow (Eds.), *Career decision making* (pp. 33-76). Hillsdale, NJ: Lawrence Erlbaum Associates.

Tinsley, H. E. (Ed.). (1992). Special Issue: Career decision making and career indecision. *Journal of Vocational Behavior, 41,* 209-211. doi: 10.1016/0001-8791(92)90022-R

Uthayakumar, R., Schimmack, U., Hartung, P. J., & Rogers, J. R. (2010). Career decidedness as a predictor of subjective well-being. *Journal of Vocational Behavior, 77,* 196-204.

Wheeler, G. (1991). *Gestalt therapy reconsidered.* New York: Gardner Press.

Whiston, S. C., & Rose, C. S. (2013). Career counseling with emerging adults. In W. B. Walsh, M. L. Savickas, & P. J. Hartung (Eds.), *Handbook of vocational psychology* (4th ed., pp. 250-272). New York, NY: Routledge.

PERSONAL GLOBE INVENTORY

Reviewed by

Terence J. G. Tracey

Arizona State University

Purpose

The Personal Globe Inventory (PGI) is designed to measure vocational and educational interests to assist in the choice of a career or educational major, as well as for exploring potential hobbies or avocational activities. The goals of the PGI are to (a) teach the user about his or her interests, (b) stimulate career exploration by presenting appropriate careers and majors that he or she might not have considered previously, and (c) confirm current career choices. The instrument is based on the Personal Globe model, which is inclusive of traditional measures (i.e., Holland's [1997] RIASEC types and Prediger's [1982] People/Things and Data/Ideas dimensions), but adds the dimension of prestige to form a more differentiated representation of the interest domain. The PGI is novel in that it includes an assessment of self-efficacy in addition to the assessment of interests. Therefore, the PGI mirrors extant measures, in terms of information provided, but goes further in providing additional information. The scales from the PGI are matched to over 900 occupational titles and 450 educational majors to assist in decision-making.

The instrument is appropriate for individuals above the age of 14 and career practitioners can use the PGI with most adults. The instrument is complex and used most appropriately in a computer or internet-based format. The PGI is available without cost on the internet at https://PGI.ASU.EDU. Although assessment takers can use the PGI in a paper and pencil format, this format is appropriate for research purposes only.

Instrument Description

There are four versions of the PGI: the extended PGI, which is available only on a standalone PC program (available at http://tracey.faculty.asu.edu/), the regular PGI and the PGI-Short, each of which are available on the internet (https://PGI.asu.edu), and the PGI-Mini. The extended PGI contains three different sets of items: 108 occupation preference, 113 activity preference, and 113 activity competence items. The regular PGI contains only the 113 activity preference items, to which users respond using a seven-point scale (1 = *very strongly dislike* to 7 = *very strongly like*), and 113 activity competence items, to which users respond using a seven-point scale (1 = *unable to do* to 7 = *very competent*) to rate perceived competence. Given that the author, Tracey (2002), found that the different scale types were equally valid, he adopted the regular PGI, omitting the occupation preference items, as the standard. Tracey (2010) developed the PGI-Short using Item Response Theory (IRT) analysis, and the PGI-S consists of only 40-activity preference and 40 activity competence items. Given its shorter length, the PGI-S does not provide all the scores of the regular PGI. Finally, the PGI-Mini is very brief (only 20 items) and focuses only on activity preference.

The PGI is based on the Personal Globe model wherein interests and self-efficacy estimates can be described using a three dimensional spherical structure (i.e., globe) defined by *People* versus *Data, Ideas* versus *Data,* and *Prestige.* The regular PGI and extended PGI have 18 scales distributed equally over this globe: eight basic interest scales (Social Facilitating, Managing, Business Detail, Data Processing, Mechanical, Nature/Outdoors, Artistic, and Helping), five high prestige scales (Financial analysis, Social Science, Science, Business systems, and Influence), and five low prestige scales (Basic service, Personal service, Construction/repair, Quality control, and Manual work). The spacing of these globe scales are presented in Figure 1, with more similar scales in closer proximity. In addition, weighted geometric composites of the 18 spherical scales are used to construct the RIASEC scales, Prediger's four poles of People, Things, Data, and Ideas, and three summary dimensional scales (People vs. Things, Data vs. Ideas, and Prestige), which results in 31 scales. These 31 scales are calculated for both interests and self-efficacy separately, thus, resulting in 62 scales. Finally, there is an interest-self-efficacy discrepancy score, which provides information on the profile similarity of the interests and self efficacy scores (i.e., congruence of interests and self-efficacy). As a check on validity, there are two validity scales provided (forced response and repeated items). All scores present in T score format based on combined gender norms, as well as same gender norms.

The score profile (combined interest and self-efficacy) is compared to the O*NET listing of occupations. The match of the PGI profile to each occupation is listed using a similarity score (100 = perfect match; 0 = very poor match). The similarity of each of the 1,000 O*NET occupations is presented in rank order. A similar procedure is used to map the PGI onto majors. Specifically, the over 450 majors listed in the National Center for Educational Statistics Classification of Instructional Program (CIP) taxonomy are presented. Finally, the PGI and PGI-Short provide matches to the 16 Career Clusters created by the Office of Vocational and Adult Education (OVAE) because this system is used in some educational programs.

Figure 1. *Personal Globe model: Proximity of the interest types represents their similarity.*

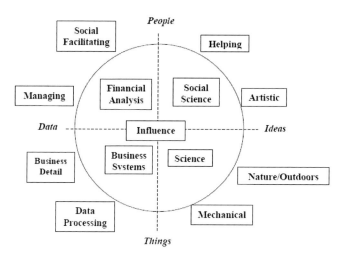

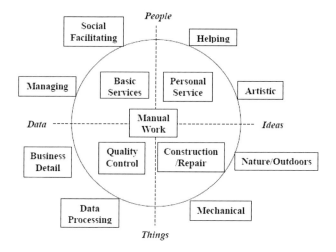

Top half represents the top hemisphere of the PGI globe, looking down at the north pole of high prestige.

The bottom represents the bottom hemisphere, looking up at the south pole of low prestige.

The equator represents the familiar general interest circle, which is the same plane as that occupied by Holland's RIASEC types.

Administration

The PGI is intended to provide useful information to individuals aged 14 to 30 relative to selecting majors and occupations or verifying choices they have made. The norms are based on a representative sample of high school and college students, but the test can provide information that many older individuals considering a career change might find helpful. The PGI is not recommended for use with adolescents under 14 because there is no research support on its application to this age group yet. For those interested in assessing children and young adolescents, Tracey and Caulum (2015) and Tracey and Ward (1998) recommend the *Inventory of Children's Activities.*

Users take the PGI regular version online, typically, because the calculations of all the scale scores are involved. Administering the PGI or the PGI-Short in a paper and pencil format is possible if the user is interested only in obtaining the raw scale scores. Completing the regular PGI takes approximately 20-30 minutes, and the PGI-Short takes roughly 10 minutes. Anyone can take the PGI in that there is no special access required, but the test is complex, and having a qualified professional assist with the interpretation would be helpful.

The primary source of the PGI is online at https://PGI.ASU.EDU. This free site offers the regular PGI (236 items) and the PGI-Short (80 items) along with a copy of the PGI manual. These are in English only. The manual contains all versions of the PGI as well as scoring rubrics. There are many versions of the PGI in other languages that have been validated but these are available only in paper and pencil versions. A benefit of the internet version is that it individualizes the profile presentation based on each respondent's score pattern. This simplifies the information presented, which is important given the number of scores provided, and highlights and graphs the scores that matter most. For example, if an individual does not endorse any high or low prestige items, then such scales are not graphed. Further, if an individual demonstrates that the interests and self-efficacy profiles are dissimilar, then, the two profiles are graphed, whereas; they would not be if these profiles matched. This individually-determined interpretation report enhances user grasp.

Users interested in using any form of the PGI for their own purposes other than those obtainable from the website (e.g., research or career intervention) should contact Terence Tracey (ttracey@asu.edu) for permission.

Technical Considerations

Instrument Development

The PGI evolved from three different studies on interests. First, Tracey and Rounds (1995) demonstrated that responses to interest items are not clustered into the six RIASEC types posited by Holland (1997). The responses are arranged uniformly around a circle implying that the division of the circle into different slices is arbitrary. Thus, interests can be categorized as valid using eight types or four types (or any other number). Second, Tracey and Rounds (1996) demonstrated that responses to interest items could be described well by three substantive dimensions: Prediger's People/Things, Data/Ideas, and the new dimension of Prestige. The interests can be conceptualized as points in a three dimensional spherical space (i.e., Personal Globe model; see Figure 2). Finally, Tracey (1997a) demonstrated that interests (what people like) and self-efficacy estimates (what people believe they can do successfully) can both be described validly using this same personal globe model. This result meant that interests and self-efficacy scores can be compared directly because the same structural model holds for each.

Figure 2. *Personal Globe model of interests and self-efficacy.*

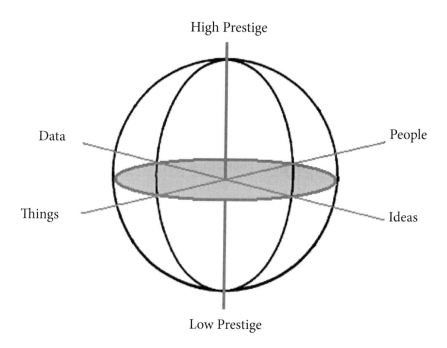

Given these results, Tracey (2002) created the Personal Globe Inventory (PGI) to represent the spherical structure. Tracey developed the PGI empirically from a principal components analysis of a vast set of items representative of the domain of occupations and vocational activities. Each item fell at a point in three-dimensional space, and Tracey formed items into scales based on their proximity to spots on the globe. The equator was comprised of Prediger's People/Things and Data/Ideas dimensions and could be represented using Holland's RIASEC scales equally spaced around the circle on these two dimensions. However, Tracey thought six sections was too broad a representation, which led to types that were too inclusive to defy intuitive understanding (e.g., the meaning of Realistic, Investigative, Enterprising or Conventional is not at all obvious to new test users). To obtain a more finely tuned representation and one that was more intuitively clear, Tracey used an eight type model and formed the items that clustered around the eight equally spaced points on the circle into scales. He based the resulting scale names on item content (i.e., Social Facilitating, Managing, Business Detail, Data Processing, Mechanical, Nature/Outdoors, Artistic, and Helping). The graphic of the spatial relations among the two dimensions and eight types versus six types is presented in Figure 3.

Figure 3. *Graphic representation of the equator of the Personal Globe model.*

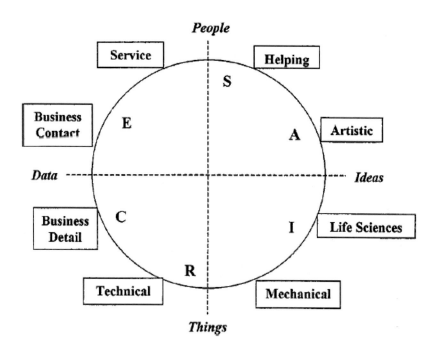

Following this, Tracey (2002) created five high prestige scales (four spaced equally around the Tropic of Cancer and one at the North Pole) and five low prestige scales (four spaced equally around the Tropic of Capricorn and one at the South Pole). He labeled the four scales at the Tropic of Cancer *Financial analysis, Social Science, Science,* and *Business systems,* with *Influence* existing at the North Pole. The four scales around the Tropic of Capricorn were *Basic service, Personal service, Construction/repair,* and *Quality control,* with *Manual* work at the South Pole. Tracey spaced the 18 Globe scales equally on the spherical surface of the interest space. Given this structure, the scales more proximate are more highly related, and those more distal are less related. Given these spatial relations, Tracey was able to construct Holland's six RIASEC scales from geometrically weighted composites of the octant scales. Tracey used an identical procedure in the creation of the scales for the self-efficacy items. The PGI presents all scores for all 31 scales separately for interests and self-efficacy, as well as for the combination. Generally, the combination is used in the summary.

Tracey (2010) developed the PGI-Short using item response theory (IRT). He examined the responses to the activity items and selected the best items to form a very brief version. Tracey designed the brief version only to provide scale scores for the basic interest circle (i.e., octant scores, Holland's six types, and the four types), as well as a simple high prestige and low prestige score. Tracey deleted the remaining high and low prestige scores. In addition, the IRT method enabled an examination of differential item functioning (DIF) of each item across gender. None of the selected items demonstrated a pattern of DIF. Therefore, the PGI-Short provides a good representation of the basic interest circle with the addition of two prestige scales only.

Finally, Tracey developed the PGI-Mini in 2016 to provide a very brief assessment of interests. He selected the best items from the activity preference scales of the PGI-Short using IRT. The scale is only 20 items and yields the same scores as the PGI-Short; the PGI-Mini scores pertain only to interests. There are no self-efficacy items.

Psychometric Support

Tracey (2002, 2010) provided the most support for the scale and summarized support in the PGI Manual (Tracey, 2016).

Reliability

Internal consistency estimates of each scale ranged from $\alpha = .88$ to .95 for the composite scales, and two week test-retest reliabilities ranged from $r = .77$ to .86 (Tracey, 2002) for the regular PGI scales. The PGI-Short was found to have internal consistency estimates ranging from α = .88 to .96 for the composite scales, and two-week test retest reliabilities ranging from r = .76 to .86 (Tracey, 2010). The PGI Mini is extremely brief (e.g., some scales have only two items), but its internal consistency is good considering the length (ω's = .62 to .91).

Structural Validity

The Personal Globe model, like Holland's model of six interest types, is based on the circular arrangement of the scales. Scales on the basic interest circle are arranged uniformly around the circle, with more similar scales closer to each other and more dissimilar ones more distant or opposite. A crucial demonstration of the validity of the instrument is the extent to which this circular structure holds in different samples. If the circular structure does not hold, then the underlying assumptions about the test, the meaning of the scales, and the basis of interpretation are inappropriate. To examine the validity of the circular model, each type of scale was examined for the extent to which it could be validly described using a circular model using the randomization test of hypothesized order relation (Hubert & Arabie, 1987; Tracey, 1997b). This test provides an inferential statistic indicating the significance of any departure in circular fit from chance as well as correlation of model-data fit (correspondence index, CI). The CI ranges from -1.0 to +1.0. A CI value of +1.0 indicates that the data perfectly fit the circle. A CI value of .00 indicates that the fit is roughly 50-50 and a value of -1.0 indicates that there is no fit to a circular structure.

The results of the randomization test demonstrated that the circular ordering of the scales was supported in both high school and college samples, across gender, and across all of the major U.S. ethnic groups. Indeed the fit of the PGI scales had CI values as great as, or greater than, the U.S. fit benchmark presented by Rounds and Tracey (1996), which indicates the PGI fit the theoretical circular model as well, or better than, existing RIASEC measures. The lack of differences in fit across age, gender, and ethnicity indicate that the model fits each group well and equally and provides support for use of the measure in cross group examinations.

The structural validity of the PGI-Short was examined because it varied across age and gender with respect to fit to the circular model. The PGI-S fits the data well and did not differ in fit from that obtained using the longer PGI (Tracey, 2010). Like the results with the longer PGI, the PGI-S fit each ethnic group well, and the values were above those yielded elsewhere for Holland type measures. Finally, examination of the structural fit of the PGI-Mini was strong with CI values far exceeding those of the RIASEC benchmark, even for such a short scale (Tracey, 2016).

A unique aspect of the PGI is the extensive validity support for international applications. The PGI has been adapted and translated for use in many countries, and there is similar and strong published validity support for the structure in Ireland (Darcy, 2004), Croatia (Sverko, 2008), Serbia, (Hedrih, 2008), China (Long, Adams, & Tracey, 2005), Caribbean (Wilkins, Ramkissoon, & Tracey, 2013), Iran (Akbarzadeh, 2010), Turkey (Vardarli, Özyüre, Wilkins-Yel, & Tracey, 2017), Germany (Etzel, Nagy, & Tracey, 2016), and Japan (Long, Watanabe, & Tracey, 2006; Tracey, Watanabe, & Schneider, 1997). Likewise, Caulum, Tracey, Gresham, & McCarty (2011) validated the PGI in Singapore, and the PGI has been used as a required part of the career planning curriculum for every secondary student in Singapore. Although the results have not been published, there is also validity support for Slovenia, Macedonia, Turkey, France, Italy, Hong Kong, Malaysia, Germany, Philippines, and Portugal. Overall, there is strong structural support for the scales in the U.S. and internationally.

Concurrent Validity

To examine the concurrent validity of the scale, the PGI Holland scales were correlated with General Occupational Theme (GOT) scales from the Strong Interest Inventory (SII, Harmon, Hansen, Borgen, Hammer, 1994), which assesses interests, and the scales form the Skills, Confidence Inventory (SCI, Betz, Borgen, & Harmon, 1996). The correlations ranged from r = .65 to .77 for similar interest scales and r = .75 to .80 for the self-efficacy scales, which demonstrated good support for the scales. Sodano (2011) found that work values are well represented in the PGI scales, which support the value and applicability of the PGI further.

Predictive Validity

A key reason for the application of interests tests is that the greater the match of one's interests to one's environment (e.g., occupation or major), the greater the career outcomes (e.g., certainty, satisfaction, performance, tenure/persistence). When using the PGI to match interests profiles to majors, the greater the match, the greater the career choice certainty (Durr & Tracey, 2009; Tracey & Tao, 2018). Leung et al. (2014) found that the PGI profiles were able to discriminate among high school students areas of study, as well as students' academic performance.

Bias

As noted above, there is support for the structural equivalence of the PGI across gender, age, ethnicity, and country. Thus, there is demonstrated strong support for use of the instrument with different groups. A key issue in interest measurement is the gender difference on the People-Things dimension (Realistic vs. Social), where the vast majority of women score high on People and men on Realistic. In a meta-analysis, Su, Rounds, and Armstrong (2009) found that this gender effect has an average Cohen's d of .93, which is huge. A hotly debated issue pertains as to the meaning of such differences (e.g., such differences perpetuate the current differences in occupational membership). The PGI has a People/Things gender difference of only d = .29, which is among the lowest of all current RIASEC measures (Tracey, 2016). Therefore, there is less gender difference in the PGI than in other instruments. Finally, the PGI-Short and PGI-Mini demonstrated that there was no differential item functioning across gender (Tracey, 2010).

Norms

The PGI regular version (i.e., the one that includes only the activity items) has a reading grade level of under sixth grade (Flesch-Kincaid reading grade level: 5.79 and a Flesch Reading ease score of 61.88) so a wide variety of individuals can use the PGI.

The PGI, the PGI-Short, and the PGI-Mini are normed using a representative sample of high school and college students (ages ranging from 16-24, with a mean of 20.5). This sample contained 500 men and 500 women and was generated to represent the 2010 U.S. census with respect to ethnicity. The instrument reports all scores in T score units (mean =50, SD=10) relative to the total norm group and relative to the same sex norm group.

Use/Interpretation/Evaluation

General utility

The PGI and the PGI Short are administered on the web site (https://PGI.asu.edu) and the reports vary across the two versions. Because the PGI is longer and has more scales, there is a greater amount of information presented. There are over 121 different scale scores reported in the regular PGI:

- 18 scales of the Personal Globe (liking and competence combined) scored using general sample norm and using same sex norms;
- 18 scales of the Liking responses;
- 18 scales of the Competence responses;
- 18 (Liking and Competence combined) raw scores;
- The four general scales of *People, Things, Data,* and *Ideas* (using both general norms and same sex norms);
- The six Holland RIASEC types (Realistic, Investigative, Artistic, Social,

Enterprising, and Conventional) and scores (both using general sample norms and same sex norms);

- The dimensional scores of the interest globe: *People* vs. *Things*, *Data* vs. *Ideas*, and *Prestige* scores (both using general sample norms and same sex norms);

- The difference between Liking scores and Competence scores (both using general sample norms and same sex norms); and

- Validity scales (liking; competence; difference).

These scores are available on a technical information page for those who desire the information. However, more generally, this number of scores is too numerous to be helpful to most users. The relevant scores are graphed to enable the user to understand the meaning better. Given the circular and spherical arrangement of the scales, circular graphs are used to portray the results. The PGI is unique in that the reports generated are tailored to each individual test taker using their responses. Specifically, information is tailored based on the differentiation of the profile. Most people get their interests graphed on the octant graph. This is the major graph provided to users. However, some users do not differentiate much among the different items, so these people who do not see too much difference in the different interest types are presented with a simpler graph of only four types (People, Things, Data, and Ideas) because this better matches how they view the world. Prestige scores (the top and bottom of the Personal Globe model) are graphed only if an individual scores above a T score of 60 on Prestige (for scales above the equator) or below a T score of 40 on Prestige) for scores below the equator. Most individuals score in the middle (T scores of 40-60) on Prestige and are, thus, stating that prestige is not especially defining for them so their scores are not graphed. Finally, although interest scores have been found to agree highly with competence perceptions (i.e., people are generally good at things they like), this is not always so. For an individual who has an unusual lack of agreement between the interest profile and the competence profile (i.e., T score greater than 60), these two profiles are graphed so that the user can see, more clearly, where the interests and competence perceptions do not align. Therefore, there are many different uniquely defined presentations of results based on the user's item responses. An asset of the PGI is that, although it is thorough, the report is adapted to each user. If a user wants to examine all the scores, there is the presentation on the *All Scores* page. Finally, on the All Scores page, there are three validity scales provided to determine whether the user was attending to the items. There are two "Mark 4 here" items to determine whether the user can respond appropriately. In addition, four items are repeated to enable an examination of response consistency. Tracey (2016) provided examples of the different profile formats and how to interpret them in the PGI Manual, which is available on the web site.

The PGI provides a match of the profile to each of the over 950 occupations in the O*NET system, over 450 academic majors, and the 16 Career Cluster created by the Office of Vocational and Adult Education (OVAE).

Users take the PGI-Short online, but given the different content, it does not report as much information. The PGI-Short yields fewer scale scores, and the main difference is the omission of all the high and low prestige scale scores, except the high prestige (north pole) and low prestige (south pole) scale scores. The PGI-Short has only 81 total scores reported for each test taker. The presentation of information is similar to that used for the PGI and provides the same occupation, major and cluster match.

The PGI-Mini is intended for a quick administration, used most easily as a paper and pencil measure, and utilizing both standardized scores or raw scores.

The PGI takes advantage of computer scoring by presenting individually tailored reports. Given that, the Personal Globe model is not familiar to all users, using the assessment might take a bit of familiarity for professionals to become used to it. However, it is a more general version of the RIASEC model with which most professionals are familiar. If practitioners prefer, they have access to RIASEC scores in the report. The PGI uses scales and scores new test takers will understand more easily.

Summary

The Personal Globe model is an empirically derived model that incorporates the prevailing models of interest but also offers new features. The PGI is an instrument that incorporates current models and scales (e.g., Holland's RIASEC types and Prediger's People/Things and Data/Ideas) but expands on these to include prestige and self-efficacy assessments. Use of the PGI has been demonstrated to have very sound reliability and validity support that exists across gender, ethnicity, age, and nationality. In addition, there is less gender bias than found in competing interest scales. The PGI is available free and online and provides an individually tailored profile report to each individual. The PGI has three different formats (PGI, PGI-Short, and PGI-Mini) that vary in length and complexity.

References

Akbarzadeh, M. (2010). *Normalization, determining validity and reliability of the Occupational Preference form of Personal Globe Inventory in students of Isfahan University.* Master's thesis, University of Isfahan, Isfahan, Islamic Republic of Iran.

Betz, N. E., Borgen, F. H., & Harmon, L. W. (1996). *Skills Confidence Inventory.* Palo Alto, CA: Consulting Psychologists Press.

Caulum, D., Tracey, T. J. G., Gresham, S., & McCarty, K. (2011, September). *Re-Validation Studies of the PGI and Other Assessments* [Technical Report]. Madison, WI: Center for Work and Education, University of Wisconsin.

Darcy, M. U. A. (2004). Examination of the structure of Irish students' vocational interests and competence perceptions. *Journal of Vocational Behavior, 67,* 321-333.

Durr, M. R., II, & Tracey, T. J. G. (2009). Relation of person-environment fit to career certainty. *Journal of Vocational Psychology, 75,* 129-138. doi:10.1016/j.jvb.2009.05.003

Etzel, J. M., Nagy, G. & Tracey, T. J. G. (2016). The spherical model of vocational interests in Germany. *Journal of Career Assessment, 24,* 701-717. doi: 10.1177/1069072715616122

Harmon, L. W., Hansen, J. C., Borgen, F. H., & Hammer, A. L. (1994). *Strong Interest Inventory.* Stanford, CA: Stanford University Press.

Hedrih, V. (2008) Structure of vocational interests in Serbia: Evaluation of spherical model. *Journal of Vocational Behavior, 73,* 13-23.

Holland, J. L. (1997). *Making vocational choices.* Odessa, FL: Psychological Assessment Resources.

Hubert, L., & Arabie, P. (1987). Evaluating order hypotheses within proximity matrices. *Psychological Bulletin, 102,* 172-178.

Leung, S. A., Zhou, S., Ho, E. Y., Li, X., Ho, K. P., & Tracey, T. J. G. (2014). The use of interest and competence scores to predict educational choices of Chinese high school students. *Journal of Vocational Behavior, 84,* 385-394. doi:10.1016/j.jvb.2014.02

Long, L., Adams, R. S., & Tracey, T. J. G. (2005). Generalizability of interest structure to China: Application of the Personal Globe Inventory. *Journal of Vocational Behavior, 66,* 66-80. doi:10.1016/j.jvb.2003.12.004

Long, L., Watanabe, N., & Tracey, T. J. G. (2006). Structure of interests in Japan: Application to the Personal Globe Inventory occupational scales. *Measurement and Evaluation in Counseling and Development, 38,* 222-235.

Prediger, D. J. (1982). Dimensions underlying Holland's hexagon: Missing link between interests and occupations? *Journal of Vocational Behavior, 21,* 259–287. doi: 10.1016/0001-8791(82)90036-7

Rounds, J., & Su, R. (2014). The nature and power of interests. *Current Directions in Psychological Science, 23*(2), 98-103. doi:10.1177/0963721414522812

Rounds, J., & Tracey, T. J. (1996). Cross-cultural structural equivalence of RIASEC models and measures. *Journal of Counseling Psychology, 43,* 310-329. doi: 10.1037//0022-0167.43.3.310

Sodano, S. M. (2011). Integrating work and basic values into the spherical model of interest. *Journal of Vocational Behavior 78,* 1-10. doi:10.1016/j.jvb.2010.09.004ts

Su, R., Rounds, J., & Armstrong, P. I. (2009). Men and things, women and people: A meta-analysis of sex differences in interests. *Psychological Bulletin, 135*(6), 859-884. doi:10.1037/a0017364

Šverko, I. (2008). Spherical model of interests in Croatia. *Journal of Vocational Behavior, 72*, 14-24.

Tracey, T. J. G. (1997a). The structure of interests and self-efficacy expectations: An expanded examination of the spherical model of interests. *Journal of Counseling Psychology, 44*, 32-43. doi: 10.1037/0022-0167.44.1.32

Tracey, T. J. (1997b). RANDALL: A Microsoft FORTRAN program for the randomization test of hypothesized order relations. *Educational and Psychological Measurement, 57*, 164–168. doi: 10.1177/0013164497057001012

Tracey, T. J. G. (2002). Personal Globe Inventory: Measurement of the spherical model of interests and competence beliefs. *Journal of Vocational Behavior, 60*, 113-172. doi: 10.1006/jvbe.2001.1817

Tracey, T. J. G. (2010). Development of an abbreviated Personal Globe Inventory using item response theory: The PGI-Short. *Journal of Vocational Behavior, 76*, 1-15. doi: 10.1016/j.jvb.2009.06.007

Tracey, T. J. G. (2016). *Personal Globe Inventory: PGI, PGI-Short, and PGI-Mini (Manual Version 1.4)*. Unpublished Manual. Retrieved from https://PGI.asu.edu

Tracey, T. J. G. & Caulum, D. (2015). Minimizing gender differences in children's interest assessment: Development of the Inventory of Children's Activities-3 (ICA-3). *Journal of Vocational Behavior, 87*, 154-160. doi: 10.1016/j.jvb.2015.01.004

Tracey, T. J. G., & Rounds, J. (1995). The arbitrary nature of Holland's RIASEC types: Concentric circles as a structure. *Journal of Counseling Psychology, 42*, 431-439. doi: 10.1037//0022-0167.42.4.431

Tracey, T. J. G., & Rounds, J. (1996). Spherical representation of vocational interests. *Journal of Vocational Behavior, 48*, 3–41. doi: 10.1006/jvbe.1996.0002

Tracey, T. J. G., & Tao, C. (2018). Response latency in interest assessment: An added tool? *Journal of Vocational Behavior, 108*, 121-131. doi: 10.1016/j.jvb.2018.07.001

Tracey, T. J. G., & Ward, C. C. (1998). The structure of children's interests and competence perceptions. *Journal of Counseling Psychology, 45*, 290-303. doi:10.1037//0022-0167.45.3.290

Vardarli, B., Özyüre, R., Wilkins-Yel, K. G., & Tracey, T. J. G. (2017). Examining the structure of vocational interests in Turkey in the context of the Personal Globe model. *International Journal for Educational and Vocational Guidance, 17*, 347-359. doi. org/10.1007/s10775-016-9338-6

Wilkins, K. G., Ramkissoon, M., & Tracey, T. J. G. (2013). Structure of interest in a Caribbean sample: Application of the Personal Globe Inventory. *Journal of Vocational Behavior, 83*, 367-372.

Vocational Meaning Survey
and
Vocational Fulfillment Survey

Reviewed by

Gary W. Peterson
John K. MacFarlane
Debra S. Osborn
Florida State University

The *Vocational Meaning Survey* (VMS; Peterson, MacFarlane, & Osborn, 2017) measures the extent to which individuals seek *importance* or *merit* in their work according to four dimensions: *Survival, Ego Centrism, Group Welfare,* and *Universalism.* The companion instrument, the *Vocational Fulfillment Survey* (VFS) measures the extent to which individuals find their present employment fulfilling according to the same dimensions. Overlapping profiles of the VMS and VFS identify consistencies and discrepancies between an individual's desired meanings in current work and the fulfillment of them.

Sometimes, individuals might express general or specific negative thoughts about tasks, duties, peers, and supervisors, as well as experience emptiness, boredom, uncertainty, ennui, and even dissatisfaction about their work, in general. They might feel as if "something is missing in my work and even life." The VMS and VFS were designed to assist individuals in exploring reasons for their discontent. Thus, from a Cognitive Information Processing (CIP) perspective (Peterson, Sampson, & Reardon, 1991; Sampson, Reardon, Peterson & Lenz, 2004), practitioners can use the VMS and VFS in the *Communication* phase of the CASVE Cycle (Communication, Analysis, Synthesis, Valuing, and Execution) to help individuals become fully "in touch" with their presenting career problem in career counseling. Practitioners can use the VMS alone in the *Valuing* phase after individuals have narrowed their list of plausible options to a select few in the preceding *Synthesis* phase. Then, for each option, the following questions are addressed, what is in this choice for me personally? for my significant others? for my community or society? and what meanings do I want to fulfill in this choice? Finally, in organizations, employers can use the VMS and VFS in human resources to help individuals, or collectively in groups, explore the extent of their engagement in the work of a unit.

Theory Base

The VMS and VFS constructs are based on the Hierarchical Model of Vocational Meaning in work (HMVM; Peterson et al., 2017). The inspiration for the model stems from the works of Maslow (1954), who developed a hierarchical theory of human needs. In the HMVM, there are four hierarchical levels of meaning in the form of psychological constructs portrayed in the form of a triangle, with *Survival* at the base, followed by *Ego Centrism*, then *Group Welfare*, and *Universalism* at the apex (See Figure 1). The HMVM is enhanced by the work of Rosso, Dekas, and Wrzesniewski (2010).

Constructs and Measures of the VMS and VFS

Survival. The base of the HMVM relates to deriving meaning through providing survival resources for meeting essential needs such as food, shelter, transportation, health care, and other necessities of daily living for the individual self and family. The measure of this construct is labeled *Basic Needs*.

Ego Centrism. This second level of the Model alludes to finding meaning in ego gratification (Freud, 1923, as cited in Strachey, 1960; Erikson, 1968) by addressing the fundamental question, "What's in this job for me?" Here, individuals derive meaning from such hygiene satisfiers (Herzberg, 1966) as salary relative to peers, recognition from supervisors, promotions, earned privileges or perks, and social status among peers. The measure of Ego Centrism is labeled, *Self-Enhancement.*

Group Welfare. At the third level, meaning is derived from the extent to which individuals derive pleasure and fulfillment from contributing to their work group or team in the attainment of group accomplishments and success. The measure of this construct is *Team Enhancement.*

Universalism. At the apex of the Model, this construct addresses the importance of individuals making community and society a better place through working for their present organization, as well as advancing the profession or the human condition itself. Further, the extent to which individuals perceive a spiritual purpose (Warren, 2002) in their work is also an important element in Universalism. The measure of Universalism is labeled *Transcendence.*

Figure 1. *Hierarchical Model of Vocational Meaning.*

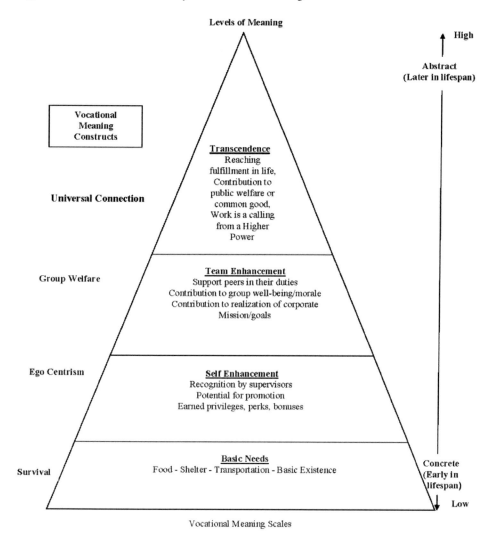

The VMS and VFS packet contains five separate sheets: (1) cover sheet, (2) VMS and VFS items and response scales, (3) scoring key, (4) Vocational Profile, and (5) Interpretation Guide. The cover sheet presents the title, authors, background data, and directions for completing, scoring, and profiling the VMS and VFS. The background data include current employment, educational attainment, gender, and ethnicity.

The second sheet contains three columns, with the response scales for the VMS in the first column on the left, the 28 common items in the center in random order, and the response scales for the VFS in the third column on the right. The directive at the top for the VMS is, *"Please rate how important it is that your current job or first choice of occupation provides opportunity or resources for each of the items in the center column."* The response scale for the VMS is: 1 = Not sure, 2 = Not important, 3 = important, and 4 = essential. The directive at the top for the VFS is, *"Please rate how adequately your current job enables you or allows you to obtain the items listed in the center column."* The response scale for the VFS is 1 = Inadequate, 2 = Less than Adequate, 3 = Adequate, and 4 = More than Adequate. Individuals completing the VMS and VFS are instructed to complete the left column first (VMS) and the right column second (VFS) by circling the appropriate number. The *Basic Needs* scale consists of six items (e.g., "Food for me and my family"); the *Self-Enhancement* scale includes six items (e.g., "Recognition by peers"); the *Team Enhancement* scale contains eight items (e.g., "Contributions to group well-being/morale"); and the *Transcendence* scale contains eight items (e.g., "Contribution to public welfare or common good").

The third sheet, the Scoring Key, has two columns, one for the VMS and one for the VFS in which the individual transposes the item scores from the second sheet onto the listing of items for each scale and then derives the sum (i.e., total score) for each scale. The fourth sheet, the Vocational Profile, contains four columns of numbers from 6 to 24 for Basic Needs and Self Enhancement, and 8 to 32 for Team Enhancement and Transcendence. The individual places a dot for each score on the VMS and a dash for each score for the VFS. The individual is then directed to create a line graph by connecting the VMS numbers with dots with one line and the VFS numbers with dashes with another line to reflect the two profiles superimposed on one another. The resulting profiles reveal the differences between the meanings the individual wishes to derive in current employment versus his or her attainment of those meanings. Finally, the fifth sheet, Interpretation Guide, describes each scale in terms of attributes of high scores and low scores. The Total Score, or profile elevation score, of the VMS is an indication of the extent of one's commitment to work in life.

Administration

The VMS and VFS exists only in English. Practitioners can obtain these by corresponding with Gary Peterson, gpeterson@fsu.edu or Debra Osborn, dosborn@fsu.edu. Then, practitioners can download the packet in print form for administering to clients or groups. Administering the VMS and VFS takes approximately 20 minutes to complete, score, and profile the instrument. Practitioners can administer the instruments individually or in groups. Practitioners can obtain the manual to assist in using and interpreting the VMS and VFS from Peterson et al. (2017). There is no cost for the using the VMS and VFS for research or practice.

Technical Considerations

Item development. We developed the items by delineating the attributes for each of the constructs (i.e., Survival, Ego Centrism, Group Welfare, and Universalism). We derived the attributes from an exhaustive review of the literature related to the topic *meaning in work*. Then, we converted the attributes into item statements. We edited the respective statements through reviews by professional colleagues and from participants engaging in one-on-one pilot testing.

Reliability. An online field test of the VMS and VFS resulted in alpha reliability coefficients spanning .76 - .92 for the VMS and .82 - .93 for the VFS. We have not pursued stability coefficients yet, although we would expect the VMS scores to be quite stable over time.

Validity. Intercorrelations among the VMS scales spanned .287 - .659, M = .423, and among the VFS scales, .125 - .677, M = .376, thus, demonstrating independence among scales. We pursued concurrent and convergent validities of the VMS through correlations with the *Work as Meaning Inventory* (WAMI; Steger, Dik, & Duffy, 2012). Correlations between the WAMI and the VMS were $r = .038$ (Basic Needs), $r = .416$ (Self-Enhancement), $r = .480$ (Team Enhancement), and $r = .317$ (Transcendence). To explore whether vocational fulfillment is related to career stress and tension, we correlated scales of VFS with the *Career Tension Scale* (CTS; Reed, 2005) and yielded the following correlates: Basic Needs, $r = .421$ ($p<.05$), Self-Enhancement, $r = -.271$ ($p > .05$), Team Enhancement, r = -.282 ($p > .05$), and Transcendence, $r = .022$ ($p > .05$). Only the Basic Needs dimension, which measures fulfillment of survival needs, was significantly ($p < .05$) related to career stress. This last finding supports the location of the Basic Needs dimension at the base of the HMVM.

Use/Interpretation/Evaluation

General utility. Peterson et al. (2017) developed the VMS and VFS to provide a conceptual framework from which individuals can explore thoughts, feelings, and reasons for engaging in their current work. Career practitioners can use the VMS and VFS easily in individual career counseling for career problem solving and decision making or in organizations to assist individuals in exploring their engagement in work in a unit. Responding to the items of the VMS and VFS has not posed any difficulties. However, sometimes, individuals require guidance in scoring and developing the respective profiles to contrast the extent of meanings they desire in their work and the extent to which they are fulfilled in them.

Presentation and interpretation. Whenever an individual expresses boredom, anxiety, dissatisfaction, or is asking the question, *Why am I working here or even why am I really working,* a counselor or human resources person could say, "*I sense you may be wondering about what your work means to you. We have an instrument that might help you explore this question.*" Many individuals find taking the instrument a rewarding experience in which they learn more about themselves. Following the completion of the VMS and VFS, we recommend the counselor describe the individual scale scores of the VMS and VFS, respectively, and differences among them (i.e., high and low scores). Next, we recommend the counselor note the general profile elevation of the VMS as an indicator of the importance of work in that person's life. Third, the counselor will want to explore the magnitude of differences or gaps between VMS and VFS scores in each dimension. Finally, the counselor will want to examine individual items for very high or low responses.

Evaluation. Thus far, anecdotal evidence from pilot testing in several dozen one-on-one administrations and interpretations has been very encouraging for us, as authors, as well as rewarding for individuals in terms of eliciting self-exploration regarding their present employment. In almost every case, the reactions have been, "*Wow, this instrument really pegs me!*" or "*These results sure give me something to think about.*" No one has acted indifferently to reviewing the results. The participants in the pilot tests were volunteers to assist the authors in test development; they were not career counseling clients. Our strong impressions, at this point in development, is that anyone who is employed or in the process of career exploration could derive some benefit from taking the VMS and VFS with a trained career counselor.

Psychometric evidence is, thus far and as stated above, also encouraging. Validity studies in progress include securing further evidence of independence of constructs, convergent validity with job satisfaction and meaning in life, and contextual factors (e.g., age, gender, ethnicity, time in current employment) that might influence the manner in which individuals respond to the items.

Career Counseling Practice Considerations

At the beginning of career counseling in the Communication phase of the CASVE Cycle (Sampson et al., 2004), practitioners can administer both the VMS and VFS to identify "gaps" between desired meanings and obtained meanings from current work. These gaps create cognitive dissonance (Festinger, 1964), which provides the motivation to engage career problem solving and decision making. Practitioners can use the VMS alone in a latter CASVE stage of career problem solving and decision making (i.e., Valuing), in which individuals have narrowed their choice viable to options to a select few to address the client question, *What meanings do I wish to derive from my work*? This information could be helpful in deriving a first choice to implement.

Summary

The Vocational Meaning Survey (VMS) and the Vocational Fulfillment Survey (VFS) were developed to assist individuals in examining the extent to which they find their current employment meaningful and fulfilling. The instruments were derived from a HMVM containing four meaning constructs in the form of a triangle with Survival at the base, Ego Centrism and Group Welfare above, and Universalism at the apex. Individual measures of the constructs include Basic Needs, Self-Enhancement, Team Enhancement, and Transcendence. Because the VMS and VFS are not fully validated and tested with clients, we emphasize that practitioners exercise caution in the use of these instruments. Nevertheless, we invite researchers and practitioners to participate in the development and use of the instruments. Practitioners can obtain a complete packet, which includes the Background Information Sheet, the VMS and VFS, the Scoring Key, the Vocational Profile and the Interpretive Guide, by corresponding with the authors, gpeterson@fsu.edu or dosborn@fsu.edu. In the request, practitioners should note the purpose for which they plan to use the instrument.

References

Erikson, J. (1968). *Life cycle completed*. New York, NY: W.W. Norton & Company.

Festinger, L. (1964). Motivations leading to social behavior. In R. C. Teevan, & R. C. Burney (Eds.), *Theories of motivation in personality and social psychology* (pp. 138-161). New York, NY: Van Nostrand.

Herzberg, F. (1966). *Work and the nature of man*. Cleveland, OH: Word Publishing.

Maslow, A. (1954). *Motivation and personality*. New York, NY: Harper & Row.

Peterson, G. W., MacFarlane, J., & Osborn, D. (2017). The Vocational Meaning Survey (VMS): An exploration of importance in current work. *Career Planning and Adult Development Journal, 33*, 49-59.

Peterson, G. W., Sampson, J. P. Jr., & Reardon, R. C. (1991). *Career development and services: A cognitive approach*. Pacific Grove, CA: Brooks/Cole.

Reed, C. (2005). *The relationships among neuroticism, dysfunctional career thoughts, and coping strategies*. (Doctoral thesis, Florida State University). Retrieved from http://etd.lib.fsu.edu/theses/available/etd-07032005-123327

Rosso, B. D., Dekas, K. H., & Wrzesniewski, A. (2010). On the meaning of work: A theoretical integration and review. *Research in Organizational Behavior, 30,* 91- 127.

Sampson, J. P., Reardon, R. C., Peterson, G. W., & Lenz, J. C. (2004). *Career counseling and services: A cognitive information processing approach.* Pacific Grove, CA: Wadsworth-Brooks/Cole.

Steger, M. F., Dik, B. J., & Duffy, R. D. (2012). Measuring meaningful work: The Work as Meaning Inventory (WAMI). *Journal of Career Assessment, 20,* 332-337.

Strachey, J. (Ed.). (1960). *The standard edition of the complete works of Sigmund Freud.* New York, NY: W.W. Norton & Company.

Warren, R. (2002). *The purpose-driven life.* Grand Rapids, MI: Zonervan.

Career Development Inventory

Reviewed by
Debra S. Osborn
Michael Morgan
Tiffany Brown
Florida State University

Introduction/Description

The Career Development Inventory (CDI; Super, Thompson, Lindeman, Jordaan, & Myers, 1979, 1981) was developed by a team of university professors, graduate students, and university personnel whose goal was the development of a "multidimensional measure of career maturity" (Thompson & Lindeman, 1981a, p. ii). Two forms exist, one for 11th and 12th grade students in high school (School Form; S Form), and one for students in higher education (College and University Form; CU Form). According to Thompson and Lindeman (1981a), the main difference is item content, which is adjusted to reflect occupations relevant to educational requirements at each level (i.e., occupations requiring a high school degree and those requiring a college degree). Super et al. (1979, 1981) designed the S Form to help individuals make career and training plans, and they designed the CU Form to help with career decision-making readiness. Thompson and Lindeman (1981a) suggested that the CU Form might be especially helpful for liberal arts majors choosing a major or for those considering graduate school. The CDI and its manuals are available at www.vocopher.com.

The CDI consists of 120 multiple choice items and is comprised of eight scales, five of which examine dimensions of career development: Career Planning (CP), Career Exploration (CE), Decision-Making (DM), World of Work Information (WW), and Knowledge of Preferred Occupational Group (PO). The final three scales consist of different combinations using the five scales, and create measures of career knowledge, attitudes, and orientation. Each of the five scales are comprised of 20 items, with the exception of the PO scale, which Super et al. (1979, 1981) developed in consultation with 40 experts and consists of 40 items. The CDI is divided into two sections, with the first part including the CP, CE, DM, and WW scale, and the second part being the PO scale. The CP Scale asks students to indicate the degree to which they have engaged in career planning, such as *"Talking about career plans with an adult who knows something about me,"* and also assesses students' knowledge of work tasks for specific occupations. Lower scores indicate less planfulness. The CE Scale is divided into two steps. In the first step, the student rates various groups (e.g., friends, professors) as career information sources on a 4-point scale. The intention is to rate how likely the student would be to go to these sources for information or help. In the second step, the student evaluates (on a 4-point scale) the quality of career information each of these sources provided in the past concerning the student's career or educational decision. Low scores suggest poor exploratory attitudes and a need to learn more about quality career information sources. The DM Scale includes 20 gender neutral scenarios and four possible answers of individuals making career decisions. This scale measures students' ability to make effective career decisions. A sample item is *"E.B. has excellent grades and very high scores on all ability tests but has no educational or vocational plans. What is the best advice to give to E.B.?"* Low scores indicate a need for learning decision making skills, including understanding what information the student needs to make an informed career decision.

The WW scale is divided into two sections and measures both career awareness and knowledge of occupational options. The first section reflects tasks associated in the Exploratory and early Establishment stages of Super's (1957) career theory. An example item with four response options is *"Which of the following changes of college major is easiest to make? (Business Administration to Biology; Physics to Business Administration; History to Physics; or Engineering to Business Administration)."* The second section measures knowledge of occupational structure (e.g., which occupations are in the same type of field), sample occupations, and job search and maintenance strategies. A sample item from this scale is *"Which of the following occupations belongs to an occupational family or field of work that is different from that of the other three? (Options: Anthropologist, Sociologist, Paleontologist, Demographer)."* Lower scores indicate a need for more information about the world of work, job search strategies, and how to be successful in the workforce.

The PO scale consists of 40 multiple choice items in 20 groups of potential occupational interests. Students begin with reading about the 20 groups to choose their occupational group of interest, and then answer the questions in this section while considering their preferred group. These questions address psychological requirements, educational and training requirements, and the degree to which the occupational group engages in work with data, people, or things. The answers are based on either objective information from the 1977 Dictionary of Occupational Titles or the combined judgment of 20 vocational psychologists. A sample item asks students to indicate which is most important to their occupational group – working with words, numbers, people, or things. This scale is meant for those students who have identified an occupational group they are interested in pursuing, and, thus, might not be as useful for those who have yet to make a career decision.

348

Those with lower scores on this scale need more specific information about their preferred career field.

The CP and CE subscales combine to create the Career Development-Attitudes (CDA) Scale, identified as a conative factor of attitudes that underlines those subscales. The DM and WW subscales combine to create the Career Development –Knowledge and Skills (CDK) Scale to provide a picture of how a student's career decision making knowledge and world of work knowledge combine to make a brief cognitive scale. The scales CP, CE, DM, and WW combine to create the Career Orientation Total (COT), which is described as a measure of career maturity, although Thompson and Lindeman (1981a) cautioned against calling it such, because it does not measure all of the constructs identified by Super as comprising career maturity.

Technical Considerations

The concept of measuring career maturity, the primary goal of the CDI, was developed during a longitudinal study of 9th graders called the Career Pattern Study (Thompson & Lindeman, 1981b). A group of researchers used exploratory factor analysis featuring six a priori categories: Orientation to Vocational Choice, Information and Planning, Consistency of Preferences, Crystallization of Traits, Vocational Independence, and Wisdom of Vocational Preferences. The developers used the results of factor analysis to create a revised set of four domains: Planning Orientation, The Long View Ahead, The Intermediate View Ahead, and The Short View Ahead. The qualitative differences between the a priori and factor analyzed domains represent a move toward assessing self-reported career exploration behaviors as an index of career maturity. Further refinement of this research yielded a set of six domains with validated constructs: Concern with Choice, Acceptance of Responsibility for Career Planning, Specificity of Information about the Preferred Occupation, Specificity of Planning for the Preferred Occupation, Extent of Planning Activity, and Use of Resources in Orientation.

The first instrument dedicated to measuring career maturity was the Career Maturity Index (CMI; Thompson & Lindeman, 1981b), with the final model of career maturity serving as the foundation of the CDI. Thompson and Lindeman detailed findings from four replications of the Career Pattern Study. Importantly, the results were validated with samples of inner city African American youth, Mexican American youth, and in Filipino youth. Thus, there is cross-cultural validity of the construct. However, given that no age differences were found in outcomes related to these samples, the idea that aging influences career maturity is not supported. Thompson and Lindeman (1981b) argued that life experience, associated with age, is the driving factor influencing the relationship between age and career maturity. Three iterations of the CDI existed prior to the current form.

Thompson and Lindeman (1981b) tested reliability of the CDI extensively for all iterations of the assessment and presented that information in the technical manual. They assessed the internal consistency of the CDI scales via Cronbach's alpha with a sample of no less than 265 per cell for the combined males and females and no less than 126 in a sex specific cell. They assessed internal consistencies for 9th-12th graders, with relatively high internal consistencies of the attitudinal scales (i.e., CP scale reliabilities ranged from .85 to .90; CE scale reliabilities ranged from .75 to .81). The WW scale reliabilities ranged from .77 to .87, and moderate reliabilities (.58 to .71) existed in the DM and PO (.53 to .71) scales. Thompson and Lindeman (1981b) argued that the reliabilities in the CP, CE, and WW scales make them most suited to analyzing difference scores, although, the practitioners should approach others with greater caution. On a theoretical level, the lower reliabilities could relate to these scales better by representing a homogenous factor while others might be more heterogeneous; this trend is reflected by the factor analysis results that indicated a third factor comprised mostly by the PO scale.

Thompson and Lindeman (1981b) reported test-retest reliability assessment for both the CDI S Form and the CU Form. They administered the high school version of the CDI at a two-week interval to 668 ninth, eleventh, and twelfth graders in two locations (i.e., one in an urban and one in a rural setting). The attitudinal loaded scales produced higher reliability consistently (i.e., CP scale test-retest reliability range from .65 to .86; CE scale test-retest reliability range from .44 to .85; CDA scale test-retest reliability range from .70 to .86) more than cognitively loaded scales (i.e., DM scale test-retest reliability range from .51 to .78; WW scale test-retest reliability range from .49 to .79; PO scale test-retest reliability range from .36 to .70; CDK scale test-retest reliability range from .58 to .86). In his 2013 review of the CDI, Pietrzak noted that the lack of stability over time on these scales, as well as the DM, WW, PO, and CDK scales on the CU form, is below what is acceptable, and "makes the use of these scales questionable in clinical and research contexts" (p. 321).

Thompson and Lindeman (1981b) reported canonical correlation analysis conducted on data collected during norming of the CDI S Form and the CDI CU Form. They developed three sets of canonical correlations (i.e., one from the urban high school, one from the rural high school, and one from the university sample). The results of analysis support five distinct canonical correlations with sufficient size to be statistically significant (i.e., test-retest reliability was significantly high to be detectable via canonical correlation). Additionally, the eigenvalues associated with the 5-factor structure agree with other analyses that the attitudinal scales display higher reliability than cognitively laden scales consistently. Standard error (SE) is a common way to describe reliability of measurement and Thompson and Lindeman (1981b) reported these figures for the CDI S Form. Most importantly, the equation for standard error (SE) is directly influenced by a reliability correlation and, thus, higher reliability yields lower SE. The SEs of the CDI range from 6.5 standard score points on the CP scale to 13.3 standard score points on the PO scale. Given the standard score mean is 100 points with a standard deviation of 20 points, the SE appears manageable, but practitioners must consider this carefully when interpreting results that are outside the mean. Calculation of SE scores with the test-retest reliability coefficients already discussed yield SE ranges of 6.78 to 15 standard points. Thus, SE is generally higher on the CDI CU Form than the CDI S Form.

Content validity of the CDI rests in the agreement of the developers of the instrument that the content is relevant to the scales being assessed. The initial a priori factor analytic structure, proposed during the Career Pattern Study, was the foundation for content validity of the CDI (Thompson & Lindeman, 1981b). Although the content validity might have been strong in 1981, the relevancy and correctness of the items needs to be re-evaluated for today, especially the WW and PO scales. For example, one item on the WW scale starts with *"By age 25 most young men and women who work have stopped changing jobs and are ready to 'settle down'. "* Likewise, the main content validity concern with the PO scale is that the knowledge presented and tested is based on the 1977 Dictionary of Occupational Titles and, thus, the job titles and specific work tasks need to be updated. A recent study using a shortened version of the CDI (Pordelan, Sadeghi, Abedi, & Kaedi, 2018) did not include the PO items. In addition, Thompson and Lindeman (1981a) stated in the user manual that the main difference between the high school and college forms is the occupations that require a high school versus college degree, and though those specific requirements might have been true in when the instrument was created, they might not hold true today for those occupations. In addition, some occupations, such as sewing machine operator and gas attendant, might be outdated, and other occupations, especially those of an online nature, are not represented.

The CDI User's Manual reports construct validity supported by both group differences and factor analysis (Thompson & Lindeman, 1981b). The greatest concern underlying construct validity remains whether career maturity represents a homogeneous construct or a heterogeneous combination. Thompson and Lindeman (1981b) posited that construct validity is supported by group differences in the domains of grade differences, gender, and academic program, as observed by: 1) mean increases in scale scores in conjunction with higher grade level, 2) higher mean scores on cognitive scales for males than for females, and 3) higher scale scores, especially on cognitive scales, in college preparatory and business students than general or vocational students. With respect to discriminant analysis, the technical manual (Thompson & Lindeman, 1981b) indicates that no longitudinal studies validated the CDI and, thus no general statements about age as a causative

351

factor can be made. However, discriminant analysis of the mean differences discussed in the User's Manual (Thompson & Lindeman 1981a) revealed two significant change patterns across age: one primarily cognitive and one primarily attitudinal. The difference in what the manuals report is contradictory and somewhat confusing. Construct validity was developed over the three iterations of the CDI via factor analysis (Thompson & Lindeman, 1981b). The CDI User's Manual reported two main factors (i.e., one attitudinal and one cognitive); however, factor structure reported during development of the CDI Form III yielded three main factors: one attitudinal and two cognitive. The attitudinal factor is related to items from the CP and the CE scale, one of the cognitive scales is related to the DM, WW, and CDI scale, and the final factor is comprised primarily of the PO scale. Another important consideration is that the correlations between the cognitive and attitudinal scales were significant, which suggests some overlap between the measures. The User's Manual (Thompson & Lindeman, 1981b) is accurate in the assertion that only two factors exist when they combine the third (PO factor) into the overall cognitive factor. The correlation between the attitudinal factors and cognitive factors might be evidence of a homogeneous career maturity construct, but the 3-factor solution used while reducing items on the CDI Form II suggests a heterogeneous combination might be more accurate.

The CDI correlates meaningfully with several related constructs. The most common construct related to CDI is intelligence. In addition, Thompson and Lindeman (1981b) reported significant correlations between reading ability and the CDI, as well as academic achievement and the CDI. These three areas are supported further by the analysis revealing different patterns of CDI scores for different academic programs (e.g., college preparatory compared to vocational). Savickas and Hartung (1996) reported more aspects of concurrent validity, such as studies that related the CDI cognitive scales to both the Wonderlic Intelligence Test and grade-point average, as well as the level of integration individuals have for their vocational schema. They also reported several aspects of predictive validity of CDI scales (i.e., CE, WW, and DM) with student perseverance. The first measure of career maturity meaningfully correlated to the CDI is the aforementioned CMI (Thompson & Lindeman, 1981b). Research indicates positive correlations between three of the CDI scales and the scales of the CMI. The attitudes scale of the CMI was correlated with the CP scale ($r = .37$), the WW scale ($r = .31$), and DM ($r = .22$). Also, the cognitive scale of the CMI was correlated with the CP scale ($r = .20$), the WW scale ($r = .45$), and DM scale ($r = .41$). Divergent validity was provided by lack of correlation between the CDI and a personality measure (i.e., decision-making style). More evidence for convergent and divergent validity is reported in the technical manual.

Thompson and Lindeman (1981b) included 5,039 high school students, between the late seventies and early eighties, in the norming process for the

CDI Form S. They did not report reading level in either manual. Thompson and Lindeman collected the sample from schools in the Eastern United States. primarily, with more than 3,000 of the sample coming from one city in New Jersey, and the students demonstrated diversity in terms of urban-suburban-rural context, inner city youth, sex, and grade level. However, given the datedness of the sample and the changes in career education since the seventies, we advise against using the CDI in counseling until the norms have been updated.

Use/Interpretation/Evaluation

Thompson and Lindeman (1981a) noted three main applications for the CDI: (a) providing diagnostic data and predictors in individual counseling and group assessment; (b) as a survey instrument in planning guidance programs; and (c) using results to measure criteria and outcomes in the evaluation of programs and research. The manual describes multiple ways to implement these applications, as well as provides an example for interpreting a sample profile. In addition, the CDI profile creates a report for an individual's career development needs and could be helpful for determining a student's readiness to make sound educational and vocational decisions. Thompson and Lindeman (1981a) recommended exploring the highest scores (75th percentile and above) and, especially, highlighting strengths, and exploring the lowest scores (25th percentile and below), indicating deficits. Additional steps for interpretation are included in the manual but are somewhat complicated. An online report, generated from responses to the online inventory at www.vocopher.com, provides a breakdown of each score on the scale. The report does not provide a specific explanation for each score (percentile), but rather a general explanation about high and low scores on those scales. Taking the assessment is relatively straight forward and does not require the administrator to be present. This increases utility and can allow for mass administration, if desired. Although Thompson and Lindeman developed the CDI in 1979 in the United States based mostly on Western society (Super et al., 1979; 1981), several others have made attempts to adapt the CDI to other cultures and settings, including the CDI-A (Australia; Lokan, 1984), the K-CII (Korean Career Indecision Inventory; Tak & Lee, 2003), and more recently, a shortened version validated for use in Iran (Pordelan et al, 2018; Sadeghi, Baghban, Bahrami, Ahmadi, & Creed, 2011). Pietrzak (2013) noted the need for the CDI to be updated because it has many outdated concepts, save for some of the core scales, which are still helpful for counselors. We agree, and due to the concerns noted in the technical section, we do not recommend use of the CDI in counseling and program evaluation at this time.

Research and Evaluation/Assessment Uses

Super et al. (1979, 1981) developed the CDI as a theory-based assessment and, thus, the CDI has the potential to contribute not only to specific constructs of career readiness, but also to Super's (1957) theory of career development and other theories that rely on the core concepts the CDI attempts to measure. Research through the years on the use of the CDI has been limited. The recent study by Pordelan et al. (2018) in Iran shows that there still might be applicability of this inventory for research and program evaluation. However, the CDI needs to be re-normed, and although some scales of the CDI might still show strong reliability and validity, others (i.e., WW and PO) are in dire need of updating prior to being used for these purposes.

References

Lokan, J. (1984). *Manual of the Career Development Inventory – Australian Edition*. Melbourne, Australia: ACER.

Pietrzak, D. (2013). Career Development Inventory [Review]. In C. Wood & D. G. Hays (Eds.), *A counselors guide to career assessment instruments, 6th ed.* (pp. 319-323). Broken Arrow, OK: National Career Development Association.

Pordelan N., Sadeghi, A., Abedi, M. R., & Kaedi, M. (2018). How online career counseling changes career development: A life design paradigm. *Education and Information Technologies, 23*, 2655–2672. doi: 10.1007/s10639-018-9735-1

Sadeghi, A., Baghban, I., Bahrami, F., Ahmadi, A., & Creed, P. (2011). Validation of the short form of the Career Development Inventory with an Iranian high school sample. *International Journal for Educational and Vocational Guidance, 11*(1), 29-38. doi: 10.1007/s10775-011-9189-0

Savickas, M. L., & Hartung, P. J. (1996). The Career Development Inventory in review: Psychometric and research findings. *Journal of Career Assessment, 4*, 171-188.

Super, D. E. (1957). *The psychology of careers: An introduction to vocational development.* Oxford, England: Harper & Row.

Super, D. E., Thompson, A. S., Lindeman, R. H., Jordaan, J. P., & Myers, R. A. (1979). *Career Development Inventory: School form.* Palo Alto, CA: Consulting Psychologists Press.

Super, D. E., Thompson, A. S., Lindeman, R. H., Jordaan, J. P., & Myers, R. A. (1981). *Career Development Inventory: College form.* Palo Alto, CA: Consulting Psychologists Press.

Tak, J., & Lee, K. (2003). Development of the Korean Career Indecision Inventory. *Journal of Career Assessment, 11*, 328-345. doi: 10.1177/1069072703254503

Thompson, A. S., & Lindeman, R. H. (1981a). *Career Development Inventory: Volume 1. user's manual.* Palo Alto, CA: Consulting Psychologists Press.

Thompson, A. S., & Lindeman, R. H. (1981b). *Career Development Inventory: Volume 2. technical manual.* Palo Alto, CA: Consulting Psychologists Press.

Career Maturity Inventory - Form C

Reviewed by

Logan Vess

John Carroll University

Introduction/Description

Super and Overstreet (1960) developed the Career Maturity Inventory (CMI – Form C) as a succinct assessment to measure career choice readiness for individuals in grades 6 through 12. Developed originally by Super and Overstreet (1960) and revised later by Crites (1965) and Crites and Savickas (1995), the most current version is the Form C, developed by Crites and Savickas (2011) and Savickas and Porfeli (2011). The purpose of the instrument is to provide career professionals with a reliable and sound measure that is both useful and brief. Specifically, the CMI-Form C allows counselors to assess an individuals' career choice readiness, which can include readiness for using different types of interest inventories.

The CMI-Form C has 24 statements, and participants respond in an *Agree* or *Disagree* response format. Instructions read "There are 24 statements about choosing the kind of job or work that you will probably do when you finish school. Read each statement. If you agree or mostly agree with it, then circle agree next to it. If you disagree or mostly disagree with it, then circle disagree next to it."

There are four scales composing the CMI-Form C. Those are *Concern, Curiosity, Confidence,* and *Consultation.* Concern refers to the extent to which an individual is oriented to and involved in the process of making career choices. Savickas and Porfeli (2011) noted that the first step in the career decision-making process is for an individual to gain awareness of the choices that must be made in the future. The intention of this process is to prompt individuals to begin making decisions that could lead to occupational choices and enhanced career development. The CMI features six items related to this scale. Sample items include:

- As far as choosing an occupation is concerned, something will come along sooner or later.
- I seldom think about the job that I want to enter.
- I really can't find any work that has much appeal to me.

Next, the Curiosity scale refers to the extent to which an individual is exploring the work world and seeking information about occupations and their requirements. Exploration of one's abilities and interests as they relate to occupations that fit personality and talents can alleviate confusion around career decision making (Savickas & Porfeli, 2011). The CMI features six items related to this scale. Sample items include:

- I don't know how to go about getting into the kind of work I want to do.
- I am having difficulty in preparing myself for the work that I want to do.
- I keep wondering how I can reconcile the kind of person I am with the kind of person I want to be in my occupation.

The Confidence scale refers to the extent to which individuals believe in their ability to make wise career decisions and practical occupational choices. Individuals who have confidence in their career decision-making also have faith in their ability to handle the complex challenges that might arise. The CMI features six items related to this scale. Sample items include:

- Everyone seems to tell me something different; as a result, I don't know what kind of work to choose.
- There are so many things to consider in choosing an occupation, it is hard to make a decision.
- I can't understand how some people can be so certain about what they want to do.

Last, the Consultation scale refers to the extent to which an individual seeks advice from others in making career and occupational decisions. Savickas and Porfeli (2011) noted that this scale examines, specifically, how individuals seek to obtain advice from others on making wise and realistic choices, rather than what specific occupation to choose. The CMI features six items related to this scale. Sample items include:

- If you have doubts about what you want to do, ask your parents or friends for advice.
- It is important to consult close friends and get their ideas before making an occupational choice.
- In making career choices, one should pay attention to the thoughts and feelings of family members.

Technical Considerations

Providing an overview on the origins of the Career Maturity Inventory (CMI), first developed and administered in 1961, Savickas and Porfeli (2011) described the instrument as the first paper-and-pencil assessment of an individual's vocational development. The authors emphasized the word *maturity* refers to *readiness*. At the time of Savickas and Porfeli's publication, the instrument consisted of 50 items with a *True* or *False* response format. Earlier, Crites (1978) developed a revision of the CMI (Form A) by adding 25 items from the original pool of 1,000 statements. Later, Crites and Savickas (1995) chose inventory items from the 1,000 statements made in educational or vocational counseling sessions from real clients. The next iteration of the CMI came in 1995, with the focus on constructing an adult version (Crites & Savickas, 1995).Ten years later, the CMI had been used in hundreds of studies and even, more so, in practice as a screening tool, mainly, for 5-12 grade clients', assessing their readiness for career interventions (Savickas & Porfeli, 2011).

Savickas and Porfeli (2011) sought to incorporate some theoretically relevant and pragmatically useful content scales that fit within the existing framework of the CMI. Specifically, they incorporated elements of career construction theory (Savickas, 2005), which includes the assumptions that individuals should have concern toward their futures, a sense of control over their careers, a curiosity to explore possible selves and social opportunities, and the confidence to execute their plans.

One shift in the CMI-Form C from previous versions refers to the emergence of the Consultation scale. Upon examining the scores on the various scales, Savickas and Porfeli (2011) noted that the 75 items in CMI Form B-1 did not provide a sufficient group of items to represent career control viewed as an intrapersonal variable, rather than an interpersonal variable. Further, the authors did not discard the items selected as representatives of career control because they did correlate with readiness. After examining the content of the Control scale items, the authors decided to rekey the Control scale, and they renamed the resulting scale Consultation instead of Control. Elevated scores on the Consultation scale refer to an individual's tendency to consult family and friends interdependently regarding career choices. Low scores mean the individual prefers to make career choices with an independent relational style. Thus, the consultation scale reflects relational style or interpersonal strategy in constructing career choices.

Reliability

Savickas and Porfeli (2011) reported the coefficient alphas for the four 6-item scales as concern = .62, consultation = .69, curiosity = .74, and confidence = .78. They noted that the scale scores appeared to be meaningful, unidimensional, and marginally reliable with good face validity.

Validity

Savickas and Porfeli (2011) noted the following results to offer some evidence for convergent validity with the Vocational Identity Scale (Holland, Johnston, & Asama, 1993): "Concern correlated most highly with orientation (.51) and involvement (.51). Curiosity correlated most highly with decisiveness (.65) and compromise (.55). Confidence correlated with decisiveness (.83). Consultation correlated .53 with independence" (p. 8). They noted their research provided initial evidence to support the face, construct, and concurrent validity of the CMI scores as indicators of career choice readiness.

Norms

Savickas and Porfeli (2011) examined results from their study, which included participants from grades 9-12 in a Midwestern urban high school. They reported the following item mean norms for high school students on the four scales: Concern = 4.6, Curiosity = 2.72, Confidence = 2.56, and Consultation = 4.94.

Use/Interpretation/Evaluation

Career professionals can use the CMI-Form C item rationales to "teach the test" to individuals once they complete it. Theorized originally by Crites (1974), Savickas and Porfeli (2011) dedicated a section of their report on the CMI to this process called *Teaching the Test*. For example, a professional might begin the process with a student by giving a general introduction on career choice readiness. From there, the professional can introduce the concepts of Concern, Curiosity, Confidence, and Consultation. This process aims at acclimating the participant to the constructs of the assessment to spark dialogue about results on the CMI. Savickas and Porfeli provided a detailed outline of this approach and included sample questions professionals can ask participants in the process. For example, the career professional might ask, "What did you have in mind when you agreed with this item?" Other ways to "teach the test" might involve role playing, verbal modeling, and instruction. Although the CMI-Form C is available on Vocopher. com, there is not an available user manual. In scoring the CMI, participants receive a credit of one point for every one of their responses that correlates with the scoring key. Savickas and Porfeli (2011) noted that the result of the CMI-Form C is five scaled scores. First, a composite score including the 18 items in the scales Concern, Curiosity, and Confidence total to readiness. Higher scores for this composite score indicate more readiness to make career decisions. Next, the scores for Concern, Curiosity, and Confidence represent specific scores for each scale. The fifth and final score represents the Consultation score, which provides a measure of individuals' willingness to seek guidance from others in their career choice process. The authors noted that elevated scores on the Consultation scale suggest a more interdependent relational style, while lower scores represent a more independent relational style.

A major strength of the CMI-Form C is its ease of use. With only 24 Agree/Disagree statements, individuals can complete the CMI quickly. Similarly, the scoring of the instrument is relatively easy for professionals. One potential drawback in administering and interpreting the CMI could be a professional's lack of understanding in the foundational theories used to represent the constructs of the inventory. Savickas and Porfeli (2011) provided an excellent overview of the theories and outlined how a professional can *Teach the Test* to a participant. An inexperienced professional might need to review the extant literature around career maturity and adaptability to interpret and utilize a participant's' results fully. Still, the CMI's scoring and interpretation is simple and effective in comparison with most career assessments.

How is the instrument used in career counseling?

As discussed previously, the CMI is an effective tool to measure an individual's readiness to make career choices and measure the individual's potential readiness to experience career interventions. Savickas (1990a; 1990b) noted that the experience of teaching the test, along with administration and interpretation of the CMI, is effective in individual career counseling sessions. Savickas and Porfeli (2011) noted that career professionals might use the CMI in group counseling but cautioned against using the measure to explore which occupational choice is right for each group member. Rather, the authors suggested that group counselors focus on the decision-making aspects of the process. As an example, certain group members might have a specific preferred attitude toward career decision-making and might receive reinforcement from other group members. Then, these members might serve as role models for those who are still in the development stages of their dispositions toward career decision making.

Presentation and Interpretation

Participants receive a point when their answers correlate with the following scoring key. Savickas and Porfeli (2011) reported the scoring key as follows:

CMI-C Scoring key Response format = Agree (A) or Disagree (D)

Concern = 1 (D), 5 (D), 9(D), 13(D), 17(D), 21(D)

Curiosity = 2(D), 6(D), 10(D), 14(D), 18(D), 22(D)

Confidence = 3(D), 7(D), 11(D), 15(D), 19(D), 23(D)

Consultation = 4(D), 8(A), 12(A), 16(D), 20(A), 24(A)

For the scales of Concern, Curiosity, and Confidence, higher scores indicate more advanced development in career decision making. Benefits of this type of scoring include the relative quickness and ease of measuring a participant's results on these scales. True to its theoretical foundation, CMI results do not match an individual to an occupational path.

Cultural Considerations and Implications

Savickas and Porfeli (2011) gave special attention to the Consultation scale for cultural considerations and implications. They suggested using the Cultural Formulation Model developed by Leong (2010). This model allows counselors to consider their clients' cultural identity, cultural concept of career choice, context, and dynamics within the therapeutic relations. The CMI Consultation scale assesses respondents' familial career conversations on a spectrum from "do as we advise" to "it is up to you." Therefore, Savickas and Porfeli (2011) suggested that exploring and discussing cultural dimensions before evaluating an individual's score on the Consultation scale is imperative.

Research and Evaluation/Assessment Uses

Prior to its revision to Form C, researchers had used the CMI in over 500 research studies (Savickas & Porfeli, 2011). Presently, the CMI has been used in many different forms of research, including studies of career maturity for students in Malaysia (Ismail, Abdullah, Mohamad, & Khairuldin, 2018), levels of career maturity for nursing students (Cheng et al., 2016), and the relationship between self-concept and career maturity in Pakistani high school students (Zahra & Malik, 2018). The CMI-Form C has potential for use in evaluating career programming and career coursework. Examining participants' scores before and after a program could serve as an indicator for the effectiveness of the program. Career professionals can use the CMI-Form C, and its accompanying forms, to serve multiple audiences in individual and group sessions (Savickas, 1990a) and as career education curricula (Savickas, 1990b; Savickas, Porfeli, Lara-Hilton, & Savickas, 2018).

References

Cheng, C., Yang, L., Chen, Y., Zou, H., Yonggang, S., & Fan, X. (2016). Attributions, future time perspective and career maturity in nursing undergraduates: A correlational study design. *BMC Medical Education, 16*(26), 1-8. doi:10.1186/s12909-0160552-1.

Crites, J. O. (1965). Measurement of vocational maturity in adolescence: I. Attitude test of the Vocational Development Inventory. *Psychological Monographs: General and Applied, 79*(2), 1-212.

Crites, J. O. (1974). A reappraisal of vocational appraisal. *Vocational Guidance Quarterly, 22,* 272-279.

Crites, J. O. (1978). *Career Maturity Inventory.* Monterey, CA: CTB/McGraw-Hill.

Crites, J. O., & Savickas, M. L. (1995). Revision of the Career Maturity Inventory. *Journal of Career Assessment, 4,* 131-138.

Crites, J. O., & Savickas, M. L. (2011). *Career Maturity Inventory – Form C.* Available from www.vocopher.com

Holland, J. L., Johnston, J. A., & Asama, N. F. (1993). The Vocational Identity Scale: A diagnostic and treatment tool. *Journal of Career Assessment, 1,* 1-12.

Ismail, M. S., Abdullah, S. S., Mohamad, M. Z., & Khairuldin, W. M. K. F. W. (2018). Student's career maturity: Implications on career counselling. *International Journal of Academic Research in Business and Social Sciences, 8,* 887–897.

Leong, F. T. L. (2010). A cultural formulation approach to career assessment and career counseling. *Journal of Career Development, 37,* 375–390.

Savickas, M. L. (1990a). The career decision-making course: Description and field test. *Career Development Quarterly, 38,* 275–284.

Savickas, M. L. (1990b, March). Developing career choice readiness. Paper presented at the annual meeting of the American Association for Counseling and Development. Cincinnati, OH.

Savickas, M. L. (2005). The theory and practice of career construction. In S. D. Brown & R. W. Lent (Eds.), *Career development and counseling: Putting theory and research to work,* (pp. 42–70). Hoboken, NJ: John Wiley & Sons.

Savickas, M. L. & Porfeli, E. (2011). Revision of the Career Maturity Inventory: The adaptability form. *Journal of Career Assessment, 19,* 355-374.

Savickas, M. L., Porfeli, E. J., Lara-Hilton, T., & Savickas, S. (2018). The student career construction inventory. *Journal of Vocational Behavior, 106,* 138-152.

Super, D. E., & Overstreet, P. L. (1960). *The vocational maturity of ninth grade boys.* Oxford: Columbia University, Teachers College.

Zahra, S. T. & Malik, A. A. (2018). Relationship between self-concept and career maturity in Pakistani high school students. *Bahria Journal of Professional Psychology, 17*(1), 1-16.

My Vocational Situation

Reviewed by
Catherine Allen
University of North Carolina at Chapel Hill

Introduction/Description

Holland and colleagues developed My Vocational Situation (MVS, Holland, Gottfredson, & Power, 1980) in an effort to combine three areas of career decision research: diagnostic methods, career indecision, and experimental research. The ultimate goal of the MVS is to identify clients who have difficulty making career related decisions based on the certainty of their vocational choice, necessary information about that choice, and barriers that affect progress.

The MVS is a two page, hard copy assessment tool composed of 20 forced-choice items: 18 True or False items and two additional sentence stems with four questions for each, all responded to in a Yes or No format. In addition, the MVS includes three open-ended responses for clients to list occupations of interest, comments, or questions. The MVS is free, and practitioners can administer the assessment in 10 minutes or less. Scores display directly on the tool itself. The MVS includes three scales, which assess for vocational identity (VI, 18 items), occupational information (OI, 4 items), and barriers perceived (B, 4 items). Vocational Identity measures a clear and stable picture of an individual's goals, interests, and talents (Holland et al., 1980). A sample item includes "I need to find out what kind of career I should follow." The OI scale assesses specific deficits in career information. An item from the common stem "I need the following information" is "More information about employment opportunities." Finally, B provides a measure of the barriers the individual identifies. This scale uses the common stem "I have the following difficulties" and a sample item is "I lack the special talents to follow my first choice."

Although each scale addresses different aspects of career decision making, information gathering, and personal career development, practitioners and users should consider the latter two scales, OI and B, as checklists for self-reporting due to reliability constraints (Holland et al., 1980).

Scoring takes place by tallying the False responses for the 18 items (VI scale) and the No responses (OI and B scales) for the two sentence stems questions

365

that include 4 responses each. The False and No responses receive one point and each scale (VI, OI, & B) is tallied separately. True and Yes responses receive zero points resulting in lower scores. Higher score amounts indicate increased levels of achieved identity (VI) and career information (OI), and lower levels of perceived barriers (B).

Technical Considerations

Holland et al. (1980) developed the MVS over a long and rigorous process and used a combination of pre-existing scales (i.e., Vocational Decision-Making Difficulty [VDMD, Holland & Holland, 1977] and the identity scale [VI; Holland & Holland, 1977]) as the basis for the VI and OI scales. The authors used a process of matching factors across scales, with correlates of .36 or higher, to construct these two MVS scales. Additionally, Holland et al. created the B scale based on items related to "environmental barriers or a clear psychological limitation" (Holland et al., 1980, p. 1194).

Holland et al. (1980) measured internal consistency reliability using two samples: first with high school sophomores and second with a combination of high school, college, and full-time workers. The KR20 results showed the VI scale to have the highest internal consistency reliability across groups and gender, with .86 for high school males (n=185) and females (n=311), .89 for college students and working males (n=291), and .88 for females (n=301). The OI scale showed varied internal consistency reliability across groups and gender. High school students, both male and female, revealed lower KR20 statistics at .39 (n= 185) and .44 (n=311), respectively. College students and workers indicated higher KR20 results, with males at .79 (n=289) and females at .77 (n=300). The B scale varied similarly to the OI scale; however, results were much lower across groups and gender, ranging from .23 to .65. Based upon the lower internal consistency reliability for the OI and B scales, Holland et al. (1980) suggested these be used as checklists, rather than true scales, because they provide little more than additional information career practitioners and clients might use in the career decision making process.

Holland et al. (1980) measured construct validity with 824 individuals across high school, college, and business settings. These age and education ranges were intentional because Holland et al. wanted a greater variation in their validation sample. The results of the intercorrelational analysis ($m = .49$) supported their hypotheses and confirmed the validity of the MVS on the sample. Additional hypotheses tested included correlations between each scale and age and the number of occupations listed. Scales VI and OI correlated positively with age of respondent, which indicated higher levels of identity and occupational information as age increased. The VI and OI scales correlated negatively with number of occupations listed, thus, signaling that clients with well-defined identities and ample occupational information listed fewer jobs and less varied occupational ambitions.

Normative data for the MVS focused on high school students, college students, full-time workers, and graduate students and faculty. Holland et al. (1980) provided mean responses by gender for each population and scale. The VI scale increased across each group; high school males had the lowest mean score of 11.20 (n=185), and graduate student/faculty females had the highest mean score of 17.71 (n=14). The OI scale decreased across groups; high school females had the highest mean at 3.67 (n=311), and college females (n=134) had the lowest mean of 1.77. The B scale was quite different and increased across groups. High school males (n=185) showed the lowest mean of 2.03, and female graduate students/faculty (n=14) held the highest mean of 3.57. Holland et al. (1980) suggested these norms might be beneficial in creating low, medium, and high score ranges for various populations. Though the VI scale norms suggest an increased clarity with age and education, Holland et al. (1980) cautioned against making assumptions about the OI and B scales due to inconsistent sampling.

Use/Interpretation/Evaluation

Given the reliability and validity constraints of two of the three scales, career practitioners should use the MVS with caution. Additionally, no new evidence exists regarding the reliability and validly of the instrument with current diverse populations or in the modern workplace. Perhaps the best use of the MVS is as a starting point for conversation and intervention with clients high school age and older. In addition, using this assessment in a pretest-posttest design might provide insight to those interventions that encourage individual identity formation for supporting career decision making specific to individual clients. Working with the client to establish goals and action plans might be a beneficial follow-up to the MVS results conversation. If practitioners use the MVS in an environment offering various services (e.g., individual, group, etc.), this tool might be helpful in identifying groups or workshops relevant to the client's career decision-making needs.

At the time of this review, the user manual for the MVS was unavailable. In spite of the low reliability for the OI and B scales and the lack of clarity regarding validity, there are still strengths with the MVS. The assessment is easily accessible online as a free download. Because of its brevity, users can complete the assessment quickly (i.e., 10 minutes or less), and practitioners can score rapidly, without additional templates, rubrics or materials, by using simple math.

Each scale has its own section on the form. The first page includes a prompt for listing considered occupations and the list of questions for the VI scale. Scoring takes place by simply totaling the number of "False" responses and placing the total in the box at the bottom of the first page. A high score represents a clearly defined sense of identity, and a low score represents the inverse (Holland et al., 1980). The second page has two sections for the OI and B scales, respectively. Practitioners calculate these scores by totaling the number of "No" responses and placing the total in the box at the end of each section. Low scores on each of these scales indicate a need for information related to occupations of interest and barriers to making career related decisions (Tinsley, Bowman, & York, 1989). Using this scoring format allows for conversation around specific scale scores, as well as responses to specific items. There is not a combined score for each scale; individuals calculate each of the three scales independently.

Even with all the limitations presented, some authors recommend use of the MVS across populations to support client career decision-making. For example, some vocational rehabilitation counselors have proposed using the MVS with spinal cord injury patients (Nitsch et al., 2017). Other professionals have used the MVS to measure adolescent career decision-making needs and how those needs might relate to certain personality characteristics (Hirschi & Herrmann, 2013).

Overall, some consider this instrument "one of the world's most frequently applied measures" (Hirschi & Herrmann, 2013). The MVS is a helpful tool for use with clients where background and action planning might be beneficial to the career development and decision-making process. However, practitioners and users will want to keep in mind that responses from the MVS represent only one part of a client's story and should not be the only variable used in supporting client career decision-making.

Research and Evaluation/Assessment Uses

Career practitioners can measure individual client change or progress with a pretest-posttest administration of the MVS. Increases in "False" or "No" responses could be a sign the client is approaching clarity around his or her career related decisions. Professionals might be able to use the MVS, in conjunction with other measures, to identify effectiveness of interventions. Individual scales could be helpful when working in programs with specific goals or outcomes.

References

Hirschi, A., & Herrmann, A. (2013). Assessing difficulties in career decision making among swiss adolescents with the German My Vocational Situation scale. *Swiss Journal of Psychology, 72,* 33-42.

Holland, J. L., Gottfredson, D. C., & Power, P. G. (1980). Some diagnostic scales for research in decision making and personality: Identity, information, and barriers. *Journal of Personality and Social Psychology, 39,* 1191-1200.

Holland, J. L., & Holland, J. E. (1977). Vocational indecision: More evidence and speculation. *Journal of Counseling Psychology, 25,* 404-414.

Nitsch, K. P., Pedersen, J., Millotto, A., Petersen, B., Robbins, S., Garcia, A.,...Janikowski, T. (2017). My Vocational Situation (MVS): Case example and psychometric review. *The American Journal of Occupational Therapy, 71,* 7102405010. Retrieved from https://doi.org/10.5014/ajot.2017.025288

Tinsely, H. E. A., Bowman, S. L., & York, D. C. (1989). Career Decision Scale, My Vocational Situation, Vocational Rating Scale, and Decisional Rating Scale: Do they measure the same constructs? *Journal of Counseling Psychology, 36,* 115-120.

ABOUT THE EDITORS

Kevin B. Stoltz, PhD, ACS, NCC, is an associate professor in the Department of Counselor Education at the University of North Alabama. He teaches graduate courses across the counseling curriculum and specializes in assessment, research, and career counseling. Kevin is a National Certified Counselor and Approved Clinical Supervisor. His research interests include psychometric methods in counseling, career assessment with early recollections and other qualitative assessment techniques, career transition, and the integration of career and mental health counseling. Kevin has published in national and international journals regarding career techniques used in counselor supervision, career transition, applications of motivational interviewing in career counseling, and Adlerian constructs used in career counseling. He has presented at national and international conferences and consults on career issues and research across the globe. His professional activities include serving as Chair of the Mentoring Committee and Research Committee for National Career Development Association (NCDA). Currently, he is a co-editor of the NCDA publication, *A Comprehensive Guide to Career Assessment.* He has provided invited editorial service to the Journal of Vocational Behavior, Clinical Supervisor, and British Journal of Guidance and Counseling. Additionally, he served or serves on the editorial boards of the Career Development Quarterly, Measurement and Evaluation in Counseling and Development, Journal of Individual Psychology, and the Lifespan Journal. He can reached at CG7@ncda.org

Susan R. Barclay, PhD, LPC-C, LPC-S, NCC, GCDF-I, is an associate professor at the University of Central Arkansas, where she teaches in the College Student Personnel Administration (CSPA) graduate program and teaches undergraduate career and life-planning courses. Susan is a licensed professional counselor (LPC) and holds certification as a Global Career Development Facilitator (GCDF) instructor. Currently, she serves on the editorial board for the Career Development Quarterly and the Journal of Student Affairs Research and Practice. Susan's research and publication experience focuses, primarily, on the implementation of career construction and life design techniques in diverse settings, including with groups. Other interests include career transitions and student identity development and success. She can be reached at CG7@ncda.org

CONTRIBUTORS

Charmayne R. Adams, MA, NCC. Charmayne Adams is a doctoral candidate at the University of Tennessee in Knoxville. She has worked in the Center for Career Development at the UTK and was a teaching assistant at Wake Forest University for the career exploration courses. She is interested in how past experiences influence career decision-making.

Yang Ai, MEd, MA. Yang Ai is a doctoral student at the University of Missouri–St. Louis. He holds an M.Ed. in Clinical Mental Health Counseling and an M.A. in Education Administration. Yang serves as a teaching assistant, the editorial assistant for the Asia-Pacific Career Development Association, and chair of the Missouri Career Development Association.

Catherine Allen, MA, GCDF. Catherine Allen is an assistant director for University Career Services (UCS) at the University of North Carolina at Chapel Hill. Previously, Catherine worked as a college and career readiness resource counselor with Albuquerque Public Schools. She received her master's degree in Community Counseling from Lenoir-Rhyne University (Hickory, NC).

Tina Anctil, PhD, CRC, CCCE, LPC. Tina Anctil is Associate Dean for Academic Affairs in the College of Education at Portland State University. She is a Licensed Professional Counselor in Oregon, a Certified Rehabilitation Counselor, and a Certified Career Counselor Educator. She is the NCDA Credentialing Commissioner for Career Counselor Educators and Clinical Career Counselor Supervisors.

Stephanie Bell, PhD, P-LPC, NCC, ACS. Stephanie Bell is an assistant professor of Counselor Education at Delta State University in Cleveland, MS. Her primary research interest is in trauma counseling, specifically with survivors of acquaintance rape in college.

Courtney R. Boddie, PhD, LPC, NCC. Courtney Boddie's career has included roles in college counseling, instruction, academic support, and accessibility services. His areas of expertise include multicultural counseling, ADHD, career development, and integrated care. He earned a doctorate in Counseling and Counselor Education at the University of Missouri and is a practitioner of Adler's Individual Psychology.

Tiffany Brown, BS. Tiffany is a first year doctoral student in the Combined Counseling and School Psychology program at Florida State University. She has a Bachelor of Science in Education from the University of Oklahoma. Her goal is to become a licensed psychologist working with children and young adults.

Zach Budesa, MA, LPC-MHSP. Zach Budesa is a doctoral student at the University of Tennessee, Knoxville. He completed his Master of Arts in Clinical Mental Health Counseling at Tennessee Technological University, and he is a Licensed Professional Counselor (LPC-MHSP) in Tennessee.

Louis A. Busacca, PhD. Louis A. Busacca is a professional counselor in Ohio and a National Certified Counselor. Currently, Louis is an adjunct associate professor of Counseling and Human Services at Old Dominion University and adjunct professor of Psychology at Lakeland Community College.

Brian Calhoun, MA. Brian Calhoun is an assistant professor at Wake Forest University in the Department of Education. Brian is an active member of the American Counseling Association and the National Career Development Association. Brian is on the NCDA research committee and a member of the 2017 NCDA Leadership Academy.

Tanya M. Campos. Tanya M. Campos is a doctoral candidate in counseling at the University of New Mexico. She is a National Certified Counselor, a Licensed Professional Mental Health Counselor, and is certified as a Global Career Development Facilitator. Tanya has worked in higher education for over twenty years.

Darrin L. Carr, PhD. Darrin Carr completed his doctorate in Counseling Psychology at Florida State University and his predoctoral internship at Kansas State University. In his postdoctoral residency in community mental health, Darrin served clients with severe and persistent mental illness. His research interests include technology in counselor training and interactions between mental health and career.

Jacks Cheng, EdM. Jacks Cheng is a doctoral candidate in Counseling Psychology at Indiana University Bloomington. Jacks is interested in the career stories of racial, sexual, gender, and linguistic minorities in oppressive workspaces, and in multicultural interventions for organizational development and human resources management.

Y. Barry Chung, PhD. Y. Barry Chung is dean of the College of Education at San Diego State University. His research interests include career development, multicultural counseling, and sexual orientation issues. He is an Eminent Career Award winner and Fellow of the National Career Development Association and a Fellow of the American Psychological Association.

S. Autumn Collins, MA, LMHC, GCDF. Autumn Collins is a doctoral student in Educational Psychology at the University of New Mexico (UNM). She is the Career Counseling Manager at UNM Career Services, and she holds an LMHC and is NMCDA Past President (2017-2018). Her research interests include utilizing career center services in retention in higher education and the career development of student-athletes.

Jenna Crabb, PhD, LPC, NCC. Jenna Crabb has worked in higher education for over 24 years and in career counseling for 17 years. Currently, she is the Director of Career Services and adjunct faculty at the University of New Mexico. Jenna earned her PhD in Counselor Education from the University of New Mexico.

Peter A. Creed, PhD. Peter Creed's research applies goal setting/self-regulation theories to understand how individuals set and adjust goals, respond to goals set by self and others, and how individuals manage the consequences of goal disruption and implement behaviour change to improve performance and reduce stress. He is particularly interested in career goal setting.

Sif Einarsdottir, PhD. Sif Einarsdóttir is a professor in the Career Guidance and Counseling program at the University of Iceland. She does research mainly on interests, personality, and cross-cultural assessment. She is a coordinator of VALA network of career guidance and counselling programs in the Nordic and Baltic countries.

Alec Eshelman, PhD. Alec Eshelman is an assistant professor of Psychology at the University of Wisconsin Platteville. He is especially interested in psychology of working perspectives and is passionate about understanding the ways in which social stratification influences work experiences across the life span.

Kathy M. Evans, PhD, LPC, CCCE. Kathy Evans is Professor Emerita from the University of South Carolina and is the President-Elect of NCDA. She has published widely in career counseling with over twenty publications devoted to career issues. From 2015-2017, Kathy served as the Trustee for Counselor Educators and Researchers for NCDA.

Nikki A. Falk, MA. Nikki A. Falk is a counseling psychology doctoral student at the University of Missouri-Columbia. Her research interests include women's career development, underrepresented student self-efficacy and persistence in STEM, and feminist psychology.

Justin R. Fields, PhD. Justin Fields is a school counselor and a counselor educator. He has experience working in large urban high schools, and he assists students and parents with issues related to personal/social development, college readiness, and career exploration.

Amanda G. Flora, PhD, NCC, GCDF, CCCE. Amanda Flora is an assistant professor at the University of Virginia's School of Education & Human Development. She teaches courses on career and professional development with a focus on diversity and equity. Dr. Flora is a former NCDA Leadership Academy participant and President-Elect of the Virginia Career Development Association.

Itamar Gati, PhD. Itamar Gati is a Fellow of the National Career Development Association and of Divisions 17 and 52 of the American Psychological Association, and a recipient of the Eminent Career Award from NCDA. He is the developer of www.cddq.org, a free, anonymous, evidence-based career assessment and planning system.

Melinda M. Gibbons, PhD. Gibbons is a professor of Counselor Education and the PhD program coordinator in the Department of Educational Psychology and Counseling at the University of Tennessee. Her research interests focus on career development for underserved populations, particularly rural Appalachian youth, prospective first-generation college students, and students with intellectual disabilities.

Madeleine Haenggli, MS. Madeleine Haenggli is doctoral student of the Department of Work and Organizational Psychology at the University of Bern, Switzerland. Her research focuses on how to create successful, satisfying, and sustainable careers using career resources. In addition, she has been responsible for the student advisory service at the university for years.

Paul J. Hartung, PhD. Paul J. Hartung is Professor of Family and Community Medicine, Northeast Ohio Medical University. He is current editor of *The Career Development Quarterly* and fellow of the American Psychological Association, International Association of Applied Psychology, and National Career Development Association.

Andreas Hirschi, PhD. Andreas Hirschi is a full professor and the chair of the Department of Work and Organizational Psychology at the University of Bern, Switzerland. His major research interests are in the field of career development and career counseling with a focus on self-directed career management, career success, and the work-nonwork interface.

Michelle Hood, PhD. Michelle Hood is an associate professor and Deputy Head (Learning and Teaching) of the School of Applied Psychology at Griffith University. She publishes on career development and assessment, higher education, and literacy development. She teaches career psychology and counselling, and psychological assessment.

Simona Ingold, MSc. Simona Ingold is a research assistant at the Department of Work and Organizational Psychology at the University of Bern, Switzerland. Her work involves research on scale development and career management.

Viktoria Kulcsar. Viktoria Kulcsar is a doctoral student at the Babeş-Bolyai University (Romania). Her qualifications are based on a strong academic background and practical research experience at Yale University (US) and the Hebrew University of Jerusalem (Israel). Her research focus is on career decision-making difficulties associated with negative dysfunctional emotions.

Yue Li, MS. Yue Li is a doctoral student who is studying Counseling Psychology at Indiana University. She received her Bachelor of Science at Shanghai Normal University and her Master of Science at University at Albany, SUNY. Her primary research interests are career development, the psychology of culture, and positive psychology.

Chad Luke, PhD, LPC-MHSP, NCC, ACS. Chad Luke is a counselor educator with experience with addictions, children and adolescents, the homeless, college students, and other adults. He has been a career services director and an associate dean of student development, and is the author of *Essentials of Career-Focused Counseling* (Cognella, 2017).

Jill A. Lumsden, NCC. Jill Lumsden is program manager at Zeiders Enterprises, where she leads the Department of Defense contract supporting military spouses with career and educational advising and coaching services. Jill has over 20 years of experience in career services in public higher education and corporate settings.

John K. MacFarlane, EdS. John MacFarlane is a doctoral candidate in the Combined Doctoral Program in Counseling Psychology and School Psychology at Florida State University. John has been researching meaning in vocation as part of his doctoral program of studies. Before entering the doctoral program, he was a decorated U.S. Navy Special Operations Officer.

Clayton V. Martin, PhD. Clayton is the Program Director for the Department of Clinical Counseling at Alvernia University, Reading, Pennsylvania. He obtained a doctorate in Counselor Education/School Counseling and Guidance Services after earning a dual Master's degree in Mental Health Counseling and Marriage and Family Therapy

Laith Mazahreh, PhD. Laith Mazahreh is an assistant professor of School Counseling at Mississippi State University. His research interests include validating instruments among Arabic speakers, stress coping resources, career development, bullying in school, and the leadership and advocacy competencies of school counselors.

Pamela McCoy, MFHC. Pamela received her Master of Arts in Mental Health Counseling at Indiana University. Pamela has worked at Milestones Clinical Health & Resources as a behavior clinician and therapist since 2014 and has received much of her clinical training working with those diagnosed with autism, intellectual disabilities, and dual diagnoses.

Carol A. Miller. Carol A. Miller is a doctoral student in Counseling at the University of Missouri – St. Louis and a counselor at Care and Counseling, a non-profit mental health agency serving the St. Louis area.

Michael Morgan, Jr., MS, NCC. Michael is a doctoral student at the Florida State University. He has an M.S. in Psychology from the Georgia Institute of Technology, and an M.S. in Counseling from Mercer University.

Spencer Niles, PhD. Spencer Niles is Professor and Dean of the School of Education at the College of William & Mary. Previously, he served as Distinguished Professor and Department Head at Penn State. His research addresses developmental aspects of career engagement with a particular emphasis on empowering others to make soul-centric career choices.

Debra S. Osborn, PhD. Debra Osborn is an associate professor in the Educational Psychology and Learning Systems Department, and the co-director for the Center for the Study of Technology in Counseling and Career Development at Florida State University. She is a Fellow and Past President of the National Career Development Association. Her research focuses on the design and use of technology, career assessments, and cognitive information processing (CIP) theory.

Gary W. Peterson. PhD. Gary Peterson is Professor Emeritus and Senior Research Associate for the Study of Technology in Counseling and Career Development, Career Center, Florida State University. He continues to conduct research in the areas of career development, career decision making, and personality and career assessment.

Mark Pope, EdD, NCC, MCC, CCC. Mark Pope is Thomas Jefferson Professor and Curators' Distinguished Professor Emeritus at the University of Missouri - St. Louis. He was president of both the National Career Development Association and the American Counseling Association. Mark received the NCDA Eminent Career Award and served as *Career Development Quarterly* Editor.

Rebekah Reysen, PhD, NCC, LPC, DCC. Rebekah Reysen is the assistant director of Academic Support Programs for the Center for Student Success and First-Year Experience at The University of Mississippi (UM). She received both her master's and her Ph.D. in Counselor Education from UM. Rebekah serves as co-editor of the *Journal of Counseling Research and Practice.*

Mary-Catherine McClain Riner PhD. Mary-Catherine is a licensed psychologist serving South Carolina and Georgia. She specializes in treating eating disorders, obsessive compulsive disorder, self-harm, and marital discord. Mary-Catherine conducts ADHD/LD evaluations for college students, provides career counseling, and performs compensation evaluations for veterans seeking benefits.

Patrick Rottinghaus, PhD. Dr. Patrick Rottinghaus is an associate professor of Counseling Psychology at the University of Missouri-Columbia. His research examines vocational interests, abilities, personality, self-efficacy, values, and career adaptability. He is a Fellow of NCDA and APA and serves on editorial boards for the *Career Development Quarterly* and *Journal of Career Assessment.*

James Rounds, PhD. James Rounds is Professor of Psychology and Educational Psychology at the University of Illinois at Urbana-Champaign. He studies the continuity and change in work values and interests.

James P. Sampson, PhD. Jim Sampson is Professor Emeritus, Department of Educational Psychology and Learning Systems, and Senior Research Associate, Center for the Study of Technology in Counseling and Career Development, Florida State University. He writes and speaks on computer technology in counseling, cognitive strategies in career interventions, and theory, research, and practice integration.

Julie Aitken Schermer, PhD. Julie Aitken Schermer (formerly Harris) is a professor in the Department of Management and Organizational Studies at The University of Western Ontario. She has authored or co-authored over 90 peer-reviewed articles, book chapters, a Canadian Business Statistics textbook, and the *Jackson Career Explorer*, and has given over 100 conference presentations.

Ryan D. Sides, MS. Ryan Sides is doctoral student in the Combined Doctoral Program in Counseling Psychology and School Psychology at Florida State University (FSU). Ryan has a Master of Science in Sport Psychology, also from FSU. His research interests include the career transition of athletes, adaptation, and negative career thinking.

Brian J. Taber, PhD. Brian Taber is an associate professor in the Department of Counseling at Oakland University. His scholarship interests are in the areas of vocational assessment and career counseling. He currently serves on the editorial boards of *The Career Development Quarterly*, *Journal of Employment Counseling*, and *Journal of Vocational Behavior*.

Terence J. G. Tracey, PhD. Terence Tracey is a professor in the Counseling and Counseling Psychology program at Arizona State University and soon to be a Visiting Professor at the University of British Columbia (June, 2019). He is a past editor of the *Journal of Counseling Psychology*.

Logan Vess, MA, LPC. Logan R. Vess serves as Assistant Director for Academic Internships in the Center for Career Services and adjunct instructor for Counseling at John Carroll University. Logan is a doctoral candidate in the Counselor Education and Supervision program at Kent State University.

Joshua C. Watson, PhD, NCC, LPC-S, ACS. Joshua C. Watson is a professor and chair in the Department of Counseling and Educational Psychology at Texas A&M University-Corpus Christi. Dr. Watson is a past-president of the Association for Assessment and Research in Counseling and current editor for the *Journal of College Counseling*.

Alyssa West, MA, LMHC. Alyssa is employed as a behavioral consultant and has focused her work on serving individuals with intellectual disability and developmental delay since graduating in 2015. An area of professional focus for Alyssa is working with youth and young adults who engage in sexually maladaptive and/or abusive behaviors.

Kerrie G. Wilkins-Yel, PhD. Kerrie Wilkins-Yel is an assistant professor at Indiana University. Her research focuses on women, underrepresented minorities, international students, and cross-cultural groups, and, in particular, the factors that enhance recruitment, retention, and career persistence among graduate women of color enrolled in STEM disciplines. Another interest is in measurement and scale development as it relates to the cross-cultural applicability of U.S. based career instruments.

ASSESSMENT AUTHOR INDEX

INDEX

M

Manifest interests, 252
MANOVA, 174
Marlowe-Crowne Social Desirability Scale
    (M-C SDS), 293
Meaning-making, 76
Member checking, 85
Metacognitions, 173
Microskills, 61
Minnesota Multiphasic Personal
    Inventory (MMPI) Versions I & II,
    8, 114
Missouri Occupational Card Sort, 92
Modernity, 4
Motivational Skills Card Sort (MSCS),
    270-273, 275
Multicultural competence, 60
Multigenerational career development
    patterns, 259, 266
Multivariate discriminant function
    analysis, 285
MVS, 365-369
Myers Briggs Type Indicator (MBTI), 63,
    214, 240

N

National Alliance on Mental Illness
    (NAMI), 51
Negative career thinking, 49
NEO, 209-217
    NEO-AC Inventory, 148
    NEO-FFI Inventory-32, 13
    NEO Personality Inventory (NEO PI),
        32, 209
    NEO Personality Inventory (NEO PI-
        3), 209-210, 213, 239, 248
    NEO Personality Inventory (NEO PI-
        4), 209, 211-213-216
    NEO Personality Inventory-Revised
        (NEO PI-R), 93, 210-211, 213-216
Neuroticism Scale, 174, 209, 211-215
Non-binary, 260
Norm referenced, 97, 204

O

OASIS, 219-229
OCCU-Find feature, 131-132, 134-135
Occupational Interest Card Sort (OICS),
    269-270, 272-273, 275
Occupational Outlook Handbook
    (OOH), 9, 117-118, 168
Occupational Scales, 92, 196
Office of Vocational and Adult Education
    (OVAE), 326, 336
O*NET OnLine, 17-18, 27, 47, 49, 117-
    118, 124, 135, 168, 184, 195, 197, 198,
    200, 202, 205, 226, 232-233, 236-237,
    239, 245-249, 264, 326, 336
O*NET Ability Profiler, 18
O*NET Interest Profiler, 18, 27, 49, 54,
    239
O*NET Work Importance Locator, 18
Open Source, viii, x, xi, 347, 357, 365
Organismic self-regulation, 318

P

P-values, 123
Peer debriefing, 85
Person-Environment (PE) fit, 5-6, 51, 214
Personal Characteristics Scale, 145
Personal Globe Model, 325-327, 329-330,
    332, 335-336
Personal Health Questionnaire (PHQ)-9,
    51
Personal Style Scales (PSS), 92
Personality tests, 92
Personality theory, 144
PGI, 325-338
Physical health factors, 77
Pictorial tests, 77
Preferred Occupation (PO) scale, 347-
    348, 350-352
Profile for American Youth Project
    (PAY97),135
Prolonged engagement, 85
Protean, iv, 17
Protean and Boundaryless Career
    Attitude Scales, 75

W